Developing Cognitive Competence

Developing Cognitive Competence: New Approaches to Process Modeling

Edited by

Tony J. Simon
Georgia Institute of Technology

and

Graeme S. Halford
University of Queensland

LEA

LAWRENCE ERLBAUM ASSOCIATES, PUBLISHERS
1995   Hillsdale, New Jersey   Hove, UK

Lawrence Erlbaum Associates, Inc., Publishers
365 Broadway
Hillsdale, New Jersey 07642

Cover design by Kate Dusza

Library of Congress Cataloging in Publication Data

Developing cognitive competence : New approaches to process modeling /
edited by Tony J. Simon and Graeme S. Halford.
    p. cm.
  Includes bibliographical references and index.
  ISBN 0-8058-1289-X (alk. paper). ISBN 0-8058-1998-3 (pbk).
  1. Cognition. 2. Cognitive styles. I. Simon, Tony J.
II. Halford, Graeme S.
BF311.D468 1995
153 – dc20   94-34726
                                        CIP

Printed in the United States of America
10 9 8 7 6 5 4 3 2 1

We dedicate this book to the late Allen Newell, who challenged us to tell him "where the issue stands on transitional mechanisms."

Contents

Preface

It should seem obvious that transition mechanisms, or how the system progresses from one level of competence to the next, ought to be the central question for investigation in cognitive developmental psychology. Yet, if one scans the literature of modern developmental studies, it appears that the question has been all but ignored. Our dedication of this book to Allen Newell refers to a challenge made in his William James lectures. This was based on the finding that Newell's many friends in developmental psychology could not tell him what the prevailing wisdom was on the subject of transition mechanisms. Perhaps the reason for this theoretical shortfall was offered by Flavell in his commentary on chapters in R. J. Sternberg's 1984 book, *Mechanisms of Cognitive Development*. To paraphrase Flavell, not much theorizing about transition mechanisms has been done since Piaget because it is very hard to do. Another reason might have been the concentration on prior, possibly more descriptive, aspects of cognitive change. Yet another factor might have been the relatively recent advent of cognitive science and the armory of theoretical and empirical tools that it has brought with it.

Whatever the reason for the delay, by the start of the 1990s, increasing numbers of researchers in the cognitive sciences were of the opinion that the tools of mathematical modeling and computer simulation make theorizing about transition mechanisms both practical and beneficial. Computational models make it possible to define the processes that lead to a system being transformed, under environmental influence, from one level of competence observed in children to the next most sophisticated level. By coding computational models into simulations of actual cognitive change, they become tangible entities that are accessible to systematic study.

Feeling that developmental psychologists should be exposed to this relatively new approach, we decided to organize a symposium at the Biennial Meeting of the Society for Research in Child Development (SRCD) that was held in Seattle in April 1991. The "cost of entry" was that speakers had to have a running computational model of a documented cognitive transition. The symposium contained four such models, including both symbolic and connectionist implementations. It was also the inspiration for this book, which contains those and two further models. At the same conference there was an invited symposium on connectionist models and child development. Perhaps SRCD 1991 will come to be seen as the start of a concerted effort to build computational accounts of developmental phenomena.

Our purpose in producing this volume was twofold. Our first aim was to introduce to a wider audience the idea of computational modeling and what we perceive to be its special advantages for developmental research. To this end we have provided an introductory chapter that discusses the computational modeling enterprise itself and its special relevance to studying change. There is also a review chapter by David Klahr at the end of the book to put the work contained here into a wider perspective. Our second aim was to collect examples of this kind of research into a single volume where different models can be read, evaluated, and compared to one another. Examples of computational models of developmental phenomena are still relatively scarce and they have not been published in places where the more traditional developmental research community will easily chance upon them. We hope that this volume will remedy that situation and provide a collection that can inform the interested researcher as well as form the basis for graduate-level courses.

In writing this book, extensive efforts have been made to make it accessible to readers other than those who specialize in computational modeling. It is intended to be of interest to psychologists, in developmental and other areas, to educationalists, and to cognitive scientists.

ACKNOWLEDGMENTS

Finally some acknowledgments are due to people without whom this book would not have come about. Thanks to Judi Amsel at Lawrence Erlbaum Associates whose advice and cajoling has brought us to a point where we have a book to publish. Thanks also to a number of reviewers who willingly gave their time to help us improve the quality of the chapters in the book, for which we are very grateful.

I (Tony Simon) wish to acknowledge the very special environment of Carnegie Mellon University in Pittsburgh where, as a postdoctoral researcher, I benefited enormously from a wide range of scientific influences and made many wonderful friends. Most directly, though, these included the Soar research group in general and the friendship and collaboration with Rick Lewis and Thad Polk in particular. Most important of all were two people. Allen Newell provided vision, guidance, friendship, and caring. I feel luckier than I could ever have imagined to have had the chance to work with Allen for 3 years. David Klahr provided guidance, challenge, and insightful analysis of my ideas and ceaselessly improved the quality of my thinking and writing. To both I am eternally grateful. Finally I would like to thank my friend and mentor, Richard Young, for giving me the chance to rise to this level in the first place and my parents, Shirley and Gad Simon, for being who they are.

I (Graeme Halford) would like to acknowledge a very widespread debt to many colleagues in both developmental and cognitive psychology, who made me aware of the need for explicit models of the developmental process. The time I spent at Carnegie Mellon University in 1985, where I had the opportunity for closer contact with colleagues like Bob Siegler and David Klahr, was particularly beneficial. I had long been interested in the influence of cognitive representations on performance, but it was when I read the planning net models of VanLehn and Brown, and of Greeno, Riley, and Gelman, that I realized a formalism was available for dealing with this problem. There was no history of work in this area in our institution, although I would like to acknowledge the stimulation and support from the simulation model BAIRN that was developed by Iain Wallace at Deakin. In the event, a group of enthusiastic researchers was assembled at the University of Queensland, and we were fortunate to have Sue Smith, who had recently completed her doctorate at Carnegie Mellon University, join us as a postdoctoral fellow at just the right time. The model was developed by this group, whose contributions are acknowledged by shared authorship. Tony Simon's decision to organize a symposium at SRCD 1991 was a crucial step in bringing both our own and others' efforts in this area into public view for the first time. Finally I would like to acknowledge the support and assistance of my wife, Lyn, whose contribution was crucial in bring this project to fruition.

1

Computational Models and Cognitive Change

Tony J. Simon
Georgia Institute of Technology

Graeme S. Halford
University of Queensland

The question we address in this chapter is, "why build computational models of developmental phenomena?" We do not use the term *developmental* to restrict our discussion to child development, which has become its default meaning. Although what follows focuses on data from transitions in children's cognition, we do not make any in principle distinction between the mechanisms underlying those and many other cognitive changes occurring later in life. Despite the focus of this chapter and volume, we do not claim that what we say applies only to cognitive developmental phenomena, as opposed to social or emotional development. We hope the progress represented here will encourage others to build computational models of transitions in those domains as well. Finally, we try to minimize the use of the term *development*. There has been a long debate in psychology regarding the nature of differences between development and learning (Piatelli-Palmarini, 1980). Because this volume adresses this issue as one of the questions to be resolved, we adopt the more neutral term of *change*. The aim of this volume is to collect a body of work that addresses the problem of specifying the mechanisms of change in human information processing through computational modeling. The aim of this chapter is to examine the special role such models can play in the study of change.

Although not generally considered an influential figure in developmental psychology, Herbert Simon clearly prescribed the role of the computational model in the field more than 30 years ago. The following quotation makes clear what computational modeling can offer to the study of mechanisms of change:

> If we can construct an information-processing system with rules of behavior
> that lead it to behave like the dynamic system we are trying to describe, then
> this system is a theory of the child at one stage of development. Having
> described a particular stage by a program, we would then face the task of
> discovering what additional information-processing mechanisms are needed
> to simulate developmental change—the transition from one stage to the next.
> That is, we would need to discover how the system could modify its own
> structure. Thus the theory would have two parts—a program to describe
> performance at a particular stage and a learning program governing the
> transitions from stage to stage. (Simon, 1962, pp. 154–155)

Today, that statement still holds true. However, we prefer to characterize
the research program in terms of three components that are required in
order to understand the central question in development: What is the nature
of the transition mechanisms that promote change? First, there needs to be
a performance model that can simulate the competence of a child or adult
at a given level of competence. Second, there needs to be a principled
mechanism that can transform the representations at the initial level into
new representations supporting some more advanced level of processing.
Finally, there must be a clear account of the activities engaged in by the
individual(s) to be modeled between the start and end states of the transition
concerned. By *activities*, we do not mean information processing operations, but the manifest behavior the person chooses, or is requested, to
engage in. Description at the information processing level is instantiated in
the model's account of changes in that higher level of behavior. Thus the
model, as it is being exercised on those same activities, should produce the
same intermediate outputs, both mental and behavioral, as do the human
subjects. In the resulting state, the model should exhibit the same knowledge and competence as the human subjects. The knowledge and processes
that were responsible for the transformation should be clearly statable in
their entirety, so that there is no mystery about how the representations at
the later point in time came to be created out of those at the initial point.
Any model that conforms to this prescription can be called a theory of
transition mechanisms in a given domain.

This chapter comprises five sections, the first three of which address the
three components of computational models of transitions just described.
The first section examines how computational models provide the opportunity to specify information processing theories in greater detail than is
usually possible. In this section, we examine the implementation of process
models in running simulations, and we discuss the advantages of doing so.
We also address the question of where, in the resulting model, the theory
resides and bring up the notion of *cognitive architecture*. In the second
section, we concentrate on the central theme of this book: the special
contribution that computational modeling can make to the study of

transition mechanisms. We highlight the issue of self-modification processes and claim that computational modeling is the only method available
for the direct study of change mechanisms. In the third section, we
investigate the issue of input, one that has not been discussed in great detail
until now. What kinds of environmental input must a computational
transition model receive in order to make its processing realistic? Issues here
include the role of training studies and the veracity of assumptions about
the nature of environmental input. Within this discussion, we consider
differences between symbolic and nonsymbolic computational approaches.
The fourth section briefly examines the impact that computational modeling can have on developing explanations of transitions described in
developmental psychology research. In the final section, we give a brief
overview of the chapters in the book, grouping them by broad themes.

PROCESS MODELING

It has become accepted during the last 20 years that information processing
theories of cognition can be implemented as computer programs to increase
theoretical rigor and conceptual specificity (McClelland, 1988; Newell &
Simon, 1972; Pylyshyn, 1984), although the practice is still somewhat
controversial (Goel, 1992; Searle, 1984). However, the vast majority of
computational studies have concentrated on phenomena associated with
adult cognition, leaving models of children's cognition and of transition
mechanisms significantly underrepresented. The state of information processing theorizing in these latter two areas was discussed in detail by Klahr
(1992) in his analysis of *soft-core* to *hard-core* accounts of cognitive
development. A soft-core account is one where processes are described with
verbal statements, but no explanation is given about how such processes are
carried out in the cognitive system or how, in the context of processing a
task, they interact with one another. Conversely, hard-core accounts take
the form of computational models of the processes involved. Such models
"independently execute the mental processes they represent. That is, rather
than leaving it to the reader to interpret a verbal statement about what is
involved in an analogical mapping or a memory search or a match between
two symbols, computational models actually do the mapping, searching and
matching so that the complex interactions of multiple processes can be
unambiguously derived" (Klahr, 1992, p. 276).

This is the critical point of computational modeling. Not only can
increased specificity of the processes be gained by the practice of implementation, but the performance of the resulting model can then be
examined. Very often, this leads to novel results or predictions emerging.
Let us examine this claim in more detail. In the middle of Klahr's

soft-core/hard-core continuum lies the use of formal notations such as flowcharts and decision trees. These have been used to increase the rigor of explanations about a wide range of processing accounts. For example, the decision trees drawn by Siegler (1981) explain the choice of rules used by children operating at different stages of competence on the balance scale task. The balance scale is a beam on a central fulcrum with an equal number of pegs on each side. On these are placed a number of weights, and children are asked which side will go down when a support is removed. Through an elegant series of experiments, Siegler generated a set of four rules that children at different levels of competence use for given tasks. The first rule takes only the weight on each side of the fulcrum into account. The second takes distance of the weights from the center into account only when the weights are equal. The third rule takes weight and distance into account, but fails in certain complex cases. The fourth rule computes torque by multiplying weight and distance and can produce a correct answer for any configuration.

These rules were quite a clear specification of the representations that the children were using at different stages of competence in the balance scale task. However, the decision trees that Siegler drew added yet another level of specification. They provided a description of the conditions under which a child at a given level would use one of the rules for the different kinds of problems that were encountered. This enabled a prediction of the likelihood of a correct answer under those circumstances. Both the rule and decision tree analyses were major advances over those carried out before, and so made a significant impact on the field. For our purposes, they illustrate that the more detailed the description one uses, the more questions one has to ask (and answer) about exactly what representations and processes are being assumed when abstract verbal statements about change are made. The result is always a deeper understanding of the processing, either in terms of a finer grained account or in a clearer set of questions. Taking this to the extreme, the task of writing a computer program that can execute a task in its finest detail requires the most rigorous analysis of one's understanding of the processing involved.

In fact, in the early days of computational modeling, one of its greatest benefits was that the methodology forced a deeper analysis of the behavior in question than had previously been required. This was necessary in order to specify the processes in sufficient detail to be able to write code so that a computer program could follow the steps and complete the task. So little was understood about cognitive processing at this microscopic level of analysis that, for most, the journey was more valuable than the models constructed upon arrival. Johnson-Laird's (1981) statement that "the single most important virtue of programming should come not from the finished product itself, or what it does, but rather from the business of developing it" (p. 186) shows that, initially, most gain came from discovering questions and answers about this finer grained analysis of processing when confronted with the task of trying to construct a computational model.

For many researchers, it is still the case that the task of specifying one's theory to the level of individual processes and their interactions is as valuable as actually building the model. Nevertheless, it is clear that producing an implementation can have even greater benefits in terms of explanatory payoff. Klahr (1992) described how he and Siegler learned even more about the processing involved in the balance scale task when they constructed computational models of each level of competence that Siegler had so clearly documented (Klahr & Siegler, 1978). Their models revealed differences in encoding patterns and working memory capacity, as well as the dynamic interaction of these factors that existed among the four levels of competence. This level of specificity and dynamic characterization was impossible to read off the decision trees or rule models that Siegler had constructed. Yet, such information comes as explicit output from the running model. Similarly, McClelland (1988) reported how early experiences with connectionist computer models helped to integrate seemingly contradictory results from studies of disparate aspects of speech perception.

Thus, as the researcher traverses Klahr's continuum from soft- to hard-core, rewards can be reaped in increasingly specified accounts of the processing involved in some cognitive activity of interest. The greatest rewards come when the processing account is implemented in a running computer program. This is not only because the processes are specified to the greatest degree, but also because their dynamic interactions can be observed directly. A further issue, for us the most critical of all, is that running computer models are the only arena in which the effects of learning mechanisms can be directly observed. For, although the indirect effects of learning manifest themselves in changed behavior, it is only in running computer models that the direct effects of transition mechanisms on underlying processes and representations can be examined. This is such a major point that the whole of the next section is reserved for its discussion.

Another benefit that arises from the construction of a computational model, and one that goes beyond the claim made by Johnson-Laird, is that the program can itself become the object of study. Even the casual observer realizes that there is never just a single model that can be constructed for any given phenomenon. Indeed, the apparent arbitrariness of the modeling process has been a cause for concern for those skeptical of the technique. It is possible to construct a number of alternative models that all appear to contain knowledge and processes sufficient to simulate the behavior of interest. Which of the candidates is closest to the human being's cognitive processes? In this regard, computational models are no different from any other verbal or flow chart model, many alternative forms of which exist for any given phenomenon (Newell, 1980). Those less formal explanatory devices are traditionally evaluated by using them to generate behavioral predictions that are tested empirically to see if the predictions were borne out. If they were, we infer that the processes described in the theory were responsible for causing the predicted behavior. Computational models can also be evaluated in the same way. However, another analytical method is to manipulate the model directly to find out which variants most closely simulate human performance on related tasks. This can be done by taking an implemented model and experimenting with the representations and processes it contains to see which ones cause the model to best match the performance of human subjects. By adding, removing, or modifying its components and observing the resulting behavior, one can more directly manipulate the relationship between hypothesized processes and representations and observable behavior.

Still another interesting characteristic of computational models is that they afford the direct investigation of multiple methods. In the course of constructing a model, one may become aware that processes used by the model to successfully carry out a task can be combined in a number of different ways. Each combination may produce the same manifest behavior under a particular set of circumstances. In other words, the model is telling the researcher that there are multiple methods for completing the task in question. However, some variants may break down in the face of different conditions. For example, learning may cause the wrong behaviors to be generated, or different variants may be able to handle only a subset of the range of tasks that humans can. Thus, not all methods may be equally effective models of human performance and learning, even though they initially seem to be adequate simulations. It may also be that not all of the methods the program can exhibit are found in humans. Tests (such as what the model learns compared to what the human subjects learn) may be used to effectively rule out some methods that are computationally plausible but psychologically implausible. More specifically, by holding some computational parameters constant, one can experiment with different types and combinations of processes in a computer model to determine the required set of processes for producing the target behavior.

Theories and Programs

There is as much scope for variety in the construction of computational models as there is in the development of soft-core models of human information processing activity. We suggested that the advantage of computational models is that they offer one way of narrowing the space of candidate theories by virtue of being runnable, and therefore testable, on a range of tasks. They also afford the opportunity to observe the effect of the interaction of component processes. This cannot be done with unimplemented models. The strongest constraint of all is in a computational model that changes through learning. Self-modification can turn a plausible-looking performance model into a disastrous failure as a transition model if implausible components are included. Thus, just any model will not do. Let us examine why.

Whether one conceives of human information processing as the manipulation of symbolic tokens, as in Newell's (1980) "Physical Symbol Systems" hypothesis, or as the propagation of activation through networks of connected simple processors without symbols, as in the connectionist approach (McClelland, Rumelhart, & PDP, 1986; Rumelhart, McClelland, & PDP, 1986), most agree that human cognition involves the processing of representations. A symbolic representation includes a structural component that encodes external data and internal products in a certain form along with dedicated processes that transform those structures according to a corresponding set of principles (Anderson, 1983). A connectionist representation is interpreted from the pattern of connectivity between individual units that encode different aspects of the overall representation. In either case, what is different about the computational form of theoretical models from all other kinds is that it makes a commitment to the specific nature of those representations and the processing system in which they are implemented.

However, just because a model is implemented in the form of a computer program does not mean that it is any less ad hoc than a verbal model, although it will be more detailed. There are two distinctions that must be made here. One is the separation of the theory from the computer, and the other is the distinction between the theory and the program. The first is rather simple, whereas the second is an issue of considerable complexity and is a theoretical question in the field of cognitive science. Klahr (1992) stated:

> It is important to distinguish between the theoretical content of a program that runs on a computer and the psychological relevance of the computer itself. Hard-core information processing theories are sufficiently complex that it is necessary to run them on a computer in order to explore their implications. However, this does not imply that the theory bears any resemblance to the computer on which it runs. Meteorologists who run computer simulations of hurricanes do not believe that the atmosphere works like a computer. Furthermore, the same theory could be implemented on computers having radically different architectures and mechanisms. Failure to make the distinction between theory and computer leads to the common misconception that information-processing approaches can be arranged along a dimension of "how seriously they take the computer as a model (Miller, 1983)." (p. 300)

Separating the theory from the program is not so easily done. Most of the earliest, and many of the current computational models were written in high level computer languages, such as Lisp. The language is neutral in the sense that it makes no commitment to any particular theory of the cognitive system. Instead, it is a means for programming a computer in a manner that was particularly suitable for the kinds of symbolic manipulations that are the focus of cognitive models. In other words, the programming language is a totally distinct entity in theoretical terms from the representations that are constructed by the program. Although the need to find ways around idiosyncratic programming constraints often affects the construction of the program, the implementation language contributes nothing to the theory. This means that none of the theoretical degrees of freedom in the resulting model can be attributed to the program itself. The programmer's job is to either construct code for, or explain away, every process that is a part of the behavior being simulated.

However, some early models used languages that did make a commitment to a particular view of the human cognitive system so that some aspects of the theory resided in the language itself. The program and the theory were not totally distinct. Perhaps the first example of such a modeling environment is Newell's (1973a) PSG language for constructing *production system* models of human cognition. A production system is a language that assumes a working memory space for doing serial processing and a long-term recognition memory consisting of a store of condition–action (or IF–THEN) rules called *productions*. One example of such a rule is: "IF today's date is December 31st THEN tomorrow is the first day of a new year."

The system contains a matcher that constantly monitors the contents of working memory, and whenever the condition pattern (or IF side) of a production is matched, the representation on its action (or THEN) side is added to the contents of working memory (see Neches, Langley, & Klahr, 1987, for a review of production systems and their applications to cognitive modeling). In such a system, the language is taken to be part of the theory, because it is utilized to take care of the implementation of certain parts of the cognitive processing system that are assumed to be universal across all tasks. Here, to a small extent, the program and the theory are inextricable; the model is like it is partly because of the characteristics of the programming language used. In other words, the programming language takes up some of the theoretical degrees of freedom. Unlike the programmer in Lisp, who would either have to ignore certain cognitive processes or account for them by constructing algorithms for memory access, matching, and so on, the production system user allows the theory underlying the language to contribute implementations of these processes and so shape the resulting program and theory.

The most extreme version of this intermingling of program and theory is the notion of cognitive architecture (Anderson, 1983; Newell, 1990) — that the human cognitive processing system comprises a number of invariant components and processes that are universal across all tasks. For Newell, these include the assumptions that all cognition takes place as tasks formulated in problem spaces (Newell, 1981), that the basic underlying memory and processing components are those of the production system described previously, and that there is a single learning mechanism, called *chunking*, that continually converts the results of processing in working memory into new recognition memory elements stored in long-term memory (Rosenbloom, Newell, & Laird, 1991). These ideas culminated in the construction of Soar, a fully programmable instantiation of Newell's unified theory of cognition (1990). Because Soar exists in the form of a computer program, the modeler begins with the language that is an embodiment of a theory of cognition at the architecture level and uses it to construct a model of his or her own phenomenon of interest.

Such architectures provide constraints on information processing theories because all models must be formulated using the same system, and all results will be transformed by the same learning mechanism. Just as all cars on the road have the same underlying architecture, yet each one has a different appearance, history, state of repair and capabilities, so does the cognitive system of each person. Furthermore, the common architecture of each individual car imposes a set of constraints. Not a single one can go sideways, none of them go backwards well for long, and few can perform well at extremely high speed. Similarly, for human beings, the cognitive architecture provides constraints on what each individual can do. A person's performance and learning at any given time is a function of the interaction of the architecture and the individual's current task, knowledge, and goals.

Thus, the notion of a fixed cognitive architecture represents one extreme end of the theory–program interaction continuum. At this end there is no theory–program dissociation. Because the theorist is adding on to the theory in the architecture, it necessarily becomes a large part of the explanation being put forth. What he or she adds is the extra knowledge and processes that are theorized to be the domain-specific resources human beings use to employ the architecture for the task in question. The benefits the theorist receives are many. First, he or she need not worry about constructing the parts of the model assumed to be universal. These are time consuming, difficult to build, and either discourage the building of a complete model in the first place, or the details tend to be neglected and so are idiosyncratic to each theorist's model. Examples of such universals are the memory access algorithm and the learning mechanism. Thus, the programmable architecture takes care of a number of theoretical and implementational degrees of freedom by providing carefully implemented, theoretically grounded processes that constitute the basic building blocks of cognitive processing. This leaves the researcher to investigate ways of analyzing, and ultimately implementing, the knowledge and processes that underlie the behavior of interest.

The outcome is that theorists and observers can be more sure of where the explanatory power of such models reside. There need be less concern that the model behaves as it does because of how its creators programmed their own memory access or learning algorithms. Rather, one can be sure that, within the bounds of the architecture, what the model does and how it does it are a consequence of the general theory plus the representations that the theorists have deemed critical and have provided for the architecture to process. Therefore, these components plus the architecture are the theory of the behavior in question. A second benefit is unification; Newell's (1990) main goal. Because all models within the architecture are couched within the same theoretical constraints, the constraints propagate from one model to another in a way that has been missing from psychological research until now (Newell, 1973b, 1981). Independent researchers can inform and constrain each other's models by providing general principles of processing within the architecture or even sharing code for the same processes in totally different tasks. This reduces the *ad hoc* nature of individual models because they share not only the same basic architecture, but also important higher level processes with many others. Such activity occurs in the Soar community and has resulted in some published accounts of multiple models being interactively combined. One example is the combination of early forms of a natural language and a relational reasoning model that could read in instructions for a variety of reasoning tasks, come up with answers, and output them back to the environment (Polk, Newell, & Lewis, 1989).

Soar is not the only example of an architecture of human cognition, although it is the most advanced instance, in that it exists in a publicly available, fully programmable form. Anderson's (1983) ACT* was an even earlier theory of the human cognitive architecture. Though extremely influential in the cognitive science community, ACT* has never existed in a widely available programmable form and so represents more of a framework for theorizing than a means of building theoretical programs. A new version, ACTr (Anderson, 1993), goes a long way toward bridging the programmability gap. PRISM (Langley & Neches, 1981) does exist as a programmable system, but not one that was committed to a specific architecture, like ACT* or Soar. Rather, its purpose was to let the programmer select from a range of variables to construct an instance of a cognitive architecture from the space of possible architectures. Thus, like Soar, its main aim was unification in the sense of communicability about a set of programs in a common language. Unlike ACT* and Soar, PRISM did not aim to constrain accounts of the entire range of phenomena through a common theory. Langley (1987) used PRISM quite successfully to create unified accounts of a number of developmental phenomena in terms of discrimination learning. Several other architectures for general intelligent processing (but not necessarily theories of the human cognitive system) have also been developed (VanLehn, 1991).

Although we just used the term *architecture* to refer to a unified set of theoretically motivated processes claimed to underlie all cognition, the terminology has been applied to other kinds of systems that can be fit onto a continuum. Having placed Soar at the most extreme (or hard-core) end of the architecture continuum, with ACT very close by, we suggest that PRISM occupies more central ground. Other authors have used architecture in different ways, and it is important to situate their view of cognitive architecture on our continuum. In their discussion of computer simulation and development, Rabinowitz, Grant, and Dingley (1987) used the term *architecture* in a weaker, more organizational sense than we defined PRISM. They described diverse entities, such as sets of production system models, exemplified by Klahr and Wallace's models of children's series completion and quantification processing (Klahr & Wallace, 1973, 1976), as well as modeling environments like PRISM as architectures. Thus, their view of architecture would be more central on the continuum. They saw architecture as a unifying construct in terms of common language, making a clear distinction between a theory and its implementational basis. They argued that "without a semiuniversal adaptation of a modifiable cognitive architecture, communication about program theories will sometimes appear unfathomable to the uninitiated and will be difficult to follow for individuals using different systems" (p. 277). This was an odd claim because, to use Klahr's (1992) example, it was like an exhortation for all researchers to use the same statistical technique so that their results are most easily communicated to others. In our view, Klahr's suggestion that scientists interested in developmental phenomena should be more widely trained to understand computational approaches is a better solution to the problem.

Finally, the softest use of *architecture* can be found in reference to connectionist models (e.g., McClelland, 1988). This use of the term neither refers to degree of theory in the programming medium nor to interprogram similarity. Instead, it refers to the topographical structure of a network of units and connections. Connectionist models are quite unlike the symbolic models we previously discussed. They are sometimes referred to as Parallel Distributed Processing (PDP) models because processing is distributed across a connected network of simple processors, whereas representations are distributed as patterns of activation on those processors and connections. Processing takes place by the propagation of activation through the network. Learning is implemented as the adjustment of weights on connections between units via feedback from the environment and other units within the network. Different units in the network denote different aspects of represented entities, and the connectivity and activation level of a settled network (one that has learned to some stable level and is no longer adjusting itself) are taken as the model's learned representations. There are variations concerning how any given network is connected, and McClelland used the term *architecture* to refer to the connectivity pattern of a given network. There are presently no forms of universal architectures in connectionist modeling, even in the sense that a production system can be seen as a weak form of a theoretical architecture. Because PDP models only made their way into the cognitive science community recently (McClelland et al., 1986; Rumelhart et al., 1986), it is unclear whether or not connectionism is suitable for the construction of cognitive architectures and that it can only be a general framework (McClelland, 1988), or whether or not such architectures will naturally emerge as more experience with connectionist modeling is gained by the scientific community.

SELF-MODIFICATION AND TRANSITION MECHANISMS

We looked in some detail at what can be gained in terms of specificity and unification by expressing information processing accounts of cognitive phenomena in the form of computer programs. In this section, we address the special relevance of computational models to the study of cognitive change. In his comments on the chapters in a book about mechanisms of change, Flavell (1984) made the observation that "serious theorizing about basic mechanisms of cognitive growth has actually never been a popular pastime. . . . It is rare indeed to encounter a substantive treatment of the problem in the annual flood of articles, chapters and books on cognitive development. The reason is not hard to find: good theorizing about mechanisms is very, very hard to do" (p. 189). Although in agreement with Flavell's statement, we believe that a large part of that difficulty stemmed from researchers not having techniques available that were suitable for examining the sorts of issues involved in the study of transition mechanisms. Here, we claim that the computational model is the single most effective and powerful tool cognitive science has to offer the researcher interested in studying how change occurs. This is because it is the only means available for studying transition mechanisms by manipulating them directly, rather than inferring their working from measures of the behavioral effects they create.

In the introduction, we outlined the three components necessary for the construction of computational models of cognitive transition mechanisms. Such models now can be built. The advance that made this possible was the development of computer languages able to autonomously modify the representations they are processing. Such a capability matches one of

Klahr's (1992) three theoretical assumptions about information processing approaches to cognitive development, that "cognitive development takes place via self-modification of the information-processing system" (p. 274).This volume represents the most advanced collection of models of this kind. Previous collections have either focused on developmental transitions but contained noncomputational accounts (Sternberg, 1984), or have presented self-modifying models of a more diverse set of learning phenomena (Klahr, Langley, & Neches, 1987).

Why Only Computational Models?

Why do we make the claim that only computational models are especially well suited to the study of transition mechanisms? The primary reason is one of direct access to the change mechanisms themselves. In recent years, many interesting studies have been carried out by researchers employing microgenetic approaches to the study of cognitive change (Karmiloff-Smith, 1979; Siegler & Crowley, 1992). Microgenetic methods involve high-density observations of children's behavior over an extended period of time and were found to be effective in providing insights into behavioral changes the children exhibit. However, the mechanisms responsible for those changes are not available to inspection. They can only be inferred from the effects they have on the initial competence of the children as a consequence of the observed activities. What is missing from the microgenetic approach, but is present in a running computer model, is a physical embodiment of the actual representations and processes with a lid one can open and look inside. This enables the theorist to unequivocally state what the set of mechanisms are that transform the initial representations into those that support the target behavior. So, whereas microgenetic or other kinds of longitudinal methodology may track the time and experience aspect of cognitive change very closely, they do not provide direct access to candidate mechanisms of change—for us, the objects of greatest interest.

The inadequacy of cross-sectional methodologies for the study of transition mechanisms is even more pronounced. Most importantly, these methodologies, whether observational, experimental or computational, do not focus on the manifest behavior in which individuals engage that causes them to move from one level of competence to the next. Computational state-models that specify processes at separate, discrete levels of competence, but that do not study intervening behavior, provided some insight into cognitive change (see review in Rabinowitz et al., 1987). Furthermore, as Klahr (1992) pointed out, such models have limited the space of possible explanations of transition mechanisms by specifying the *before* and *after* representations to the extent that good guesses at the transformational processes could be made. Nevertheless, they were unable to directly specify the actual transition mechanisms that could take those *before* representations as inputs, undergo a specific set of experiences, and output only the *after* representations that had been specified.

An obvious question that arises in response to the previous claim is, "what more can be understood from a specification of the transition mechanisms?" There are a number of answers to this question. The most important one is that transition models provide an account of how change is taking place. The theorist can state not only what is changing in terms of the competence a child or adult possesses but also the representations being transformed and the processes responsible for that transformation. The benefit of this knowledge is to make it possible to predict the effects of certain experiences in terms of producing cognitive change. It should also enable us to harness that knowledge into interventions that will produce change, such as instruction and training. Another outcome from specifying transition mechanisms is the ability to understand when change will occur, or put another way, under what conditions the transition mechanisms are called into play to transform existing representations.

This question was addressed by Neches, Langley, and Klahr (1987) in the context of when, during the processing cycle, self-modifying production systems cause knowledge to be altered. A more general treatment of the issue arose in Newell's (1990) consideration of the types of *impasses* that arise during Soar's processing. Soar's learning mechanism, chunking, is called into play whenever an impasse arises during processing in any of Soar's current problem spaces. For Soar, an impasse is any point where the knowledge retrieved from long-term memory does not lead to an unequivocal indication of what to do next. In response, Soar establishes a subgoal whose purpose is to resolve the difficulty at hand. Although we make use of Newell's discussion of impasses in relation to Soar, we employ the notion of impasses here as an instance of the more general set of cases when an intelligent agent will have cause to learn. Newell (1990) distinguished four types of impasses. These are the *tie, no-change, reject,* and *conflict* impasses. A tie impasse arises when an action must be taken and more than one option is retrieved from memory. In other words, the learner has sufficient *applicability* knowledge to be able to decide what things could be done at this particular point in time. What is missing is sufficient *desirability* knowledge to be able to decide which of the possible actions should be selected in the current situation. Learning the results of choosing an option in the present context is clearly a useful thing to do and it increases the learner's problem solving efficiency.

The learner experiences a no-change impasse when, having reached some decision point, no obvious next step is suggested from the collection of things the learner has stored in memory. In other words, nothing is known that is immediately applicable to the current problem. The learner must try alternative approaches to resolve the difficulty until something that is known becomes an appropriate step to take. Again, learning the results of this sort of problem solving would result in new applicability knowledge. Here, the learner discovers new ways to apply existing knowledge to the problem at hand. Reject impasses occur when a learner first recalls one or more actions applicable to the current situation. These subsequently cause recall of learned knowledge that, under the current circumstances, those actions are undesirable. For example, when locked out of the house, breaking a window and calling the police may both have been retrieved, considered, and then rejected. The learner must then begin the search for new things to try and so becomes open to acquiring new applicability and/or desirability knowledge. Finally, a conflict impasse will arise where more than one applicable action is recalled but knowledge learned at different times tells the learner both that Option A is better than Option B under the current circumstances, and that Option B is better than Option A. At this point, the learner must try to decide if there are more conditions that might help choose between the two, or whether a totally new option should be sought, again leaving the way open to learn either applicability or desirability knowledge or both. (For an extended discussion of impasses in Soar, see Newell, 1990, chap. 4).

Klahr (1992) presented a detailed discussion of the variety of self-modifying mechanisms that were developed for symbolic computational modeling systems, and McClelland (1988) discussed some of the learning algorithms developed for connectionist models of change. Whatever form these models take, the implementation of a theory of change in a self-modifying computer program is the most direct method for examining the workings of proposed cognitive transition mechanisms. Two other benefits of self-modifying cognitive models should also be mentioned here. The first is a methodological issue discussed in the previous section: A self-modification mechanism provides a strong constraint on the representations and processes of candidate models of cognitive phenomena. The other is a far more theoretical issue: the claim that self-modifying programs offer an empirical examination of the old debate of whether or not there are qualitatively different mechanisms that underlie different kinds of change, such as the distinction between learning and development. We briefly discuss each of these issues.

In the previous section, we saw how computational models support increased specification of the knowledge and processes that theorists claim to be supporting cognitive activity. We also saw how, like any other form of theorizing, there can be multiple computational models for any one phenomenon. However, those theorists who have built their own self-modifying models have found that self-modification is a very constraining characteristic of a program. At the risk of being repetitive, we restate that cognition is the ability to execute information processing activities based on internally generated representations. Both self-modifying and static models are usually provided with usable representations by the programmer. What distinguishes the self-modifying system is that little of its overall processing is carried out using those initial representations once it has begun working in a given domain. That is because the initial representations it is given, and the tasks it is carrying out, become inputs to the self-modification mechanism. The outputs of that mechanism will be new representations that will quickly supersede the old ones and become the basis for new processing and, of course, the construction of new representations.

Models based on theoretically sound self-modification mechanisms will create meaningful new representations only to the extent that the original representations and task specifications are realistic characterizations of human competence. Such a transition mechanism will take implausible representations and create structures that may be meaningless in terms of human cognition. Based on these modified representations, the model will quickly diverge from simulating realistic processing, making it behave in a manner inconsistent with human behavior, if it is able to continue to behave at all. Many modelers have built convincing static performance models of human cognition only to see their simulations collapse when subjected to a theoretically plausible self-modification mechanism. This means that a self-modifying model is likely to be far more accurate as a simulation of human cognition than a static performance model. A second, and more theoretical reason for demanding self-modification in a cognitive model is realism. Self-modifying systems are more realistic because almost all competence exhibited by human beings is constructed out of their previous experience. Thus, when any account of cognition is presented in detailed information processing terms, an important question to ask is "how did the system get to be like that?". Along with a credible explanation of the processing that is the basis for a given cognitive competence, the theorist must be pressed to say how the human being came to have knowledge and processes in that particular form. This question of learnability is beginning to have an important impact in may areas of cognitive science from developmental psychology (Carey & Gelman, 1991) to linguistics and language learning (Pinker, 1979). Another way to say this is that human beings do not have self-modification as an option. Their learning switch is permanently in the on position and, therefore, change must always be accounted for.

Self-modifying systems also contribute to the learning–development debate (Piatelli-Palmarini, 1980). This is too large a debate to review here, but for some (notably Piaget), there was a clear distinction between mechanisms of learning and of development. The distinction was not only in terms of the time course of change, but also in terms of structural organization of cognitive components and their implications for behavior. Our claim is that self-modifying simulations of cognitive change can contribute to this debate in an important and meaningful way. As more simulations of cognitive change are constructed and reported, we will be able to evaluate whether or not such a dichotomy exists. Because computational models offer unequaled identifiability and examinability of processes and representations, it is possible to scrutinize the mechanisms that account for the change concerned and ask some critical questions. Do these models credibly simulate phenomena traditionally associated with development? If so, what kinds of self-modification mechanisms are they using? Have these same mechanisms been used to explain other changes traditionally associated with so-called learning phenomena? We believe that a growing body of self-modifying models of change will show that one can empirically demonstrate the lack of any dissociation between mechanisms of learning and development. This volume is an example of such a body of work. It contains simulations of developmental phenomena implemented in systems that use self-modification mechanisms that equally well explain nondevelopmental phenomena. Examples of these are chunking in Soar, weight adjustment in PDP models, and symbolic models of association strength adjustment. Other examples exist, such as Jones and VanLehn's (1994) use of concept formation algorithms to model strategy change. We expect that the learning–development debate will most likely be resolved via computational modeling research.

ENVIRONMENTAL INPUT

We discussed what the practice of constructing a computational model can contribute in terms of process specification, and we claimed there is a special role for such models in the study of cognitive change. We said very little about the activities in which the model must engage, such that it is able to modify its initial representations into the ones of the target level of competence. Though the statement may seem a truism, it is essential that the model undergo the same experiences that the human being does during the transition in question. This is because the learning and processing that the model engages in during self-modification must be a consequence of the same general activities as the human subject being modeled. If the child and the model undergo the same set of experiences and the model simulates the child's intermediate and ending states then we can say, with a high degree of confidence, that we have created a good account of the transition in question. To put it another way, when experimenting on a computational model, the task and environmental input are independent variables. The dependent variables are the representations provided for the model that create its initial performance, and the self-modification mechanism that transforms them into representations that support the target behavior. If all else is held constant and the simulation is successful, then we can hold up those representations and self-modification mechanism as a sufficient account of the transition in question. If, however, the model's task or input are not accurate reflections of those experienced by the human, then the model's credibility is severely limited.

In other words, if the model and the child take a different set of experiences as input, then we can say nothing about the model's transition mechanism as an account of the child. They are creating new representations that support the same end state of behavior, but doing it by different means. As an example, imagine Chris and Pat who start out with identical cameras and film and who both take a picture of the same flower. Their initial behavior is identical and is supported by the same resources (camera, film, light, flower). Chris takes the film to a store to have it processed, spends the rest of the day buying groceries and visiting friends. The next day, Chris goes to the store and pays for the print and takes it home. Pat, however, takes the film home and spends the rest of the day in a darkroom developing the film, setting up an enlarger, making test prints and finally creating an identical print to the one Chris has. So Chris and Pat end up with the same observable results in the form of a print of the flower. However, in getting from start to end state, a different set of intermediate results was created. Chris' life may have been enriched by an increased stock of food and positive feelings from interacting with friends. Pat's activity created more experience and expertise in the darkroom, as well as a feeling of having achieved a job well done. It is clear that the intervening processes and their results are different in the cases of Chris and Pat, despite the perfect match of their observable start and end states. Any model that does not directly simulate its human counterpart's activity has not undergone the same transition.

Minimizing Weakening Assumptions

This is not a problem with a simple solution. It is rarely possible to exactly specify the set of experiences a child or adult undergoes in the course of a transition, often spread over an extended period of time. Nevertheless, there is danger in merely assuming the set of experiences critical to the transition, lest the model carry out a completely irrelevant set of self-modifications. However, short of picking up a video camera and following individuals around for the years it might take them to learn to play chess, or the violin, or master mental arithmetic, what are we to do? One solution is to find some way of specifying a set of identical experiences for the model and human subjects to undergo.

One way to do this is to employ training studies. Subjects can be tested to find out which capabilities form the foundational competencies for training on the target ability. We call this state in the human subject *Sh1*, and a computational model that accurately simulates this level of competence can be built, called *Sc1*. Both Sh1 and Sc1 should produce the same responses during identical training experiences (Sh2 and Sc2). Note that an examination of the representations that Sc2 now has provides an account of Sh2's increasing competence. Also, an examination of the processes that created Sc2 from Sc1 provides an account of the transition mechanisms involved. If, at the end of training, Sh3 and Sc3 equate in terms of performance, then Sc3's representations exist as a specification of Sh3's knowledge that resulted from the training and the transition mechanisms embodied in the model. This was the approach taken by Simon and Klahr (this volume) to account for the acquisition of number conservation knowledge. Further empirical tests can then be run to determine whether or not these are the kinds of representations human subjects have after training. If they are, then an account of how they come to be naturally constructed can be sought. This could be done by simulating the change that occurs during seminaturalistic interventions of the sort carried out by Saxe, Gearhart, and Guberman (1984) or Shrager and Callanan (1991). Training studies do have well-known shortcomings. Problems such as lack of transfer and temporary nature of learning sometimes result. However, these issues are identifiable and so should also become topics for investigation. By employing training studies we can be confident that the transitions result from the same activities engaged in by the model and the human subjects.

A similar point about the importance of environmental input was made by McClelland (1989) in his discussion of the contribution of PDP models to the study of cognition and development. He stated that "the environment plays a crucial role in determining exactly what is learned. Thus models that aim to capture aspects of cognitive development through connectionist learning include among their assumptions a specification of the details of the experience that gives rise to the resulting developmental sequence. In many cases, these assumptions play a major role in the success or failure of the modeling effort" (p. 15). We agree with McClelland that the input to the model is a critical factor in the resulting developmental sequence. However, as we argued, it is possible that leaving the structure of that input to assumption (however well-founded) introduces the danger that one of the strongest theoretical contributions of a computational model of transition mechanisms could be undermined.

We offer one other resolution of this issue. It is not always possible to design training studies that adopt the suggested methodology. Also, in many cases the assumptions about the structure of environmental input may be strongly grounded. Nevertheless, even if the simulation does produce the same transitional and target states as do human subjects, the transition mechanism can be taken as an explanation of the change only if it can be shown that human subjects receive their input in the same form that the model does. In other words, the form of that input becomes a prediction of the model based on the behavior of the particular transition mechanism involved. This prediction should be tested with experiments where the transition mechanism is the independent variable and various forms of input are the dependent variables.

A case in point is McClelland's simulations of the same balance scale transitions simulated by Klahr and Siegler's (1978) production system models. McClelland's (1989) models were "based on the assumption that the environment for learning about balance problems consists of experiences that vary more frequently on the weight dimension than they do on the distance dimension" (p. 27). Such an assumption was tested by Schmidt and Shultz (1992), who built a series of connectionist models with different structures and learning algorithms to test this and other McClelland assumptions. Schmidt and Shultz found the input assumption to be critical to the learning of the models. Only the models whose input was most heavily biased in terms of a greater number of weight trials produced psychologically plausible learning. Furthermore, the best learning came from the biggest bias. McClelland (1989) went on to say that his environmental assumption "is meant as a proxy for the more general assumption that children generally have more experiences with weight than with distance as a factor in determining the relative heaviness of something" (McClelland, 1989, p. 27). That may be true, but along with an input assumption, McClelland is importing an assumption about the goals of the processing — something that is not explicitly represented in a PDP model. In the domain of balance, the goal of the learner has a great impact on what is perceived as the primary dimension to take into consideration.

In all of the balance scale work (e.g., Siegler, 1981) it is evident that subjects view weight as the primary dimension for the problem. It is the basis of the first rule used by children, and one of the main transitions is the shift of attention to the distance dimension. However, in this task, children are given the goal of telling the experimenter which arm of the balance will fall (i.e., determining which is the heavier). In an almost identical task, Karmiloff-Smith and Inhelder (1974) gave 4- to 9-year-old children differently weighted blocks and asked them to try to balance them on a bar. This switched the children's goal to one of finding a balance point and, for them, the primary dimension became distance. Just as with the balance scale, a great deal of effort was then required to make the children understand that weight was also important in balancing the blocks. Thus, it is clear that the learner's goal has a significant impact on the encoding of the task. So, if assumptions related to goals are to be made, they must also become explicit predictions of the model and must be empirically tested. We do not present these arguments as a critique of McClelland's models. Rather, our purpose is to show that the more assumptions are introduced into a model, the less one can tell about the contribution of its transition mechanisms in accounting for the change in question. The authors of these and other models are well aware of these issues and have already begun to address them in detail, as can be seen in the chapters by McClelland and Shultz et al. in this volume.

One of the main contributions of computational models of cognitive transitions is to allow the researcher to appreciate the complex interactions between different processes, the model's self-modification mechanism, and the experiences on which it is exercised. None of these can be examined using a static model such as a flow chart or decision tree. In other words, computational models enable the researcher to understand more about cognitive transitions than was possible before. However, researchers new to simulating transitions must be careful not to come to the practice with fixed ideas about how transitions occur and then look for simulation techniques that are consistent with those ideas. Such research would not be discovering transition mechanisms, it would merely be confirming prior assumptions about them. The characteristics of certain computational approaches can encourage this. There are sound reasons for the adoption of connectionist modeling techniques for investigating transition mechanisms, as the chapters by McClelland and Shultz et al. show. Principal among these is that these models are able to exhibit the gradual, nondiscrete transitions between levels of competence and the U-shaped behavior that are often observed in cognitive change. However, a superficial understanding of the technique may lead to its selection for the wrong reasons. The researcher may begin by reasoning that development is a slow and gradual process, where knowledge builds up over a long period of time and across many experiences. This, it is assumed, is why so many transitions take so long. However, rather than making this assumption an empirical matter for research, it instead becomes a required characteristic of any modeling technique that is to be adopted. As they learn, connectionist models usually require many thousands of trials to settle into a stable network, with errors being made until that stability is reached. This superficial similarity may make connectionism seem to be a natural computational method for transition modeling.

However, this similarity is not necessarily valid. Connectionist models typically begin with random connections between units or weights set to random levels. This means that their initial output, before learning, is also random. As developmentalists know, there is considerable evidence (Carey & Gelman, 1991) that not even the neonate's world is such a blooming, buzzing confusion as that of an untrained PDP network. PDP models start out tabula rasa and take time to form representations based on input and feedback. That model of development is very outdated indeed! Furthermore, it may not be correct to assume that all development does take time just because many trials are required. The young child is simultaneously learning a great deal across different domains. Experience in any single one may be temporally distributed, meaning that much time is required to collect just a few experiences in that domain. Such temporal distribution may mean that many potential pieces of information are lost due to the memory load of relating new experiences to old ones, even assuming that the child is even paying attention to the right thing at the right time. A good test would be to ask if the transition in question has ever been successfully trained. If so, the sufficient number of experiences may be found to be quite small and the question then returns to how these are collected and related together over time in the case of naturalistic development.

The exhortation we are making here is not to decide the solution ahead of time and look for a model that might fit. It is precisely because the problem of specifying transition mechanisms is so complex that we are claiming that the computational methodology is so useful. We cannot assume that we know the answer ahead of time. Rather, we must use this methodology to help us discover how cognitive transitions occur. In that enterprise, both symbolic and nonsymbolic approaches have their place. The field of cognitive science, having popularized the computational approach to explaining cognitive processes, has a special contribution to offer to the developmental scientist. We hope that the collection represented in this volume signals the beginning of an exciting new wave in research on cognitive change.

COMPUTATIONAL MODELING AND COGNITIVE DEVELOPMENT RESEARCH

In this section we consider ways that specifying processes in cognitive tasks might influence research in cognitive development, beyond the computational modeling process. We consider how computational modeling might become integrated with, and both influence and be influenced by empirical research in the field. We suggest that there are at least three ways in which cognitive development research might benefit from more attention to process models. It can assist in the interpretation of children's performance, help resolve theoretical issues, and suggest new research questions.

Many issues in cognitive development center on the way performances should be interpreted. Much of the early controversy about Piagetian tests was not so much concerned with what children did, as with the interpretation of their behavior. In the case of conservation, for example, there is little doubt that young children behave as Piaget reported. Considerable doubts were raised, however, about whether or not Piaget's interpretation was valid. It was suggested that children's failures might not have reflected lack of understanding of quantity, but other factors, such as conflict, misleading perceptual cues, or ambiguous instructions. A protracted controversy resulted, and it does not appear to have been resolved. We suggest that it would be easier to resolve this issue if we could precisely specify what processes are entailed in a task such as conservation. This is not a matter of arguing that computational modeling will automatically clarify every issue, but it can remove ambiguity and channel research along more productive lines.

This point is illustrated more clearly with a simpler and less controversial task than conservation. There are a number of paradigms in the literature that go under the name of *false belief*. One was devised by Wimmer and Perner (1983) and entails a person seeing an object hidden in Place A, then the person leaves the room, and the object is removed to a new hiding Place B. The child is asked where the person will look for the object. This task requires the child to infer that because the person saw the object in Place A, and did not see it moved to Place B, the person should look at Place A. Another false belief task was devised by Wellman and Bartsch (1988). The child is told that Sam thinks his puppy is in Place A, whereas it is really in Place B. The child is then asked where Sam will look for his puppy. Unlike the Wimmer and Perner task, the Wellman and Bartsch task does not require the child to infer where Sam thinks the puppy is, because the child is told that directly. The inferences required in the Wellman and Bartsch task cannot be assumed to be the same as those in the Wimmer and Perner task.

Considerable controversy surrounded the age of attainment of false belief and related paradigms. We do not wish to take a position on that issue, but we draw attention to the problem of specifying what is entailed in performing these tasks. Failure to do this can lead to considerable confusion. The two false belief tasks outlined in the last paragraph may entail different cognitive processes. However, they tend to be treated as equivalent because the same verbal tag, false belief can be attached to each of them. This common label may mask important differences that could have unrecognized consequences. For example, a manipulation that improves performance on one task might not improve the other. Furthermore, it is not necessarily appropriate to expect that children would attain both performances at the same age. It might be that the task entailing the simpler inferences would be attained first. The problem is that we do not know what to expect, or how to interpret out findings, until we know what processes are entailed in performing each task.

Much controversy in cognitive development has revolved around the age of attainment of certain concepts. There have been many instances where children have been found to perform one version of a task earlier than another, leading to some protracted polemic. It seems that much of this discussion might have been unnecessary, and other parts of it might have been more productive, if we had been working from process models of the tasks in question. Issues concerned with children's performance of some of the important Piagetian tasks (such as transitivity and class inclusion) hinges on the processes entailed.

There are also substantive issues in cognitive development that might be transformed by a computational approach. A good example is the important but difficult problem of processing capacity. It is arguable that we will never have an adequate account of cognitive development until we understand capacity, and can clearly answer the question whether or not capacity changes with age. Our progress on this problem has been hampered by lack of a clear and realistic concept of human capacity limitations. Processing capacity limitations have lacked plausibility as an explanatory factor because we think in terms of primitive and inappropriate concepts, such slots or stores. If we are trying to store books on a shelf, there is no increase in difficulty of storing as we add more books until capacity is reached, when it suddenly becomes impossible to add another book. Human capacity limitations do not appear to exhibit this discontinuous quality. Rather, it seems that as the amount of information to be processed increases, there is a continuous decline in performance, but it never totally ceases. That is, we do not have anything equivalent to a filling up of the available store. This makes it implausible that human performance has anything to do with processing capacity.

This whole argument is completely changed when we adopt a different conception, based on PDP accounts. Models based on distributed representations have the property of *graceful saturation*, meaning that there is a gradual decline in performance, but no total cessation. Performance can decline to the point where it is no better than chance, just as it does with humans. Thus, distributed models provide a concept of capacity limitations that is much more intuitively plausible than outdated metaphors based on slots or stores. Some implications of this conception for cognitive development were explored elsewhere (Halford, 1993), but our concern here is to illustrate the way computational models can have very real and substantial implications for fundamental issues in our field.

Research in other fields is driven by process models more than is cognitive development. For example, research questions in vision and memory tend to be generated by the dominant process models. In contrast, many research questions in cognitive development continue to be generated by the conflict between Piagetian psychology in its various forms, and a competing approach that seems to owe much to neobehaviorism. The cognitive revolution has had less influence on the field of cognitive development than on many related fields. Successful process models have been built, but they have not been used as a source of research questions as much as they could have been.

We hope that this volume will assist in drawing attention to new and potentially productive research. As discussed previously, a whole set of questions concerning the nature of transition mechanisms now seem ripe for both theoretical and empirical investigation. The development of new models of learning, induction, strategy and skill acquisition, as well as models of the way information is encoded, opens up a whole array of new areas for the cognitive development researcher. New conceptions of the way information is represented, especially those that employ the parallel distributed processing, or connectionist architecture, give us fundamental new insights into the bases of human performance. These conceptions permit us to reformulate old questions, one of the most central of which is the nature of processing capacity. More will be said on each of these issues in later chapters.

OVERVIEW OF CHAPTERS IN THIS VOLUME

Following this introduction, the first two chapters are concerned with models of how children choose among existing strategies and acquire new ones.

Chapter 2, by Siegler and Shipley, reports a model of the way children choose the most adaptive strategy for arithmetic tasks. They emphasize that all children have more than one strategy available for a task. Therefore, rather than asking what strategy a child is using, it makes more sense to ask how children choose the best strategy in the prevailing circumstances. They have also demonstrated that children have biases toward certain classes of strategies, thereby accounting for individual differences. They offer the Adaptive Strategy Choice Model (ASCM—pronounced "Ask-em"), which builds on Siegler's earlier Distributions of Associations model. It is implemented as a running computer program that simulates choices among strategies on the basis of strength—a function of past speed and accuracy on all problems in the class, on problems with features in common with the current one, and on problems the same as the current one. This provides a mechanism for storing problem solving experience as a basis for future adaptive strategy choices. The strategies adopted by the simulation model correspond closely with children's choices on the same tasks.

Chapter 3, by Halford et al., presents a model of strategy development in transitive inference tasks, called the Transitive Inference Mapping Model (TRIMM). The model chooses strategies on the basis of strength, as with Siegler and Shipley's model, but where no strategy is available that matches the current situation, it develops a new strategy. This development is guided by a concept of the task acquired in past experience, not necessarily in the same context. Previous knowledge is used by analogy, but the analogical mappings are subject to a processing load factor, that simulates human capacity limitations. However, this factor operates only where it is necessary to develop new strategies. Where existing strategies are adequate, they are performed automatically and the processing load is considerably reduced. Thus, the model blends associative and metacognitive strategy development mechanisms. The model is implemented as a self-modifying production system, and new strategies are added by creating new productions. Once formed, productions are strengthened or weakened, depending on their success in performing transitive inference tasks. The model simulates adult and child performance on a representative set of transitive inference tasks.

The next two chapters are concerned with connectionist (parallel distributed processing, or PDP) models of cognitive development.

Chapter 4, by McClelland, offers a connectionist model of the balance scale task. It simulates progression through the four rules defined by Siegler (1981) as a function of experience with the balance scale. However, it also accounts for other effects not incorporated into previous models, but well established empirically. These include the magnitude of the torque difference, and cue familiarity and complexity. The model also conceptualizes the difference between implicit knowledge that can mediate balance judgments, and explicit knowledge in the form of verbalizable rules. The model architecture comprises three layers of units. The bottom layer is used to code the weights and distances on each side of the balance. The middle or hidden layer codes relations between weights (or distances) on each side of the balance. The output layer represents the judgment as to which side will go down, or whether the beam will balance. Learning consists of adjusting the connection weights between the layers. The model first learns to perform in accordance with Siegler's weight rule because it is more strongly represented in the input, and because it is more complex than the distance rule. Its progression through the remaining rules is consistent with empirical observations.

Chapter 5, by Shultz, Schmidt, Buckingham, and Mareschal, describes a set of connectionist models using a technique called *cascade-correlation*. This style of modeling differs from other PDP approaches in that it does not start with a fixed set of units and connections that are randomly connected. Instead these models recruit new intervening or hidden units as they are required to cope with qualitative and quantitative changes in representation and processing. Shultz et al. show the advantages of such an approach by presenting models of a range of tasks, such as the balance scale; the acquisition of concepts of space, time, and velocity; developments in causal reasoning; the acquisition of personal pronouns; and development in seriation reasoning. Among other results, cascade correlation modeling shows its advantages in the balance scale task by producing better coverage of the human data and requiring fewer theoretical assumptions than were required by previous models. In the seriation task, not only is the developmental progression produced, but some predictions emerge about the kind of events that provoke learning and about how children decompose the task into independent *what* and *where* processing. Similarly the models of personal pronoun learning make some interesting predictions about the nature of the input and learning environment children require in order to master the tricky task of correctly using terms that refer to different people at different times.

Two further chapters address the topic of representation change in terms of constructing of new conceptual understandings out of existing knowledge and processes.

Chapter 6, by Gentner, Ratterman, Markman, and Kotovsky, presents a representation change view of the development of analogical reasoning. They focus on the *relational shift*, a transition from judging the similarity of entities based on the objects involved, to judging similarity based on the relations between those objects. A series of empirical studies and computational models based on the Structure Mapping Engine provide evidence that this shift relies on changes in domain-specific knowledge and not on advances in global competence or processing capacity. Two main mechanisms are proposed to underlie the relational shift. One is the processing of relational language that promotes the representation and learning of relational structure. The other is the act of making comparisons between entities that creates structural alignments from which relational learning can occur. In modeling the data they present, Gentner et al. are able to make explicit two of the main representational changes critical for the relational shift. One of these is the use of higher order relations. Although not yet able to provide an account of the acquisition of these relations beyond suggesting a role for language, the authors' models show that older children's ability to map beyond literal similarity could result from their use of higher order relations, like monotonic increase in size, that younger children have not yet been able to construct. The other critical change is the developing child's ability to move from comparing values in a dimensionally embedded fashion such as (longer x,y) to a dimensionally analytic representation like {Greater-than[length(x), length(y)]}. This latter form enables analogies to be made across quite different domains. The authors suggest that the process of comparison and alignment promotes re-representation of holistic relations into analytical relational structures.

Chapter 7, by Simon and Klahr, presents a model of the construction of number conservation knowledge by preschool children. In order to tightly constrain the processing account, the model simulates a published training study where 3- and 4-year-old children who initially failed conservation problems were trained to successfully make conservation judgments. The model was built using the Soar cognitive architecture and is called *Q-Soar* to reflect the fact that conservation knowledge is shown to be primarily based on the process of quantification. The central point of Q-Soar is that arrays of objects are quantified before and after a transformation is observed and then the resulting representations are compared. The quantitative outcome is then attributed to the transformation as its effect. Subproblems of the whole task, such as quantifying an array or comparing the two results, create impasses and these determine the learning that Soar's learning mechanism, chunking, carries out. The result of the processing executed as a function of the impasses creates new and more general knowledge that Q-Soar can later use to simply recognize, rather than compute, the conserving or nonconserving effects of familiar transformations. The model learns from the same trials as the children in the published study. It also embodies an account of the differences between the younger and older subjects in terms of the knowledge and processes that are being used by the two age groups to solve the problems with which they are presented.

In the final chapter, Klahr reviews the work presented in this book in the light of general progress toward computational models of developmental phenomena.

ACKNOWLEDGMENT

We would like to thank John Dunlosky for his comments on an earlier draft of this chapter.

REFERENCES

Anderson, J. R. (1983). *The architecture of cognition.* Cambridge, MA: Harvard University Press.

Anderson, J. R. (1993). *Rules of the mind.* Hillsdale, NJ: Lawrence Erlbaum Associates.

Carey, S., & Gelman, R. (Eds.). (1991). *The epigenesis of mind.* Hillsdale, NJ: Lawrence Erlbaum Associates.

Flavell, J. H. (1984). Discussion. In R. J. Sternberg (Ed.), *Mechanisms of cognitive development* (pp. 187–209). New York: Freeman.

Goel, V. (1992). Are computational explanations vacuous? *Proceedings of 14th Annual Conference of the Cognitive Science Society.* Hillsdale, NJ: Lawrence Erlbaum Associates.

Halford, G. S. (1993). *Children's understanding: The development of mental models.* Hillsdale, NJ: Lawrence Erlbaum Associates.

Jones, R. M., & VanLehn, K. (1994). Acquisition of children's addition strategies: A model of impasse-free, knowledge-level learning. *Machine Learning, 16,* 11–36.

Johnson-Laird, P. N. (1981). Mental models in cognitive science. In D. A. Norman (Ed.), *Perspectives on cognitive science.* Norwood, NJ: Ablex.

Karmiloff-Smith, A. (1979). Micro and macro developmental changes in language acquisition and other representational systems. *Cognitive Science, 3,* 91–117.

Karmiloff-Smith, A., & Inhelder, B. (1974). If you want to get ahead, get a theory. *Cognition, 3,* 195–212.

Klahr, D. (1989). Information-processing approaches. In R. Vasta (Ed.), *Annals of child development* (pp. 131–185). Greenwich, CT: JAI.

Klahr, D. (1992). Information-processing approaches to cognitive development. In M. H. Bornstein & M. E. Lamb (Eds.), *Developmental psychology: An advanced textbook* (3rd ed., pp. 273–335). Hillsdale, NJ: Lawrence Erlbaum Associates.

Klahr, D., Langley, P., & Neches, R. (1987). *Production system models of learning and development.* Cambridge, MA: MIT Press.

Klahr, D. & Siegler, R. S. (1978). The representation of children's knowledge. In H. W. Reese & L. P. Lipsitt (Eds.), *Advances in child development* (pp. 61–116). New York: Academic Press.

Klahr, D., & Wallace, J. G. (1973). The role of quantification operators in the development of the conservation of quantity. *Cognitive Psychology, 4,* 301–327.

Klahr, D. & Wallace, J. G. (1976). *Cognitive development: An information processing view.* Hillsdale, NJ: Lawrence Erlbaum Associates.

Langley, P. (1987). A general theory of discrimination learning. In D. Klahr, P. Langley, & R. Neches (Eds.), *Production system models of learning and development* (pp. 99–162). Cambridge, MA: MIT Press.

Langley, P., & Neches, R. (1981). *PRISM user's manual.* Computer Science Department, Carnegie Mellon University, Pittsburgh, PA.

McClelland, J. L. (1988). Connectionist models and psychological evidence. *Journal of Memory & Language, 27,* 107–123.

McClelland, J. L. (1989). Parallel distributed processing: Implications for cognition and development. In R. G. M. Morris (Ed.), *Parallel distributed processing: Implications for psychology & neurobiology* (pp. 8–45). Oxford, England: Clarendon.

McClelland, J. L., Rumelhart, D. E., & the PDP Research Group (1986). *Parallel distributed processing: Explorations in the microstructure of cognition* (Vol. II). Cambridge, MA: MIT Press.

Neches, R., Langley, P., & Klahr, D. (1987). Learning, development and production systems. In D. Klahr, P. Langley & R. Neches (Eds.), *Production system models of learning and development* (pp. 163–220). Cambridge, MA: MIT Press.

Newell, A. (1973a). Production systems: Models of control structures. In W. G. Chase (Ed.), *Visual information processing* (pp. 463–526). New York: Academic Press.

Newell, A. (1973b). You can't play 20 questions with nature and win: Projective comments on the papers of this symposium. In W. G. Chase (Ed.), *Visual information processing* (pp. 283–308). New York: Academic Press.

Newell, A. (1980). Physical symbol systems. *Cognitive Science, 4,* 135–183.

Newell, A. (1981). Reasoning, problem solving and decision processes: The problem space as a fundamental category. In R. Nickerson (Ed.), *Attention & Performance* (Vol. 8, (pp. 693–718). Hillsdale, NJ: Lawrence Erlbaum Associates.

Newell, A. (1990). *Unified theories of cognition.* Cambridge, MA: Harvard University Press.

Newell, A., & Simon, H. A. (1972). *Human problem solving.* Englewood Cliffs, NJ: Prentice-Hall.

Piatelli-Palmarini, M. (Ed.), (1980). *Language and learning: The debate between Jean Piaget and Noam Chomsky.* Cambridge, MA: Harvard University Press.

Pinker, S. (1979). Formal models of language learning. *Cognition, 1,* 217–283.

Polk, T. A., Newell, A., & Lewis, R. L. (1989). Toward a unified theory of immediate reasoning in Soar. *Proceedings of the 11th Annual Conference of the Cognitive Science Society* (pp. 506–513). Hillsdale, NJ: Lawrence Erlbaum Associates.

Pylyshyn, Z. W. (1984). *Computation and cognition: Toward a foundation for cognitive science*. Cambridge, MA: MIT Press.

Rabinowitz, F. M., Grant, M. J., & Dingley, H. L. (1987). Computer simulation, cognition, and development: An introduction. In J. Bisanz, C. J. Brainerd, & R. Kail (Eds.), *Formal methods in developmental psychology: Progress in cognitive development research* (pp. 263–301). New York: Springer-Verlag.

Rosenbloom, P. S., Newell, A., & Laird, J. E. (1991). Towards the knowledge level in Soar. In K. VanLehn (Ed.), *Architectures for intelligence* (pp. 75–111). Hillsdale, NJ: Lawrence Erlbaum Associates..

Rumelhart, D. E., McClelland, J. L., & the PDP Research Group (1986). *Parallel distributed processing: Explorations in the microstructure of cognition* (Vol. I). Cambridge, MA: MIT Press.

Saxe, G. B., Gearhart, M., & Guberman, S. R. (1984). The social organization of early number development. In B. Rogoff & J. V. Wertsch (Eds.), *Children's learning in the zone of proximal development: New directions for child development* (Vol. 23, pp. 19–30). San Francisco: Jossey-Bass.

Schmidt, W., & Shultz, T. (1992). An investigation of balance scale success. In *Proceedings of 14h Annual Conference of the Cognitive Science Society* (pp. 72–77). Hillsdale, NJ: Lawrence Erlbaum Associates.

Searle, J. R. (1984). *Minds, brains and science*. Cambridge. MA: Harvard University Press.

Shrager, J., & Callanan, M. (1991). Active language in the collaborative development of cooking skill. In *Proceedings of 13th Annual Conference of the Cognitive Science Society* (pp. 394–399). Hillsdale, NJ: Lawrence Erlbaum Associates.

Siegler, R. S. (1981). Developmental sequences within and between concepts. *Monographs of the Society for Research in Child Development, 46,* 1–84.

Siegler, R. S., & Crowley, K. (1992). The microgenetic method: A direct means for studying cognitive development. *American Psychologist, 46,* 606–620.

Simon, H. A. (1962). An information processing theory of intellectual development. *Monographs of the Society for Research in Child Development, 27 (2, Serial No. 82).*

Sternberg, R. J. (Ed.). (1984). *Mechanisms of cognitive development*. New York: Freeman.

VanLehn, K. (Ed.). (1991). *Architectures for intelligence*. Hillsdale, NJ: Lawrence Erlbaum Associates.

Wellman, H. M., & Bartsch, K. (1988). Young children's reasoning about beliefs. *Cognition, 31,* 239–277.

Wimmer, H., & Perner, J. (1983). Beliefs about beliefs: Representation and constraining function of wrong beliefs in young children's understanding of deception. *Cognition, 13, 103–128.*

2

Variation, Selection, and Cognitive Change

Robert S. Siegler
Christopher Shipley
Carnegie Mellon University

Cognitive development is usually described in terms of a sequence of 1:1 relations between ages and ways of thinking. This is evident in both classical domain-general stage theories and in recent domain-specific approaches. First, consider the stage theories. Within Piaget's theory, the reasoning of young children is said to be preoperational; that of somewhat older ones, concrete operational; that of yet older ones, formal operational. Within Vygotsky's theory, young children are said to form thematic concepts; somewhat older ones, chain concepts; yet older ones, true concepts. Within Bruner's theory, infants are said to form sensorimotor representations; somewhat older children, iconic representations; yet older ones, symbolic representations.

Current cognitive development has moved away from many aspects of stage theories, particularly their domain generality and their overly conservative estimates of infants' and young children's cognitive capacities. One feature that has been retained, however, is the emphasis on 1:1 relations between ages and ways of thinking. In descriptions of the development of competence in forming past tense verbs, children are said first to use correctly a small range of regular and irregular past tense forms, then to overgeneralize the standard past tense rule to irregular as well as regular verbs, then to form correctly both regular and irregular verbs (Brown, 1973; Rumelhart & McClelland, 1986). In descriptions of the development of addition skill, 5-year-olds are said to count from 1; 7-year-olds to count from the larger addend; 10-year-olds to retrieve answers from memory (Ashcraft, 1982; Neches, 1987). In descriptions of the development of serial recall strategies, 5-year-olds are said not to rehearse; 8-year-olds to rehearse in a simple way; 11-year-olds to rehearse in a more elaborated way (Flavell, Beach, & Chinsky, 1966; Schneider & Pressley, 1989).

Although these 1:1 equations between ages and ways of thinking are omnipresent in the literature, few would defend them as literally meaning that young children of a given age or developmental level *always* use one approach, older ones *always* use another approach, and so on. Instead, their widespread and enduring use seems due to their having several pragmatic advantages: They are interesting, sometimes dramatic, easy to describe, easy to remember, and straightforward to discuss in textbooks and lectures.

The 1:1 equations also entail two serious problems, though, one obvious, the other less so. The obvious problem is that the 1:1 equations are inaccurate. For example, detailed studies of each of the previously described domains show that individual children, by definition of a single age, generate a variety of past tense verb forms, arithmetic strategies, and serial recall strategies (Maratsos, 1983; McGilly & Siegler, 1990; Siegler & Robinson, 1982). Such inaccuracy is a serious problem. Still, if it were the only one, many might still judge the trade-off worthwhile.

A less obvious but equally pernicious consequence of this oversimplification is that it impedes understanding of change. The 1:1 equations between age and way of thinking make it extremely difficult to go beyond a superficial understanding of change. How can preoperational reasoning turn into concrete operational reasoning, chain concepts into true concepts, iconic concepts into symbolic concepts? How can a child who always overregularized past tense verbs become one who correctly uses both regular and irregular forms? Portraying children's thinking as monolithic at each point in the developmental sequence has the effect of segregating change from the ebb and flow of everyday cognitive activity. It makes change a rare, almost exotic, event that demands an exceptional explanation. Thus, we often speak of brief "transition periods" that separate long-lived stages, theories, strategies, or rules. Yet, if children of a given age have for several years been in a particular stage, had a particular theory, or used a particular strategy or rule, why should they suddenly change? From this perspective, it is no accident that both traditional and current depictions of development have been so consistently faulted for being vague, unclear, mysterious, or silent concerning how transitions occur. The problem is that the 1:1 equations that the accounts of change seek to explain are fundamentally flawed, root and branch.

The central theme of this chapter is that recognizing the roles of variation and selection in cognitive development, and transcending the omnipresent 1:1 equation between age and thought, will lead to a better understanding of how change occurs. We illustrate this perspective in the context of children's strategy choices, particularly their choices among alternative strategies for adding numbers. We first note key empirical phenomena that any model of strategy choice must explain. Then we describe three generations of models in this area and their successes and failures in accounting for the empirical phenomena. Finally, we consider their contributions to understanding how change occurs and the issues they raise for future investigation.

BASIC PHENOMENA

Variability

Although innumerable studies have depicted development in terms of a 1:1 correspondence between children's age and the strategy they use, recent trial-by-trial analyses indicate that children of a single age often use a variety of strategies. One task in which we observed such strategy discovery is elementary school children's single-digit addition. Examination of both videotaped records of ongoing behavior and immediately retrospective self-reports reveals five relatively common strategies (each used on 3% to 36% of trials among the kindergartners, first and second graders in Siegler, 1987b). Sometimes children use the *sum strategy*, in which they count from one; to solve 3 + 6, a child using this strategy might put up 3 fingers, then 6 more, and then count from 1 to 9. Other times, children use the *min strategy*, which involves counting from the larger addend the number of times indicated by the smaller addend. Here, a child would solve 3 + 6 by counting "6, 7, 8, 9" or "7, 8, 9." On other occasions, children use *decomposition* — translating the problem into an easier form and then making the necessary adjustment. A child solving 3 + 6 via decomposition might think, "3 + 7 = 10, 6 is 1 less than 7, so 3 + 6 = 9." Still other times, children use *retrieval* or *guessing* to generate an answer. These strategies are described in Table 2.1.

These diverse strategies are not artifacts of one child consistently using one of the strategies and another child consistently using a different one. The majority of kindergartners, first and second graders use at least three of the five strategies; a substantial minority use more (Siegler, 1987b). This multiple strategy use is apparent within classes of similar problems, and even on the same problem presented to the same child on consecutive days. In two studies, one on addition (Siegler & Shrager, 1984), and one on time telling (Siegler & McGilly, 1989), fully one-third of the children used different strategies on the identical problem on two successive days. Only a small part of this day-to-day variability could be explained by learning, because the progression of strategies was not consistently from less to more

TABLE 2.1
Early Elementary School Students' Main Addition Strategies

Strategy	Typical Use of Strategy to Solve 3 + 5
Sum	Put up 3 fingers, put up 5 fingers, count fingers by saying "1, 2, 3, 4, 5, 6, 7, 8."
Min	Say "5, 6, 7, 8" or "6, 7, 8," perhaps simultaneously putting up one finger on each count beyond 5.
Retrieval	Say an answer and explain it by saying, "I just knew it."
Guessing	Say an answer and explain it by saying, "I guessed."
Decomposition	Say "3 + 5 is like 4 + 4, so it's 8."

advanced. For example, in the study of addition, almost as many children retrieved the answer on the first day, and used the sum strategy on the second, as did the reverse (45% vs. 55%).

This strategy diversity is not limited to any particular domain or age group. Consider findings from our own studies. When multiplying, 8- to 10-year-olds sometimes repeatedly add one of the multiplicands, sometimes write the problem and then recognize the answer, sometimes write and then count groups of hatch marks that represent the problem, and sometimes retrieve the answer from memory (Siegler, 1988b). To tell time, 7- to 9-year-olds sometimes count forward from the hour by ones and/or fives, sometimes count backwards from the hour by ones and/or fives, sometimes count from reference points such as the half hour, and sometimes retrieve the time that corresponds to the clock hands' configuration (Siegler & McGilly, 1989). To spell words, 7- and 8-year-olds sometimes sound out words, sometimes look them up in dictionaries, sometimes write out alternative forms and try to recognize which is correct, and sometimes recall the spelling from memory (Siegler, 1986). To serially recall lists of unrelated stimuli, 5- to 8-year-olds sometimes repeatedly recite the names of items within the list during the delay period, sometimes recite the names once and stop, and sometimes just wait (McGilly & Siegler, 1989, 1990).

Similar strategy diversity has been observed by other investigators of arithmetic (Cooney, Swanson, & Ladd, 1988), causal reasoning (Shultz, Fisher, Pratt, & Rulf, 1986), number conservation (Church & Goldin-Meadow, 1986), spatial reasoning (Ohlsson, 1984), referential communication (Kahan & Richards, 1986), language development (Kuczaj, 1977), and motor activity (Goldfield, in press). These diverse strategies have been observed among adults as well as children, and in Japan and China as well as in North America and Europe (Geary, Fan, & Bow-Thomas, 1992; Kuhara-Kojima & Hatano, 1989). These studies call into question the typical description that at Age N, children are in Stage X, have Rule X, have Theory X, use Strategy X; at Age N + 2 they are in Stage Y, have Rule Y, have Theory Y, use Strategy Y; and so on. Instead, over a wide range of ages and tasks, children know and use multiple approaches.

Adaptive Strategy Choices

Children's strategy choices are adaptive in several ways. One involves their choice of whether to state a retrieved answer or to use a *backup strategy* (any approach other than retrieval, such as the sum and min strategies in addition). As shown in Fig. 2.1, the more difficult the problem, the more often children use backup strategies to solve it. This pattern of strategy choice is adaptive, because it enables children to use the faster retrieval approach on problems where that yields correct answers and to use the slower backup strategies on problems where they are necessary to produce accurate performance. Consistent with this analysis, forcing children to retrieve on all trials by imposing a short time limit (4 sec) produces a sharp fall-off in accuracy, with the fall-off largest on precisely the problems on which children most often use backup strategies when allowed to choose freely (Siegler & Robinson, 1982).

This pattern of choices between retrieval and backup strategies is extremely general. It holds true with problem difficulty defined either by percentage of errors or by length of solution times; with preschoolers, elementary school-aged children, college students, and senior citizens; with high achieving and low achieving students; with suburban White and inner-city African-American children; and with addition, subtraction, multiplication, time telling, spelling, and word identification (Geary & Burlingham-Dubree, 1989; Geary & Wiley, 1991; Kerkman & Siegler, 1993; Maloney & Siegler, 1993; Siegler, 1986, 1988a, 1988b; Siegler & Shrager, 1984).

Children also choose adaptively among alternative backup strategies. For example, when choosing between the min and sum strategies, children most often select the min strategy on problems where differences between addends are large (Siegler, 1987b). Thus, when solving single-digit addition problems, they are most likely to use the min strategy on problems such as 9 + 2. Problems with large differences between addends are the ones on which the min strategy produces the greatest savings in amount of counting, relative to the main alternative approach, the sum strategy; thus, it makes sense to use it most often on them.[1]

Change

Three main changes in strategy use occur with age and experience: changes in relative frequency of use of existing strategies, changes in the effective-

---

[1]It might seem that using the min strategy would always be more advantageous than using the sum strategy, because it always involves less counting. However, at the time when they learn the min strategy, children are much more practiced at counting from one than from other starting points, and do so more accurately and efficiently. Thus, the advantage of the min over the sum strategy is not as great as the savings in number of counts would suggest, and some problems at first are solved more quickly via the sum strategy (Siegler & Jenkins, 1989).

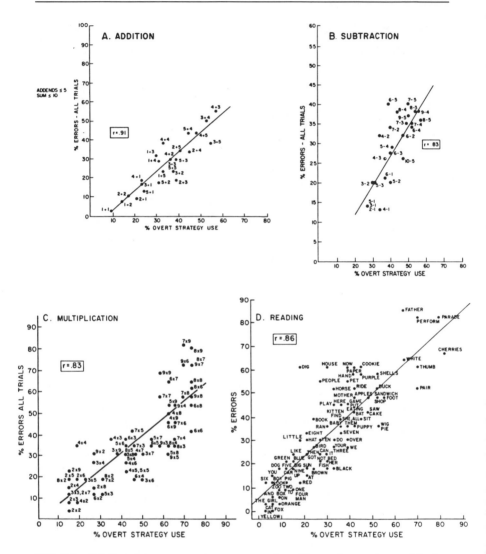

FIG. 2.1.   Relations between percent errors on each problem and percent use of backup strategies on that problem on four tasks.

ness with which each strategy is executed, and changes involving acquisition of new strategies.

Table 2.2 illustrates the changes in strategy use that occur in kindergartners', first, and second graders' single-digit addition. Frequency of retrieval, the min strategy, and decomposition increase; frequency of the sum strategy and guessing decrease.

Changes in the skill with which each strategy is executed are also evident.

TABLE 2.2
Percent Use of Each Strategy by Children of Each Age

	Strategy				
Grade Level	Retrieval	Min	Decomp	Count all	Guess or no response
Kindergarten	16	30	2	22	30
Grade 1	44	38	9	1	8
Grade 2	45	40	11	0	5

Note. From "The Perils of Averaging Data Over Strategies: An Example From Children's Addition" by R. S. Siegler, 1987, *Journal of Experimental Psychology: General, 116*, 250–264. Copyright 1987 by the American Psychological Association.

Older children are faster and more accurate than younger ones in their execution of each addition strategy. For example, in Siegler (1987b), mean time to execute the min strategy decreased from 6 sec among kindergartners to 4 sec among second graders, and percent errors using the strategy decreased from 29% to 7%. Thus, the general improvements in speed and accuracy that characterize acquisition of arithmetic include both changes in frequency of use of different strategies and in efficiency of execution within each strategy.

A third type of change involves acquisition of new strategies. Even after children know strategies that consistently yield correct performance on a class of problems, they continue to invent new strategies for solving them. For example, children who competently solve simple addition problems by using the sum strategy or retrieval go on to discover the min strategy (Siegler & Jenkins, 1989). In class inclusion, children who competently solve problems by comparing the number of objects in the larger subordinate class with the number in the superordinate class later realize that the superordinate class must be larger, whatever the particular numbers involved (Markman, 1979). In using causal verbs, deeper linguistic analysis leads children who for years have made such grammatically correct statements as "she killed him" and "he dropped it," to start introducing ungrammatical forms such as "she died him" and "he falled it" (Bowerman, 1982). Together with imitation and direct instruction from other people, such strategy discovery is among the ultimate sources of variability in children's strategy use.

Generalization

Children generalize their strategies beyond the particular problems on which they acquired them. Observation of children in the weeks after they first discover a new strategy indicates that this generalization process often takes a long time, at least when children possess other strategies that work well (Kuhn, Schauble, & Garcia-Mila, 1992; Schauble, 1990; Siegler & Jenkins, 1989). However, generalization of new strategies can be considerably hastened if children encounter conditions that highlight the new strategy's advantages over previous approaches.

Both the typical slow generalization and a condition that produced much faster generalization were observed in a study of 4- and 5-year-olds' discovery of the min strategy (Siegler & Jenkins, 1989). At the beginning of the experiment, the preschoolers knew how to add via the sum strategy and retrieval, but did not yet know the min strategy. They were then presented with 7 weeks of practice on small number problems, where neither addend exceeded 5. During this period, most of the children discovered the min strategy, in the sense of using it at least once. These early uses were often accompanied by insightful explanations of why the strategy was useful (e.g., "If you count from 4, you don't need to count all those numbers").

Despite these insights, the children showed little generalization of the newly discovered strategy, instead continuing to rely mainly on the sum strategy when they could not retrieve the answer. Therefore, in Week 8, they were presented with challenge problems, such as 3 + 22, that included a small and a very large addend. The logic was that such problems would serve as both a carrot, encouraging use of the min strategy, and as a stick, discouraging use of the sum strategy or retrieval.

Children who had not yet discovered the min strategy did not benefit in any way from encountering such challenge problems; most could not cope with them. However, those who had previously discovered the min strategy (in the sense of using it at least once) generalized it much more widely than they had before. The amount of generalization continued to increase in the three remaining weeks of the experiment, on small addend problems as well as on the challenge problems. By the end of the experiment, the min strategy was the dominant backup strategy, being used on more than 90% of trials where retrieval was not. Both the slow generalization that occurs in the absence of experiences that highlight the advantages of new strategies, and the rapid generalization that can take place when such experiences occur, are important phenomena for models of strategy choice to explain.

Individual Differences

Recognizing the variability of strategy use within individuals raises the issue of whether strategy use also varies in interesting ways across individuals. Although research on broad cognitive styles has not identified many strong consistencies in strategy use (Kogan, 1983; Sternberg, 1985), studies of more narrowly defined strategy choices have yielded more encouraging results. For example, examination of the choice between stating a retrieved answer and using a backup strategy revealed consistent individual patterns in first graders' addition, subtraction, and word identification (Kerkman & Siegler, 1993; Siegler, 1988a). The research delineates three characteristic patterns: the good student, not-so-good student, and perfectionist patterns. Good students are children who usually rely on retrieval and answer quickly and accurately. Not-so-good students sometimes use retrieval but usually answer slowly and inaccurately. Perfectionists are fairly fast and very accurate, but use retrieval even less often than the not-so-good students; instead, they rely heavily on backup strategies.

These patterns of individual differences in addition, subtraction, and word identification have been found in four different experiments, some involving high income, predominantly White, suburban children, and others involving low income, predominantly African-American inner-city children. They also have proved predictive of standardized test scores and of future classroom placements; not-so-good students score significantly lower than the other two groups, are more likely to be classified as learning disabled, and are more likely to need to repeat a grade (Kerkman & Siegler, 1993; Siegler, 1988a; Siegler & Campbell, 1990). Thus, the differences between not-so-good students and the other two groups are of the type that are detected by standard psychometric tests. However, the differences between the strategy choices of good students and perfectionists are not apparent on these tests; they are more akin to cognitive style differences.

Summary

The present perspective brings to center stage a different set of phenomena than those emphasized in traditional developmental accounts. Rather than focusing on *the* problem solving approach children use at each age, our perspective focuses on the *set of approaches* children use. Highlighting this variability brings into the spotlight how children choose among the alternative approaches and what adaptive purposes those choices serve. Our perspective also calls attention to several different types of changes: changes in the frequency of use of existing strategies, in the effectiveness with which these strategies are used, and in the acquisition of new strategies. Beyond this, our perspective spotlights how strategies are generalized beyond their initial contexts, and how individuals vary in their strategy choices. We now describe and evaluate three generations of models that have attempted to account for these phenomena.

GENERATION 1: METACOGNITIVE MODELS
OF STRATEGY CHOICE

Children's strategies first became a major topic of research in the 1960s (e.g., Flavell, Beach, & Chinsky, 1966; Keeney, Cannizzo, & Flavell, 1967).

The early research documented large changes in memory strategies between ages 5 and 8. Five-year-olds were said to rarely use strategies such as rehearsal and organization; 8-year-olds were said to consistently use them. Especially interesting were efforts to teach such strategies to 5- and 6-year-olds who did not spontaneously use them. Such children often learned the strategies, and their performance improved when they used them. Despite these benefits, the children usually did not continue to use the strategies later, even in similar situations.

This puzzle was an important impetus for the first generation of models of strategy choice. These models were labeled *metacognitive*, because they focused on how knowledge about cognition could be used to control cognitive activities. Their fundamental assumption was that young children's failure to use new strategies reflected their limited understanding of their own cognitive capacities and of why the new strategies were needed.

The metacognitive models originally proposed, the type being discussed in the next section, focus on explicit, rationally derived, conscious metacognitive knowledge. The term *metacognitive* also at times has been used to refer to processes that are implicit, not derived from rational consideration, and unconscious. Greeno, Riley, and Gelman's (1984) planning networks, Van Lehn's (1982) repair models, and Halford's (1993) mental models, like our own models of strategy choice, fit into this category. In the present context, however, the term *metacognitive* is used only in its original sense of explicit, rationally-derived, conscious knowledge that influences the workings of the cognitive system. This allows a clearer contrast between the two approaches to strategy choice.

Two Metacognitive Models

Metacognitive approaches assume that strategy choices are made through the cognitive system's explicit knowledge of its own workings. This knowledge is often said to be used by an *executive processor,* that decides what the cognitive system should do (Case, 1978; Kluwe, 1982; Sternberg, 1985). Schneider and Pressley (1989) described the executive processor's role as follows:

> This executive is aware of the system's capacity limits and strategies. The executive can analyze new problems and select appropriate strategies and attempt solutions. Very importantly, the executive monitors the success or failure of ongoing performance, deciding which strategies to continue and which to replace with potentially more effective and appropriate routines. In addition, the efficient executive knows when one knows and when one does not know, an important requirement for competent learning. (p. 91)

Similarly, Kuhn (1984) described the way in which metacognitive knowledge influences strategy selection as follows: "In order to select a strategy as appropriate for solving a particular problem, the individual must understand the strategy, understand the problem, and understand how the problem and strategy intersect or map onto one another" (p. 165).

Models of the executive processor that are based on such conceptions of how metacognitive knowledge exercises its effects have been high level, rather abstract characterizations of types of relevant knowledge used to govern cognition. A less and a more elaborate model of this type are shown in Fig. 2.2.

Such metacognitive models are useful for conveying hypotheses about relations among different types of knowledge and for pointing to one way in which intelligent strategy choices can be generated. However, they also have a number of weaknesses, both theoretical and empirical (Brown & Reeve, 1986; Cavanaugh & Perlmutter, 1982; Siegler, 1988b). As statements of theory, they generally have been vague regarding the mechanisms that produce the phenomena of interest. Do people make explicit judgments about their intellectual capacities, available strategies, and task demands every time they face a task they could perform in multiple ways? If not, how do they decide when to do so? Do they consider every strategy they could use on the task, or only some of them? If only some, how do they decide which ones? How do people know what their cognitive capacity will be on a novel task or what strategies they could apply to it? The apparent simplicity of metacognitive models masks a world of complexity.

Empirical evidence has also raised questions about the fundamental assumption that underlies the models. Relations between explicit, verbalizable metacognitive knowledge and cognitive activity have proven weaker than originally expected (Cavanaugh & Perlmutter, 1982; Schneider, 1985; Schneider & Pressley, 1989), casting doubt on whether such metacognitive knowledge plays a central role in children's strategy choices.

On the other hand, the questions addressed by metacognitive research are important, and research stimulated by the approach has yielded intriguing data. We now review findings from this research that are relevant to the five phenomena noted in the previous section.

Variability

Metacognitive research has documented that even quite young children have conscious, statable knowledge about diverse strategies. For example, Kreutzer, Leonard, and Flavell (1975) asked 5- to 10-year-olds what they could do to remember to bring their skates to school the next day. At all ages, children often described multiple strategies. Studies of other tasks

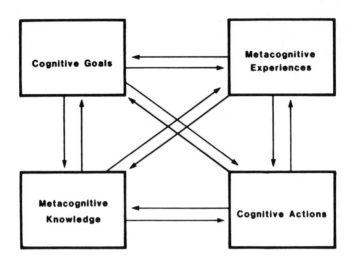

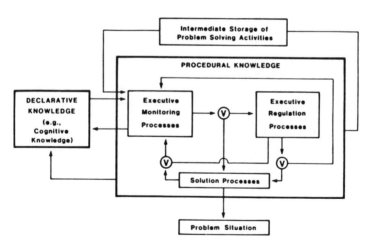

FIG. 2.2.   Two metacognitive models of the executive processor: Flavell's (1981) model (top) and Kluwe's (1982) model (bottom).

(e. g., ways of remembering a forgotten idea) have obtained similar results at young ages and have demonstrated that the number of strategies described increases at least into early adolescence (Yussen & Levy, 1977).

Adaptive Strategy Choices

The metacognitive perspective suggests a way of thinking about how children choose among alternative strategies. The models are often not explicit, but the implicit causal pathway is:

Metacognitive knowledge → *Strategy choice* → *Performance*

For example, knowledge about alternative memory strategies, task demands, and personal capacities would lead the executive to choose a particular memory strategy, that in turn, would influence memory performance.

The type of research suggested by this approach is exemplified in an experiment reported by Justice (1985). Children were presented with videotapes of a 10-year-old executing different strategies that might benefit recall, and were then asked to judge the likely effectiveness of the strategies. Older children's judgments of the strategies' relative value were more accurate. The conclusion was that older children's superior choice of strategies and superior memory performance largely stemmed from their superior knowledge about the strategies.

However, even when children know abstractly that one strategy is superior to another, they often do not choose that strategy. Flavell and Wellman (1977) and Wellman (1983) suggested a number of explanations for this discrepancy: for example, lack of motivation, lack of time, overreliance on sheer effort, and beliefs that the strategy is unnecessary. Supporting this view, Fabricius and Hagan (1984) found that among a sample of children taught a new strategy that consistently improved their performance, only a minority continued to use it when no longer instructed to do so. The children who continued to use it were predominantly those who attributed their improved success to adopting the strategy. Other children, who attributed their improvement to trying harder, luck, or other factors, generally did not continue to use the new approach.

Even when significant relations between metacognitive knowledge and strategy choices are present, they often do not seem sufficient to account for the strong relations between problem difficulty and strategy choices that have been observed (Siegler, 1986). This can be seen in the specific area of focus in this chapter, children's arithmetic. Recall that the frequency with which children choose to use backup strategies on a given arithmetic problem is highly correlated with the problem's difficulty. This relation might have been mediated by metacognitive judgments of problem difficulty. Actual problem difficulty could give rise to metacognitive judgments of problem difficulty, which in turn could direct strategy choices. A difficult problem could lead a child to think, "This is a difficult problem; I'd better use a strategy such as X that can solve problems like that." However, Siegler and Robinson (1982) found that children's judgments of the difficulty of a set of arithmetic problems correlated only $r = .51$ with their strategy choices (the percentage of trials on which they used backup strategies on the problem). Further, the metacognitive judgments of problem difficulty correlated only $r = .47$ with actual problem difficulty (measured as percent errors the problem elicited). These correlations were significant, but not nearly sufficient to account for the very strong correlation ($r = .92$) between problem difficulty and strategy choices (25% vs. 85% variance accounted for). Young children's moderate amount of conscious, explicit, metacognitive knowledge may contribute to their extremely adaptive strategy choices in arithmetic and other domains, but cannot alone account for them.

Change

Metacognitive knowledge increases greatly during childhood and adolescence. Older children know more strategies, are often better at choosing among them, and are better at learning new approaches as well (Schneider & Pressley, 1989). They are more realistic in assessing their own memory capacities, more accurate in assessing the relative importance of different parts of a task, and more knowledgeable about interactions among factors that influence performance. This increasing metacognitive knowledge provides a database on which children increasingly can rely to choose strategies. Whether reliance on such knowledge to choose among strategies increases with age, however, remains unknown.

Generalization

When children learn a strategy, they often do not generalize it to new situations. One reason may be that they often realize fewer benefits in increased accuracy and incur greater costs in cognitive effort from using new strategies than they will when the strategies become better practiced (Guttentag, 1984; Miller, 1990). Thus, they have less reason to generalize, at least in the short run.

Even with well-practiced strategies, however, it is surprisingly difficult to override usual selection procedures through metacognitive means in order to produce wider generalization of a given approach. This was shown in the domain of children's arithmetic by an experiment reported in Siegler

(1989a). Second graders were given subtraction problems under conditions in which they were told that only accuracy, only speed, or both speed and accuracy were important. The children heeded the instructions; they were fastest and least accurate when told that only speed was important, and slowest and most accurate when told that only accuracy was important. However, the instructions had no effect on their frequency of use of any of the four most common strategies in the experiment. Instead, the children just executed the same strategies more carefully or more quickly, depending on the instructions. Thus, at least in domains such as arithmetic, in which children have substantial experience, strategy choice seems to be a relatively automatic, hard-to-change process. This may underlie the slow generalization of newly taught strategies that has been so frequently observed and lamented (e.g., Brown, Bransford, Ferrera, & Campione, 1983). As noted by Kuhn, Schauble, and Garcia-Mila (1992), learning not to use old strategies may often be as large a challenge as learning to use new ones.

Individual Differences

A great deal of research has been devoted to testing relations between individual children's metamnemonic knowledge and their memory performance. This research has produced varying results. Early studies often yielded no significant relations between the two (Cavanaugh & Perlmutter, 1982). More recent research, such as the studies by Justice described earlier, has found significant relations. However, these relations also have tended not to be very strong. For example, two meta-analyses of the literature, one weighted by sample size and the other unweighted, revealed identical average correlations of $r = .41$ between individual children's metacognitive knowledge about memory and their recall (Schneider, 1985; Schneider & Pressley, 1989). Thus, the fact that an individual child knows a lot about memory is not extremely helpful in predicting how much the child will remember.

Even these modest to moderate correlations may overstate the relation between long-term metacognitive knowledge and performance. The studies in the meta-analyses included ones in which the assessments of metacognitive knowledge were done after the relevant performance, as well as before. The timing made a big difference: When metamemory was measured after memory performance, the correlations averaged $r = .54$, whereas when it was measured before, the correlations averaged only $r = .25$ (Schneider & Pressley, 1989). The higher correlations produced when metacognitive knowledge was measured after the child performed the task suggests that children use short-term recall of their situation-specific experience to guide their metacognitive judgments, rather than the usual assumption that enduring general metacognitive knowledge governs the judgments.

Evaluation

These first generation models, that emphasized explicit, verbalizable meta-cognitive knowledge, were clearly insufficient to account for strategy choices. Different investigators drew different conclusions about how to proceed. Some emphasized the need for better assessments of metacognitive knowledge (e.g., Cavanaugh & Perlmutter, 1982). Others argued that because many factors influence strategy choice and cognitive performance, the moderate relations were all that could be expected (e.g., Flavell, 1981; Schneider & Pressley, 1989). Yet others emphasized the need to go on to determine where and when metacognitive knowledge is most strongly related to cognitive activity (e.g., Wellman, 1983).

Another, more radical, conclusion was that enduring, statable, meta-cognitive knowledge has less impact on strategy choices than we think. This interpretation led Flavell (1985) and Brown and Reeve (1986) to suggest that strategy choices may often be generated by unconscious, automatic, nonrational processes, rather than the types of explicit, conscious, rational ones usually thought of as metacognitive. For example, Flavell (1985) wrote:

> Your reactions to external or internal memory materials and to your own metacognitive experiences regarding them may often be automatic or reflex-like. Through years of experience as a rememberer (and forgetter), you have learned to recognize and respond adaptively to numerous "patterns" of memory-relevant materials and feelings—and to do so quickly and automat-ically with little or no conscious reflection. (pp. 234–235)

If this is the case, then abstract, rational knowledge about cognition may not be the place to look for the factors that typically drive strategy choices. Instead, intelligent strategy choices may arise from application of simpler, more basic processes. This was the perspective that motivated development of the second generation strategy choice model.

GENERATION 2: THE DISTRIBUTIONS
OF ASSOCIATIONS MODEL

The distributions of associations model was developed by Siegler and Shrager (1984) to show how simple cognitive processes could produce adaptive strategy choices without anything resembling an executive proces-sor. It was specifically aimed at accounting for preschoolers' strategy choices in solving simple addition problems. In this section, we describe the model's basic structure and functioning, the mechanisms that produced changes in its performance, and the performance and changes that the model produced.

The Model's Basic Structure

As shown in Fig. 2.3, the two main parts of the distributions of associations model are a representation of knowledge about particular problems, and strategies that operate on the representation to produce answers. The answers, in turn, reshape the representation; the model learns by doing.

Within this model, the representation of knowledge is hypothesized to include associations between problems and potential answers, both correct and incorrect. For example, 3 + 5 would be associated not only with 8, but also with 6, 7, and 9 (Fig. 2.4). Each problem's associations with various answers can be classified along a dimension of *peakedness*. In a problem with a *peaked distribution*, such as that on the left in Fig. 2.4, most of the associative strength is concentrated in a single answer, ordinarily the correct answer. At the other extreme, in a *flat distribution*, such as that on the right of Fig. 2.4, associative strength is dispersed among several answers, with none of them forming a strong peak.

The process that operates on the representation involves three sequential phases, any one of which can produce an answer: retrieval, elaboration of

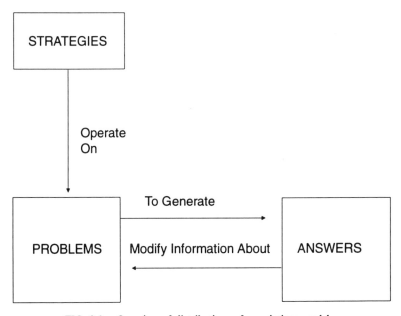

FIG. 2.3. Overview of distributions of associations model.

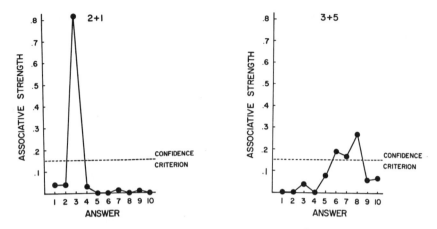

FIG. 2.4.   A peaked (left) and a flat (right) distribution of associations.

the representation, and application of an algorithm. In the specific case of preschoolers' addition, children would first try to retrieve an answer. If not sufficiently confident of any answer, they would elaborate the representation of the problem, perhaps by putting up fingers to represent the two addends. If they still did not know the answer, they would use the algorithm of counting the objects in the elaborated representation—in this case, the fingers that were up. All distributions of associations models include these three phases. The way in which retrieval occurs is also constant across the models, though the particulars of the other two phases are specific to each task.

The retrieval mechanism is central. When presented with a problem, children are hypothesized to set a *confidence criterion*, which determines how sure they must be to state a retrieved answer, and a *searchlength*, which determines how many attempts they will make to retrieve an answer before trying a different approach to solving the problem. Then the child retrieves an answer. Probability of retrieving any given answer to a problem is proportional to that answer's associative strength relative to the total associative strength of all answers to the problem. For example, if a given answer had an associative strength of .4, and the total associative strength of all answers was .8, then that answer would be retrieved on 50% of retrieval efforts. This retrieval procedure closely paralleled that hypothesized by Gillilund and Shiffrin (1984).

The retrieved answer is stated if its associative strength exceeds the confidence criterion. For example, if a girl had a distribution of associations and a confidence criterion like that shown for 3 + 5 in Fig. 2.4, she would state the answer if she retrieved 6, 7, or 8, but not if she retrieved any other answer.

If the answer's associative strength does not exceed the confidence criterion, and the number of retrieval attempts has not exceeded the searchlength, the child again retrieves an answer from the distribution of associations. She states it if its associative strength exceeds the confidence criterion. If the retrieval process fails to yield such an answer within the allocated number of searches, the child elaborates the representation. In the case of simple addition, this occurs through putting up fingers corresponding to the number of objects in each addend or forming a mental image of objects corresponding to that number of objects. A single further retrieval attempt is made, to see if the the kinesthetic and/or visual cues associated with such elaborations allow an answer to be retrieved whose strength exceeds the confidence criterion. If this criterion is met, the answer is stated; if not, the child uses an algorithmic procedure to solve the problem. In the case of addition, this involves counting the number of objects in the elaborated representation.

The distributions of associations model has been formalized within running computer simulations of 4- and 5-year-olds' addition (Siegler & Shrager, 1984), 5- and 6-year-olds' subtraction (Siegler, 1987a), and 8- and 9-year-olds' multiplication (Siegler, 1988b). The simulation of preschoolers' addition is representative. It can be described as follows:

1. The simulation is presented the 25 problems with both addends between 1 and 5, in accord with estimates of their relative frequency obtained through empirical studies of parental presentation of problems (or in the case of older children's arithmetic, through empirical studies of textbook presentation rates).

2. Before each problem, the simulation generates a confidence criterion and a searchlength, whose values vary randomly within the limits set by the simulation.

3. The probability of retrieving an answer is proportional to its associative strength, compared to the associative strengths of all answers to the problem. A retrieved answer is stated if its associative strength exceeds the current confidence criterion. Retrieval attempts continue until either the associative strength of a retrieved answer exceeds the confidence criterion or the number of searches matches the search length.

4. If no answer has been stated and the search length has been reached, the program generates an elaborated representation. The particular elaboration varies with the operation being modeled; in all cases, though, it may lead directly to a statable answer. In the case of addition, the elaboration involves either forming a mental image of counters corresponding to the addends, or putting up one's fingers to represent each addend. The visual and/or kinesthetic cues associated with these elaborations add associative strength to the answer corresponding to the number of fingers that have been put up—usually the correct answer.

5. If no answer has been stated, the model uses an algorithmic backup strategy, which again is specific to the operation being modeled. This algorithmic strategy always yields a statable answer. In the case of addition, the algorithm involves counting the objects in the mental image or the fingers that were put up.

6. Crucial to the overall working of the model is the learning mechanism. Every time the system advances an answer, the association between that answer and the problem increases. The increment is twice as great for correct answers, that presumably are reinforced, as for incorrect answers, that presumably are not. The change in the association value is identical regardless of whether the answer is produced through retrieval or through use of a backup strategy.

The Model's Performance

The model's functioning can be understood in terms of how it generates the key strategy choice phenomena previously described.

Variability. Variability of strategy use is built into the distributions of associations model. For example, the Siegler and Shrager (1984) simulation of preschoolers' addition included four strategies: retrieval, fingers, counting fingers, and counting. The strategies are particular to preschoolers' addition, and their specifics are less important in the present context than is the organization of strategies and the way in which this organization generates variability. The model considers the strategies in a fixed order in which it first tries retrieval; then, if retrieval is unsuccessful, it tries the fingers strategy (elaboration of the representation); then, if both retrieval and fingers have failed to yield an answer, it uses either the counting fingers strategy or the counting strategy (algorithmic approaches).

This organization yields variability of strategy use within as well as between problems. Each strategy can be, and is, applied to any problem. Siegler and Shrager (1984) found that in the course of the simulation's run, all 4 strategies were applied to each of the 25 problems. This assignment of strategies to problems is not random; problems with peaked distributions of associations elicit greater reliance on retrieval, and problems with flatter distributions elicit greater reliance on the three backup strategies. Nonetheless, strategy use is variable within as well as between problems.

Adaptive strategy choices. At the heart of the model is its procedure for choosing whether to use retrieval or a backup strategy on a problem. The procedure illustrates how adaptive strategy choices can be generated without any homuncular executive processor.

Within the model, adaptive strategy choices between retrieval and backup strategies arise because the peakedness of a given problem's distribution of associations determines both problem difficulty and the likelihood of using a backup strategy. To understand this view, it is useful to compare the model's workings on problems with peaked and flat distributions of associations.

Relative to a peaked distribution, a flat distribution elicits a higher percentage of use of backup strategies (because flat distributions, by definition, lack a strongly associated answer that has a high probability of being retrieved and a high probability of exceeding the confidence criterion once it is retrieved. The absence of such a strongly associated answer will lead to children often being unable to state any retrieved answer and instead using a backup strategy). The flat distribution will also elicit a higher percentage of errors (because the difference between the strength of association of the correct answer and incorrect ones will be smaller in the flatter distribution, leading to statement of a greater proportion of wrong answers on retrieval trials). Finally, the flatter distribution will lead to longer solution times (because the flatter the distribution, the less likely that an answer whose associative strength exceeds the confidence criterion will be retrieved and stated on an early retrieval attempt). Thus, within this model, backup strategies will be used primarily on the most difficult problems because the peakedness of the distribution of associations determines both problem difficulty and how often retrieval of a statable answer will be possible.

The data on children's performance supported these predictions and demonstrated the sufficiency of the hypothesized mechanism to generate adaptive choices between retrieval and backup strategies. Within the simulation, correlations between strategy choices (percent use of backup strategies on each problem) and the measures of problem difficulty (percent errors on that problem; length of solution times on each problem) exceeded $r = .90$. The simulation's strategy choices paralleled those of children; the correlation of percent backup strategies on each problem of the simulation and of the children in Siegler and Shrager (1984) exceeded $r = .80$. The most difficult problems elicited the highest percentage of backup strategies in both cases. Thus, the simulation generated adaptive strategy choices similar to those of children.

The model also made a specific, nonintuitive prediction regarding the sources of these correlations: The predicted high correlations between percent backup strategies, percent errors, and length of solution times on each problem was really a prediction regarding percent backup strategy use, percent errors on retrieval trials, and length of solution times on retrieval trials on each problem. The reason is that only on retrieval trials do percent errors and length of solution times stem from the peakedness of the distributions of associations. On backup strategy trials, they derive from the difficulty of executing the backup strategies.

Analyses of 4- and 5-year-olds' performance supported this prediction

(Siegler & Shrager, 1984). Correlations between percent backup strategy use and percent errors on retrieval trials on each problem were significantly higher than correlations between percent backup strategy use and percent errors on backup strategy trials on the problem. The same was true for the corresponding predictions regarding solution times. These nonintuitive predictions arose specifically from the distributions of associations model; it is unlikely that they would have been made without it.

Change. The distribution of associations model focused on a single change process: how increasingly peaked distributions of associations lead to faster and more accurate performance and more frequent use of retrieval. This view raises the question of how some problems come to have more peaked distributions than others—that is, how some problems come to elicit higher percentages of errors, longer solution times, and higher percentages of backup strategies than others.

The basic assumption of the model regarding creation of these distributions is that people associate whatever answer they state, correct or incorrect, with the problem on which they state it. This assumption reduces the issue of what factors lead children to develop a particular distribution of associations on each problem to what factors lead them to state particular answers on each problem.

Three factors that seem to lead to differences among problems in peakedness are differences in difficulty of executing backup strategies on the problem, different influences of related problems, and differences in frequency of encountering problems. First, consider differences in difficulty of executing backup strategies on each problem. In preschoolers' addition, the most common backup approach is the sum strategy. Children are more likely to correctly execute this backup strategy on problems with small addends, because such problems can be solved via the sum strategy with fewer operations and therefore less chance of error than can other problems. Generating the correct answer via backup strategies on a greater percentage of attempts on these problems leads to their having more peaked distributions of associations.

Intrusions from related operations also influence the rate of acquiring peaked distributions. Knowledge from one numerical operation often intrudes on performance on another; for example, $4 + 3$ fairly often elicits the answer 12, and 4×3, the answer 7 (e.g., Miller & Paredes, 1990). With preschoolers, knowledge of the counting string often intrudes into addition, leading them to wrong answers (e.g., $3 + 4 = 5$, $3 + 5 = 6$) but also to right ones (e.g., $1 + 2 = 3$, $1 + 3 = 4$). These counting string associations interfere with learning of answers to the first pair of problems, but may facilitate learning of answers to the second pair.

Children also encounter some problems more often than others. For example, tie problems, such as 2 + 2 and 3 + 3, seem to be presented especially often to preschoolers by their parents (Siegler & Shrager, 1984). More frequent presentation of these problems contributes to their more quickly coming to have peaked distributions.

The effects of these factors—ease of execution of backup strategies, intrusions from related operations, and frequency of problem presentation—have been examined empirically in addition, subtraction, and multiplication. Each of the three factors hypothesized to contribute to learning in these areas has been found to do so. For example, in analyses of preschoolers' addition errors on different problems, each of the three factors added significant independent variance to that which could be accounted for by the other two factors. Together, they accounted for more than 80% of the variance in percentage of errors on the 25 problems (Siegler & Shrager, 1984).

The correlations between the simulation's behavior and that of children increased substantially during its run. Before the learning phase, the correlation between the model's and the children's frequency of use of backup strategies on each problem was $r = -.03$; the correlation between their solution times was $r = .00$. After the learning phase, the corresponding correlations were $r = .87$ and $r = .80$. Thus, not only did the model's absolute level of performance change in the way that children's did, but the relative performance it generated on different problems also closely resembled that of children.

Generalization and Individual Differences.   Simulations embodying the distributions of associations model were silent about both generalization and individual differences, but for different reasons. Their silence about generalization was due to their inherently not being able to generalize. All learning was specific to the particular problems that were encountered. Thus, strategy choices on a newly encountered problem would reflect only experience with that problem, regardless of what had happened with previously learned problems.

The silence regarding individual differences was not due to any such conceptual difficulty. Rather, it reflected a lack of implementation within the simulations of ideas regarding individual differences. Such implementations could have been undertaken, but they were not.

Evaluation

The distributions of associations model had a number of strengths. It was far more explicit than the previous metacognitive models of strategy choice. It accounted straightforwardly for a number of key phenomena regarding strategy choices and made specific, testable, nonintuitive predictions that proved to be correct. It illustrated the viability of an alternative to the metacognitive perspective: Rather than adaptive strategy choices implying a knowledgeable and insightful executive processor, the choices could arise through the operation of simple cognitive processes such as retrieval.

However, the model had certain weaknesses as well. It was too inflexible, too limited in its explicitness, and too dumb.

Inflexibility. The distributions of associations model was rigid. It always considered strategies in the same order, regardless of the circumstances. It also did not provide any obvious way in which new strategies could be integrated into the strategy choice process.

Both properties are at odds with what is known about human strategy choices. People do not always attempt retrieval before other strategies. Instead, they at times first consider the strategy that seems the most likely to pay off, even when that strategy is not retrieval (Reder, 1982). Further, adults under time pressure often choose to use calculational strategies in less than the amount of time that retrieval requires (Reder & Ritter, 1992). People's strategy choice procedures clearly are more flexible than those described within the distributions of associations model.

Another way in which the distribution of associations model was inflexible involved the fixed three phase process of retrieval, elaboration of the representation, and use of a solution algorithm. This three phase approach fit the particular strategies used in preschoolers' addition (and in somewhat older children's beginning subtraction and multiplication, as well), but seemed too restrictive to capture strategy choices in general. Even within basic addition, the min strategy does not fit in any natural way into the three phase structure. Thus, the goal of generating a more general model of strategy choice demanded a more flexible structure.

Limited Explicitness. The distribution of associations model was far more explicit than previous metacognitively oriented models of how strategy choices are made. However, the explicitness lay primarily in the depiction of the choice between stating a retrieved answer or using a backup strategy. Procedures for choosing among alternative backup strategies were left vague. For example, the choice between elaborating the representation by putting up fingers or by forming an internal representation was simply stated as a pair of probabilities. There was no account of how this decision was made.

Dumbness. The distributions of associations model was considerably less intelligent than children are in at least two ways. First, it could not draw any generalizations from its experience. No matter how much experience it had with solving problems, it could not draw any implications regarding other problems, even the most closely related. Its learning was all literal. It would not even draw the generalization that a strategy that was useful on 5 + 3 might also be useful on 3 + 5. Yet, even infants generalize problem solving approaches to related problems (Rovee-Collier, 1989).

The model also had no abstract knowledge about the usefulness of strategies or the difficulty of problems. As described earlier, children's judgments of problem difficulty correlated about $r = .50$ with the actual difficulty of the problems (Siegler & Shrager, 1984). This is insufficient to account for their very adaptive strategy choices, but it also is not negligible. The model did not include any data that would provide a basis for such judgments.

In response to these limitations in flexibility, range of explicit depictions of strategy choice mechanisms, and breadth of knowledge, we recently built a new simulation—the Adaptive Strategy Choice Model (ASCM, pronounced "Ask-em"). The goal was to create a more flexible, more precise, and more intelligent model of strategy choice. We also wanted to simulate acquisition of knowledge not just of small addend problems in the preschool years, but of all single-integer problems over the preschool and elementary school period. Thus, the simulation is intended to depict the mastery of single-digit addition over the period from roughly 4 to 12 years of age.

GENERATION 3: ASCM

The Model's Basic Structure

Fig. 2.5 illustrates ASCM's overall organization. Strategies operate on problems to generate answers. The solution process yields information not only about the answer to the particular problem, but also about the time required to solve the problem using that strategy and the accuracy of the strategy in answering the problem. This information is used to modify the database regarding the strategy, the problem, and their interaction.

The Database. The type of information that gets entered into the database is illustrated in Fig. 2.6. Through their experience solving problems, children gain knowledge of both strategies and problems. Knowledge of each strategy can be divided into knowledge based on actual data and knowledge based on projections (inferences) from that data.

The actual data include each strategy's past speed and accuracy aggregated over all problems (*global data*), its speed and accuracy on problems with a particular feature (*featural data*), its speed and accuracy on each particular problem (*problem-specific data*), and its newness (*novelty data*).

ASCM

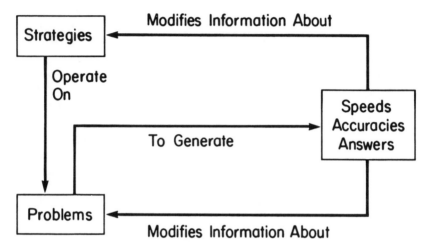

FIG. 2.5.   Overview of ASCM.

The roles of the first three types of data should be easy to comprehend, but that of the novelty data may require some explanation. Inclusion of these data was motivated by an attempt to answer the question: How do new strategies come to be used in situations where existing strategies work well? In the context of young children's addition, if a child can consistently solve a problem by using the sum strategy, why would the child ever try the min strategy on the problem? ASCM deals with this issue by assigning novelty points to newly discovered strategies. These novelty points temporarily add to the strength of new strategies, and thus allow the new strategies to be tried even when they have little or no track record. With each use of a new strategy, some of its novelty strength is lost, but information about its speed and accuracy is gained. This leads to the strategy's probability of use increasingly being determined by the expanding database on its effectiveness. The idea of novelty being a kind of strength was suggested by the observation that people (especially children) are often interested in exercising newly acquired cognitive capabilities (Piaget, 1970) and by the realization that without a track record, a newly acquired strategy might otherwise never be chosen, especially if reasonably effective alternatives were available.

Whenever ASCM is presented a problem, it uses these speed, accuracy, and novelty data for each strategy to make projections concerning how well

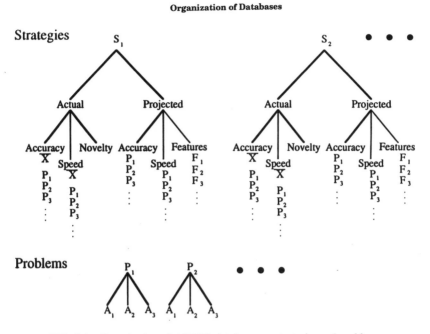

FIG. 2.6.   Organization of ASCM's databases on strategies and problems.

the strategy is likely to do in solving the problem. If a strategy has never been used on a particular problem, ASCM's projections are based solely on global and featural data. If the strategy has never been used on the particular problem or on any problem with that feature, only global data are used to derive the projection.

The Model's Operation.   ASCM is implemented as a running computer simulation. Because this simulation has not been described previously, its operating assumptions are explained here in some detail.

1. At the beginning of its run, ASCM knows only the two strategies that are common among 4-year-olds — retrieval and the sum strategy — and basic procedures for choosing strategies, collecting data on the outcomes they generate, and projecting their future usefulness. These latter competencies are hypothesized to be basic properties of the human information processing system and to be present from birth.

2. During the learning phase, the simulation is repeatedly presented the 81 basic addition facts formed by all possible combinations of addend values 1–9, inclusive. The problems are presented equally often. In the absence of data on presentation rates over the large age range being modeled, this seemed the most conservative assumption.

3. After a number of exposures to each problem (60 trials/problem in the simulation runs reported here), the min strategy is added to those initially available. This is done to correspond to the time, usually sometime during first grade, when children add the min strategy to their repertoire. The process of discovery of the min strategy is not yet modeled. Like its predecessor, the new simulation focuses on choices among existing strategies, rather than on how new strategies are constructed.

4. Strategy choices are based on the projected strength of each strategy. As shown in Table 2.3, projected strength is a function of the strategy's past speed and accuracy on problems as a whole, on problems with features in common with the current one, and on the particular problem being solved. For new strategies, the strategy's novelty boosts its strength beyond what its past performance alone would justify.

5. A logistic equation weights these sources of data according to the amount of information they reflect. When a strategy has rarely been used on a particular problem, global and featural data are weighted most heavily. As more information becomes available about how well the strategy works on the problem, problem-specific information receives increasing weight, eventually exercising the largest influence. The reasoning is that data derived from a few uses of a strategy is inherently noisy, but problem-specific information based on a substantial database is the best predictor of a strategy's future effectiveness on that problem. A similar logistic equation is used to weight data according to how recently it was generated. The reasoning underlying this decision was similar: Recent performance is given greater weight because it is likely to better predict future performance.

6. Each time a problem is presented, these weighted sources of information provide the input to a stepwise regression equation that computes the projected strength of each strategy on the problem.

7. Probability of choosing a particular strategy is proportional to that strategy's projected strength relative to that of all strategies combined. The simulation attempts to execute whichever strategy is chosen. If a backup strategy is chosen, it is executed to completion. If retrieval is chosen, a

TABLE 2.3
General Equations Governing ASCM's Operation

Strength $(strategy_a)$ = f (speed, accuracy, and novelty)	
P(retrieve $strategy_a$) =	$\dfrac{\text{Strength } (strategy_a)}{\text{Strength of all strategies}}$
P(retrieve $answer_a$) =	$\dfrac{\text{Strength } (answer_a)}{\text{Strength of all answers}}$

procedure identical to that within the distribution of associations model is followed. This means that when an answer is retrieved with associative strength that exceeds the confidence criterion, the answer is stated.

8. If no statable answer is retrieved and the searchlength has been reached, the model returns to the strategy choice phase and chooses among the backup strategies. The process is the same as at the beginning of the trial, except for the exclusion of retrieval from the set of strategies under consideration (because it has already been tried). Thus, the probability of a given backup strategy being chosen at this point reflects its projected strength relative to that of all backup strategies combined.

9. Probabilities of errors using the sum and min strategies are proportional to the number of counts required to execute the strategy on that problem. The errors arise through double counting or skipping an object in the representation of the problem. Each count entails a probability of error; thus, the greater the number of counts, the more likely that an error will be made. On retrieval trials, errors arise through an incorrect answer being retrieved and having sufficient associative strength to be stated.

10. Solution times on backup strategy trials are proportional to a constant times the number of counts that are executed. The constant is smaller for the sum than for the min strategy, because children take less time per count in counting from one than in counting from other numbers (Siegler, 1987b). Times on retrieval trials reflect a constant multiplied by the number of searches prior to locating a statable answer. This constant is much smaller than those used with the backup strategies, reflecting the fact that retrieval is much faster than the sum or min strategies.

11. As in the distributions of associations model, each time an answer is advanced, ASCM increases the association between that answer and the problem. Unlike in the earlier model, ASCM also adds information regarding the speed and accuracy with which the answer was generated to the database for the strategy.

12. Each execution of a backup strategy also brings an increase in the strategy's speed and a decrease in its probability of generating an error. Thus, strategy execution improves with practice.

There are clear similarities between ASCM and the distributions of associations model; in a sense, ASCM is a generalized version of the principles inherent in its predecessor. Several differences between the two should also be noted, though. ASCM is smarter: It possesses mechanisms for generalizing its experience to unfamiliar problems. It also is explicit about a broader range of strategy choices, in that it describes how choices among alternative backup strategies are made. Further, it is more flexible in allowing strategies to be considered in any order.

The Model's Performance

As in the tests of the distributions of associations model, the tests of ASCM's performance involved a *learning phase* of a given length and then a *test phase* that indicated the performance generated by the simulation after that amount of experience. During the learning phase, performance on each trial altered the database regarding strategies, problems, and answers. The analogy was to the experience that children would have had prior to entering the experimental situation. During the test phase, in contrast, the database remained constant. The analogy was to children's performance in the experimental situation, after their having had a given amount of pre-experimental experience.

The learning phases ranged from 60 to 1,250 trials per problem. This latter figure may at first sound high. However, to put it in perspective, 1,250 trials per problem works out to approximately 100 simple addition operations per school day over 6 years of elementary school (6 years, 180 school days/year, 81 problems). Given the torrent of addition problems that elementary school students receive from textbooks, workbooks, handouts, fact quizzes, and magic minutes, plus the embedding of simple addition within the multidigit addition and multiplication algorithms (a typical 3-digit by 3-digit multiplication problem entails 16 adding operations), this number does not seem unreasonable. Where not otherwise specified, the values reported for the simulation will be those attained after a learning phase of 750 exposures per problem, a point at which performance is very good, but where ceiling effects are not a serious difficulty.

Regardless of the length of the learning phase, the test phase included 3,700 trials per problem (300,000 total trials). Because the simulation did not undergo any change during the test phase, the only effect of this large number of trials was to approximate closely the expected values the simulation would produce after that length learning phase. The other key parameter values within the simulation are shown in Table 2.4.

TABLE 2.4
ASCM's Main Parameter Values

- Learning phase length: 60, 120, 250, 500, 750, or 1,250 trials/problem
- Test phase length: 3,700 trials/problem
- Range of confidence criteria: .01–.95
- Range of search lengths: 1–3
- Timing of min strategy introduction: After 60 trials/problem
- Range of min strategy percent correct: 30%–95%
- Range of sum strategy percent correct: 20%–85%
- Increment in associative strength for statement of correct answer: .0002
- Increment in associative strength for statement of incorrect answer: .0001

As with the distributions of associations model, ASCM can be understood in terms of its treatment of variability, strategy choice, change, generalization, and individual differences. Its performance on these dimensions highlights both its similarities to and its differences from its predecessor.

Variability. ASCM generates variability in the senses that the earlier model did, and in some additional senses as well. Like the distributions of associations model, it uses diverse strategies both within and between problems. It tends to most often use strategies on the problems where they work best, but strategy use varies within as well as between problems.

ASCM also generates some types of variability that the distributions of associations model did not. In the distributions of associations model, strategies were always executed in a fixed order, with retrieval invariably being tried first. Within ASCM, in contrast, any strategy can be tried first. In practice, retrieval comes to be tried first in the large majority of cases (99% after a learning phase of 750 trials/problem). This is due to its always being the fastest strategy and usually being accurate when it is used. However, the same mechanism that allows the novelty points to add associative strength to a strategy also opens ASCM to situational influences that can temporarily boost the strength of competing strategies (e.g., through instructions encouraging their use or through a child consciously thinking that it would be a good idea to try a particular strategy). Further, the order in which the backup strategies are considered varies in practice as well as in theory from trial-to-trial, unlike in the distributions of associations model, where their order was fixed.

Adaptive Strategy Choices. ASCM produced performance that was adaptive in the same ways as the performance generated by the distributions of associations model, and in an additional sense as well. Like the earlier model, it produced extremely high internal correlations between each problem's percent use of backup strategies and percent errors ($r = .98$) and between each problem's percent use of backup strategies and its mean solution time ($r = .99$).

We also compared ASCM's performance to that of children. The children were 120 students at a middle class suburban school, tested near the end of first grade. Speed, accuracy, and strategy use on each trial were assessed as in previous studies (e.g., Siegler, 1987b, 1989b). For each problem, percent correct, median solution time, and percent use of retrieval was computed over the set of 120 children.

As shown in Table 2.5, the simulation's percentages of use of backup strategies on each problem initially were almost uncorrelated with those of the children. However, as the simulation gained experience, the patterns of

TABLE 2.5
Correlations Between ASCM's and Children's Performance on Each Problem

Measure	Learning Trials/Problem				
	60	250	500	750	1,250
Percent errors	.27	.78	.85	.85	.50
Mean solution times	.12	.55	.77	.90	.81
Percent retrieval	.06	.21	.76	.93	.78

performance grew increasingly similar. After 750 trials per problem, ASCM's percentages of use of backup strategies on each problem correlated $r = .93$ with those of the children. After this point, the correlations decreased, for a reason that is easy to understand. After a learning phase with 1,250 trials per problem, the percentage of test-phase errors made by the simulation was extremely low (1%) and the percentage of strategies other than retrieval was also quite low (5%). This led to there being too little variance to produce the high correlations seen after shorter learning phases. Nonetheless, even in this advanced state, the simulations still produced adaptive choices between use of a backup strategy or retrieval much like those of children.

This type of adaptive strategy choice was also made by the distributions of associations model. However, ASCM also made a second type of adaptive choice, the choice of which backup strategy to use, that the earlier model did not. The adaptiveness of ASCM's choices is evident in the frequency of use of the min strategy relative to that of both backup strategies (percent min strategy/percent min + sum strategies). After relatively brief learning phases (e.g., 120 trials per problem), the best predictor of min strategy use on a problem was the size of its smaller addend; the smaller this value, the higher the percentage of min strategy use on the problem. After greater numbers of trials, the best predictor of percentage of min strategy use on a problem was the difference between the problem's addends; the larger the difference, the greater the percentage of min strategy use. These are the same variables that best predict min strategy use (given that retrieval was not used) in empirical data on children (Siegler, 1987b). It also makes intuitive sense for the min strategy to be used most often on problems with small smaller addends, where it is easiest to execute correctly, and on problems with large differences between the addends, where the min strategy produces the greatest reduction in counting relative to the sum strategy.

Change.   Perhaps the single most essential property of a simulation of acquisition of arithmetic knowledge is that it progress from the inaccurate performance characteristic of children just beginning to add, to the virtually perfect performance that characterizes children by fifth or sixth grade. ASCM met this test. After a learning phase of 60 trials per problem, its performance was 31% correct, whereas after a learning phase of 1,250 trials per problem, its performance was 99% correct. As shown in Fig. 2.7, this improvement did not occur in sudden jumps; rather it came steadily with a substantial amount of experience. Children show similar gradual improvement with experience in the accuracy of their addition (Kaye, Post, Hall, & Dineen, 1986; Siegler, 1987b).

As shown in Fig. 2.8, ASCM's changes in frequency of use of the three strategies also paralleled children's. At first the simulation used only the

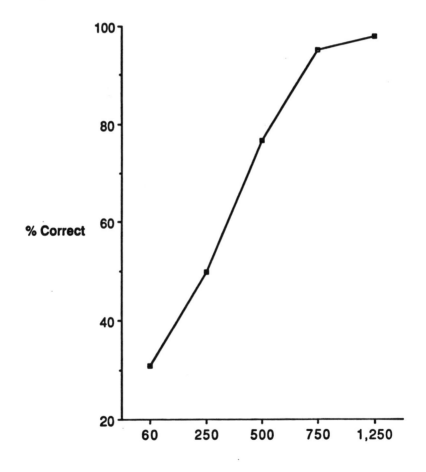

Learning Trials / Problem

FIG. 2.7.   ASCM's percent correct after different length learning phases.

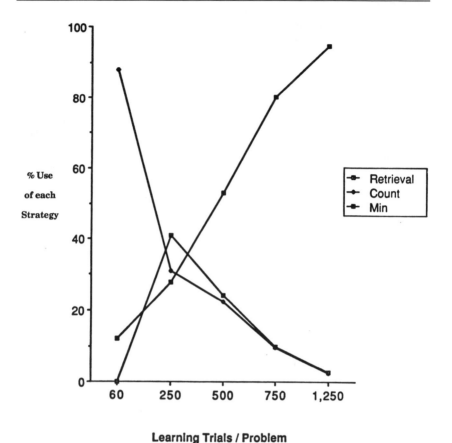

Learning Trials / Problem

FIG. 2.8.   ASCM's percent use of the min strategy, sum strategy, and retrieval after learning phases of different lengths.

sum strategy and retrieval (the only strategies it knew), with the sum strategy being employed on the large majority of trials. After the min strategy was added, it became the most frequently used strategy, with the sum strategy and retrieval also being used on substantial numbers of trials. This corresponds to children's performance at around first grade. Beyond this point, use of both sum and min strategies decreased, and retrieval became increasingly dominant. After a learning phase of 1,250 trials per problem, retrieval was used on 95% of trials.

A third key type of progress involved decrements in solution times. The overall decrement in times was produced by two factors: shifts from the slower backup strategies to the faster retrieval approach, and faster execution of each strategy. Along with this general speedup, ASCM produced changes in the pattern of solution times on different problems, changes that paralleled those in the pattern of children's times on different problems. Empirical studies of children's arithmetic have demonstrated that the best predictor of children's solution times on addition problems changes with age in a regular way. In the preschool period, the size of the sum is the best predictor (Siegler & Robinson, 1982; Siegler & Shrager, 1984); in first and second grade, the size of the smaller addend is the best predictor (Groen & Parkman, 1972; Groen & Resnick, 1977; Svenson & Broquist, 1975). Beyond this time, the product of the two addends tends to be most predictive (Geary, Widaman, & Little, 1986; Geary, Widaman, Little, & Cormier, 1987; Miller, Perlmutter, & Keating, 1984). Accounting for these changes in the best predictors of solution times is a considerably more rigorous test of the simulation than simply producing improvements in the absolute levels of the times.

As shown in Table 2.6, the simulation underwent the same type of changes in the predictors of its solution times as did children. At first, the best predictor of solution times was the sum of the addends; later, the size of the smaller addend was the best predictor; still later, product size became the most predictive variable.

The reasons for these predictive relations also appear to be the same for the simulation and the children. The sum was the best predictor at first because the predominant strategy that was used, the sum strategy, generated solution times that are a linear function of the sum (Siegler, 1987b). Smaller addend size became the best predictor of solution times when the min strategy was most often used, because it generated solution times that are a linear function of the size of the smaller addend (Siegler, 1987b).

The reasons why the product was the best predictor of both the children's and the simulation's times are both less intuitive and more interesting. The only previous explanation of the phenomenon was Widaman, Geary, Cormier, and Little's (1989) spreading activation model. Within this model, arithmetic knowledge is represented much like the type of facts table often seen in elementary school textbooks. In such tables, the numbers 0–9 head

TABLE 2.6
Best Predictor of ASCM's Solution Times After Learning Phases of Different Lengths

Learning Trials per Problem	Best Predictor	% Variance Accounted for
60	Sum	91
120	Smaller addend	88
250	Product	93
500	Product	91
750	Product	79
1,000	Product	93
1,250	Product	92

the columns and the rows and the sum of the two addends at each intersection, so that 0 is in the top left hand corner and 18 is in the bottom right hand corner. Geary and Widaman hypothesized that presentation of an addition problem X + Y causes activation to spread from the origin to cover a rectangle whose vertices are 0, 0; X, 0; 0, Y; and X, Y. The time to activate this rectangle was hypothesized to be proportional to its area, thus leading to the product XY determining solution times to X + Y.

Such fact table explanations were faulted on a number of grounds (e.g., Ashcraft, 1987; Pellegrino & Goldman, 1989; Siegler, 1988b). Among the criticisms, the fact-table model renders problematic why factors other than problem size (e.g., presence of 5 as an addend or multiplicand) should make problems easier than their size would suggest. It also makes problematic how people would ever retrieve answers that are not part of the arithmetic table (e.g., $7 \times 8 = 58$).

ASCM generated the same result (solution times being best predicted by the product of the addends) through an entirely different, and we believe more plausible, mechanism. Within ASCM, as within the distributions of associations model, relative difficulty of problems reflects the relative difficulty of executing backup strategies on them. In the case of addition, the two most common backup strategies are the sum and min strategies. Solution times on retrieval trials ultimately reflect the distribution of associations generated by the backup strategies. Because min and sum are the main backup strategies used, solution times should reflect the history of the simulation having sometimes solved the problems using one approach and sometimes the other.

To demonstrate the sufficiency of this explanation to account for the phenomenon, we generated several artificial data sets. In one, we had the simulation use both the min strategy and the sum strategy on exactly half of trials on each problem. Within this run, the solution time predicted for each problem was an unweighted average of the time that would arise from use of each strategy.

The results illustrated that such a history would lead to the product being an excellent predictor of solution times in absolute terms, accounting for 98% of the variance in times on the 81 single-digit problems, and also to the product being more predictive than the other variables that were examined: the smaller addend, larger addend, first addend, second addend, sum, and sum squared.

This result was not dependent on the frequency of strategy use being equal for the two backup strategies. The product was just as good a predictor in absolute terms, and the best predictor in relative terms, on a test in which the min strategy was used on two-thirds of trials on each problem and on a test in which the sum strategy was used on two-thirds of trials on each problem. These results suggest that the product is the best predictor of both the children's and the simulation's solution times because it reflects the combined influences of the most frequent backup strategies in shaping strengths of associative connections between problems and answers. The results hold over a range of assumptions about the history of learning that shaped the associative network.

This example illustrates how simulations can suggest alternative explanations of empirical phenomena that would not otherwise be generated. The simulation was not designed with the intention of explaining why the product was the best predictor of older children's and adults' solution times. When the pattern emerged, however, we recognized it as the same one that had emerged in the empirical literature. The result allowed us to say with certainty that such a pattern could arise in the absence of a tabular representation; we know for a fact that ASCM does not have such a representation. The simulation thus served as a tool analogous to animal models in medicine — a system believed to work similarly along the relevant dimensions, but one amenable to much more precise experimental manipulation than the system being modeled. This function seems to us to be one of the most valuable that simulations can serve in the study of cognitive development.

Generalization.   As noted earlier, a key requirement for a realistic model of arithmetic is that it be able to generalize its knowledge of strategies to new problems. A first or second grader who, for the first time, needed to mentally calculate 4 + 38 would be unlikely to know the answer, but almost certainly would choose to count from 38 rather than from 1. Inability to generalize in this way was one of the major limits of the distributions of associations model.

To test ASCM's ability to generalize, we presented it with 50 learning-phase exposures to each of 10 single-digit problems, and then, during the test phase, examined its strategy choices on the other 71 problems. We then repeated the procedure with 500 learning-phase trials per problem for each of the 10 problems, to see if generalization improved with experience. The 10 problems were generated randomly, subject to the stipulation that each integer was included once as the first addend and once as the second addend. We chose to have a low ratio of example problems to generalization problems to mimic the situation that children encounter, in which there are very large numbers of problems that they occasionally need to solve (e.g., 3 + 29).

In this test of ASCM's ability to generalize, we were interested in whether it would choose the min strategy most often on problems where it was easiest to execute and/or where its advantage in reduced counting over the sum strategy was greatest. For example, would it choose the min strategy especially often on 9 + 1, a problem that has both of these properties?

ASCM showed exactly this pattern of generalization. On the 71 problems that had not been presented in the learning phase, the best predictor of percentage of trials on which the min strategy was used was the difference between the addends (Table 2.7). What this meant can be illustrated by considering the use of the min and sum strategies on two specific problems: 9 + 8 and 9 + 1. On the former problem, where the difference between addends was only 1, the min strategy was used on 33% of trials during the generalization phase and the sum strategy on 67% (after the simulation had been given 500 exposures to each of the 10 original problems). In contrast, on 9 + 1, where the difference between the addends was 8, the min strategy was used on 76% and the sum strategy on only 24% of trials.

The differentiation between problems on which the min strategy was more and less helpful increased with learning; differences between the addends was a better predictor of amount of generalization of the min strategy after a learning phase of 500 trials per problem than after one of 50 trials per problem. This made sense, because the model was obtaining increasingly valid data about each strategy's effectiveness on different problems. Even at the first point of measurement, however, ASCM produced generalizations similar to those shown by children.

Individual Differences.   As noted earlier, Siegler (1988a) found substantial individual differences in children's approaches to addition, subtraction, and word identification tasks. The children could be classified into three distinct groups: the *good students,* the *not-so-good students,* and the *perfectionists.* As the names suggest, the good students were both more accurate and more likely to retrieve answers than the not-so-good students. The perfectionists were as accurate as the good students, but used retrieval even less often than the not-so-good students.

Both the distributions of associations model and ASCM suggested a simple means through which the three individual difference groups could arise: parametric variation in peakedness of the distributions of associations and in confidence criteria. The more peaked the distribution of associations, the more likely that a correct answer will be retrieved, and the more likely that if retrieved, its associative strength will exceed the confidence criterion and be stated. The higher the confidence criteria, the greater the

TABLE 2.7
Generalization of Min Strategy Use

Learning Phase Trials/Problems	Best Predictor of Min Strategy Use on Generalization Problems	% Variance Accounted for
50	Difference between addends	62
500	Difference between addends	83

associative strength of the retrieved answer must be to exceed it, and therefore, the fewer retrieved answers will be stated.

This view suggests an interpretation of each group's pattern of performance. The good student pattern would arise from a combination of peaked distributions of associations and a wide range of confidence criteria. This would lead to both high accuracy and frequent use of retrieval, because the highly peaked distributions would result in frequent retrieval and statement of the correct answer. The not-so-good student pattern would arise from flat distributions of associations and low confidence criteria. This would generate inaccurate performance and medium-to-low amounts of retrieval, because incorrect answers would often be retrieved and would sometimes exceed the low confidence criteria. The perfectionist pattern would arise from peaked distributions and very high confidence criteria. This would lead to accurate performance, but to low amounts of retrieval, because only the most peaked distributions would have correct answers with enough associative strength to exceed the very high confidence criteria.

To test this interpretation, we created three variants of the simulation. They differed only in their values of the two parameters hypothesized to underlie the individual differences: probability of correct execution of backup strategies (which influenced the peakedness of distributions that were formed) and range of confidence criteria. The simulation of the not-so-good students' performance executed backup strategies less accurately than did the simulations of the perfectionists' and good students' performance, which were identical to each other in accuracy of execution of these strategies. The confidence criteria of the not-so-good students were consistently low (.10–.50), those of the perfectionists consistently high (.50–.90), and those of the good students included both low and high values (.10–.90). Other than these two parameter values, the simulations of the three groups were identical.

Results indicated that the variations in these two parametric values were sufficient to account for the observed pattern of individual differences. As shown in Table 2.8, ASCM's simulation of the not-so-good students produced lower percentages correct than its simulations of the good students and perfectionists, which did not differ. As with children, ASCM's good student simulation produced the greatest amount of retrieval, its not-so-good student simulation the next most, and its perfectionist simula-

TABLE 2.8
Performance Generated by ASCM Simulations of Individual Differences

Group	% Correct	% Retrieval
Good students	96	84
Not-so-good students	76	76
Perfectionists	96	69

tion the least. The simulations thus illustrate how qualitatively different patterns of performance can arise through parametric variations within the same basic processing framework.

CONCLUSIONS

The central thesis of this chapter is that transcending the typical 1:1 equation between age and way of thinking, and recognizing the importance of variation and selection in cognitive development, will lead to a better understanding of change. To support this thesis, we identified a set of key phenomena regarding children's strategy choices and examined how three generations of models accounted for them. The increasing ability of the models to account for change reflects two types of progress: broadening of the types of variability and selection that are accounted for, and increasingly precise specification of how the variability and selection are produced.

The first-generation metacognitive models represented an initial effort in this direction. They reflected the recognition that individual children often know multiple strategies and that they use them under some circumstances and not others. They depicted choices among the strategies in terms of an executive processor using explicit, conscious knowledge about cognitive capacities, strategies, and situational variables to decide which strategy to use. Change in this knowledge was what led to better choices among the strategies. The key insight of these first generation models was that choices among strategies was a key issue to be explained. The key weaknesses were their questionable assumption that strategy choices are in general produced by explicit, rational analyses of situations, capacities, and strategies, and their lack of specificity regarding how the choice process works.

The second-generation attempt to explain strategy choices — the distributions of associations model — recognized a broader range of variability: variability not just in strategies known to each child but also in answers associated with the problem and in individual children's strategy choices. Within this model, choosing whether to use a backup strategy or retrieval was viewed as reflecting an interaction between the organization of the strategies and the peakedness of the distributions of associations for the particular problem. Change in the peakedness of the distributions of associations changed the frequency with which each strategy was selected, as well as the speed and accuracy of performance. The key insight embodied within the distributions of associations model was that intelligent strategy choices did not require an intelligent executive processor. The model was also far more explicit than the metacognitive models had been about how strategy choices are made and about the factors that contribute to changes in the choices. However, it was too inflexible, not explicit about how choices among backup strategies are made, and incapable of generalizing its strategy choices to new problems.

The third generation model, ASCM, further expanded the range of variability that was recognized. It not only attempted to account for variability in strategies, answers, and individual patterns of performance, but also for variability in the order in which strategies were considered. Its choices among strategies made use of a considerably broader range of data – not just associations between problems and answers, but also global, featural, local, and novelty data about the strategies. These data allowed ASCM to make adaptive choices on novel as well as familiar problems, and to choose between alternative backup strategies as well as between retrieval and some backup strategies. Relative to its predecessors, ASCM also specified a larger set of contributors to change in strategy choices – not just changes in the peakedness of the distributions of associations, but also changing knowledge about all of the types of data regarding strategies that contribute to adaptive choices at any one time. The key insight was that the principles used by the distributions of associations model to choose between retrieval and a backup strategy could be used to choose among any set of strategies, and provided a basis for generalization as well. However, ASCM had its limits: Additional sources of variation and selection that need to be explained.

An important source of variation that remains to be accounted for is strategy acquisition. ASCM provides a general account of how choices among existing strategies are made, but does not indicate how the strategies come to be present. Yet, acquisition of new strategies is what makes strategy choice both possible and necessary.

This limit may soon be overcome. Jones and VanLehn (1991) formulated a simulation, GIPS, that models the data on preschoolers' discovery of the min strategy reported by Siegler and Jenkins (1989). If the models can be integrated, GIPS may provide a kind of "front end" to ASCM, providing it with the strategies that it would then choose among.

An important source of selection that remains to be accounted for is explicit, conscious, metacognitive judgment. This may not play a large role when people have had experience in a domain, as is the case in children's arithmetic. However, this type of knowledge seems likely to be more influential when children are presented with a novel problem and need to decide what to do. Metacognitive models may have overestimated the influence of conscious, explicit knowledge, but this does not mean that such knowledge has no influence. Understanding when and how metacognitive knowledge is used to choose among alternative strategies seems essential for a general understanding of strategy choice.

One final comment on a basic assumption underlying the present research effort seems essential. Science progresses not only through increasingly precise description of an increasing range of phenomena, but also through repeated efforts to explain the phenomena. We believe that models are critical in this effort, because they indicate the range of phenomena that can be accounted for at any one time, and thus provide a benchmark against which the successes and failures of alternative explanations can be measured. Such models never have the solidity of facts and are never complete. Still, they seem to us extremely valuable, because they make clear both what we have achieved and the much larger tasks that remain.

ACKNOWLEDGMENTS

This research was supported by a grant from the Mellon Foundation, by a grant from the Spencer Foundation, and by grant HD-19011 from the National Institutes of Health.

APPENDIX
ASSOCIATIVE STRENGTH VALUES FOR 0–9 + 0–9

		FIRST ADDEND									
		0	1	2	3	4	5	6	7	8	9
	0	53	53	52	52	52	52	52	52	53	51
	1	51	53	51	52	50	53	50	53	51	53
	2	53	51	52	47	50	50	50	50	45	47
SECOND	3	52	53	52	53	46	46	42	45	42	46
ADDEND	4	53	50	45	47	53	45	38	31	31	26
	5	53	52	48	40	46	53	35	24	18	19
	6	53	52	44	44	36	37	49	26	9	11
	7	53	51	48	39	23	26	19	51	21	11
	8	52	50	46	41	28	12	7	18	38	18
	9	53	52	43	45	24	18	11	8	24	40

REFERENCES

Ashcraft, M. H. (1982). The development of mental arithmetic: A chronometric approach. *Developmental Review, 2*, 213–236.

Ashcraft, M. H. (1987). Children's knowledge of simple arithmetic: A developmental model and simulation. In J. Bisanz, C. J. Brainerd, & R. Kail (Eds.), *Formal methods in developmental psychology* (pp. 302–338). New York: Springer-Verlag.

Bowerman, M. (1982). Starting to talk worse: Clues to language acquisition from children's late speech errors. In S. Strauss (Ed.), *U-shaped behavioral growth* (pp. 101–145). New York: Academic Press.

Brown, A. L., Bransford, J. D., Ferrara, R. S., & Campione, J. C. (1983). Learning, remembering, and understanding. In P. H. Mussen (Ed.), *Handbook of child psychology: Cognitive development* (Vol. 3, pp. 77–166). New York: Wiley.

Brown, A. L., & Reeve, R. A. (1986). Reflections on the growth of reflection in children. *Cognitive Development, 1,* 405–416.

Brown, R. (1973). *A first language.* Cambridge, MA: Harvard University Press.

Case, R. (1978). Intellectual development from birth to adulthood: A neo-Piagetian interpretation. In R. S. Siegler (Ed.), *Children's thinking: What develops?* (pp. 37–72). Hillsdale, NJ: Lawrence Erlbaum Associates.

Cavanaugh, J. C., & Perlmutter, M. (1982). Metamemory: A critical examination. *Child Development, 53,* 11–28.

Church, R. B., & Goldin-Meadow, S. (1986). The mismatch between gesture and speech as an index of transitional knowledge. *Cognition, 23,* 43–71.

Cooney, J. B., Swanson, H. L., & Ladd, S. F. (1988). Acquisition of mental multiplication skill: Evidence for the transition between counting and retrieval strategies. *Cognition and Instruction, 5,* 323–345.

Fabricius, W. V., & Hagen, J. W. (1984). The use of causal attributions about recall performance to assess metamemory and predict strategic memory behavior in young children. *Developmental Psychology, 20,* 975–987.

Flavell, J. H. (1981). Cognitive monitoring. In P. Dickson (Ed.), *Children's oral communication skills,* (pp. 35–60). New York: Academic Press.

Flavell, J. H. (1985). *Cognitive development,* (2nd ed.). Englewood Cliffs, NJ: Prentice-Hall.

Flavell, J. H., Beach, D. R., & Chinsky, J. M. (1966). Spontaneous verbal rehearsal in a memory task as a function of age. *Child Development, 37,* 283–299.

Flavell, J. H., & Wellman, H. M. (1977). Metamemory. In R. V. Kail & J. W. Hagen (Eds.), *Perspectives on the development of memory and cognition* (pp. 3–33). Hillsdale, NJ: Lawrence Erlbaum Associates.

Geary, D. C., & Burlingham-Dubree, M. (1989). External validation of the strategy choice model for addition. *Journal of Experimental Child Psychology, 47,* 175–192.

Geary, D. C., Fan, L., & Bow-Thomas, C. C. (1992). Numerical cognition: Loci of ability differences comparing children from China and the United States. *Psychological Science, 3,* 180–185.

Geary, D. C., Widaman, K. F., & Little, T. D. (1986). Cognitive addition and multiplication: Evidence for a single memory network. *Memory and Cognition, 14,* 478–487.

Geary, D. C., Widaman, K. F., Little, T. D., & Cormier, P. (1987). Cognitive addition: Comparison of learning disabled and academically normal elementary school children. *Cognitive Development, 2,* 249–269.

Geary, D. C., & Wiley, J. G. (1991). Cognitive addition: Strategy choice and speed-of-processing differences in young and elderly adults. *Psychology and Aging, 6,* 474–483.

Gillilund, G., & Shiffrin, R. M. (1984). A retrieval model for both recognition and recall. *Psychological Review, 92,* 1–67.

Goldfield, E. C. (in press). Dynamical systems in development: Action systems. In L. B. Smith & E. Thelen (Eds.), *Dynamic systems approaches to development.* Cambridge, MA: MIT Press.

Greeno, J. G., Riley, M. S., & Gelman, R. (1984). Conceptual competence and children's counting. *Cognitive Psychology, 16,* 94–143.

Groen, G. J., & Parkman, J. M. (1972). A chronometric analysis of simple addition. *Psychological Review, 79,* 329–343.

Groen, G. J., & Resnick, L. B. (1977). Can preschool children invent addition algorithms? *Journal of Educational Psychology, 69,* 645–652.

Guttentag, R. E. (1984). The mental effort requirement of cumulative rehearsal: A developmental study. *Journal of Experimental Child Psychology, 37,* 92–106.

Halford, G. S. (1993). *Children's understanding: The development of mental models.* Hillsdale, NJ: Lawrence Erlbaum Associates.

Jones, R. M., & VanLehn, K. (1991). Strategy shifts without impasses: A computational model of the sum-to-min transition. *Proceedings of the Thirteenth Annual Conference of the Cognitive Science Society* (pp. 358-363). Hillsdale, NJ: Lawrence Erlbaum Associates.

Justice, E. M. (1985). Categorization as a preferred memory strategy: Developmental changes during elementary school. *Developmental Psychology, 21*, 1105-1110.

Kahan, L. D., & Richards, D. D. (1986). The effects of context on children's referential communication strategies. *Child Development, 57*, 1130-1141.

Kaye, D. B., Post, T. A., Hall, V. C., & Dineen, J. T. (1986). The emergence of information retrieval strategies in numerical cognition: A developmental study. *Cognition and Instruction, 3*, 137-166.

Keeney, F. J., Cannizzo, S. R., & Flavell, J. H. (1967). Spontaneous and induced verbal rehearsal in a recall task. *Child Development, 38*, 953-966.

Kerkman, D. D., & Siegler, R. S. (1993). Individual differences and adaptive flexibility in lower-income children's strategy choices. *Learning and Individual Differences, 5*, 113-136.

Kluwe, R. H. (1982). Cognitive knowledge and executive control: Metacognition. In D. Griffin (Ed.), *Animal mind-human mind* (pp. 201-224). New York: Springer.

Kogan, N. (1983). Stylistic variation in childhood and adolescence: Creativity, metaphor, and cognitive styles. In P. H. Mussen (Ed.), *Handbook of child psychology: Vol. III. Cognitive development* (pp. 630-706). New York: Wiley.

Kreutzer, M. A., Leonard, C., & Flavell, J. H. (1975). An interview study of children's knowledge about memory. *Monographs of the Society for Research in Child Development, 40* (Serial No. 159).

Kuczaj, S. (1977). The acquisition of regular and irregular past tense forms. *Journal of Verbal Learning and Verbal Behaviour, 16*, 589-600.

Kuhara-Kojima, K., & Hatano, G. (1989). Strategies for recognizing sentences among high and low critical thinkers. *Japanese Psychological Research, 31*, 1-19.

Kuhn, D. (1984). Cognitive development. In M. H. Bornstein & M. E. Lamb (Eds.) *Developmental psychology: An advanced textbook* (pp. 133-180). Hillsdale, NJ: Lawrence Erlbaum Associates.

Kuhn, D., Schauble, L., & Garcia-Mila, M. (1992). Cross-domain development of scientific reasoning. *Cognition and Instruction, 9*, 285-327.

Maloney D. P., & Siegler, R. S. (1993). Conceptual competition in physics learning. *International Journal of Science Education, 15*, 283-295.

Maratsos, M. (1983). Some current issues in the study of the acquisition of grammar. In P. H. Mussen (Ed.), *Handbook of child psychology: Vol. III. Cognitive development* (pp. 707-786). New York: Wiley.

Markman, E. M. (1979). Realizing that you don't understand: Elementary school children's awareness of inconsistencies. *Child Development, 50*, 643-655.

McGilly, K., & Siegler, R. S. (1989). How children choose among serial recall strategies. *Child Development, 60*, 172-182.

McGilly, K., & Siegler, R. S. (1990). The influence of encoding and strategic knowledge on children's choices among serial recall strategies. *Developmental Psychology, 26*, 931-941.

Miller, K. F., & Paredes, D. R. (1990). Starting to add worse: Effects of learning to multiply on children's addition. *Cognition, 37*, 213-242.

Miller, K., Perlmutter, M., & Keating, D. (1984). Cognitive arithmetic: Comparison of operations. *Journal of Experimental Psychology: Learning, Memory, and Cognition, 10*, 46-60.

Miller, P. (1990). The development of strategies of selective attention. In D. F. Bjorklund (Ed.), *Children's strategies: Contemporary views of cognitive development* (pp. 157-184). Hillsdale, NJ: Lawrence Erlbaum Associates.

Neches, R. (1987). Learning through incremental refinement procedures. In D. Klahr, P. Langley, & R. Neches (Eds.) *Production system models of learning and development* (pp. 163-219). Cambridge, MA: MIT Press.

Ohlsson, S. (1984). Induced strategy shifts in spatial reasoning. *Acta Psychologica, 57*, 47-67.

Pellegrino, J. W., & Goldman, S. R. (1989). Mental chronometry and individual differences in cognitive processes: Common pitfalls and their solutions. *Learning and Individual Differences, 1,* 203-225.

Piaget, J. (1970). *Psychology and epistemology.* New York: Viking.

Reder, L. M. (1982). Plausibility judgments versus fact retrieval: Alternative strategies for sentence verification. *Psychological Review, 89,* 250-280.

Reder, L. M., & Ritter, F. E. (1992). What determines initial feeling of knowing? Familiarity with question terms, not with the answer. *Journal of Experimental Psychology: Learning, Memory, and Cognition, 18,* 435-451.

Rovee-Collier, C. (1989). *The "memory system" of prelinguistic infants.* Paper presented at the Conference on the Development of Neural Bases of Higher Cognitive Functions, Chestnut Hill, PA.

Rumelhart, D. E., & McClelland, J. L. (1986). On learning the past tenses of English verbs. In J. L. McClelland & D. E. Rumelhart (Eds.), *Parallel distributed processing: Vol. 2: Psychological and biological models* (pp. 216-271). Cambridge, MA: MIT Press.

Schauble, L. (1990). Belief revision in children: The role of prior knowledge and strategies for generating evidence. *Journal of Experimental Child Psychology, 49,* 31-57.

Schneider, W. (1985). Developmental trends in the metamemory–memory behavior relation-ship: An integrative review. In D. L. Forrest-Pressley, G. E. MacKinnon, & T. G. Waller (Eds.), *Cognition, metacognition, and human performance* (pp. 57-109). New York: Academic Press.

Schneider, W., & Pressley, M. (1989). *Memory development between 2 and 20.* New York: Springer.

Shultz, T. R., Fisher, G. W., Pratt, C. C., & Rulf, S. (1986). Selection of causal rules. *Child Development, 57,* 143-152.

Siegler, R. S. (1986). Unities across domains in children's strategy choices. In M. Perlmutter (Ed.), *Perspectives on intellectual development: The Minnesota symposia on child psychology* (Vol. 19, pp. 1-48). Hillsdale, NJ: Lawrence Erlbaum Associates.

Siegler, R. S. (1987a). Strategy choices in subtraction. In J. Sloboda & D. Rogers (Eds.), *Cognitive process in mathematics* (pp. 81-106). Oxford: Oxford University Press.

Siegler, R. S. (1987b). The perils of averaging data over strategies: An example from children's addition. *Journal of Experimental Psychology: General, 116,* 250-264.

Siegler, R. S. (1988a). Individual differences in strategy choices: Good students, not-so-good students, and perfectionists. *Child Development, 59,* 833-851.

Siegler, R. S. (1988b). Strategy choice procedures and the development of multiplication skill. *Journal of Experimental Psychology: General, 117,* 258-275.

Siegler, R. S. (1989a). How domain-general and domain-specific knowledge interact to produce strategy choices. *Merrill-Palmer Quarterly, 35,* 1-26.

Siegler, R. S. (1989b). Mechanisms of cognitive development. *Annual Review of Psychology, 40,* 353-379.

Siegler, R. S., & Campbell, J. I. D. (1990). Diagnosing individual differences in strategy choice procedures. In N. Fredriksen, R. Glaser, A. Lesgold, & M. G. Shafto (Eds.), *Diagnostic monitoring of skill and knowledge acquisition* (pp. 113-139). Hillsdale, NJ: Lawrence Erlbaum Associates.

Siegler, R. S., & Jenkins, E. (1989). *How children discover new strategies.* Hillsdale, NJ: Lawrence Erlbaum Associates.

Siegler, R. S., & McGilly, K. (1989). Strategy choices in children's time-telling. In I. Levin & D. Zakay (Eds.), *Time and human cognition: A life span perspective* (pp. 185-218). The Netherlands: Elsevier.

Siegler, R. S., & Robinson, M. (1982). The development of numerical understandings. In H. W. Reese & L. P. Lipsitt (Eds.), *Advances in child development and behavior* (Vol. 16, pp. 241-312). New York: Academic Press.

Siegler, R. S., & Shrager, J. (1984). Strategy choices in addition and subtraction: How do children know what to do? In C. Sophian (Ed.), *Origins of cognitive skills* (pp. 229–293). Hillsdale, NJ: Lawrence Erlbaum Associates.

Sternberg, R. J. (1985). *Beyond IQ: A triarchic theory of human intelligence.* New York: Cambridge University Press.

Svenson, O., & Broquist, S. (1975). Strategies for solving simple addition problems: A comparison of normal and subnormal children. *Scandinavian Journal of Psychology, 16,* 143–151.

Van Lehn, K. (1982). Bugs are not enough: Empirical studies of bugs, impasses, and repairs in procedural skills. *The Journal of Mathematical Behavior, 3, 3–71.*

Wellman, H. M. (1983). Metamemory revisited. In M. T. H. Chi (Ed.), *Trends in memory development research* (pp. 31–51). Basel, Switzerland: Karger.

Widaman, K. F., Geary, D. C., Cormier, P., & Little, T. D. (1989). A componential model for mental addition. *Journal of Experimental Psychology: Learning, Memory, and Cognition, 15,* 898–919.

Yussen, S. R., & Levy, V. M. (1977). Developmental changes in knowledge about different retrieval problems. *Developmental Psychology, 13,* 114–120.

3

Modeling the Development of Reasoning Strategies: The Roles of Analogy, Knowledge, and Capacity

Graeme S. Halford
Susan B. Smith
J. Campbell Dickson
Murray T. Maybery
Mavis E. Kelly
John D. Bain
J. E. M. Stewart
University of Queensland

Cognitive development is about the process of change, and a major component of change is the acquisition of skills and strategies for reasoning. In this chapter, we propose a model of the development of reasoning strategies. The model uses transitivity as a prototypical task, but is based on processes that generally apply to the acquisition of reasoning. One such process is analogy, and because analogy entails mapping of structures, the model is called the Transitive Inference Mapping Model (TRIMM).

There are several reasons for using transitivity as a prototypical reasoning task. First, it has the main features that are basic to reasoning. It includes representation, storage, conversion and integration of premises, and entails making an inference based on the integrated representation. Second, there is an extensive and high-quality database on transitivity in both the general cognition and cognitive development literatures, that can constrain theory. Furthermore, there are a number of good models of the processes entailed in transitive inference (Foos, Smith, Sabol, & Mynatt, 1976; Sternberg, 1980a, 1980b), although there is no model of how these reasoning processes develop. There is also less dispute about these processes than occurs in some areas, such as class inclusion or conservation. This provides a solid foundation on which to build.

Acquisition of transitivity is an important developmental landmark. It was regarded as an indicator of concrete operational thought (Piaget, 1950), and continues to be an important phenomenon for cognitive developmental theories to explain (Halford, 1989, 1993a). However, recognition of the developmental importance of transitivity does not commit us to adoption of Piagetian or any other stage theory. Implications for the stage issue will be considered in the final discussion, but the TRIMM model does not rest on assumptions of either continuity or discontinuity in cognitive development.

An example of a transitive inference is: if a > b, and b > c, then a > c. Transitivity has a strict mathematical definition,[1] but the way it is understood psychologically may be different from the mathematical concept of transitivity. The best course is to consider both the mathematical and psychological concepts of transitivity.

To relax the mathematical definition, transitivity means that if R is a transitive relation, and if R exists between a and b and also between b and c, then the relation R will exist between a and c; that is, aRb and bRc implies aRc. Examples of transitive relations include those concerned with size, weight, distance, and measurable properties. On the other hand, "lover of" is nontransitive; if a is the lover of b, and b is the lover of c, it is unlikely that a is the lover of c.[2]

The psychological significance of transitivity rests on the fact that it is part of the definition of the psychologically important concept of *serial order*. Mathematically, an ordered set is one on which an asymmetric, transitive, binary relation is defined. For example, if we take the ordered set (a, b, c, d), where a is the biggest and d is the smallest, then it will be true that a > b, b > c, c > d, but also a > c, a > d, b > d. The relation "bigger than" is asymmetric (because a > b implies b > a cannot be true), and transitive.

The concept of order is important in many situations. Understanding the numbering of houses in a street depends on understanding order, as also does understanding positions in a competition and a multitude of other concepts. Order is also important to all but the most primitive concepts of quantification. Only the lowest level of scale, the nominal scale, does not depend on order. An ordinal scale clearly entails a concept of order, an interval scale entails the concept of order plus a definition of the distance between the elements and, therefore, an addition operation. A ratio scale entails everything that is in the interval scale, plus a zero point and a multiplication operation. Thus, understanding of quantification beyond the nominal scale entails a concept of order that in turn entails transitivity.

---

[1]A relation R defined on a set S is transitive if aRb and aRc imply aRc for every a, b, c in S.

[2]A relation is nontransitive if aRb and bRc implies aRc for some, but not all, a, b, c. A relation is intransitive if aRb and bRc does not imply aRc for any a, b, c.

Transitivity tasks are examples of a larger class called *N-term series tasks*. N-term series tasks are presented as a set of premises of the form aRb, bRc, cRd, and so on (where R is asymmetric and transitive), with a question that asks for the rank order of one or more terms (e.g. which is the largest element, which is larger, b or d?). The TRIMM model is designed to apply to N-term series tasks.

REASONING PROCESSES

Models of N-Term Series Reasoning

There are already a number of reviews of work in this field (Breslow, 1981; Halford, 1982, 1989; Maybery, 1987; Thayer & Collyer, 1978), and a number of theoretical models. Two of the best known models of children's performance on these tasks were proposed by Sternberg (1980b) and Trabasso (1977). Sternberg offered a mixed model that integrates a number of previous theories, and accounts for a high proportion of the variance in solution times. The essence of it is that the premises are first processed to obtain the linguistic deep structural base strings that represent their meaning. These strings are then converted to images of ordered pairs. For example, in the problem *Tom is happier than Bill, Bill is happier than John,* the premises would be coded as the pairs (Tom, Bill) (Bill, John). The pivot or common term (Bill) is then located, and the pairs are integrated into an ordered triple (Tom, Bill, John). Trabasso's (1977) model also proposed that the problem elements are placed in an ordered array, from which the ordinal position of any term can be read.

The model of Foos, et al. (1976) originally applied only to adults, but was recently extended to children (Maybery, Halford, Bain, & Kelly, submitted). It assumes that the problem is solved by constructing an ordered array in short-term memory (STM). The first premise is stored in STM, then an element is sought in the second premise that matches one of the elements in STM, and the new premise is integrated with the one that is stored. Then further premises are processed in the same way, and an ordered string grows in STM. Several operators for performing the integration process were proposed and empirically confirmed, and we consider these later.

Sternberg's model applies only to three-term series, whereas the Trabasso and Foos et al. models are not restricted in this respect. With the exception of the Maybery et al. (submitted) formulation, all of these models were applied to problems with premises only between adjacent elements, such as a > b, b > c. Problems with nonadjacent premises (e.g., a > c) were not considered, although they do have ecological validity, because real life ordering tasks normally entail nonadjacent relations. For example, if we are rank-ordering students according to grade, we may know that Martin is better than Wendy, but it does not follow that Martin and Wendy are adjacent. There may be other students in between. The TRIMM model will not be restricted to three-term problems, and will take account of adjacent and nonadjacent relations.

All of these models agree that premise elements are organized into an ordered set, so the raw premise information is not retained. This is also consistent with the fuzzy-set theory of Brainerd and Kingma (1984). Therefore, short-term memory for the raw premises is not likely to be a major factor in the solutions, but retention of the ordered set should be necessary. The core of the problem is construction of the ordered set. Once this is done, the inference is almost perceptual (Thayer & Collyer, 1978). Therefore, the TRIMM model focuses on construction of the ordered set.

All of these models propose a single strategy that has been treated as the whole explanation for the observed performances. There are two reasons for wanting to go beyond single strategy models. The first is that they beg the question of how strategies originate. Second, it is possible that people do not have a strategy for every conceivable task, or even every N-term series task, but have instead some general- or domain-knowledge that can be used to construct strategies that meet task demands. Third, the question of how children acquire strategies is vital to understanding cognitive development. This paper presents a model of strategy development. In this respect, it is allied to models of strategy and skill development in counting, addition, multiplication, and arithmetic word problems, which we will consider next.

Strategy Development Models

Strategy selection mechanisms can be divided into two kinds—metacognitive and associative. With metacognitive mechanisms, the participant makes strategy choices based on an understanding of the problem. With associative selection, the participant has a set of possible strategies, each of which is associated with a particular strength or confidence level that the task can be successfully performed.

Siegler and Shipley (this volume) argue that some metacognitive models overemphasize the role of knowledge and conscious reasoning in strategy choice. In their model, strategy selection depends on the relative strength of competing associations, and is not influenced by conceptual knowledge of the task. Thus, strategy selection is automatic.

Metacognitive selection mechanisms are based on understanding the task. The most explicit models of this kind were by Van Lehn and Brown (1980) applied to subtraction, Greeno, Riley, and Gelman (1984) to counting, and Greeno and Johnson (1984), to arithmetic word problems. In each of these models, declarative knowledge is used to construct strategies applicable to particular task contexts. The idea is that people do not have strategiesready-made for every situation, but devise strategies based on their knowledge of the relevant concept and the demands of the task.

The model of Van Lehn and Brown (1980) was based on *planning nets*, which are directed graphs, the nodes of which represent plans for strategies, and the links represent inferences concerning how well each proposed strategy conforms to declarative knowledge. Each proposed strategy is checked against the relevant declarative knowledge and adjusted if it does not fit. In this way, a strategy is devised that is consistent with the participant's knowledge of the task.

The concept of planning net is a sophisticated and powerful one. Van Lehn and Brown (1980) showed how a model of the planning process can provide more fundamental insights into the nature of a task or concept than models based on surface structure, or the actual procedures used. The reason is that procedures may vary considerably even though the essential concept remains the same. The procedural differences are often trivial or even irrelevant, with the result that models of specific processes may fail to capture the essence of a task. It may be preferable to adopt a model based on the underlying logic of the task. Planning net models enable this to be done.

The model of Greeno, Riley, and Gelman (1984) was based on the planning net approach, and was designed to model the influence of children's implicit knowledge of the logic of counting on the development of counting strategies. Gelman and Gallistel (1978) observed that young children could perform unconventional counts, in which the second object in a row was the "one," or even the "two," "three, " and so on. Because it is unlikely they would have learned such unconventional procedures by rote as a skill, their above-chance performance suggests they understood something about the logic of counting, and could devise a strategy to fit the constraints imposed. Greeno et al. (1984) produced a computational model of the development of counting strategies under the dual constraints of conceptual knowledge and task demands.

The way conceptual competence is formulated in the Greeno et al. (1984) model implies that these principles are understood in a form that is equivalent to logical rules of general validity. Set theoretic notation is used in the formal specification of the schemata and it is still true that understanding of logical, generally valid, principles is attributed to the children.

This model is capable of accounting for the development of counting knowledge, but if the planning nets approach is to be applied more widely to acquisition of cognitive skills, it is desirable that a way be found to use it with conceptual representations that are not innate, and are not based on universally valid logical rules. It should be possible for conceptual representations and mental models to be acquired through experience, and the present theory goes beyond existing planning net models in proposing a way for this to be achieved.

It remains to consider the relationship between associative and metacognitive mechanisms of strategy selection. Our proposal is that associative strategy selection is the mechanism of first resort, and it is only when it fails to produce a viable strategy that metacognitive mechanisms are employed. When a task is attempted in a particular context, the strategy that became dominant through successful use in that or similar contexts, is tried first. If the answers it produces have insufficiently high confidence ratings (or strength, to be defined later), it is abandoned and the next most dominant strategy tried, and so on. If no adequate strategy is found, then declarative knowledge is examined to see whether a modified strategy can be produced, using planning net-type mechanisms. Thus, metacognitive processes are only invoked where usual or habitual techniques fail. In familiar situations we do not think about what to do, we simply perform. The reason is that, although understanding confers immense power for development of new strategies to deal with changed conditions, it is cognitively effortful. Therefore it tends to be used only where habitual strategies are found to be inadequate.

The TRIMM model will therefore use associative strategy selection mechanisms as a first resort, and will employ metacognitive mechanisms where associative mechanisms fail. It is unique among contemporary models in blending the two types of mechanism in this way. Our next step is to consider the origin of the conceptual knowledge that forms the basis of metacognitive strategy development.

Origin of Conceptual Knowledge

Metacognitive strategy development is constrained by the conceptual knowledge of the task. In the planning net model of Greeno et al. (1984), counting strategies were constrained by a concept of number. Strategies for N-term series reasoning should be constrained by a concept of order, because the essence of the task is to assemble the premise elements into an ordered set. We therefore need to consider the nature and origin of the concept of order.

Features of a Concept of Order

Mathematically, an ordered set is defined, as noted earlier, as a set with an asymmetric binary relation. However, a more psychologically realistic definition of a concept of order would have the following features:

Understanding of one or more asymmetric binary relations (e.g., *larger than, better than*). Note that it is not implied that the child knows the relation to be asymmetric and binary. The child simply knows examples of such relations; that is, knows that Object a can be larger than Object b, entailing that b is not larger than a, and so on.

Each element occurs once and only once in an ordered string.

End elements have the same relation to all other elements; for example, a > b, a > c, a > d, and so on.

The position of an internal element is defined by relations to elements on both sides of it; for example, b < a, b > c.

The same relation must exist between all pairs, both adjacent and nonadjacent; e.g., a > b, b > c, .. a > c, and so on.

All of these features can be instantiated in any ordered set of at least three elements. Therefore, a child who has a mental representation of any ordered set of three or more elements has a concrete example of the concept of order. We show in a later section that a concrete example can be used to constrain performance by using it as an analogy and mapping it into the problem.

Children have no shortage of experience with ordered sets because they abound in the environment. Some child-appropriate experiences are order of children in a family, stackable blocks or other toys that vary in size, and positions in a race. The three bears also constitute an ordered set, consisting of Daddy, Mummy, and Baby Bear. It seems reasonable to assume then that children as young as 3 to 4 years would have plenty of concrete instances of ordered sets stored in memory. The TRIMM model aims to demonstrate that such knowledge can serve as a basis for a concept of order, and can be applied to strategy development through analogical mapping. The model does not assume that the child knows these are ordered sets. All that is necessary is that the child stores a representation of the elements together with the relations between them; for example, he or she represents at least three objects varying in (a relation such as) size, and knows that object a > object b, object b > object c, and so on.

Origins of Manipulative Knowledge

The environment also provides abundant experience in manipulating ordered sets. For example, it is easy to learn that if three objects (e.g., blocks) are in the order acb, switching the last two results in the order abc. That is, given acb as an initial state, the switching operator applied to b and c produces abc as a final state. We assume that manipulative experience with real objects results in a store of knowledge of the effect of operators on ordered sets in this way. These operators, together with their initial and final states, are the building blocks of strategies.

Application of Conceptual Knowledge

It is necessary to find a mechanism that would enable experience with ordered sets to be utilized in strategy development. Analogical mapping has the power and flexibility required for this task. According to Gentner (1983), an analogy is a structure-preserving map from a base or source to a target. For example, in the analogy *man is to house as dog is to kennel, man is to house* is the source and *dog is to kennel* is the target. *Man* is mapped into *dog* and *house* into *kennel*. The relation *lives in* between man and house is mapped into the corresponding relation between dog and kennel.

The essence of an analogy is that relations (multiplace predicates) in the source are mapped into the target. Attributes (single-place predicates) tend not to be mapped. For example, the attribute of man *wears clothes* is not mapped into dog. Analogies are influenced more by structural similarity between base and target than by element similarity.

Analogies can be formed between structurally similar, but otherwise quite different, situations. An important implication of this for the TRIMM model is that experiences with different kinds of ordered sets can be used as analogies for other ordering tasks. The ordered sets experienced in the past might have quite different elements to those in the task, but this will not necessarily prevent the experience from serving as a source for the task. Element similarity between source and target may facilitate discovery of an analogy, but dissimilarity does not constitute a logical impediment to mapping (Holyoak & Koh, 1987).

MODELS OF ANALOGY

There are a number of process models of human analogical reasoning (Bakker & Halford, 1988; Falkenhainer, Forbus, & Gentner, 1990; Halford et al., 1994; Holyoak & Thagard, 1989; Hummel, Burns, & Holyoak, in press). However, because the model of Halford et al. was specifically designed to incorporate realistic processing capacity limitations, it enables this factor to be incorporated in the TRIMM model.

The STAR Analogical Reasoning Model

The Structured Tensor Analogical Reasoning (STAR) model (Halford et al., 1994) uses a parallel distributed processing (PDP) architecture because the properties of graceful saturation and graceful degradation of these models (Rumelhart & McClelland, 1986) make them particularly suitable for modeling capacity limitations. However, because analogies entail mapping base predicates and their arguments into target predicates and their arguments, the representation of predicate–argument bindings as distributed representations is at the core of a PDP model of analogies. Following Smolensky's (1990) proposal that the variable-binding problem could be handled in terms of tensor products, Halford et al. (1994) showed that predicate–argument bindings could be represented as tensor products of vectors representing predicates and arguments. The essence of this approach is shown in Fig. 3.1, which also provides a numerical example of a rank 3 tensor product (i.e., with three input vectors).

Consider the simple analogy: *woman:baby::mare:foal.* This depends on the fact that a similar relation MOTHER-OF exists in the base (with arguments woman and baby) and in the target (with arguments mare and

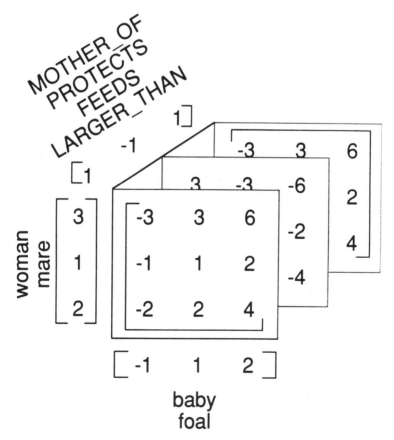

FIG. 3.1.   Tensor product representation of predicate–argument binding.

foal). The analogy requires the predicate MOTHER-OF, as well as other predicates that can take woman–baby or mare–foal as arguments to be represented. The other predicates include PROTECTS, FEEDS, and LARGER-THAN. Figure 3.1 shows how this information is represented in the STAR model. There is a predicate vector that represents all the predicates, superimposed. Then there are argument vectors representing the predicates woman and mare (superimposed) and baby and foal (superimposed). The tensor product of these vectors (represented by the activation values within the figure) represents the binding of the predicates to the arguments.

The solution process for a simple proportional analogy is shown in Fig. 3.2, using the *woman:baby::mare:foal* analogy as an illustration. The vectors for woman and baby are used as inputs to the net, and the vector for the predicate MOTHER-OF(-,-) appears as output on the appropriate "side" of the tensor product net. In the next phase of the reasoning process,

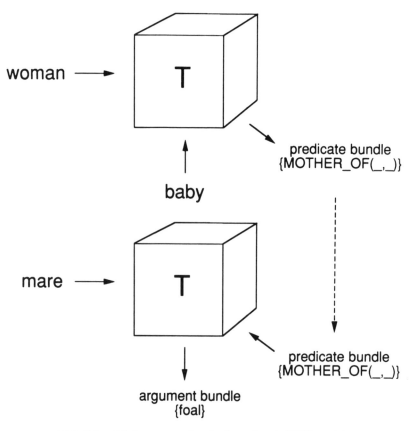

FIG. 3.2.   Solution process for simple analogy in STAR model.

mare is substituted for woman, and MOTHER-OF(-,-) becomes an input vector rather than an output. The argument 2 slot now produces the output vector, representing foal.

The analogical reasoning model is based on PDP architectures, whereas the TRIMM model is based on production rules. There is no PDP basis for production rules that is adequate for our purposes, even though progress was made in that direction (Dolan & Smolensky, 1988; Lebiere & Anderson, 1993; Touretzky & Hinton, 1988). There are additional problems in that the analogy model is simulated in a different language, and on a different computer, from the TRIMM model. Because of these constraints, the simulations must remain distinct until developments in the field, such as a fully adequate PDP model of production rules, permit their integration. Consequently the analogical reasoning process used in the TRIMM model is based on production rules, and amounts to a "black box" implementation of the relevant features of the analogical reasoning model.

However, the representations used in the STAR model do provide insights into the reason why more complex relations impose processing loads. More complex relations are those with more arguments and require tensor products of higher rank; that is, they require tensor products with more vectors. We consider this question in the next section.

COMPLEXITY OF RELATIONS

Some theorists have proposed that cognitive development in general, and acquisition of transitive inference in particular, are influenced by changes in processing capacity over age (Case, 1985, 1991; Chapman, 1987, 1990; Halford, 1993a). The TRIMM model, like the STAR model discussed in the last section, is based on the definition of capacity in terms of the complexity of relations that can be processed (Halford, 1993a; Halford & Wilson, 1993; Halford et al., 1994). This approach has also been used to define interspecies differences (Holyoak & Thagard, 1994) and the nature of certain deficits in the frontal lobes (Robin & Holyoak, in press).

Relational complexity is defined in terms of the number of elements that are related; that is, the number of arguments the relation has. A unary relation has one argument, and corresponds to an attribute—for example, LARGE(dog). A binary relation relates two elements, and has two arguments—for example, LARGER-THAN(dog,mouse). A ternary relation has three arguments, and relates three elements. An everyday example would be *love-triangle,* in which two persons love a third person. Ternary relations are particularly important for transitive inference models, because the ordered triple formed by integrating premises, as discussed earlier, is a ternary relation; that is, R(a,b) and R(b,c) are integrated into the ternary relation: R(a,b,c). Quaternary relations relate four elements and have four arguments.

Each argument of a relation can be instantiated in more than one way. For example, LARGER-THAN(-,-) has two argument slots, each of which can be filled with a number of elements, such as (dog,mouse), (whale,fish), (sun,planet). Therefore, each argument corresponds to a source of variation or dimension, and the number of arguments corresponds to the dimensionality of the concept. Mathematically, the number of arguments corresponds to the number of dimensions of the cartesian product space on which the relation is defined. There is evidence that the number of dimensions processed in parallel is related to processing load. Using secondary task indicators, Maybery, Bain and Halford (1986) and Halford, Maybery and Bain (1986) showed that premise integration, which entails representing a ternary relation, imposes a higher processing load than processing individual premises, which entails representing a binary relation.

To see why there is a processing load in premise integration, consider the transitive inference *Tom is happier than Bill, Bill is happier than John.* Who is happiest? We want to assign Tom, Bill, and John to the correct ordinal positions. From Premise 1, we can only assign Tom to either top or middle position. To decide the correct assignment, we must also take account of the other premise. The same is true for assigning the other premise elements to ordinal positions. Each assignment requires both premises to be considered, meaning that more information is being processed than when individually processing premises.

Representation of relations as tensor products, as in the STAR model in the last section, provides a possible explanation for the association between processing load and dimensionality. This is that the rank of the tensor product increases with dimensionality. Thus, unary relations are represented by a tensor product of Rank 2, binary relations by Rank 3 tensor products, ternary relations by Rank 4, and quaternary relations by Rank 5. The number of units required for the representation increases exponentially with rank; processing load increases with the dimensionality of the representation (Halford, 1993a; Halford & Wilson, submitted; Halford et al., 1994). We illustrate this point by contrasting the representation of the binary relation in Fig. 3.1 with the ternary relation in Fig. 3.3a–c.

A PDP representation of transitivity, based on the STAR model, is shown in Figure 3.3a. Because transitivity is a ternary relation, the representation is a rank 4 tensor product. This represents the entire structure, but component relations, aRb, bRc, aRc can be recovered by collapsing over the remaining vector (Humphreys, Bain, & Pike, 1989). The mapping of premises into an ordering schema, as in Fig. 3.4a, is shown for the STAR architecture in Figure 3.3c. The ordering schema, top–middle–bottom, is shown as the tensor product of four vectors, representing the predicate *monotonically higher*, and the arguments, top, middle,

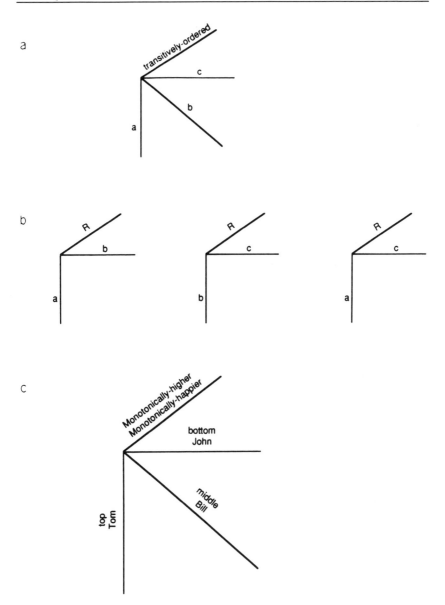

FIG. 3.3.   Tensor product representation of transitive inference.

bottom. The problem is represented as the predicate *monotonically happier,* with arguments Tom, Bill, John. The two structures are superimposed on the tensor product representation. Comparison of the PDP representation of transitivity in Figure 3.3a–c with the representation of the binary relation *larger-than* in Fig. 3.1 shows that the former is represented by a

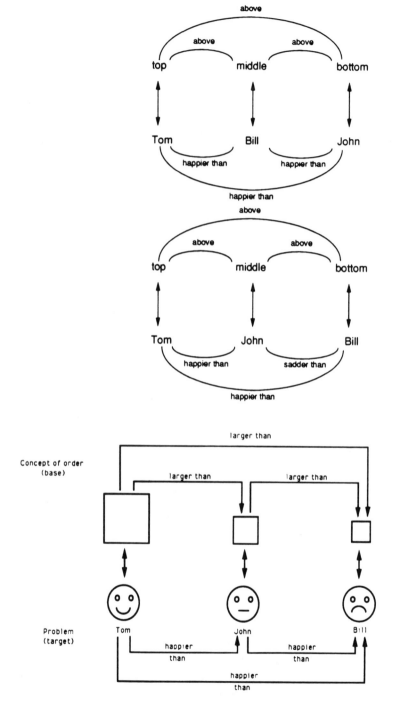

FIG. 3.4. Consistent (a) and inconsistent (b) mapping of transitive inference problem into top-down schema, or (c) into concrete representation.

tensor product of higher rank. The increased processing load associated with the ternary relation is attributable to the number of binding units in the tensor product. For example, if the predicate and argument(s) are each represented by vectors with 3 units, then the number of binding units is 27 for the binary relation (as shown in Fig. 3.1), but is 81 for the ternary relation involved in transitivity. The number of binding units determines the amount of activation, which in turn determines processing load.

We proposed (Halford, 1993a; Halford & Wilson, submitted; Halford et al., 1994) that dimensions are like chunks, in that both are independent units of information of arbitrary size. From a review of the literature, we suggested that human adults are limited to processing approximately four dimensions in parallel. Concepts with more than four dimensions are either processed serially, or a process called *conceptual chunking* is used to pack high dimensional representations into one dimension, albeit with loss of ability to represent some of the structure (Halford, 1993a; Halford & Wilson, submitted; Halford et al., 1994).

From a review of the literature (Halford, 1993a) we proposed that the number of dimensions that are typically processed in parallel increases with age, being 1 at age 1 year, 2 at age 2 years, 3 at age 5 years, and 4 at age 11 years. Because premise integration normally requires representation of ternary relations, it is likely to be difficult for children under 5 years of age. This factor will mean an interaction between age and relational complexity. Given appropriate experience, children under 5 will have no difficulty dealing with binary relations, but will have considerable difficulty with ternary relations. This difference will be considerably reduced in children over 5 years.

Relational Complexity and Levels of Structure Mapping

Because structure mapping in analogies depends on representation of relations, each level of relational complexity corresponds to a level of structure mapping. Four levels of structure mapping were defined by Halford (1987) based on earlier work by Halford and Wilson (1980). Element, Relational, System, and Multiple-system mappings depend on unary, binary, ternary, and quaternary relations, respectively. We consider each level of mapping in turn.

Element mappings are based on 1-dimensional structures, and are defined as:

$$\text{M: } R(e_i) \leftrightarrow R(e'_i)$$

It is a mapping between two structures, each of which is based on a unary relation. The elements, e, of one structure are mapped into the elements of the other structure, so that the unary relations, R, correspond. Because unary relations are predicates with one argument, they correspond to attributes in Gentner's (1983) terms, so mappings based on one-place predicates are validated by attribute similarity.

Relational mappings are based on 2-dimensional structures, and are defined as:

$$M: R(e_i, e_j) \leftrightarrow R(e'_i, e'_j)$$

The elements in Structure 1 are mapped into the elements in Structure 2 so that the binary relations in both structures correspond. At this level, there need not be any similarity between elements in the structures, and mappings are validated by similarity of binary relations. Simple proportional analogies of the form A:B::C:D belong to this level. For example, the analogy *woman:baby::mare:foal* is validated by the similar relation, *mother of* in source and target.

System mappings are based on three-dimensional structures, and can be defined as:

$$M: R(e_i, e_j, e_k) \leftrightarrow R(e'_i, e'_j, e'_k)$$

Elements are mapped so that ternary relations correspond. At this level, there need not be any resemblance even between the binary relations in the structures. The structure of source and target is defined as a ternary relation, but may also be expressed as a binary operation, $*(e_i, e_j \rightarrow e_k)$, or as a composition of two or more binary relations, $(e_i \; R \; e_j)$, $(e_j \; R \; e_l)$, $(e_i \; R \; e_l)$. System mappings permit a high degree of flexibility and abstraction, because they can be used to establish correspondences between structures that have only formal similarities. They also permit analogies to be recognized between superficially dissimilar situations (Halford & Leitch, 1989). However, this flexibility and generality is obtained at the cost of higher information processing loads.

Multiple system mappings are based on 4-dimensional structures, and are defined as:

$$M: R(e_i, e_j, e_k, e_l) \leftrightarrow R(e'_i, e'_j, e'_k, e'_l)$$

Elements are mapped so that quaternary relations correspond. The quaternary relations may be interpreted as compositions of ternary relations, binary operations, or bivariate functions. Like system mappings, multiple system mappings are validated by structural correspondence, and are independent of element or relational similarity. They differ only in the complexity of the structures represented.

In theory, mappings based on predicates with more than four arguments are possible, but it is difficult to attach any psychological meaning to such structures, because processing capacity limitations prevent structures of higher dimensionality being mapped.

Representation of Transitivity

As noted earlier, a number of contemporary models agree that transitive inferences are made by integrating the premise elements into an ordered string. We suggest that this is a case of analogical reasoning, because it entails using a familiar schema, such as top-down (or left-right) ordering as a basis for organizing the premise elements. The premise elements and relations are mapped into a representation of the top-down schema. This is shown in Fig. 3.4a for the problem *Bill is happier than John, Tom is happier than Bill.* The problem elements are assigned to, or mapped into the three positions — top, middle, bottom — and there is a structural correspondence between the spatial arrangement and the problem. The top position corresponds to Tom, middle to Bill, and bottom to John.

This is a system mapping, because both structures are based on ternary relations. The mapping is independent of element and relational similarity and convention. It is validated solely by structural correspondence.

An example of the type of mapping that children might use is shown in Fig. 3.4c. The base is an ordered set retrieved from memory, consisting of three blocks ordered for size. The hypothetical problem comprises the premises *Tom is happier than John, John is happier than Bill,* and the conclusion *Tom is happier than Bill.* The analogy is formed by mapping Tom, John, and Bill into the large, medium, and small blocks, respectively. The relation *happier than* consistently corresponds to the relation *larger than.*

The validity of the mapping does not depend on any resemblance between Tom, John or Bill and the blocks into which they are mapped, or on resemblance between *larger than* and *happier than,* other than the properties of transitivity and asymmetry. The mapping is validated by consistent structural correspondence. That is, each element in the problem is mapped into one and only one element in the base and vice versa (uniqueness), the relations in the source are mapped consistently into relations in the target (*larger than* is always mapped into *happier than*), and the arguments of the relations in the source are mapped into the arguments of the relations in the target (in each case, the arguments of *larger than* are mapped into the arguments of *happier than*).

With system mappings, validity depends on consistency over two or more relations, requiring that elements be mapped in sets of at least three. This is illustrated by Fig. 3.4b. Notice that if we consider only two elements in each structure (deleting the element at one end), there is no apparent inconsistency in the mapping. For example *middle above bottom* mapped into *John sadder than Bill,* meets the criteria for a valid mapping. Recognition of the inconsistency requires that all three elements be considered together with the relations between them.

The importance of structure mapping of premises into an ordering schema is that an ordered set stored in long term memory can be used as a mental model, purely on the basis of the structural correspondence to the task. In principle, any ordered set of three or more elements stored in long-term memory, can be used for this purpose. However, there are psychological advantages to sets that do resemble the target, or to sets that are prototypical in the sense that they represent the common properties of many ordered sets, because it is then easier to see the possibility of the mapping being made. However, once the mapping has been recognized as possible, similarity does not facilitate the actual mapping process, which can be based purely on structural correspondence, as in Fig. 3.4c (Holyoak & Koh, 1987).

Once the mapping is made, it is fused into a single representation, the ordered set Tom, John, Bill. The analog provides the structure of the representation, and effectively provides a criterion for the correct way to organize the information in the problem. The fact that Tom, John, Bill is self-evidently the right order to us conceals the fact that at some time children had to come to this understanding. If they do not innately possess logical rules, a likely explanation is that they can use previous experience as an analog.

Recognition of Indeterminacy

Mapping into a mental model consisting of an ordered set of (at least) three objects can also lead to recognition that a problem is indeterminate. Suppose, for example, that the premise *Bill happier than John* were missing from Fig. 3.4a or 3.4c. It is clear that two different mappings are possible: Bill could be mapped into either middle or bottom, implying the orders Tom, Bill, John or Tom, John, Bill. A mental model in the form of an ordered set can provide a criterion for deciding when another set is ordered. The target set is ordered when it can be mapped in one, and only one, way into the base ordered set.

Children's Transitive Inference Abilities

The question of when children can make transitive inferences is a major issue in cognitive developmental theory, and there are already several reviews of the literature (Breslow, 1981; Halford, 1982, 1989; Thayer & Collyer, 1978; Trabasso, 1975, 1977). Piaget's (1950) contention that transitive inferences were not understood by young children was challenged by Bryant and Trabasso (1971), who obtained evidence that 3- to 4-year-olds made above-chance transitive inferences. However, reassessments of this research by Halford (1989) and Bryant (1989) led to the conclusion that there is no valid evidence of transitive inferences before age 5. The problem with studies conducted in the Bryant–Trabasso paradigm was that procedures were used that unduly aided children in constructing an ordered set, and that children who were unable to do so were deleted (Halford, 1989). When these factors were eliminated, preschool children failed the task (Halford & Kelly, 1984; Kallio, 1982).

Two reasons were advanced as to why young children find transitive inferences difficult. One is that young children encode premises in absolute terms, whereas older children encode them in relative terms. For example, given the premise *Tom is happier than Bill,* young children would encode Tom as happy and Bill as sad. When the premise *Bill is happier than John* is processed, Bill is encoded as happy, contradicting the earlier encoding. This hypothesis was proposed by Perner and Mansbridge (1983), Siegler (1989), and Sternberg and Rifkin (1979).

The other hypothesis is that preschool children have difficulty integrating premises. For example, Halford (1984; Andrews & Halford, submitted) presented ordering tasks that could be performed by considering either one or two premises in a single decision, and found 100% success by 3- to 4-year-olds on the former task, but chance performance on the latter. Furthermore, Halford et al. (1986) provided evidence that the failure was due to inability of young children to process the loads imposed by premise integration. Halford and Kelly (1984) required children to learn either overlapping pairs (a > b, b > c, c > d) or nonoverlapping pairs (a > b, c > d, e > f). The former would be easier if integrated, because they would be learned as the string a, b, c, d. If not integrated, however, the overlapping condition would lead to conflict because of elements b and c being smaller in one premise but larger in another. Preschool children learned the nonoverlapping pairs but not the overlapping pairs, suggesting that they were unable to integrate the premises.

Recent evidence suggests that 4-year-olds can integrate premises in certain transitive inference tasks. Pears and Bryant (1990) presented premises in the form of colored blocks placed one above the other; for example, block A above B, B above C, and so on. Childen were required to build a tower with another set of blocks of the same color as the premise blocks, with a top–down order, A, B, C, D, E, consistent with the premises. Before building the tower, they were asked inferential questions, such as whether Block B would be above or below Block D. Four-year-olds performed significantly above chance in two experiments, suggesting that they can perform transitive inferences.

Pears and Bryant acknowledged that the task might be performed by manipulating images of the premises. For example, it is possible to imagine pair B–C sitting on top of pair C–D, and it would then be apparent that in a tower B would be above D. This is a legitimate way to make a transitive inference in these circumstances.

The study shows that 4-year-old children can integrate premises in certain conditions, but the Pears and Bryant task did not entail mapping from one representation to another. It, therefore, did not entail analogical reasoning. In this respect, it is instructive to compare Pears and Bryant's procedure with that of Halford (1984). Both used color-coded premises, both obviated the need for retention of premises in memory, and both used tasks that were appropriate for young children. However Halford's task had premises coded in the form of colored pegs in a board. Children were asked to arrange tubes whose colors matched those of the pegs in an order consistent with the pairs of pegs on the board.

Pears and Bryant suggested that the difficulties children experienced in Halford's study may have been because it was hard for them to translate spatial position into length. Actually, however, this cannot be true in its entirety, because Halford's data showed that even 3-year-olds could order the tubes without error, consistent with the pegboard, provided the ordering task was constructed so they could process the premises serially. Therefore, they were able to translate the pegboard information into the task of ordering the tubes. What they could not do is make this translation by processing two premises jointly. When they had to order tubes using information from two premises in a single decision, 3- to 4-year-olds failed. Therefore the comparison of Halford's study with that of Pears and Bryant shows that 3- to 4-year-olds had trouble mapping from one representation to another when this mapping depended on two premises that expressed two relations. The traditional seriation task entails mapping across dimensions: for example, mapping lengths into spatial positions.

This hypothesis was recently tested in our laboratory (Andrews & Halford, submitted). We used the tower of five blocks employed by Pears and Bryant (1990) and an isomorphic sticks task that required children to order sticks from left to right, with left defined as closer to a stuffed toy frog. We also employed two mapping tasks, in which children had to use pairs of blocks to determine the order of sticks, or vice versa. The number of binary premise relations required for the mapping was also manipulated.

Pears and Bryant's finding of above-chance transitive inference in 3- to 4-year-olds was replicated for the blocks task, but the performance was only marginally better than chance. The 3- to 4-year-olds failed on the inference task based on mapping of two relations, even though they succeeded on all tasks that required only one relation to be processed. Despite the great ingenuity shown by Pears and Bryant in devising a transitive inference task that is eminently suitable for young children, we found that tasks that require ternary relations to be processed, where premise integration is required, pose major difficulties for young children. It is clear that relational complexity is a significant factor in performance, particularly with children under 5 years.

Both encoding and integrating are processes that improve with age, but it is unlikely that young children are completely unable to encode relations. Both Bullock and Gelman (1977) and DeLoache (1989) provided evidence that 2- to 3-year-old children encode relations between objects. For example, DeLoache showed that young children could locate a hidden toy in a room after seeing a model toy hidden in a model of the room. Presumably this task entails encoding the relation between the model toy and a model piece of furniture (e.g. behind the lounge), then mapping this relation into the real room. It is a good example of a relational mapping task (Halford, 1993a). There is evidence, however, that children under age 5 have difficulty integrating relations. Progress in transitive inference and ordering between approximately 2 and 7 years depends to a considerable extent on switching from processing relations independently to processing them in an integrated way. This will, therefore, be one of the major developments that the model will attempt to simulate. Integrated representation of the premises is expected to result in a shift toward relational encoding. Therefore, the question of whether development of transitive inference depends on relational encoding or on premise integration may turn out to be a nonissue.

Working Memory Architecture

Baddeley (1986, 1990) and Schneider and Detweiler (1987) provided sophisticated reviews of the working memory literature. Working memory consists of more than one system, and the aggregate capacity is much greater than the small number of items in short term memory span. Our model does not make strong assumptions about working memory limitations, but it provides for this factor to be manipulated.

THE MODEL

Outline of the TRIMM Model

The model has the following major objectives:

1. To simulate development of N-term series strategies, under the constraint of a concept of order that could be acquired through experience.

2. To integrate associative and metacognitive strategy selection mechanisms.

3. To simulate a major acquisition in middle childhood: the ability to integrate premises.

Main Features of the Model

1. Transitive inferences are made by constructing an ordered set of premise elements, as in the models of Sternberg (1980b) and Foos et al. (1976). The ordered set, called a *working memory resultset* is stored in short-term memory.

2. There are no strategies as such, the role of strategies being filled by productions. Each production corresponds approximately to a single problem solving step. Thus, development proceeds by acquiring steps independently, rather than by acquiring intact strategies.

3. If productions exist that match the current state, they are invoked without metacognitive processing. If no productions match the current state of the problem, new productions are created by metacognitive processes, constrained by the concept of order.

4. It is assumed that operators are learned by manipulative experience, and are stored in long-term memory, together with initial and final states, so they can be used in means–end analysis. An example would be the switch operator (Table 3.1), that reverses the order of two elements. It is assumed that children have learned during manipulative play that if two objects are in the order AB, and then are switched around, that the order will be BA. Thus the initial state is AB and the final state is BA.

5. It is assumed that a concept of order is acquired through experience (such as play with blocks that form series), and can be instantiated as an ordered set of at least three elements, stored in long-term memory. The essential features of the concept of order were previously outlined.

6. Analogical mapping of the ordered set in long-term memory into the strategy output is used to assess validity of strategies. This constrains the strategies to produce an output consistent with the concept of order. This mapping produces a high processing load that causes difficulty for children and adults, but the magnitude of the difficulty is greater at younger ages.

7. Strength of productions is increased if they produce correct orders, and decreased if they produce incorrect orders (associative strategy development). Strength of productions is defined in the next section, and it affects the likelihood that a production will be used.

8. Negative feedback leads to increased effort, resulting in higher level structure mapping processes being invoked.

9. If relational level structure mapping is invoked, strategies are produced that do not integrate premises. If system-level structure mapping is invoked, strategies are produced that do integrate premises.

TABLE 3.1
Operators Used in the Model

Name (Args)	Preconditions	Effect
delete (ob; list)	ob is a member of the list.	Remove one occurence of ob from list.
Join(list1; list2)	neither list is empty.	Combine ob1 and ob2 into a single list.
get_front(ob; list)	ob is an element of the list.	Return the part of list preceding ob.
get_rest(ob; list)	ob is an element of the list.	Return the part of the list following ob.
append(ob1; ob2; list)	ob1 in list; ob2 not in list.	Make ob2 the immediate successor of ob1.
insert(ob1; ob2; list)	ob1 not in list; ob2 in list.	Make ob1 the immediate predecessor of ob2 in the list.
delete_append(ob1; ob2; list)	ob1 and ob2 both in list.	Make ob1 the immediate successor of ob2.
delete_insert(ob1; ob2; list)	ob1 and ob2 both in list.	Make ob1 the immediate predecessor of ob2.
switch(ob1; ob2; list)	ob1 and ob2 both indeterminate.	Exchange position of ob1 and ob2 and place markers around the indeterminate parts of a list.
mark_indet(ob1; ob2; list)	no markers currently in list.	
remove_indet_markers(list)	—	Remove indeterminacy markers from a list.
append_indet(ob1; ob2; list)	ob2 not in list; ob1 in list.	Make ob2 the immediate successor ob1 and mark ob2 as indeterminate with respect to the tail of the list.
insert_indet(ob1; ob2; list)	ob1 not in list; ob2 in list.	Make ob1 the immediate predecessor of ob2 and mark ob1 as indeterminate with respect to the preceding portion of the list.
concat_indet(ob1; ob2; list)	neither object already in list	Create new list segment (ob1 ob2) marking it as indeterminate with respect to existing list.

10. Strategies that do not integrate premises produce correct solutions on some problems, but produce errors on other problems. This leads to negative feedback that increases effort, leading to system mapping being invoked, and strategies are then developed that do integrate premises.

Architecture

The model was programmed in the production system language PRISM II (Ohlsson & Langley, 1986). The whole model described in this chapter is based on productions. The program does not have access to the PDP-based STAR model of analogical reasoning described earlier. Instead, structure mapping is carried out by productions that perform the same functions as relational and system mappings specified for the STAR model.

A production system is composed of a set of condition–action pairs, each of which specifies that if a certain state occurs in working memory, then a mental or physical action should be performed. For example, the traffic rule *stop on a red light* could be coded as a production of the form:

if a traffic light is red → stop

The left-hand side of the production refers to a condition; in this case, a red traffic light. The right-hand side refers to an action; in this case, stopping. When production systems are used to model problem solving, the actions are usually mental; for example, entering information in, or retrieving it from, working memory, manipulating information in working memory, setting goals, and so on.

PRISM II is based on the ACT* model of cognition (Anderson, 1983), and the model we present has a number of features in common with Anderson's approach. Some of these are structural, such as the use of productions and hierarchical goal structures (Fig. 3.5). However, more significant similarities occur in the way strategies or cognitive skills are acquired. The current model, like that of Anderson (1987), proposes that strategies are first acquired through domain-independent, general processes such as analogical reasoning and means–end analysis (the so-called "weak" methods). Once acquired, strategies are strengthened or weakened according to their success in solving problems. PRISM II has many parameters and structures that can be altered by the programmer, so it does not constrain the model builder to adopt the assumptions of the ACT* theory. Furthermore, no attempt is made to either conform to or depart from Anderson's theory, and the model is constrained solely by data on N-term series problems and related cognitive phenomena.

The productions that have been programmed into the model are basically domain-general, in the sense that they are not specifically related to N-term

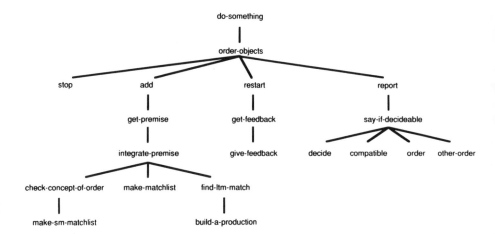

FIG. 3.5.   Goal hierarchy.

series problems. One set performs such functions as setting and removing goals, requesting feedback, starting new problems, and building new productions. Another set searches for, compares, and codes elements into features. Domain-specific productions that are specialized for performing N-term series problems are built by the model in the course of solving problems.

A working memory stores the current state of the problem, including goals. This information is subject to decay over time. When items are added to working memory, they are given an initial activation value of 1.0 — activation decays on subsequent cycles, delta $x = -0.1x$. However, goals are not subject to decay, because it is assumed that goals have highest priority and will always be maintained.

Domain-general productions are stored in a procedural memory, and their strength does not vary. It is assumed that their use has been so general that their strength will be negligibly affected by processing these problems. Domain-specific productions that are built in the course of problem solving are stored in new procedural memory, and have a strength that varies in two ways. First, strength is increased following successful performance of a problem according to the formula:

delta $S+ = .1(1-S)$,

and decreased following unsuccessful performance, according to the formula:

delta $S- = .25S$.

Second, there are small random fluctuations according to the formulas:

delta $S+ = v(1-S)$
delta $S- = vS$

where v fluctuates randomly between 0 and .2.

This causes strength values to asymptote at either 0 or 1. The random fluctuations cause strength values to tend toward a common value of .5. The net effect of these formulae is that reductions in strength following unsuccessful performance are more pronounced than increases in strength following successful performance, but the random fluctuations allow for serendipidity and the recovery of useful productions whose strength has been driven down through being combined with others in incorrect solutions.

The threshold strength level for a production to be fired can be temporarily lowered to enable a weakened production to fire, thereby obviating the need to rebuild the same production, or to abandon a problem because no production can be found that matches the conditions in working memory. This rule can be applied to productions that have the same conditions and actions as the production that is required for the current step. Where this happens, a successful production can be strengthened and can re-enter the list of active productions. An unsuccessful production will be further weakened to the point where it cannot fire again. This rule provides a damping effect on the removal of productions, to ensure they are not removed with excessive haste.

A declarative memory stores the goal hierarchy, shown in Fig. 3.5, and the information about conditions and consequences of operators (listed in Table 3.1). As noted earlier, it is assumed these operators were learned through manipulative experience, such as play. For example, the append operator has preconditions that Object 2 is not in the list, and Object 1 is in the list. The operator has the effect that Object 2 is appended to Object 1 in the list. This is assumed to be a primitive function that would have been learned manipulatively.

The effect of different memories is to categorize contents so that, for example, declarative memories contain different kinds of information from procedural memories. This is a matter of programming efficiency, and does not imply that these types of information occupy physically different memories in a human being. The categorization function in human memory is more likely to be achieved by linking stored information to context (Humphreys, Bain, & Pike, 1989; Schneider & Detweiler, 1987), than by assignment to distinct memories.

Operation of the Model

Overview. We illustrate the model using a sample problem as shown in Fig. 3.6. The first premise is a $>$ b. The model checks whether or not there is an ordered string already in working memory, finds there is not, and adds

Constructed Order	Premise	Action
- - -	a > b	insert in WM
a b	b > c	append
a b c		

FIG. 3.6.   Sequence of steps in simple transitive inference problem.

the string ab to working memory. This can be done because the model is set up with domain-general productions for storing information in working memory. When the premise b > c is presented, there is no production that has a string in working memory plus a premise in its condition side, because the model is not initially equipped with productions for dealing with transitive inference.

This puts the model into a modification phase. First, it searches for a concept appropriate to its present goal, ORDER OBJECTS. This causes the concept of order to be retrieved from memory. Analogical reasoning is used to determine the correct order, by mapping the premises a > b and b > c into an ordered set retrieved from memory, as explained previously. It is recognized that the ordering abc would be consistent with the concept of order. Means–end analysis is then used to select an operator that will produce the order abc. Then a new production is built that includes the APPEND operator, as shown in Fig. 3.7.

This production will match any state in which working memory contains one or more objects in a string, and the first object in the premise matches the last object in the string. On the action side, the APPEND operator will place the second object in the premise on the end of the string.

When a subsequent problem occurs that requires this production, it will fire, without the effortful process of having to build it. Thus strategies, which in this model consist of productions, can operate in relatively

Production built:

(((constructed order   (<relation> <obj 1 . . . . . . obj n>))

(new premise   <obj 1>   <relation>   <obj 2>)

(match   obj 1   obj n))

—————————▶

(add-to WM (perform APPEND <obj n>   <obj 2>)))

Instantiation:

working-memory contents	premise	new working-memory contents
ab	b>c	abc

FIG. 3.7.   Production built in performing problem a > b, b > c.

automatic fashion once they are acquired. Understanding is not required for problems of a type that the model has already learned to solve.

When a correct solution is obtained, positive feedback increases the strength of the productions involved in the solution. Negative feedback results in weakened productions. Productions that lead to errors are gradually weakened below threshold, and cease to fire. This clears the way for construction of new productions that avoid the errors.

When the model first builds productions, some lead to errors. Some of these errors occur because of the processing load imposed by system mappings; that is, mapping both premises into an analog, as in Fig. 3.4. This can result in a tendency to focus on the most recent premise, ignoring the implications of earlier premises. We call this the *relational strategy*, because it uses only relational mappings, as defined earlier, and processes only one relation at a time. The operation of relational and system strategies are illustrated in Fig. 3.8.

	constructed order	premise	action
Relational Strategy	- - -	c > d	insert in WM
	c d	a > b	concatenate
	c d a b	b >c	delete - insert
	b c d a		
System Strategy	- - -	c d	insert in WM
	c d	a > b	concat indet
	ˆ(cd)^(ab)	b > c	switch
	a b c d		

* indeterminacy marker

FIG. 3.8.   Steps in relational and system strategies.

105

The first premise, c > d results in the string cd being stored in working memory. The next premise, a > b contains no element that matches any element in cd. If the model is operating at a low level of cognitive effort, either because of low arousal, competition for resources, or inadequate processing capacity, then it pays attention only to the most recent premise, and performs a relational mapping. That is, it maps a > b into the analog of an ordered set, ignoring c > d. Therefore, the production that is built simply inserts ab after cd, yielding the order cdab, without recognizing that the order of the pairs is indeterminate. When b > c is presented, attention is again paid to only the most recent premise, resulting in a production that simply switches b to the front of the list, yielding the order bcda. Data from Foos et al.'s (1976) study, and from our own laboratory, show this is a common error for children, and for adults under high processing load.

This error leads to negative feedback, which weakens the productions involved in the incorrect solution, clearing the way for new productions to be built. The negative feedback also increases effort, that causes the most recent premise to be integrated with previous premises when a new production is being built. This leads to a production based on system mapping as defined earlier.

When a > b is presented, the model attempts to map c > d and a > b into the concept of order, and it is recognized that more than one ordering is possible, as explained earlier. Therefore, a marker is inserted to indicate that the order of the pairs is indeterminate. Then when b > c is presented, a production is built that switches ab to the front of the string, yielding abcd. Correct feedback strengthens this production.

The model makes these errors when it first builds strategies, but then builds new productions that provide correct solutions to problems with all permutations of premises. It also recognizes when a problem is unsolvable, because it codes indeterminacies in the ordered set in working memory.

Productions. The productions that are built into the system before it begins operation are listed in Appendix A. The productions that are built in the course of the run to be described in this section are listed in Appendix B.

Two parameters are defined: effort level and strength of productions. *Effort* is used in Kahneman's (1973) sense, and affects the type of structure mapping that is performed. Because system mapping employs two relations and imposes a higher processing load, it will only be performed if the effort level is sufficiently high. We assume people employ the minimum effort required, so effort level is initially set at a low value. This means relational mappings will be employed first, leading to correct performance only where premise integration is not required. However when integration is required errors will occur, and the resulting negative feedback eventually causes effort to be raised to a level that produces system mapping. On this run, the threshold level was set at 1.30.

Strength affects the likelihood of a production firing. As is standard in production systems, a precondition for a production to fire is that its conditions match elements in working memory. If more than one production matches, the one with the greatest strength fires.

The strength of productions involved in producing a solution is increased when it is correct, and decreased when it is incorrect. The names of productions that have contributed to a solution by altering the working memory result set are placed in a list. Following feedback, the strengths of all productions in the list are adjusted according to the formula given in the previous section. Productions that are below threshold (initially .50 on this run) will not fire. There is also a random component in the strength parameter, that varies according to the formula given in the previous section. This has the effect of causing differences in strength to be gradually reduced, thereby permitting recently weakened productions to eventually reappear.

Run of the model.   The model was run on the set of problems shown in Table 3.2. The first six problems entail adjacent and nonadjacent relations, and consist of all permutations of the premises a > b, b > c, a > c. Problems 7 through 12 do not entail nonadjacent premises, but contain a fourth term, and comprise all permutations of the premises a > b, b > c, c > d. The value of the fourth term is that it requires the system to iterate the ordering processes. For example, having integrated b > c with a > b, producing abc, it then must integrate c > d with abc to produce abcd. A

TABLE 3.2
Hypothesized Processes for 3-Term and 4-Term Problems

		Problem Form	Solution With Integration	Most Common Solution Without Integration
Three-term adjacent-and-non-adjacent	1.	AB, BC, AC	ABC	ACB
	2.	BC, AB, AC	ABC	ACB
	3.	AB, AC, BC	ABC	ABC
	4.	BC, AC, AB	ABC	ABC
	5.	AC, AB, BC	ABC	ACB
	6.	AC, BC, AB	ABC	ACB
Four-term adjacent only	7.	AB, BC, CD	ABCD	ABCD
	8.	AB, CD, BC	ABCD	ABCD
	9.	BC, AB, CD	ABCD	ABCD
	10.	BC, CD, AB	ABCD	ABCD
	11.	CD, AB, BC	ABCD	BCDA
	12.	CD, BC, AB	ABCD	ABCD

model that can do this can produce series of any length, provided they are based on adjacent relations only and subject to a memory capacity that is adequate for storing the resulting string. The problem is different with nonadjacent relations, because series of more than three terms cannot be constructed simply by iterating processes used in three-term problems. Pilot work showed that series of more than three terms with nonadjacent relations cannot normally be handled by human participants without external aids. The fact that the model can handle series of any length with adjacent relations, and can process adjacent and nonadjacent relations, gives it a high degree of generality. The generality is increased by the fact that elements and relations in production rules are defined as variables. This means that any type of element or relation can be handled. However, for the sake of clarity, specific instantiations are discussed in the run to be described.

When the operation of the model begins, the goal *order objects* is set. This is equivalent to participants attempting to perform a N-term series task. The next production requests instructions: *stop, restart new problem* or *add a premise*. The instruction can be supplied interactively by the user, or read in from a file. If the instruction is *stop*, the flag *halt* is set so no new productions will be fired, and the goal *order-objects* is deleted. If the instruction is *restart new problem*, the initial goal is reset, and further instructions are requested. If the instruction is *add a premise*, then a goal is set to integrate that premise into the working memory result set.

If the working memory result set is empty, then the elements of the new premise are simply placed in working memory in the correct order. For example, if the first premise were $a > b$, then ab would be placed in working memory. Then the next premise is requested.

If there is already a premise in working memory, then one or more *match* productions are fired. These productions seek elements that are common to the working memory result set and the premise. For example, if ab were in the working memory result set, and the premise were $b > c$, then the match element would be b. The *matchlist* is then placed in working memory.

This is as much as can be done using productions that are prewired into the system. That is, the system has productions for obtaining and comprehending premises, storing and retrieving information in working memory, and comparing new premises with the working memory result set. It can identify elements common to the new premise and the working memory result set, and mark the position of the common elements. For example, with ab in the working memory result set and $b > c$ as the new premise, the common element is b and it is at the "back" of the string in the working memory result set. Strategies for proceeding beyond this point are constructed by the system. Once constructed, they are stored and can be used on future problems without having to be constructed again.

The comprehension of premises is not modeled in detail, it being assumed that the system is capable of extracting the semantic information in the premises and storing it in short-term memory, or using it in construction of ordered sets. The reason is that this aspect of the task was modeled in Sternberg's (1980a, 1980b) formulation, and in this project we wanted to concentrate on the development of strategies for premise integration. This formulation is quite compatible with Sternberg's account of premise comprehension, and if the premise comprehension process could be simulated, it could be integrated with the TRIMM model.

A run of the model through the 12 problem forms over two cycles is shown in Table 3.3 (the run was over four cycles, but no significant changes occurred after Cycle 2). An overview of the run is given before considering the details. Additional runs have been made with problems in random order and the outputs have been essentially the same. The main difference was that in some cases, strategy shifts occurred more readily. This occurs when a number of problems happen close together, causing incorrect productions to be weakened. However, for convenience we examine two cycles through the 12 problem forms of Table 3.2. These two cycles are shown in Table 3.3. The problems were run in the order shown in Table 3.3. The effort level is initially set low (.6), so relational structure mapping will be used.

On the first cycle, the model is building productions to deal with N-term series problems. Effort level for structure mapping is initially low because of the high demands of other processes and because the need for system mappings is not recognized. The first set of productions built produce correct responses to most problem forms. However, because of the low effort level, incorrect orders are initially produced on those problem forms that are sensitive to premise integration. Specifically, on problem Forms 1 and 2, the incorrect order acb is produced. These are errors that were commonly found in previous research (Maybery, et al., submitted). Processes that lead to this error in problem Form 1 were explained in an earlier section. The same error in problem Form 2 results from first combining b > c and a > b to produce abc, then when a > c is presented, c is placed after a, yielding acb. As with the first problem form, this error results from processing the final premise by itself, not integrating it with earlier premises. The order produced is incompatible with the second premise, a > b, but this is not recognized by the model at this point in its development, because it only maps premises into the concept of order one-at-a-time.

The error on Problem 1 results in negative feedback, reducing the strength of the productions that fired for that problem, and increasing effort level to .95. However, this is below the threshold for system mapping (1.30), so the model will continue to operate at the relational level, resulting in further errors on some problem forms.

On Problem 2, a new production is built to process the second premise, because (a > b) was not previously processed following (b > c). The result set after the second premise will be a,b,c, as with Problem 1. When (a > c)

TABLE 3.3
Two Sets of Twelve Problem Forms

Premise	Result Set	Effort	Production Fired
a > b	a b	0.6	
b > c	a b c	0.6	token-1
a > c	a c b	0.6	token-2
b > c	b c	0.95	
a > b	a b c	0.95	token-3
a > c	a c b	1.213	token-2
a > b	a b	1.409	
a > c	a < <c ∧ b> >	1.409	token-12
b > c	a b c	1.409	token-13
b > c	b c	1.402	
a > c	< <b ∧ a> >	1.402	token-14
a > b	a b c	1.402	token-15
a > c	a c	1.395	
a > b	a < <b ∧ c> >	1.395	token-12
b > c	a b c	1.395	token-16
a > c	a c	1.388	
b > c	< <a ∧ b> > c	1.388	token-14
a > b	a b c	1.388	token-17
a > b	a b	1.381	
b > c	a b c	1.381	token-1
c > d	a b c d	1.381	token-1
a > b	a b	1.374	
c > d	< <a b ∧ c d> >	1.374	token-18
b > c	a b c d	1.374	token-19
b > c	b c	1.368	
a > b	a b c	1.368	token-3
c > d	a b c d	1.368	token1
b > c	b c	1.361	
c > d	b c d	1.361	token-1
a > b	a b c d	1.361	token-3
c > d	c d	1.354	
a > b	< <c d ∧ a b> >	1.354	token-18
b > c	a b c d	1.354	token-13
c > d	c d	1.347	
b > c	b c d	1.347	token-3
a > b	a b c d	1.347	token-3
a > b	a b	1.34	
b > c	a b c	1.34	token-1
a > c	a b c	1.34	token-20
b > c	b c	1.334	
a > b	a b c	1.334	token-3
a > c	a b c	1.334	token-20

(*Continued*)

110

TABLE 3.3 (*Continued*)

Premise	Result Set	Effort	Production Fired
a > b	a b	1.327	
a > c	a < <c ∧ b> >	1.327	token-12
b > c	a b c	1.327	token-13
b > c	b c	1.32	
a > c	< <b ∧ a> > c	1.32	token-14
a > b	a b c	1.32	token-15
a > c	a c	1.314	
a > b	a < <b ∧ c> >	1.314	token-12
b > c	a b c	1.314	token-16
a > c	a c	1.307	
b > c	< <a ∧ b> > c	1.307	token-14
a > b	a b c	1.307	token-17
a > b	a b	1.301	
b > c	a b c	1.301	token-1
c > d	a b c d	1.301	token-1
a > b	a b	1.294	
c > d	< <a b ∧ c d> >	1.294	token-18
b > c	a b c d	1.294	token-19
b > c	b c	1.288	
a > b	a b c	1.288	token-3
c > d	a b c d	1.288	token-1
b > c	b c	1.281	
c > d	b c d	1.281	token-1
a > b	a b c d	1.281	token-3
c > d	c d	1.274	
a > b	< <c d ∧ a b> >	1.275	token-18
b > c	a b c d	1.275	token-13
c > d	c d	1.269	
b > c	b c d	1.269	token-3
a > b	a b c d	1.269	token-3

is presented, the production that processed it with the same conditions in Problem 1 will have been weakened, below threshold. However, the model is not yet ready to build a system-level production. To avoid rebuilding failed productions or abandoning problems because no adequate production can be built, the model now checks whether or not a production was built with the same conditions and actions. Such a production exists — token-2. The threshold is temporarily lowered, to permit the production to fire again, resulting in the same error as before. The effort level was increased in the search for a production. Thus, there is competition between processes that lead to new productions and processes that reinstate old productions.

The error on Problem 2 raises the effort level to 1.409, which allows system-level productions to be built. On Problem 3, premise (a > b) is processed as before. In an attempt to build a production to process premise (a > c), system mapping is employed, and a > b, a > c are mapped into the concept of order. It is then recognized that the order is indeterminate because, as noted earlier, this can be recognized when system mapping is used. A production is then built that inserts an indeterminacy marker, < <c ∧ b> >, showing that the order of c and b is indeterminate. This is resolved by premise (b > c), yielding the result set abc.

The remaining problems are processed using productions developed under system-level mapping where necessary (i.e., where productions developed with relational mapping have led to errors), resulting in productions that take account of the current premise and the most relevant, previous premise. This means that indeterminacies are noted where they occur after the second premise, and the remaining problem forms are processed without error. On Cycle 2 (i.e., starting with the 12th problem in Table 3.3), all problem forms are processed without error. The sequence of productions that fire on problem Forms 1–3 in Table 3.2 is given in Appendix C.

The model is not designed, at this stage, to simulate solution latencies or parameters such as learning rate. However it is tightly constrained by a wide range of qualitative performance indicators, such as error patterns, mapping ordered sets across dimensions, recognition of indeterminacy, and strategies used. These are considered in the next section.

To summarize the run of the model, it began with domain-general productions, then built domain-specific productions appropriate for the N-term series problems presented. Metacognitive processes, entailing mapping of premise information into a concept of order, instantiated as an ordered set of three elements, was used to guide the creation of new productions. Once created, productions were subject to strengthening or weakening by associative learning mechanisms, depending on their success in producing correct problem solutions.

EXPERIMENTS

The design of the model was constrained by an extensive database in the literature, including studies from our own laboratory. To test the model after it was developed, seven experiments were performed with child participants to determine whether or not their performance matched the output of the model. These experiments were detailed elsewhere (Halford et al., 1992; Maybery et al., submitted), and are summarized here. Details of the model's performance in matching the performance of participants in the experiments was also given by Halford et al. (1992).

Experiment 1 tested whether or not 10- and 13-year olds could construct ordered sets using premise sets based on the 12 problem forms in Table 3.2. Experiment 2 made the same assessment with 9- and 10-year-olds. Children generally constructed a series consistent with the premises, the most common error being acb in problem Forms 1 and 2, and either bcda or dabc on problem form 11. Both of these errors are consistent with the principles incorporated in the model, and reflect attention to the final premise, a > c, or b > c, without integration with previous premises. Experiments 1 and 2 confirm that children's construction of ordered sets is consistent with the model.

Experiment 3 tested whether or not children of 5 years and older can map one ordered set into another. This is important because strategy development in the model depends on analogical mapping and (because 5-year-olds can develop adequate transitive inference strategies) the model implies they should be able to map ordered sets.

Children were shown an ordered set as standard, and required to say which of two comparison sets, one ordered and one not, was like the standard. This required children to recognize the correspondence between two ordered sets, equivalent to mapping one ordered set into the other. On each trial, a set of of three cards was presented, and each card contained three objects (bottles, drums, or rockets) in a row. The bottom card was the standard, and the two cards above it were the comparisons. The standard was ordered with respect to one dimension, such as height, width, or saturation. One comparison was ordered and one was not. The participant's task was to say which comparison card was ordered. On training trials the correct comparison was ordered on the same dimension as the standard, although it differed in a secondary dimension, so standard and comparison stimuli were not identical. On transfer trials, the correct comparison was ordered only on a different dimension from the standard.

Children aged 6 to 7 years were all successful in choosing the ordered set (on 5 out of 6 trials), and 75% of the 5-year-olds did so. These successes were maintained on the transfer trials. This suggests that the ability to map one ordered set into another is present in a majority of children from 5 years of age. This supports the assumption of the model that children of this age could use analogical mapping of ordered sets to guide the development of ordering strategies. This experiment is similar to the second investigation reported by Gentner, Rattermann, Markman, and Kotovsky (this volume). Both required children to distinguish ordered from unordered sets. Their 4-year-old sample performed above chance after they had been trained with relational labels, such as more-and-more for montonic increase. They chose the relational (ordered) alternative on 72% of trials.

This task requires mapping of a ternary relation and, as such, would amount to a system mapping, as discussed earlier. The norms from the developmental literature indicate that the median age at which system mappings are first performed is 4.5 to 5 years. Performance was improved in the 4-year-olds used by Gentner et al. (this volume) through training with relational encoding. The present theory, as expressed in this volume and elsewhere (Halford, 1993), agrees that appropriate encoding is necessary for adequate performance, but postulates that relational complexity influences processing load, that in turn, influences performance of both children and adults.

The developmental literature, and our own specific studies of the issue (Halford & Leitch, 1989; Halford et al, 1986) indicate that the cumulative percentage of children who can process ternary relations increases gradually with age, being low at 2 to 3 years, reaching 50% at about age 5, and asymptoting near 100% at about 10 years. Gentner et al. (this volume) found that 4-year-olds chose the ordered alternative 72% of the time in a binary choice task—significantly above chance, but far from perfect performance. It presumably represents about 44% correct after correction for guessing, consistent with the developmental norms for ternary relations.

This task might also be compared with the task used in the first investigation by Gentner et al. (this volume) in which children were required to choose one of three objects in an ordered set. This task was performed very well by 3-year-olds after they were taught relational encoding. However, more refined analysis shows that it does not necessitate ternary relations, and can be performed using simpler coding. The end items can be identified as such, particularly when they always occur at the beginning and end of the row, as in these studies. The middle item can be encoded as a binary relation with one of the end items: *right of the end item, bigger than the smallest item,* and so on. The general principle here (Halford & Wilson, 1993) is that when a relation is defined between one item and a set of others, and no relation is defined between the others, the other items can be chunked. This refers to conceptual chunks, as defined by Halford (1993a), and Halford et al. (1994).

If we want to represent a relation between an element a and a set of other elements, $R(a,\{b,c, . . ,n\})$, and no relation is represented between any of $\{b,c, . . ,n\}$, then $\{b,c, . . ,n\}$ can be combined into one conceptual chunk, and R is a binary relation. As with other binary relations, it can be represented by a Rank 3 tensor product, with one vector representing the relation, one vector representing a, *and one representing* $\{b,c,. . ,n\}$. *This represents the relation between a* and $\{b,c, . . ,n\}$ collectively, but represents no relation between any of $\{b,c, . . ,n\}$. This is the situation when one item has to be discriminated in an ordered set, because this only requires a relation between that one item and the remaining items, that can be chunked. Training with relational encoding, as used by Gentner et al. (this volume) would facilitate this conceptual chunking. The fact that the elements are ordered does not prevent chunking, because the ordering is provided by the experimenter, and the participant does not have to process the relations entailed in the ordering.

The situation is quite different, however, when the task is to recognize whether or not the set as a whole is ordered, because this cannot be reduced to a single binary relation. For example, consider the set {3,7,5}. This is not ordered because 7 > 3, but it is not true that 5 > 7. In this case, both the relation between 3 and 7 and the relation between 7 and 5 must be processed, so conceptual chunking is not possible, and the representation cannot be reduced to a binary relation. It is a ternary relation and requires a Rank 4 tensor product, with one vector representing the relation, and vectors representing each of 3, 7, and 5. This represents relations between 3 and 7, 7 and 5, 3 and 5, as well as the three-way relation between 3, 7, and 5. This can be done in essentially the same way as in Fig. 3.3a.

The need to process both relations makes the task of recognizing whether or not a set is ordered more complex. The model of Halford (1993) and Halford and Wilson (1993) predicts that the task of detecting whether or not a set is ordered is more complex than the task of recognizing one item in an ordered set of three. Given equal amounts of training, the age of attainment of the former task should be greater, as Gentner et al.'s (this volume) data suggest. It is difficult to see how Gentner et al.'s model can generate this prediction. This is another example of how relational complexity influences cognitive performance. This prediction is quite counterintuitive, yet it is quite clear from the underlying theory. It illustrates the point made in chapter 1, that theoretical arguments should be based on process models.

Experiment 4 assessed recognition of indeterminacy. As noted earlier, the model predicts that children should be able to recognize when the order of premise elements is indeterminate. Children aged either 7 or 10 years were presented with either determinate (a > b,b > c; b > c,a > b) or indeterminate (a > b,a > c; b > c,a > c) problem forms. Participants were asked to judge determinacy after both premises were presented, and were asked to construct orders only for problems they judged to be determinate. Both age groups reliably discriminated determinate from indeterminate problem forms. The model can recognize determinacy in these problem forms after it has progressed to using system-level strategies. The performance of these children is therefore consistent with the model.

Experiment 5 assessed construction of ordered sets, as well as recognition of indeterminacy. It was found that both 7 to 9 and 10 to 12-year-olds could discriminate significantly between determinate and indeterminate N-term series problems, without the benefit of an additional prompt. However, with benefit of a prompt that asks whether or not a specific element could go in another position, their accuracy becomes high in absolute terms, and this is not due to false alarms. They also find the correct order of elements in both four-term adjacent-only and three-term adjacent-and-nonadjacent problems with high accuracy. This experiment confirms Experiment 4 in showing that the processes children use in constructing ordered sets do permit them to recognize indeterminacy. After experience with a number of problems, the model also routinely recognizes indeterminacy when constructing ordered sets.

Experiment 6 attempted to analyze strategies used on problems of the types we have been assessing, using a response pattern analysis (sometimes known as a *rule assessment*) technique similar to that of Levine (1966) or Siegler (1981). The result showed that 8- to 9- and 12- to 13-year-olds, where they used a consistent strategy, tended to integrate premises. Where they failed to do so, this was by default, rather than due to a consistent tendency to employ an alternate strategy. The data are consistent with the model insofar as they indicate that early performance does not correspond to an incorrect strategy, so much as to incomplete strategies. Recall that the model does not entail strategies as such, but only components of strategies in the form of productions, each of which can be acquired independently. Thus, early in acquisition of transitive inference reasoning, neither the model nor the children possess strategies that are specifically incorrect. It is more accurate to say that they possess a number of independent processing steps, or productions that, collectively, yield partially correct performance.

Experiment 7 used the same technique with 5- to 7-year-old children. Similar results to those in Experiment 6 were obtained, except that fewer children showed any tendency to use a consistent strategy.

The results of Experiments 6 and 7 indicated that acquisition of transitive inference was a matter of an adequate strategy gradually developing, with early performance based on rules that worked some but not all the time, and gradually being replaced by progressively more adequate rules. The evidence is consistent with the theory that N-term series reasoning processes are acquired piecemeal, on a problem-by-problem basis. Incorrect performances are not caused by incorrect strategies, in the sense of generalized procedures that apply to all problems, but simply reflect inadequately developed skills. These skills are acquired gradually, as experience with a variety of problem forms accumulates.

GENERAL DISCUSSION

This chapter presented a computer simulation of the development of a problem solving skill in a particular domain, N-term series reasoning or transitive inference. However, the principles incorporated in this model are likely to apply to other domains, and to that extent it might be regarded as a general theory of the development of reasoning skills. We consider the implications of the model for several topics, N-term series reasoning, strategy development, capacity and complexity, and cognitive development.

N-term Series Reasoning

The immediate aims of the model were to account for previous data on N-term series reasoning, and to predict some hitherto unobserved aspects of the process. In respect of the first aim, it has been shown that the model can account for the way people acquire the ability to construct an ordered set in working memory. This construction process has been central to previous models of N-term series reasoning (Foos et al., 1976; Sternberg, 1980b; Trabasso, 1977). What the TRIMM model adds is an account of how this ability can be acquired. The specific strategies or skills required to construct an ordered set consistent with the premises are not assumed, but are developed as the system gains experience with the task.

Another aspect of previous work on N-term series is the difficulty of integrating premises. There is evidence that young children, and adults when unfamiliar with the task or under high processing loads, tend to process premises singly, without taking sufficient account of previous premises (Baylor & Gascon, 1974; Halford, 1984; Halford & Kelly, 1984). More sophisticated, or more competent performers integrate premises, finding a solution that is consistent not only with the most recent premise but also with previous ones. It was shown that premise integration is associated with high processing loads (Halford et al., 1986; Maybery et al., 1986). These premise integration phenomena were incorporated into the model through the variable of effort level. Mapping two premises into the concept of order to determine consistency requires more effort than mapping one premise. This produces a tendency to map one premise, leading to strategies that take account of only the most recent premise. Because these strategies lead to errors on some problem forms, the productions they entail are weakened, and eventually fail to be used because they fall below threshold. At the same time, effort level is raised, causing relations to be mapped in pairs, leading to strategies that integrate premises.

Another source of failure in N-term series reasoning is the tendency to encode premises in absolute rather than relational terms (Perner & Mansbridge, 1983; Siegler, 1989; Sternberg & Rifkin, 1979). Simulation of premise encoding would require a natural language processing model and is beyond the scope of the present project. However, the type of encoding might well be a consequence, rather than a cause, of difficulty in integrating premises. The reason is that if premises are processed separately there is no need to avoid absolute labels. For example, if we say *Bill is taller than John*, no conflict results from coding Bill as tall and John as short. Conflict does occur, however, if we consider two premises jointly. Consider *Bill is taller than John and John is taller than Mike.* The problem now is that John is coded as both tall and short. Absolute coding causes conflict when premises are considered jointly. If participants are unable to process premises jointly because of processing loads, as discussed previously, and are therefore restricted to processing them serially (one at a time) there is less incentive to avoid absolute encoding. Thus absolute encoding could be a consequence of information processing demands. If however premises are processed jointly, a coding scheme must be adopted which avoids conflict; for example, large, medium, small, or top, middle, bottom. Coding might be a consequence of the amount of information that can be processed in a single decision.

The TRIMM model assumes that young children have the ability to map one ordered set into another, and this structure mapping ability is a core feature of the model. This may have seemed rather unlikely, because a previous investigation (Gentner & Toupin, 1986) suggests children have difficulty mapping structures based on complex relations. Gentner and Toupin's study was concerned with structures involving systematicity, where there is a higher order relation between binary relations. Mapping ordered sets does not entail explicitly representing a higher order relation, but it does entail a structure composed of more than one binary relation. It is therefore more structurally complex than proportional analogies in which there is a binary relation between terms in base and target. Despite this added complexity, Experiment 3, and the study of Gentner et al. (this volume) show that most 5-year-old children succeed.

The model also entails recognition of indeterminacy of N-term series. Experiments 4 and 5 indicate that this feature is consistent with children's capabilities. Recognition of indeterminacy was postulated in the model of Sternberg (1981), but children's ability to perform this task was not tested. Doubt as to whether or not they can do so is caused by controversy as to whether or not they can recognize that a logical argument (based on two categorical premises) is determinate (see Halford, 1989, for a review). Experiments 2 and 3 show that they can do so, consistent with the model. This does not necessarily imply that they can recognize when a logical argument is determined or can recognize logical necessity, because the tasks are too different to permit extrapolation from one to the other. Further analysis of this problem was presented elsewhere (Halford, 1993).

Strategy Change

The model implies that strategies should not be treated as the cause of behavior, but as phenomena that need to be explained. It is consistent in this respect with the planning net models of Van Lehn and Brown (1980) and Greeno et al. (1984). Planning nets were used by Greeno et al. (1984) to develop a model of how a child's concept of number constrains counting strategies. Our model shows how a concept of order can constrain the development of N-term series reasoning skills. Experiments 6 and 7 suggest that progress is not a matter of incorrect strategies being replaced by correct ones, but of gradual development of an adequate strategy through the accumulation of context-specific skills.

However, the TRIMM model differs from previous planning net models in two significant ways. The first is that it permits concrete experience with specific content to provide the declarative knowledge base for development of reasoning skills. That is, experience with specific ordered sets can be used as the basis for a concept of order, constraining the development of N-term series reasoning skills. By contrast, Greeno et al. (1984) postulated knowledge of universally valid logical rules — probably innate. We do not object to postulating the existence of such knowledge, but believe that a role must be provided for empirical knowledge as well, because not all reasoning skills can be based on innate knowledge. Furthermore, logical reasoning principles have limited power to explain human reasoning (Halford, 1990).

Use of content-specific, experience-based knowledge to constrain acquisition of reasoning skills is made possible in the TRIMM model by the use of analogical mapping. This is the second way that the TRIMM model differs from previous planning net models. Analogies have the advantage that they permit concrete instances of concepts to be used as a basis for inferences that go beyond those instances. They therefore make it unnecessary to postulate knowledge of abstract, universally valid, logical rules or principles, because specific instantiations of those principles can suffice. In the TRIMM model a representation of an ordered set of at least three elements serves as a concept of order, and permits children to reason as though they understood the abstract concept of order.

One problem that remains to be explored is how an appropriate analog is selected. It is unlikely to be based on element similarity, because this principle lacks the required generality. It is possible that relational similarity plays a role. For example, in the type of mapping shown in Fig. 3.4a–c, the fact that *happier than* entails comparisons might cue the selection of a schema that entails comparing objects. This could lead to the schema in which blocks of different size are placed in some sort of orderly arrangement. The fact that the same relation is repeated in the premises might cue selection of schemas where this is true. More sophisticated persons might recognize that some schemas are suitable for measurement; for example, *happier than, larger than, above,* and *left of* are all relations that are suitable for ordering and measuring things. Still more sophisticated persons might recognize that a schema entailing an asymmetric, transitive relation, is required. However, inappropriate schemas are chosen on occasion, and this accounts for some well-known error patterns (Halford, 1993a).

The third way that the TRIMM model differs from previous planning net models is that it does not postulate that understanding operates throughout all performances of a cognitive task. Previous planning net models modeled the role of understanding in the sense that they showed how a concept of the task constrains the development of strategies. The present theory entails a role for understanding in this way, but it also postulates that once skills, modeled as production rules, are acquired, understanding is no longer required. When a production exists for a particular task it simply fires, equivalent to automatically performing a task we already know how to do. Understanding is only invoked when it is necessary to acquire a new problem solving skill. The current model is consistent with that of Siegler and Shipley (this volume) in that it does not place exclusive reliance on metacognitive processes in strategy development, but resorts to them only where new strategies must be created, and associative processes are inadequate.

The model is generally consistent with Anderson's (1983) ACT* model, and with Anderson's (1987) theory of skill acquisition. It postulates the use of domain-general methods such as analogical reasoning and means-end analysis to construct skills, based on previously acquired declarative knowledge. In its present form, it does not incorporate the compilation and proceduralization postulated by Anderson (1987). These processes could be used to explain gains in efficiency as a result of further experience with the task. However, the aim of the present project is to simulate the acquisition of basic reasoning skills in the domain of N-term series. It also has the aim of providing a sufficiency test for some basic developmental mechanisms, to be considered in the next two sections.

The model also blends metacognitive and associative strategy selection mechanisms. Planning net models are essentially metacognitive models, in that they model the way strategies and skills are developed under the constraint of declarative knowledge. However as Siegler and Shipley's work (this volume) shows, a great deal of strategy growth and development can be accounted for by associative mechanisms. In the TRIMM model, strategies are strengthened or weakened, once they are acquired, by associative learning mechanisms. Furthermore, associative mechanisms are the first resort, because performance is based on existing skills where they are applicable, and development proceeds by strengthening or weakening the processes underlying these skills. It is only if existing skills are not applicable one resorts to metacognitive mechanisms.

The TRIMM model does not imply that strategies develop automatically through the acquisition of metacognitive knowledge. Knowledge alone does not produce strategies, but knowledge is used where task demands make it necessary in order to develop new strategies. The concept of order, which entails previous knowledge of ordered sets, was accessed when it was necessary to devise new ordering steps. Thus knowledge interacts with experience to guide the development of new strategies where they are needed. Siegler and Shipley (this volume) note that instructions do not change strategies. The TRIMM model predicts that strategies would not be changed where they are found to be effective, unless they incur excessive processing loads. In the TRIMM model, a production fires if its condition matches the current state of the problem, and if its strength indicates a history of success. Strategy change operates through problem solving experience.

Capacity and Complexity

The model posulates that processing loads play a role in skill acquisition. The specific mechanism postulated in this chapter entails using a previously experienced ordered set as an analog of the order that must be constructed to perform the task. As was previously explained, this entails structure mapping, imposing a processing load. The general principle is that analogical reasoning imposes a high processing load when more than one binary relation must be processed in a single mapping decision. A lot of N-term series reasoning entails mapping two or more relations into an ordering schema, and the joint processing of two binary relations imposes a high processing load.

This processing load is separate from memory loads that might apply during other aspects of task performance. It is distinct from the short term memory load imposed when an ordered set is stored in working memory during processing of the premises. The short-term storage load applies whenever information has to be stored for later use, and is distinct from processing load, imposed by information that is actually being processed. This distinction was considered in more detail, together with supporting evidence elsewhere (Halford, 1993a). Structure mapping, which occurs when reasoning skills are being developed, imposes a processing load. This particular load does not occur once skills are acquired.

Guttentag and Ornstein (1990) also concluded that metacognitive processes entailed in strategy selection and use impose processing loads. The TRIMM model provides a specific mechanism through which the processing loads of metacognitive processes can operate. In this application it occurred when premises had to mapped into the concept of order. More generally, it occurs when subjects must represent the structure of a task and map it into a representation of the current situation in order to decide what must be done. The concept of order should be thought of as a specific instantiation of task structure, that in this project took the form of an ordered set of three elements together with the relations between them. Other tasks obviously entail different structures, but the important point is that metacognitive strategy development in any task requires that the structure of the task be represented, and be mapped into problem solving situations as they arise, in order to select appropriate problem solving steps. This entails a processing load that varies with the complexity of the structure that must be mapped.

Transitive inference has been associated with a history of failure in young children, the causes of which have been the subject of much controversy (Halford, 1989). It has been proposed that there are a number of sources of false negatives in the tests that have been used, but Halford (1992, 1993a) argued that these factors, although important, do not completely explain the difficulties experienced, especially the rather persistent problems exhibited by young children. Furthermore, Halford et al. (1986) and Maybery et al. (1986) showed that the processing load associated with premise integration is a source of difficulty for both children and adults.

The representation of relational concepts in PDP architectures explains why processing load should be a positive function of relational complexity, as previously discussed. It implies that because transitivity is a 3-dimensional concept (based on a ternary relation), representation of the transitivity principle requires a computationally costly Rank-4 tensor product. This produces a tendency to default to lower dimensional representations, in which only one binary relation can be represented at a time.

The TRIMM model implies that one of the things that develops is the ability to represent integrated relations. Young children, as well as older children and adults under lower effort or high conflicting loads, tend to represent only one relation. This can be compared to Siegler's (1981) principle that children first represent a variety of tasks, including proportion, balance scale, and conservation, in terms of a single, dominant dimension, and only later integrate this with the second, subordinate dimension. For example, in the balance scale, early representations tend to be based on weight, progressively integrated with distance.

The progression observed in this research from representations based on one relation to those that integrate two relations, and Siegler's finding of progression from representation of a single, dominant dimension to integration of dominant and subordinate dimensions, are two cases of a common principle. Both imply that development entails progression to representations of higher dimensionality. This is emerging as one of the fundamentally important principles of cognitive development. It can be related to the structural complexity of representations in PDP models, that tend to provide a natural explanation for the processing loads imposed. The explanatory value of relational complexity for cognitive development was explored elsewhere (Halford, 1993a).

Transitive inference was associated with Piaget's (1950) concrete operational stage of cognitive development. The TRIMM model, unlike Piaget's, is not based on "psycho-logic," but emphasizes learning and reasoning mechanisms more in keeping with the theory of Anderson (1983, 1987). Nevertheless, the TRIMM model can explain why transitive inference has been found to be a difficult task for young children. The high processing load imposed by the requirement to map premises into an ordering schema would place an especially heavy burden on young children. Note that the basic mechanisms are the same at all ages, and the processing load imposed by premise integration occurs with both children and adults. Young children cannot construct representations of sufficiently high dimensionality to understand transitivity. As Halford (1993b) suggested, the observations that gave rise to Piaget's stage theory might reflect the development of representations of higher dimensionality, and might entail correspondingly more complex representations in PDP models. In the STAR model (Halford et al., 1994) this structural complexity corresponds to the rank of a tensor product of vectors.

The TRIMM model provides a mechanism through which processing capacity factors operate. It is not merely a predictor variable, as in past models, but plays a role in a set of mechanisms that are precise enough to be simulated. In particular, it influences ability to represent the structure of concepts, such as ordered sets, which in turn affects ability to devise effective strategies. Where children's capacity is less than the task demands, performance is not terminated. Rather, a lower level representation is used by default. This does not produce chance performance, but leads to strategies that are correct a high proportion of the time. There are telltale errors however, caused by processing one premise at a time, that do not occur if strategy development is guided by more adequate representations. Thus, children who can only represent two dimensions in parallel will be restricted to processing binary relations, which will prevent their adoption of strategies that integrate premises into ternary relations. As we have seen, this produces predictable error patterns on certain problem forms. The capacity analysis used here also generates predictions, some of them counterintuitive, about the relative difficulties of deciding whether or not a set as a whole is ordered, as against recognizing one item in an ordered set. These predictions have a bearing on the work of Gentner et al. (this volume), and were discussed under Experiment 3.

Although the present model has a role for capacity as an enabling factor, it is a model of learning and strategy development, and gives a central role to experience. This underlines how misconceived is the widespread assumption that models that have a role for capacity are ipso facto simple maturation models. In the present model, as with the rest of Halford's formulations on cognitive development (Halford, 1980, 1982, 1987, 1989,

1993a; Halford & Wilson, 1980), experience and processing capacity interact. There was, therefore, always a role for effects of training in accounting for children's cognitive performance.

It is obvious enough that the question of cognitive development cannot be a matter of learning or maturation. However, it is equally inappropriate to propose the question in any other form. For example, it makes no sense to ask whether cognitive development is a matter of capacity or knowledge acquisition, capacity or expertise, capacity or relational encoding, and so on. All of these are really alternate forms of the learning or maturation question. We take it as self-evident that experience-driven processes such as accumulation and organization of a knowledge base, skill acquisition, and efficient encoding, are all important in cognitive development. Modeling some of those processes in detail is what this book is about. The question of capacity is not whether it is an alternative to any of these processes, but whether, and how, it interacts with them. This chapter proposed one model of that interaction.

Implications for Cognitive Development

A fundamental problem for cognitive development is to explain how children acquire cognitive processes that are autonomous and adaptive, so the child can deal with situations and problems that could not have been anticipated. This implies the ability to develop strategies that meet task demands as they arise. It is not sufficient to explain children's performance by describing the strategies they use, because the important problem is to account for the development of the strategies. To account for children's transitive inferences by defining their strategies is undoubtedly useful, especially if the strategy is precisely defined, and rigorously validated. Some earlier models of this kind formed an important foundation for this project. But to treat the strategy as the explanation for the performance is tantamount to assuming that the strategy somehow pre-existed, specifically for performing that task. There is no reason why a child should be equipped to perform transitive inference tasks in a laboratory. Such performances are of interest only because they reflect the autonomous, adaptive processes by which a child manages to cope with a multitude of problems in real life. Research on these performances is useful to the extent that it tells us about these adaptive processes.

We began, therefore, with the assumption that there is no reason why children or adults should have pre-existing strategies for performing laboratory-based transitive inferences. When asked to do so, they build strategies that draw on past knowledge, and that meet the unanticipated demands of the task. That knowledge was not acquired with the purpose of using it in this way. It might have been acquired for a quite different purpose, or might have been acquired through relatively aimless exploration of the world. The problem then was to explain how knowledge of the world, acquired for a different purpose or without any purpose, can be adapted to meet the demands of an unanticipated problem. This seems to us to be more a "real-life" situation than most experimental paradigms.

The task demanded that children take a set of relational premises, and make certain inferences that follow from the set, but that cannot be made from any premise taken alone. This entails integrating the premises into an ordered set. The knowledge required to do this includes the concept of an ordered set. It was necessary therefore to explain the nature and origin of this concept. For reasons given earlier, it is unlikely that children have a formal mathematical definition of an ordered set, or even domain-general principles that relate to it.

The solution that seemed plausible to us was to assume that children acquire experience with specific, concrete examples of ordered sets through play and general interaction with their world. Those experiences would be stored in memory, not for the purpose of solving N-term series problems, but simply as part of the child's world knowledge. The next problem was to explain how such knowledge could be used to guide the development of reasoning strategies.

Analogical reasoning proved very useful. Analogies are by no means new in models of skill acquisition. For example, Anderson's (1987) model incorporated analogies between the current problem solving step and a step taken previously in a related context. However, our use of analogy differs in that it enables knowledge acquired in a completely unrelated context to be used to guide the building of strategies for an unanticipated task. We believe this feature of the TRIMM model captures an important aspect of the autonomous, adaptive processes fundamental to cognitive development.

This step also imposes the processing load. Learning, in the sense of building up a store of representations of the world, does not appear to impose a significant processing load. We appear to be well equipped with efficient mechanisms that detect regularities in the environment, and mental models of such regularities can be built up in small increments without apparent effort. Processes by which this occurs have been discussed elsewhere (Halford, 1993a; Holland et al., 1986). Significant processing loads are observed when it is necessary to map such experiences into new problems. The size of the loads depends on the complexity of structure that must be mapped. According to the STAR model of Halford et al. (1994), the load occurs because of the type of representation that is required for these structures. The important point here is that it is the need to map one structure into another that imposes the load.

This means that very young children might well have examples of ordered sets stored in memory, and might be able to learn N-term series strategies if appropriately taught. However they might find it difficult to map their stored experiences into the tasks demanded of them. Thus, they find it difficult to develop strategies for structurally complex tasks autonomously, based on their own representation of the task. That is, they find it difficult to develop strategies with understanding.

There are other aspects of autonomous, adaptive behavior that are also captured by the model. One is that children should recognize when strategies are inappropriate. A clear case is that they should not be applied mindlessly to N-term problems that are unsolvable. Our data show children can do this, and the model shows that strategies based on knowledge of the world can reproduce this aspect of adaptive cognition. Thus, the model is adaptive and autonomous in this sense, also. Therefore, we suggest that the computational model provides a sufficiency test for a theory of processes underlying adaptive, autonomous strategy and skill acquisition.

APPENDIX A

Productions existing before the model begins operation.

```
;       Productions   -for getting premises
;                     - for reporting on solution states
;                     - for retrieving info from ltm
; If there is nothing else to do, do something.
(READY
(
 (FLAG (wm waiting))
 (<not> (FLAG (get feedback)))
)
- >
(
 ($clear-dm wm)
 ($add-to wm (GOAL (do-something)) 1 1 1)
)
)
0.4
;if the goal is to do something, read in more input
(GET_NEW_INPUT
(
 (GOAL (do-something))
)
- >
(
 ($add-to wm (INPUT (($input-line))) 1 1 0)
 ($delete-from wm (GOAL (do-something)))
)
)
0.3
```

```
; If the new input is recognised as a command, accept it
; as a goal to fulfill.
; Valid commands:- add, restart, stop, report, say, other.
(NEXT_COMMAND
 (
  (INPUT (=new-input))
  @ltm (recognized-commands !f =new-input !b))
 )
 ->
 (
  ($add-to wm (GOAL (=new-input)) 1 1 1)
  ($delete-from wm (INPUT (=new-input)))
 )
)
; Get next premise interactively and set goal to integrate-premise.
(ASK_FOR_PREMISE
 (
  (GOAL (=reply) )
  (*or(*equal =reply add)(*equal =reply ADD) )
 )
 ->
 (
  ($writecr Enter the premise: )
  ($add-to wm
   (premise (($input-line))) 1 1 0
   (GOAL (integrate-premise)) 1 1 1
  )
  ($delete-from wm (GOAL (=reply)))
 )
)

; If result set is empty add first premise directly.

(INTEGRATE_FIRST_PREMISE
 (
  (GOAL (integrate-premise))
  (<not> (result set (=rel =rset)))
  (premise (=ob1 =rel =ob2))
 )
 ->
  (
  ($delete-from wm
   (GOAL (integrate-premise))
   (premise (=ob1 =rel =ob2))
  )
  ($add-to wm
   (GOAL (do-something)) 1 1 1
   (result set (=rel (=ob1 =ob2))) 1 1 0
  )
  ($trace-results (=ob1 =rel =ob2) (=ob1 =ob2))
  )
)
```

```
; If result set is not empty add a goal to search for
; premise elements in resultset.
(INTEGRATE_OTHER_PREMISES
 (
  (GOAL (integrate-premise) )
  (<not> (MATCHLIST !matchlist))
  (<not> (FLAG (result-set-modified)));23-3-91
  (result set (=rel =resultset) )
 )
 ->
 (
  ($add-to wm (result set (=rel =resultset)) 1 1 0 )
  ($add-to matchmem
   (GOAL (make MATCHLIST)) 1 1 1
   (MATCHSET =resultset) 1 1 0
  )
  ($call mm)
 )
)


(TRY_EXISTING_STRATEGIES

;check new-pm for existing strategies,
;if there are none,
;production STRATEGIES_TRIED sets the goal to build a new production.

 (
  (GOAL (integrate-premise))
  (MATCHLIST =list1 =list2)
  (result set (=rel =resultset))
  (<not> (FLAG (STRUCTURE MAPPER called)))
 )
 ->
 (
  ($call pm new-pm )
 )
)


; This production allows the model to continue though
; no strategy already exists.

(STRATEGIES_TRIED
 (
  (MATCHLIST =list1 =list2)
  (<not> (GOAL (build a production)))
 )
 ->
 (
  ($add-to wm (GOAL (build a production)) 1 1 1)
  ($call pm)
 )
```

```
)
0.5

; Production which fires in pm after new-pm strategy is applied.
; This prevents another premise integration cycle beginning.
; It would fail as some conditions are removed by new-pm strategy productions.

(STRATEGY_APPLIED
 (
 (FLAG (result-set-modified))
 (result set (=rel =resultset))
 (premise =premise)
 )
 ->
 (
 ($trace-results =premise =resultset)
 ($delete-from wm
  (FLAG (result-set-modified))
  (GOAL (integrate-premise))
  (GOAL (build a production))
  (premise =premise)
 )
 ($add-to wm (GOAL (do-something)) 1 1 1)
 )
)

; Once premise is integrated, set goals to look for
; fresh input.

(READY_FOR_NEW_PREMISE
 (
 (<not> (premise =premise))
 (result set (=rel =resultset))
 )
 ->
 (
 ($delete-from wm (GOAL (integrate-premise)))
 ($add-to wm (GOAL (do-something)) 1 1 1)
 )
)

; If trying to achieve a goal, and there is nothing else
; to do, find a concept that is linked with that goal in ltm.

(MAP_GOAL_TO_CONCEPT
 (
 (GOAL (build a production))
 (<not> (FLAG (STRUCTURE MAPPER called)))
 (<not> (FLAG (result-set-modified)))
 (@ltm
  (=name
```

```
!headlist
(strategy !head (=goal (map-concept =concept) !rest) !tail)
!taillist)
)
)
->
(
($add-to wm (GOAL (check =concept)) 1 1 1)
)
)
```

; If wanting to check the current state of wm against a concept of order,
; call the Structure Mapper, giving it the current premise and resultset.

```
(CALL_STRUCTURE_MAPPER
(
(GOAL (check concept-of-order))
(premise =premise)
(result set (=rel =resultset))
(<not> (FLAG (STRUCTURE MAPPER called)))
)
->
(
($add-to wm
(FLAG (STRUCTURE MAPPER called)) 1 1 1
(result set (=rel =resultset)) 1 1 0
(premise =premise) 1 1 0
)
($delete-from wm
(result set (=rel =resultset))
(premise =premise)
(GOAL (check concept-of-order))
)
($consider sm)
($call sm)
)
)
```

; Elements are added to the matcher memory so that a feature-list
; will be built.

```
(MATCH_ON_SMRESULT
(
(smresult set =smresult)
(FLAG (STRUCTURE MAPPER called))
(premise (=ob1 =rel =ob2) )
(<not> (GOAL (find-ltm-match)))
(<not> (SM_MATCHLIST !list1))
)
->
(
```

```
($delete-from wm (smresult set =smresult))
($add-to matchmem
 (GOAL (make SM_MATCHLIST)) 1 1 1
 (GOAL (find-ltm-match)) 1 1 1
 (MATCHSET =smresult) 1 1 0
 )
 ($call mm)
)
)
(BUILD_A_NEW_BODY
(
 (GOAL (build a production))
 (NEWPERFORM =perform)
 (MATCHLIST (=ob1 !rest1) (=ob2 !rest2))
)
->
(
 ($delete-from wm (NEWPERFORM =perform))
 ($add-to wm (BODY
 (=name
 (
 (result set (/ =rel / =resultset))
 (MATCHLIST (/ =ob1 !rest1 ) (/ =ob2 !rest2 ))
 )
 ->
 (
 (/$delete-from wm (MATCHLIST (/ =ob1 !rest1) (/ =ob2 !rest2)))
 (/$delete-from wm (result set (/ =rel / =resultset)))
 (/$add-to wm (result set (/ =rel
   ((/$perform =perform / =ob1 / =resultset / =ob2 )))) 1 1 1)
 (/$writecr =perform performed)
 (/$add-to wm (FLAG (result-set-modified)) 1 1 1)
 )
 )
 ) 1 1 0)
)
)


(BUILD_A_PRODUCTION
(
 (GOAL (build a production))
 (BODY =body)
 (*not (*already-built =body new-pm))
 (SM_MATCHLIST (=ob1 =E =F)(=ob2 =G =H))
)
->
(
 ($build-in new-pm =body)
 ($delete-from wm
   (GOAL (build a production))
   (GOAL (do-something))
```

```
(FLAG (STRUCTURE MAPPER called))
(BODY =body)
(SM_MATCHLIST (=ob1 =E =F)(=ob2 =G =H))
)
)
)
```

; Retrieve an operator from ltm to make transition from
; current to goal state.

```
(MATCH_AGAINST_LTM
 (
  (consider =a-number-of =relations)
  (MATCHLIST (=ob1 =A =B)(=ob2 =C =D))
  (SM_MATCHLIST (=ob1 =E =F)(=ob2 =G =H))
  (GOAL (find-ltm-match))
  (@ltm
  ((considering =a-number-of =relations)
   ((=ltm-ob1 !front1 =A !mid1 =B !end1 )
    (=ltm-ob2 !front2 =C !mid2 =D !end2 )
    =perform
    (=ltm-ob1 !front3 =E !mid3 =F !end3 )
    (=ltm-ob2 !front4 =G !mid4 =H !end4 ))))
 )
 ->
 (
  ($add-to wm (NEWPERFORM =perform) 1 1 0)
  ($delete-from wm (GOAL (find-ltm-match)))
 )
)
```

; If the command is to stop, call the finishing prod's

```
(FINISH
 (
  (GOAL (=reply) )
  (*or(*equal =reply stop) (*equal =reply STOP) )
 )
 ->
 (
  ($end-trace)
  ($add-to wm
   (FLAG (halt)) 1 1 1
   (FLAG (wm waiting)) 1 1 1
   (FLAG (get feedback)) 1 1 1
   (=reply) 1 1 0
  )
 )
)
```

; Call an explicit halt.

```
(HALT
 (
  (FLAG (halt))
 )
 ->
 (
  ($delete-from wm (FLAG (halt)) )
  ($halt)
 )
)


(RESTART_NEW_PROBLEM
 (
  (GOAL (=reply) )
  (*or(*equal =reply restart)(*equal =reply RESTART) )
 )
 ->
 (
  ($trace-new-problem)
  ($add-to wm
   (FLAG (wm waiting) ) 1 1 1
   (GOAL (get-feedback)) 1 1 1
  )
 )
)


(FEEDBACK_COMMAND
 (
  (GOAL (get-feedback))
  (<not> (FLAG (no-feedback)))
 )
 ->
 (
  ($delete-from wm (GOAL (get-feedback)))
  ($add-to wm
   (FLAG (get feedback)) 1 1 1
   (GOAL (do-something)) 1 1 1
  )
 )
)
0.7


(GET_FEEDBACK
 (
  (INPUT (=reply))
  (result set (=rel =resultset) )
  (FLAG (get feedback))
 )
 ->
 (
  ($writecr)
```

```
($writecr "result set =" =resultset )
($writecr)
($writecr "enter the correct result eg. (a b c) or (indeterminate)")
($add-to wm
 (correctset is =reply) 1 1 0
 (GOAL (give feedback )) 1 1 1
 (GOAL (do-something )) 1 1 1
 )
 ($delete-from wm
 (FLAG (get feedback))
 (INPUT (=reply))
 )
)
)
0.65


(GIVE__POS__FEEDBACK
 (
 (GOAL (give feedback))
 (result set (=rel =resultset) )
 (correctset is =correctset)
 (*equal =resultset =correctset)
 )
 ->
 (
 ($writecr "GIVING FEEDBACK TO LATEST ACTION")
 ($delete-from wm (GOAL (give feedback)))
 ($strength-feedback new-pm + 0.1)
 ($writecr "STRENGTH FEEDBACK DONE")
 ($writecr)
 ($update-effort + )
 ($writecr "EFFORT UPDATE DONE")
 ($writecr)
 ($delete-from wm (correctset is =correctset))
 )
)
0.65


(INDET__RESULT__POS__FEEDBACK
 (
 (GOAL (give feedback))
 (result set (=rel (!f < < !m1 ∧ !m2 > > !b)) )
 (correctset is (indeterminate))
 )
 ->
 (
 ($writecr "GIVING FEEDBACK TO LATEST ACTION")
 ($delete-from wm (GOAL (give feedback)))
 ($strength-feedback new-pm + 0.1)
 ($writecr "STRENGTH FEEDBACK DONE")
 ($writecr)
```

```
($update-effort + )
($writecr "EFFORT UPDATE DONE")
($writecr)
($delete-from wm (correctset is (indeterminate)))
)
)
0.65

(GIVE_NEG_FEEDBACK
(
(GOAL (give feedback))
(result set (=rel =resultset) )
(correctset is =correctset)
(*not (*equal =resultset =correctset))
)
–>
(
($writecr "GIVING FEEDBACK TO LATEST ACTION")
($delete-from wm (GOAL (give feedback)))
($strength-feedback new-pm - 0.25)
($writecr "STRENGTH FEEDBACK DONE")
($writecr)
($update-effort - )
($writecr "EFFORT UPDATE DONE")
($writecr)
($delete-from wm (correctset is =correctset))
)
)
0.65

; A series of productions for coping with exceptions.

; If no ltm match is found, raise effort and relax strategy
; selection threshold to increase likelihood of a match in future.

(LTM_MATCH_FAILURE
(
(MATCHLIST (=ob1 =A =B)(=ob2 =C =D))
(SM_MATCHLIST (=ob1 =E =F)(=ob2 =G =H))
(GOAL (find-ltm-match))
)
–>
(
($up-effort)
($alter-new-pm-selection-threshold -0.05)
($delete-from wm
 (GOAL (find-ltm-match))
 (FLAG (STRUCTURE MAPPER called))
 (BODY =body)
 (GOAL (build a production))
 )
```

```
($add-to wm (bad-choice =new-sym) 1 0 1
 )
 )
 )
```

; Two competing processes are working here. On one hand effort is increased
; so that if the model is close to a strategy transition threshold, it has the
; opportunity to cross.
; On the other, the criterion for considering unsuccessful productions is
; relaxed so that in the absence of fitter strategies, some existing strategy
; may operate.
; A third point is that there is a cut-off applied so that if the model is
; completely unable to solve a problem it escapes by abandoning it.

```
(BAD_CHOICE
 (
 (BODY =body)
 (*already-built =body new-pm)
 )
 - >
 (
 ($up-effort)
 ($alter-new-pm-selection-threshold -0.05)
 ($print-new-pm-selection-threshold)
 ($delete-from wm
 (FLAG (STRUCTURE MAPPER called))
 (BODY =body)
 )
 ($add-to wm (bad-choice =new-sym) 1 0 1)
 )
 )
```

; If the current result set contains an indeterminacy,
; and the model has alreday failed to recover any appropriate
; operator, try ignoring the indeterminacy.

```
(ABANDON_INDET
 (
 (MATCHLIST !f (=ob =indic indet) !b)
 (result set (=rel =resultset))
 (bad-choice =c1)
 (bad-choice =c2)
 (*not (*equal (bad-choice =c1) (bad-choice =c2)))
 )
 - >
 (
 ($delete-from wm
 (MATCHLIST !f (=ob =indic indet) !b)
 (result set (=rel =resultset))
 )
 ($add-to wm
```

```
((($lose-matchlist-indet (MATCHLIST !f (=ob =indic indet) !b))) 0.5 1 0
(GOAL (find-ltm-match)) 1 1 1
(result set (=rel ($remove-old-indeterminacy (=resultset)))) 1 1 0
 )
 )
 )

(ABANDON_CURRENT_PROBLEM
 (
 (GOAL (integrate-premise))
 (MATCHLIST =list1 =list2)
 (bad-choice =c1)
 (bad-choice =c2)
 (bad-choice =c3)
 (*not (*equal (bad-choice =c1) (bad-choice =c2)))
 (*not (*equal (bad-choice =c1) (bad-choice =c3)))
 (*not (*equal (bad-choice =c2) (bad-choice =c3)))
 )
 ->
 (
 ($delete-from wm
  (bad-choice =c1)
  (bad-choice =c2)
  (bad-choice =c3)
  (main goal (=goal))
  (GOAL (integrate-premise))
  (MATCHLIST =list1 =list2)
 )
 ($add-to wm
  (FLAG (problem-abandoned)) 1 1 1
  (GOAL (do-something)) 1 1 1
 )
 ($setq latest-action* nil);ensure no feedback given in error
 )
 )

(LOOK_FOR_RESTART
 (
 (premise =arg)
 (FLAG (problem-abandoned))
 (INPUT (=reply) )
 (*or (*equal =reply restart)(*equal =reply RESTART)
  (*equal =reply stop)(*equal =reply STOP)
 )
 )
 ->
 (
 ($delete-from wm (FLAG (problem-abandoned)))
 ($add-to wm (FLAG (no-feedback)) 1 1 1)
 ($input-line);throw away feedback info from input file
 )
 )
```

```
(IGNORE_OTHER_GOALS
 (
  (FLAG (problem-abandoned))
  (GOAL (=reply) )
  (@ltm (recognized-commands !f =reply !b))
 )
 ->
 (
  ($delete-from wm (GOAL (=reply)))
  ($add-to wm (GOAL (do-something)) 1 1 1)
 )
)
```

; If a problem has already been abandoned as insoluble,
; ignore further information.

```
(IGNORE_INPUT
 (
  (INPUT (!new-input))
  (FLAG (problem-abandoned))
 )
 ->
 (
  ($delete-from wm (INPUT (!new-input)))
  ($add-to wm (GOAL (do-something)) 1 1 1 )
 )
)
```

```
(RemoveSMFlag
 (
  (smresult set =smresult)
  (FLAG (STRUCTURE MAPPER called))
 )
 ->
 (
  ($delete-from wm (FLAG (STRUCTURE MAPPER called)))
 )
)
0.5
```

; Productions which output a judgement on the state of the result set.

```
(JUDGE
 (
  (GOAL (=reply))
  (*or (*equal =reply judge) (*equal =reply JUDGE))
 )
 ->
 (
  ($delete-from wm (GOAL (=reply)))
  ($add-to wm (GOAL (say-if-compatible)) 1 1 1)
```

```
)
)

(ASK—FOR—ORDER
 (
  (GOAL (say-if-compatible))
 )
 - >
 (
  ($writecr possible order please, in the form : (x y z) )
  ($add-to wm (correct? ($input-line)) 1 1 1)
  ($delete-from wm (GOAL (say-if-compatible)))
 )
)

(ACCEPT
 (
  (correct?  = order)
  (result set ( = rel  = order))
 )
 - >
 (
  ($judgement-trace = order accepted)
  (writecr Order: !order is correct)
  ($add-to wm (GOAL (do-something)) 1 1 1)
  ($delete-from wm (correct?  = order))
 )
)

(INDETERMINATE
 (
  (correct?  = order)
  (result set ( = rel  = resultset))
  (*or (*equal  = order (*perform remove—indet ob1  = resultset ob2))
   (*equal  = order (*perform switch ob1  = resultset ob2)))
 )
 - >
 (
  ($judgement-trace = order order-indeterminate)
  ($dm-dump wm dmfile)
  (writecr Order: !order is indeterminate)
  ($add-to wm (GOAL (do-something)) 1 1 1)
  ($delete-from wm (correct?  = order))
 )          .
)

(REJECT
 (
  (correct?  = order)
  (result set ( = rel  = order2))
  (*not (*equal  = order  = order2))
```

```
)
->
(
($judgement-trace =order rejected)
(writecr Order: !order is incorrect)
($add-to wm (GOAL (do-something)) 1 1 1)
($delete-from wm (correct? =order))
)
)
```

```
(OUTPUT_AN_ORDER
(
(GOAL (say-order))
(result set (=rel =resultset))
(*not (*member ∧ =resultset))
)
->
(
($writecr order is =resultset)
($judgement-trace "order is " =resultset)
($delete-from wm (GOAL (say-order)))
($add-to wm (GOAL (do-something)) 1 1 1)
)
)
0.4
```

```
(OUTPUT_ONLY_ORDER
(
(GOAL (other-order))
(result set (=rel =resultset))
(*not (*member ∧ =resultset))
)
->
(
($judgement-trace "there is no other order" " " )
($delete-from wm (GOAL (other-order)))
($add-to wm (GOAL (do-something)) 1 1 1)
)
)
0.4
```

```
(OUTPUT_BEST_INDET
(
(GOAL (say-order))
(result set (=rel (!f ∧ !b)))
)
->
(
($writecr order is ($perform remove_indet ob1 (!f ∧ !b) ob2))
($judgement-trace "order is" (($perform remove_indet ob1 (!f ∧ !b) ob2)))
($delete-from wm (GOAL (say-order)))
```

```
  ($add-to wm (GOAL (do-something)) 1 1 1)
  )
)


(OUTPUT_OTHER_INDET
  (
  (GOAL (other-order))
  (result set (=rel (!f ∧ !b)))
  )
  ->
  (
  ($writecr order is ($perform switch ob1 (!f ∧ !b) ob2))
  ($judgement-trace "order is " (($perform switch ob1 (!f ∧ !b) ob2)))
  ($delete-from wm (GOAL (other-order)))
  ($add-to wm (GOAL (do-something)) 1 1 1)
  )
)


(SAY_ORDER
  (
  (GOAL (=reply))
  (*or (*equal =reply say) (*equal =reply SAY))
  )
  ->
  (
  ($add-to wm (GOAL (say-order)) 1 1 1)
  ($delete-from wm (GOAL (=reply)))
  )
)


(OTHER_ORDER
  (
  (GOAL (=reply))
  (*or (*equal =reply other) (*equal =reply OTHER))
  )
  ->
  (
  ($add-to wm (GOAL (other-order)) 1 1 1)
  ($delete-from wm (GOAL (=reply)))
  )
)

; report on the state of the problem.

(REPORT
  (
  (GOAL (=reply))
  (*or (*equal =reply report) (*equal =reply REPORT))
  )
  ->
  (
```

```
($add-to wm (GOAL (say-if-decidable)) 1 1 1)
)
)
```

; Print a message if a problem is undecideable,
; i.e. the result set is indeterminate.

```
(UNDECIDABLE_PROBLEM
(
(GOAL (say-if-decidable))
(result set (=relationx (!front < < !ob1 ∧ !ob2 > > !rest)))
)
- >
(
($writecr The problem is undecidable. The order of !ob1 and !ob2 is unknown.)
($delete-from wm (GOAL (say-if-decidable)))
($add-to wm (GOAL (do-something)) 1 1 1)
)
)
```

; Print a message if a problem has an unambiguous solution.

```
(DECIDABLE_PROBLEM
(
(GOAL (say-if-decidable))
(result set (=relationx !resultset))
(<not> (result set (=relationx (!front < < !ob1 ∧ !ob2 > > !rest))))
)
- >
(
($writecr The order is determinate. The order is )
($write !resultset)
($delete-from wm (GOAL (say-if-decidable)))
($add-to wm (GOAL (do-something)) 1 1 1)
)
)
```

```
);end build-in pm
```

; The following productions fire sequentially to build up a feature list for each object
; in the current premise, based on its position in the current result set.

; The two elements: (GOAL (make =matchlist)) and (MATCHSET !REST) are placed
; in matchmem by the productions, INTEGRATE_OTHER_PREMISES and
MATCH_ON_SMRESULT,
; which call the matching memory (mm).

; Indet is first noted, then removed before finding the other features.
; So the matchlist has the form:
;   ((ob1 absent|present|front|back unmarked|indet)
         (ob2 absent|present|front|back|in-front unmarked|indet))

(build-in mm

; If you have a goal to find the features associated with the
; objects in the current premise, as they occur in the result set,
; then tag each object so it can be fed through the matching productions.

```
(ASSERT_MATCH_ELEMENTS
 (
  (GOAL (make =matchlist))
  (@wm (premise (=ob1 =rel =ob2)))
 )
 ->
 (
  ($add-to matchmem (=matchlist)
           matchmem (match =ob1)
           matchmem (match =ob2))
 )
)


(REMOVE_INDET

; If the MATCHSET contains an indeterminate part, then add it to matchmem
; as a new element and remove the indeterminacy markers from MATCHSET.
 (
  (GOAL (make =matchlist))
  (MATCHSET (!front < < !m ∧ !m2 > > !back))
 )
 ->
 (
  ($delete-from matchmem (MATCHSET (!front < < !m ∧ !m2 > > !back)))
  ($add-to matchmem (MATCHSET (($remove-old-indeterminacy (!front < < !m ∧ !m2
> > !back))))
           matchmem (INDET (!m))
           matchmem (INDET (!m2))
 )
 )
)


(MATCH_OBJ_INDET
 (
  (GOAL (make =matchlist))
  (match =ob)
  (match =other_ob)
  (=matchlist !f (=ob =pos) !b)
  (INDET (!front =ob !back))
  (*not (*member =other_ob ( !front !back)))
  (<not> (=matchlist !f (=ob =pos indet) !b))
 )
 ->
 (
  ($delete-from matchmem (=matchlist !f (=ob =pos) !b))
```

($add-to matchmem (=matchlist !f (=ob =pos indet) !b))
)
)

(MATCH__OBJ__UNMARKED
(
 (GOAL (make =matchlist))
 (match =ob)
 (MATCHSET !REST)
 (=matchlist !f (=ob =pos) !b)
 (<not> (INDET (!front =ob !back)))
)
– >
(
 ($delete-from matchmem (=matchlist !f (=ob =pos) !b))
 ($add-to matchmem (=matchlist !f (=ob =pos unmarked) !b))
)
)

(MATCH__OBJ__ABSENT
(
 (GOAL (make =matchlist))
 (MATCHSET !REST)
 (=matchlist !list)
 (match =ob)
 (<not> (MATCHSET (!front =ob !back)))
 (<not> (=matchlist !f (=ob absent !other) !b))
 (<not> (MATCHSET (!front < < !middle > > !back)))
)
– >
(
 ($delete-from matchmem (=matchlist !list))
 ($add-to matchmem (=matchlist !list (=ob absent)))
)
)

(MATCH__OBJ__PRESENT
(
 (GOAL (make =matchlist))
 (=matchlist !list)
 (match =ob)
 (MATCHSET (!front =ob !back))
 (<not> (=matchlist !f (=ob !other) !b))
 (<not> (MATCHSET (!front < < !middle > > !back)))
)
– >
(
 ($delete-from matchmem (=matchlist !list))
 ($add-to matchmem (=matchlist !list (=ob present)))
)
)

```
(MATCH_OBJ_FRONT
(
 (GOAL (make =matchlist))
 (=matchlist !f (=ob =pos !other) !b)
 (<not> (=matchlist !f (=ob front !other) !b))
 (<not> (=matchlist !f (=ob in-front !other) !b))
 (match =ob)
 (MATCHSET (=ob !back))
 (<not> (MATCHSET (!front << !middle >> !back)))
 )
 ->
 (
 ($delete-from matchmem (=matchlist !f (=ob =pos !other) !b))
 ($add-to matchmem (=matchlist !f (=ob front !other) !b))
 )
)


(MATCH_OBJ_BACK
(
 (GOAL (make =matchlist))
 (=matchlist !f (=ob present !other) !b)
 (match =ob)
 (MATCHSET (!front =ob))
 (<not> (MATCHSET (!front << !middle >> !back)))
 )
 ->
 (
 ($delete-from matchmem (=matchlist !f (=ob present !other) !b))
 ($add-to matchmem (=matchlist !f (=ob back !other) !b))
 )
)


(MATCH_OBJ_IN-FRONT
(
 (GOAL (make =matchlist))
 (@wm (premise (=ob1 =rel =ob2)))
 (MATCHSET (!front =ob2 !middle =ob1 !back))
 (=matchlist (=ob1 =pos1 =other1) (=ob2 =pos2 =other2 ))
 (*not (*equal =pos2 in-front))
 )
 ->
 (
 ($delete-from matchmem
   (=matchlist (=ob1 =pos1 =other1) (=ob2 =pos2 =other2 )))
 ($add-to matchmem
   (=matchlist (=ob1 =pos1 =other1) (=ob2 in-front =other2)))
 )
)


; Ensure that the objects are in the correct positions in the
; matchlist. If they are not, then switch them.
```

```
(ORDER_MATCHLIST
(
 (GOAL (make =matchlist))
 (@wm (premise (=ob1 =rel =ob2)))
 (=matchlist (=ob2 !pos2) (=ob1 !pos1))
)
->
(
 ($delete-from matchmem (=matchlist (=ob2 !pos2) (=ob1 !pos1)))
 ($add-to matchmem (=matchlist (=ob1 !pos1) (=ob2 !pos2)))
)
)


(FINISHED_MATCHING
(
 (GOAL (make =matchlist))
 (=matchlist (=ob1 !pos1) (=ob2 !pos2))
)
->
(
 ($add-to wm (=matchlist (=ob1 !pos1) (=ob2 !pos2)) 1 1 1)
 ($clear-dm matchmem)
 ($call pm);return to main series productions
)
)

);build-in mm
```

APPENDIX B

List of Productions Produced During Run of Model on 4 Sets of Problem Forms 1 to 12

```
(token-1 ((result set (=rel =resultset))
  (MATCHLIST (=ob1 back unmarked) (=ob2 absent unmarked)))
  ->
 (($delete-from wm
       (MATCHLIST (=ob1 back unmarked)
          (=ob2 absent unmarked)))
  ($delete-from wm (result set (=rel =resultset)))
  ($add-to wm
    ($newadd
     (result set
       (=rel (($perform append =ob1 =resultset =ob2))))))
  ($writecr append performed)
  ($add-to wm ($newadd (FLAG (result-set-modified)))))))
1.6 2.775

(token-2 ((result set (=rel =resultset))
```

(MATCHLIST (=ob1 front unmarked) (=ob2 back unmarked)))
- >
(($delete-from wm
    (MATCHLIST (=ob1 front unmarked)
        (=ob2 back unmarked)))
 ($delete-from wm (result set (=rel =resultset)))
 ($add-to wm
    ($newadd
    (result set
        (=rel
        (($perform delete_append
        =ob1
        =resultset
        =ob2))))))
 ($writecr delete_append performed)
 ($add-to wm ($newadd (FLAG (result-set-modified))))))
0.2725 0.75

(token-3 ((result set (=rel =resultset))
    (MATCHLIST (=ob1 absent unmarked) (=ob2 front unmarked)))
 - >
(($delete-from wm
    (MATCHLIST (=ob1 absent unmarked)
        (=ob2 front unmarked)))
 ($delete-from wm (result set (=rel =resultset)))
 ($add-to wm
    ($newadd
    (result set
        (=rel (($perform insert =ob1 =resultset =ob2))))))
 ($writecr insert performed)
 ($add-to wm ($newadd (FLAG (result-set-modified))))))
1.44 2.575

(token-12 ((result set (=rel =resultset))
    (MATCHLIST (=ob1 front unmarked) (=ob2 absent unmarked)))
 - >
(($delete-from wm
    (MATCHLIST (=ob1 front unmarked)
        (=ob2 absent unmarked)))
 ($delete-from wm (result set (=rel =resultset)))
 ($add-to wm
    ($newadd
    (result set
        (=rel
        (($perform append_indet
        =ob1
        =resultset
        =ob2))))))
 ($writecr append_indet performed)
 ($add-to wm ($newadd (FLAG (result-set-modified))))))
0.826 1.8

(token-13 ((result set (=rel =resultset))
 (MATCHLIST (=ob1 back indet) (=ob2 in-front indet)))
 - >
 (($delete-from wm
     (MATCHLIST (=ob1 back indet) (=ob2 in-front indet)))
 ($delete-from wm (result set (=rel =resultset)))
 ($add-to wm
   ($newadd
    (result set
     (=rel
      (($perform switch =ob1 =resultset =ob2))))))
 ($writecr switch performed)
 ($add-to wm ($newadd (FLAG (result-set-modified))))))
 0.9975 1.8

(token-14 ((result set (=rel =resultset))
 (MATCHLIST (=ob1 absent unmarked) (=ob2 back unmarked)))
 - >
 (($delete-from wm
     (MATCHLIST (=ob1 absent unmarked)
      (=ob2 back unmarked)))
 ($delete-from wm (result set (=rel =resultset)))
 ($add-to wm
   ($newadd
    (result set
     (=rel
      (($perform insert__indet
        =ob1
        =resultset
        =ob2))))))
 ($writecr insert__indet performed)
 ($add-to wm ($newadd (FLAG (result-set-modified))))))
 0.7835 1.8

(token-15 ((result set (=rel =resultset))
 (MATCHLIST (=ob1 present indet) (=ob2 in-front indet)))
 - >
 (($delete-from wm
     (MATCHLIST (=ob1 present indet)
      (=ob2 in-front indet)))
 ($delete-from wm (result set (=rel =resultset)))
 ($add-to wm
   ($newadd
    (result set
     (=rel
      (($perform switch =ob1 =resultset =ob2))))))
 ($writecr switch performed)
 ($add-to wm ($newadd (FLAG (result-set-modified))))))
 0.7417 1.4

(token-16 ((result set (=rel =resultset))
    (MATCHLIST (=ob1 present indet) (=ob2 back indet)))
    ->
    (($delete-from wm
        (MATCHLIST (=ob1 present indet) (=ob2 back indet)))
    ($delete-from wm (result set (=rel =resultset)))
    ($add-to wm
        ($newadd
        (result set
        (=rel
        (($perform remove__indet
            =ob1
            =resultset
            =ob2))))))
    ($writecr remove__indet performed)
    ($add-to wm ($newadd (FLAG (result-set-modified))))))
0.7185 1.4

(token-17 ((result set (=rel =resultset))
    (MATCHLIST (=ob1 front indet) (=ob2 present indet)))
    -> ·
    (($delete-from wm
        (MATCHLIST (=ob1 front indet) (=ob2 present indet)))
    ($delete-from wm (result set (=rel =resultset)))
    ($add-to wm
        ($newadd
        (result set
        (=rel
        (($perform remove__indet
            =ob1
            =resultset
            =ob2))))))
    ($writecr remove__indet performed)
    ($add-to wm ($newadd (FLAG (result-set-modified))))))
0.7283 1.4

(token-18 ((result set (=rel =resultset))
    (MATCHLIST (=ob1 absent unmarked) (=ob2 absent unmarked)))
    ->
    (($delete-from wm
        (MATCHLIST (=ob1 absent unmarked)
            (=ob2 absent unmarked)))
    ($delete-from wm (result set (=rel =resultset)))
    ($add-to wm
        ($newadd
        (result set
        (=rel
        (($perform concat__indet
            =ob1
            =resultset

```
    =ob2))))))
($writecr concat__indet performed)
($add-to wm ($newadd (FLAG (result-set-modified))))))
0.8235 1.8


(token-19 ((result set (=rel =resultset))
    (MATCHLIST (=ob1 present indet) (=ob2 present indet)))
    ->
    (($delete-from wm
        (MATCHLIST (=ob1 present indet)
            (=ob2 present indet)))
    ($delete-from wm (result set (=rel =resultset)))
    ($add-to wm
        ($newadd
        (result set
        (=rel
        (($perform remove__indet
            =ob1
            =resultset
            =ob2))))))
    ($writecr remove__indet performed)
    ($add-to wm ($newadd (FLAG (result-set-modified))))))
0.7334 1.4


(token-20 ((result set (=rel =resultset))
    (MATCHLIST (=ob1 front unmarked) (=ob2 back unmarked)))
    ->
    (($delete-from wm
        (MATCHLIST (=ob1 front unmarked)
            (=ob2 back unmarked)))
    ($delete-from wm (result set (=rel =resultset)))
    ($add-to wm
        ($newadd
        (result set
        (=rel
        (($perform leave__alone
            =ob1
            =resultset
            =ob2))))))
    ($writecr leave__alone performed)
    ($add-to wm ($newadd (FLAG (result-set-modified))))))
0.9019 1.6
```

Note. As new productions are built, names are assigned by the running model. In these appendices a consistent renaming has been applied so that the names always refer to the same production.

APPENDIX C

Sequence of Productions Fired in the Solution of Problem Forms 1, 2, and 3

READY
GET_NEW_INPUT
FINISHED_MATCHING
NEXT_COMMAND
ASK_FOR_PREMISE
INTEGRATE_FIRST_PREMISE
GET_NEW_INPUT
NEXT_COMMAND
ASK_FOR_PREMISE
INTEGRATE_OTHER_PREMISES
ASSERT_MATCH_ELEMENTS
MATCH_OBJ_PRESENT
MATCH_OBJ_ABSENT
MATCH_OBJ_BACK
MATCH_OBJ_UNMARKED
MATCH_OBJ_UNMARKED
FINISHED_MATCHING
TRY_EXISTING_STRATEGIES
STRATEGIES_TRIED
MAP_GOAL_TO_CONCEPT
CALL_STRUCTURE_MAPPER
MATCH_ON_SMRESULT
ASSERT_MATCH_ELEMENTS
MATCH_OBJ_PRESENT
MATCH_OBJ_PRESENT
MATCH_OBJ_FRONT
MATCH_OBJ_UNMARKED
MATCH_OBJ_BACK
MATCH_OBJ_UNMARKED
FINISHED_MATCHING
MATCH_AGAINST_LTM
BUILD_A_NEW_BODY
BUILD_A_PRODUCTION
TRY_EXISTING_STRATEGIES
STRATEGIES_TRIED
token-1
STRATEGY_APPLIED
GET_NEW_INPUT
NEXT_COMMAND
ASK_FOR_PREMISE
INTEGRATE_OTHER_PREMISES
ASSERT_MATCH_ELEMENTS
MATCH_OBJ_PRESENT
MATCH_OBJ_PRESENT
MATCH_OBJ_FRONT

MATCH_OBJ_UNMARKED
MATCH_OBJ_BACK
MATCH_OBJ_UNMARKED
FINISHED_MATCHING
TRY_EXISTING_STRATEGIES
STRATEGIES_TRIED
MAP_GOAL_TO_CONCEPT
CALL_STRUCTURE_MAPPER
MATCH_ON_SMRESULT
ASSERT_MATCH_ELEMENTS
MATCH_OBJ_PRESENT
MATCH_OBJ_PRESENT
MATCH_OBJ_FRONT
MATCH_OBJ_UNMARKED
MATCH_OBJ_BACK
MATCH_OBJ_UNMARKED
FINISHED_MATCHING
MATCH_AGAINST_LTM
BUILD_A_NEW_BODY
BUILD_A_PRODUCTION
TRY_EXISTING_STRATEGIES
STRATEGIES_TRIED
token-2
STRATEGY_APPLIED
GET_NEW_INPUT
NEXT_COMMAND
RESTART_NEW_PROBLEM
FEEDBACK_COMMAND
GET_NEW_INPUT
GET_FEEEDBACK
GIVE_NEG_FEEDBACK
READY
GET_NEW_INPUT
NEXT_COMMAND
ASK_FOR_PREMISE
INTEGRATE_FIRST_PREMISE
GET_NEW_INPUT
NEXT_COMMAND
ASK_FOR_PREMISE
INTEGRATE_OTHER_PREMISES
ASSERT_MATCH_ELEMENTS
MATCH_OBJ_ABSENT
MATCH_OBJ_PRESENT
MATCH_OBJ_UNMARKED
MATCH_OBJ_FRONT

MATCH_OBJ_UNMARKED
FINISHED_MATCHING
TRY_EXISTING_STRATEGIES
STRATEGIES_TRIED
MAP_GOAL_TO_CONCEPT
CALL_STRUCTURE_MAPPER
MATCH_ON_SMRESULT
ASSERT_MATCH_ELEMENTS
MATCH_OBJ_PRESENT
MATCH_OBJ_PRESENT
MATCH_OBJ_FRONT
MATCH_OBJ_UNMARKED
MATCH_OBJ_BACK
MATCH_OBJ_UNMARKED
FINISHED_MATCHING
MATCH_AGAINST_LTM
BUILD_A_NEW_BODY
BUILD_A_PRODUCTION
TRY_EXISTING_STRATEGIES
STRATEGIES_TRIED
token-3
STRATEGY_APPLIED
GET_NEW_INPUT
NEXT_COMMAND
ASK_FOR_PREMISE
INTEGRATE_OTHER_PREMISES
ASSERT_MATCH_ELEMENTS
MATCH_OBJ_PRESENT
MATCH_OBJ_PRESENT
MATCH_OBJ_FRONT
MATCH_OBJ_UNMARKED
MATCH_OBJ_BACK
MATCH_OBJ_UNMARKED
FINISHED_MATCHING
TRY_EXISTING_STRATEGIES
STRATEGIES_TRIED
MAP_GOAL_TO_CONCEPT
CALL_STRUCTURE_MAPPER
MATCH_ON_SMRESULT
ASSERT_MATCH_ELEMENTS
MATCH_OBJ_PRESENT
MATCH_OBJ_PRESENT
MATCH_OBJ_FRONT
MATCH_OBJ_UNMARKED
MATCH_OBJ_BACK
MATCH_OBJ_UNMARKED
FINISHED_MATCHING
MATCH_AGAINST_LTM
BUILD_A_NEW_BODY
BAD_CHOICE
TRY_EXISTING_STRATEGIES
MAP_GOAL_TO_CONCEPT

token-2
STRATEGY_APPLIED
GET_NEW_INPUT
NEXT_COMMAND
RESTART_NEW_PROBLEM
FEEDBACK_COMMAND
GET_NEW_INPUT
GET_FEEDBACK
GIVE_NEG_FEEDBACK
READY
GET_NEW_INPUT
NEXT_COMMAND
ASK_FOR_PREMISE
INTEGRATE_FIRST_PREMISE
GET_NEW_INPUT
NEXT_COMMAND
ASK_FOR_PREMISE
INTEGRATE_OTHER_PREMISES
ASSERT_MATCH_ELEMENTS
MATCH_OBJ_PRESENT
MATCH_OBJ_ABSENT
MATCH_OBJ_FRONT
MATCH_OBJ_UNMARKED
MATCH_OBJ_UNMARKED
FINISHED_MATCHING
TRY_EXISTING_STRATEGIES
STRATEGIES_TRIED
MAP_GOAL_TO_CONCEPT
CALL_STRUCTURE_MAPPER
MATCH_ON_SMRESULT
REMOVE_INDET
ASSERT_MATCH_ELEMENTS
MATCH_OBJ_PRESENT
MATCH_OBJ_PRESENT
MATCH_OBJ_INDET
MATCH_OBJ_FRONT
MATCH_OBJ_UNMARKED
MATCH_OBJ_BACK
FINISHED_MATCHING
MATCH_AGAINST_LTM
BUILD_A_NEW_BODY
BUILD_A_PRODUCTION
TRY_EXISTING_STRATEGIES
STRATEGIES_TRIED
token-12
STRATEGY_APPLIED
GET_NEW_INPUT
NEXT_COMMAND
ASK_FOR_PREMISE
INTEGRATE_OTHER_PREMISES
REMOVE_INDET
ASSERT_MATCH_ELEMENTS

MATCH__OBJ__PRESENT	MATCH__OBJ__UNMARKED
MATCH__OBJ__INDET	MATCH__OBJ__BACK
MATCH__OBJ__PRESENT	MATCH__OBJ__UNMARKED
MATCH__OBJ__INDET	FINISHED__MATCHING
MATCH__OBJ__In-FRONT	MATCH__AGAINST__LTM
MATCH__OBJ__BACK	BUILD__A__NEW__BODY
FINISHED__MATCHING	BUILD__A__PRODUCTION
TRY__EXISTING__STRATEGIES	TRY__EXISTING__STRATEGIES
STRATEGIES__TRIED	STRATEGIES__TRIED
MAP__GOAL__TO__CONCEPT	token-13
CALL__STRUCTURE__MAPPER	STRATEGY__APPLIED
MATCH__ON__SMRESULT	GET__NEW__INPUT
ASSERT__MATCH__ELEMENTS	NEXT__COMMAND
MATCH__OBJ__PRESENT	FINISH
MATCH__OBJ__PRESENT	HALT

ACKNOWLEDGMENT

This work was supported by a grant from the Australian Research Grants Scheme.

REFERENCES

Anderson, J. R. (1983). *The architecture of cognition*. Cambridge, MA: Harvard University Press.

Anderson, J. R. (1987). Skill acquisition: Compilation of weak-method problem solutions. *Psychological Review, 94,* 192–210.

Baddeley, A. D. (1986). *Working memory*. Oxford: Clarendon.

Baddeley, A. D. (1990). *Human memory: Theory and practice.* Needham Heights, MA: Allyn & Bacon.

Bakker, P. E., & Halford, G. S. (1988). *A basic computational theory of structure-mapping in analogy and transitive inference* (Tech. Rep. No. 88-1). Brisbane: University of Queensland, Centre for Human Information Processing and Problem Solving.

Baylor, G. W., & Gascon, J. (1974). An information processing theory of aspects of the development of weight seriation in children. *Cognitive Psychology, 6,* 1–40.

Brainerd, C. J., & Kingma, J. (1984). Do children have to remember to reason: A fuzzy-trace theory of transitivity development. *Developmental Review, 4,* 311–377.

Breslow, L. (1981). Reevaluation of the literature on the development of transitive inferences. *Psychological Bulletin, 89,* 325–351.

Bryant, P. (1989). Commentary on Halford (1989). *Human Development, 32*(6), 369–374.

Bryant, P. E., & Trabasso, T. (1971). Transitive inferences and memory in young children. *Nature, 232,* 456–458.

Bullock, M., & Gelman, R. (1977). Numerical reasoning in young children: The ordering principle. *Child Development, 48,* 427–434.

Case, R. (1985). *Intellectual development: Birth to adulthood.* New York: Academic Press.

Case, R. (1991). *The mind's staircase.* Hillsdale, NJ: Lawrence Erlbaum Associates.

Chapman, M. (1987). Piaget, attentional capacity, and the functional limitations of formal structure. *Advances in Child Development and Behaviour, 20,* 289–334.

Chapman, M. (1990). Cognitive development and the growth of capacity: Issues in neoPia-getian theory. In J. T. Enns, (Ed.), *The development of attention: Research and theory,* (pp. 263-287). Amsterdam: North Holland.

DeLoache, J. S. (1989). Young children's understanding of the correspondence between a scale model and a larger space. *Child Development, 4,* 121-139.

Dolan, C. P., & Smolensky, P. (1988). Implementing a connectionist production system using tensor products. In D. Touretzky, G. Hinton, & T. Sejnowski (Eds.), *Proceedings of the Proceedings of the Connectionist Models Summer School, June 17-26, 1988* (pp. 265-272). San Mateo, CA: Morgan Kaufmann.

Falkenhainer, B., Forbus, K. D., & Gentner, D. (1990). The structure-mapping engine: Algorithm and examples. *Artificial Intelligence, 41,* 1-63.

Foos, P. W., Smith, K. H., Sabol, M. A., & Mynatt, B. T. (1976). Constructive processes in simple linear order problems. *Journal of Experimental Psychology: Human Learning and Memory, 2,* 759-766.

Gelman, R., & Gallistel, C. R. (1978). *The child's understanding of number.* Cambridge, MA: Harvard University Press.

Gentner, D. (1983). Structure-mapping: A theoretical framework for analogy. *Cognitive Science, 7,* 155-170.

Gentner, D., & Toupin, C. (1986). Systematicity and surface similarity in the development of analogy. *Cognitive Science, 10,* 277-300.

Greeno, J. G., & Johnson, W. (1984, August). *Competence for solving and understanding problems.* Paper presented at the XXIII meeting of the International Congress of Psychology, Acapulco, Mexico.

Greeno, J. G., Riley, M. S., & Gelman, R. (1984). Conceptual competence and children's counting. *Cognitive Psychology, 16,* 94-143.

Guttentag, R. E., & Ornstein, P. A. (1990). Attentional capacity and children's memory strategy use. J. T. Enns (Ed.), *The development of attention: Research and theory,* (pp. 305-320). Amsterdam: North-Holland.

Halford, G. S. (1980). A learning set approach to multiple classification: Evidence for a theory of cognitive levels. *International Journal of Behavioral Development, 3,* 409-422.

Halford, G. S. (1982). *The development of thought.* Hillsdale, NJ: Lawrence Erlbaum Associates.

Halford, G. S. (1984). Can young children integrate premises in transitivity and serial order tasks? *Cognitive Psychology, 16,* 65-93.

Halford, G. S. (1987). A structure-mapping approach to cognitive development. *International Journal of Psychology, 22,* 609-642.

Halford, G. S. (1989). Reflections on 25 years of Piagetian cognitive developmental psychol-ogy, 1963-1988. *Human Development, 32,* 325-387.

Halford, G. S. (1990). Is childrens' reasoning logical or analogical? Further comments on Piagetian cognitive developmental psychology. *Human Development, 33,* 356-361.

Halford, G. S. (1992). Analogical reasoning and conceptual complexity in cognitive develop-ment. *Human Development, 35*(4), 193-217.

Halford, G. S. (1993a). *Children's understanding: The development of mental models.* Hillsdale, NJ: Lawrence Erlbaum Associates.

Halford, G. S. (1993b). Competing, or perhaps complementary, approaches to the dynamic-binding problem, with similar capacity limitations. *Behavioral and Brain Sciences, 16*(3), 461-462.

Halford, G. S., & Kelly, M. E. (1984). On the basis of early transitivity judgements. *Journal of Experimental Child Psychology, 38,* 42-63.

Halford, G. S., & Leitch, E. (1989). Processing load constraints: A structure-mapping approach. In M. A. Luszcz & T. Nettelbeck (Eds.), *Psychological development: Perspec-tives across the life-span* (pp. 151-159). Amsterdam: North-Holland.

Halford, G. S., Maybery, M. T., & Bain, J. D. (1986). Capacity limitations in children's reasoning: A dual task approach. *Child Development, 57,* 616–627.

Halford, G. S., Maybery, M. T., Smith, S. B., Bain, J. D., Kelly, M. E., Stewart, J. E. M., & Dickson, J. C. (1992). *Acquisition of reasoning: Children's strategy development in transivity* (Tech. Rep. No. 92–1). Brisbane: Centre for Human Information Processing and Problem-Solving. University of Queensland.

Halford, G. S., & Wilson, W. H. (1980). A category theory approach to cognitive development. *Cognitive Psychology, 12,* 356–411.

Halford, G. S., & Wilson, W. H. (1993). *Processing capacity defined by relational complexity: Implications for comparative, developmental, and cognitive psychology.* Unpublished manuscript, University of Queensland, Brisbane, Australia.

Halford, G. S., Wilson, W. H., Guo, J., Gayler, R., Wiles, J., & Stewart, J. E. M. (1994). Connectionist implications for processing capacity limitations in analogies. In K. J. Holyoak & J. Barnden (Eds.), *Advances in connnectionist and neural computation theory: Vol. 2. Analogical connections.* Norwood, NJ: Ablex.

Holland, J. H., Holyoak, K. J., Nisbett, R. E., & Thagard, P. R. (1986). *Induction: Processes of inference, learning, and discovery.* Cambridge, MA: MIT Press.

Holyoak, K. J., & Koh, K. (1987). Surface and structural similarity in analogical transfer. *Memory and Cognition, 15,* 332–340.

Holyoak, K. J., & Thagard, P. (1989). Analogical mapping by constraint satisfaction. *Cognitive Science, 13*(3), 295–355.

Holyoak, K. J., & Thagard, P. (1994). *Mental leaps.* Cambridge, MA: MIT Press.

Hummel, J. E., Burns, B., & Holyoak, K. J. (1994). Analogical mapping by dynamic binding: Preliminary investigations. In K. J. Holyoak & J. Barnden (Eds.), *Advances in connectionist and neural computation theory, Vol. 2: Analogical connections.* Norwood, NJ: Ablex.

Hummel, J. E., & Holyoak, K. J. (1992). Indirect analogical mapping. In *Proceedings of the 14th Annual Conference of the Cognitive Science Society* (pp. 121–127). Hillsdale, NJ: Lawrence Erlbaum Associates.

Humphreys, M. S., Bain, J. D., & Pike, R. (1989). Different ways to cue a coherent memory system: A theory for episodic, semantic and procedural tasks. *Psychological Review, 96*(2), 208–233.

Kahneman, D. (1973). *Attention and effort.* Englewood Cliffs, NJ: Prentice-Hall.

Kallio, K. D. (1982). Developmental change on a five-term transitive inference. *Journal of Experimental Child Psychology, 33,* 142–164.

Lebiere, C., & Anderson, J. R. (1993). A connectionist implementation of the ACT-R Production System. In *Proceedings of the 15th Annual Conference of the Cognitive Science Society* (pp. 635–640). Hillsdale, NJ: Lawrence Erlbaum Associates.

Levine, M. (1966). Hypothesis behaviour by humans during discrimination learning. *Journal of Experimental Psychology, 71,* 331–338.

Maybery, M. T. (1987). *Information processing models of transitive inference.* Unpublished doctoral dissertation, University of Queensland, Brisbane, Australia.

Maybery, M. T., Bain, J. D., & Halford, G. S. (1986). Information processing demands of transitive inference. *Journal of Experimental Psychology: Learning, Memory and Cognition, 12,* 600–613.

Maybery, M. T., Halford, G. S., Bain, J. D., & Kelly, M. E. (submitted). Children's construction of series. Unpublished manuscript, University of Queensland, Brisbane, Australia.

Ohlsson, S., & Langley, P. (1986). *PRISM tutorial and manual.* Irvine: University of California Press.

Pears, R., & Bryant, P. (1990). Transitive inferences by young children about spatial position. *British Journal of Psychology, 81*(4), 497–510.

Perner, J., & Mansbridge, D. G. (1983). Developmental differences in encoding length series. *Child Development, 54,* 710–719.

Piaget, J. (1950). *The psychology of intelligence* (M. Piercy & D. E. Berlyne, Trans.). London: Routledge & Kegan Paul. (Original work published 1947)

Robin, N., & Holyoak, K. J. (in press). Relational complexity and the functions of prefrontal cortex. In M. S. Gazzanisa (Eds.), *The cognitive neurosciences.* Cambridge, MA: MIT Press.

Rumelhart, D. E., & McClelland, J. L. (1986). *Parallel distributed processing: Explorations in the microstructure of cognition: Vol. 1: Foundations.* Cambridge, MA: MIT Press.

Schneider, W., & Detweiler, M. (1987). A connectionist/control architecture for working memory. *The Psychology of Learning and Motivation, 21,* 53–119.

Siegler, R. S. (1981). Developmental sequences within and between concepts. *Monographs of the Society for Research in Child Development, 46,* 1–84.

Siegler, R. S. (1989). Mechanisms of cognitive development. *Annual Review of Psychology, 40,* 353–379.

Smolensky, P. (1990). Tensor product variable binding and the representation of symbolic structures in connectionist systems. *Artificial Intelligence, 46*(1–2), 159–216.

Sternberg, R. J. (1980a). The development of linear syllogistic reasoning. *Journal of Experimental Child Psychology, 29,* 340–356.

Sternberg, R. J. (1980b). Representation and process in linear syllogistic reasoning. *Journal of Experimental Psychology: General, 109,* 119–159.

Sternberg, R. J. (1981). Reasoning with determinate and indeterminate linear syllogisms. *British Journal of Psychology, 72,* 407–420.

Sternberg, R. J., & Rifkin, B. (1979). The development of analogical reasoning processes. *Journal of Experimental Child Psychology, 27,* 195–232.

Thayer, E. S., & Collyer, C. E. (1978). The development of transitive inference: A review of recent approaches. *Psychological Bulletin, 85,* 1327–1343.

Touretzky, D. S., & Hinton, G. E. (1988). A distributed connectionist production system. *Cognitive Science, 12,* 423–466.

Trabasso, T. (1975). Representation, memory, and reasoning: How do we make transitive inferences? In A. D. Pick (Ed.), *Minnesota symposia on child psychology* (Vol. 9, pp. 135–172). Minneapolis: University of Minnesota Press.

Trabasso, T. (1977). The role of memory as a system in making transitive inferences. In R. V. Kail & J. W. Hagen (Eds.), *Perspectives on the development of memory and cognition* (pp. 333–366). Hillsdale, NJ: Lawrence Erlbaum Associates.

Van Lehn, K., & Brown, J. S. (1980). Planning nets: A representation for formalizing analogies and semantic models of procedural skills. In R. E. Snow, P. A. Federico, & W. E. Montague (Eds.), *Aptitude learning and instruction: Vol. 2. Cognitive process analyses of learning and problem solving* (pp. 95–137). Hillsdale, NJ: Lawrence Erlbaum Associates.

4

A Connectionist Perspective on Knowledge and Development

J. L. McClelland
Carnegie Mellon University

Questions about how our knowledge changes in response to experience lie at the heart of efforts to understand cognitive development. In this chapter, I approach these questions from a connectionist perspective. I contrast a connectionist approach to these questions with traditional symbolic or propositional approaches. I suggest that thinking about the development of knowledge has been heavily influenced by the assumption that knowledge is symbolic, and I argue that a connectionist approach leads to new conceptualizations of the processes through which developing children come to know more and more about the world.

These issues are explored by considering a connectionist simulation model that is applied to the balance scale task studied by Siegler and others. The graded nature of the representations used by the model allows it to account for several aspects of the empirical data, including the Torque Difference Effect (Ferretti & Butterfield, 1986).

The incremental nature of connectionist learning—the fact that current learning builds on what has already been learned—allows the model to account for stagelike developmental progressions and for differences in readiness to learn from particular experiences at different points in development. The chapter also shows how the connectionist framework allows one to capture effects of cue complexity as well as cue familiarity on the course of development. The discussion considers the essential features of the connectionist account of performance and development in the balance scale task, and considers open questions, such as the nature of the initial constraints necessary to lead to successful development, and the relationship between the implicit knowledge that is captured by connectionist models and explicit knowledge such as verbalizable propositions and rules.

WHAT IS KNOWLEDGE?

Let us begin with the fundamental question: What is knowledge, anyway? According to the symbolic approach, knowledge takes two forms: a set of propositions, involving specified relations among specified symbols standing for objects or classes of objects; and a system of rules for using knowledge to make inferences and guide actions. Propositional knowledge can be acquired through encoding experienced events into propositional form and through inferences applied to encoded propositions. Thus, if I know *All men are mortal*, and I learn through experience or direct instruction that *Socrates is a man*, and if I know the appropriate rule of inference, then I can infer that *Socrates is mortal*. Much theoretical work in developmental psychology explicitly or implicitly adopts this symbolic approach without questioning it. Thus Siegler, in his seminal papers on development in the balance scale task, characterized children's knowledge in terms of a set of rules; Spelke, Breinlinger, McComber, and Jacobson (1992) characterized infants' knowledge of intuitive physics in terms of innate principles with which children reason; and Pinker (1991) characterized children's knowledge of morphology in terms of a simple rule system, complemented by a separate associative system used for exceptions.

This chapter explores the view that much of the knowledge that developmental psychologists study may not be propositional. Instead, I suggest the knowledge may be stored in the form of connections: that is, graded parameters embedded in specific processing structures that use them. This conception of the nature of knowledge itself leads to a change in thinking about how knowledge is acquired; not by inference as in the symbolic case, but by gradual parameter adjustment. I do not mean to suggest that no knowledge is symbolic or that no discovery of new knowledge occurs by inference; I only mean to argue that the knowledge that underlies children's performance in many developmental tasks may have this graded, embedded, nonsymbolic character.

To begin our exploration of this connectionist approach, it is useful to start with an overview of the connectionist framework. The framework is now quite familiar (see Rumelhart, McClelland, and the PDP Research Group, 1986, for an introduction), so the overview is brief. On this approach—also sometimes called the parallel-distributed processing (PDP) approach—information processing takes place through the interactions of large numbers of simple, neuronlike processing units, arranged into modules. An active representation—such as the representation one may have of a current perceptual situation, for example, or of an appropriate overt response—is a distributed pattern of activation, over several modules, representing different aspects of the event or experience, perhaps at many levels of description. Processing in such systems occurs through the propagation of activation among the units, through weighted excitatory and inhibitory connections.

As already noted, the knowledge in a connectionist system is stored in the connection weights: it is the connections that determine what representations we form when we perceive the world and what responses these represenations will lead us to execute. Such knowledge has several essential characteristics: (a) it is incohate, implicit, and completely opaque to verbal description; (b) even in its implicit form it is not necessarily accessible to all tasks—rather, it can be used only when the units it connects are actively involved in performing the task; (c) it can arbitrarily approximate symbolic knowledge but it need not—it admits of states that are cumbersome at best to describe by rules; and (d) its acquisition can proceed gradually, through a simple, experience-driven process. At certain times during acquisition, knowledge may be approximately characterizable in terms of one or another system of symbolic rules, but transition between such states of knowledge may be completely seamless, governed by a completely homogeneous learning process.

Let us consider the learning process in more detail, because it is the heart of the process of developmental change in connectionist systems (McClelland, 1989). Various approaches to learning have been taken within the PDP framework, but the one that appears to be most promising for understanding cognitive development is a procedure that learns from the mismatch between expected and observed events. In this approach, we imagine that the cognitive system is continually engaged in making implicit predictions for the immediate future, based on its representation of the current situation (cf. Rescorla & Wagner, 1972). The representation of the current situation is a pattern of activation over a set of internal units, and the prediction is represented as a pattern of activation over a set of output units. These predictions are compared to a pattern that represents what actually happens in the world, and the dicrepancy is used to adjust the weights. The actual rule for connection strength adjustment takes the following form:

Adjust each parameter in proportion to the extent that its adjustment will reduce the discrepancy between predicted and observed events.

This is equivalent to a procedure for adjusting connection weights:

Adjust each connection weight in proportion to the extent that its adjustment will reduce the discrepancy between the output the network produces and the desired output specified by the environment.

This approach to learning in connectionist systems was pioneered by Rosenblatt (1959) and Widrow and Hoff (1960); the generalization, known as *backpropagation*, was developed by Rumelhart, Hinton, and Williams (1986). These procedures perform a search process called *gradient descent:* The process of connection adjustment is seen as a process of search across a surface in a large space, in which the height of the surface represents the error, and in which the surface is defined over a large number of other dimensions, one for each connection weight. Each point in the space represents a possible entire set of connection weights and the corresponding error, and from each point there is one direction that represents the steepest direction downhill in the error measure. This direction is called the *gradient* (it represents the negative of the slope of the error surface at that point), and gradient descent simply amounts to moving down the gradient. It is useful to define the gradient in terms of an entire ensemble of possible events and experiences in the environment. In this case, each particular event gives a random sample of the gradient, rather than a true picture of the entire gradient. If we adjust connection weights based on this sample, the learning procedure is more properly called *stochastic gradient* to indicate that learning is based, not on the exact gradient, but on a random sample of it (see White, in press, for a discussion).

In this chapter I explore the effects of using the stochastic gradient approach to learning in connectionist systems that are exposed to environments that exhibit regularities in the predictions that can be made from representations of certain situations to subsequent outcomes. I show how this approach offers a new way of thinking, not only about the knowledge that underlies performance in cognitive tasks, but also about the process of developmental change. And I demonstrate that the approach has considerable appeal in accounting for a wide range of findings obtained in studies based on the balance scale task used by Siegler (1976, 1981) and others. I show how the connectionist approach is consistent with a considerable body of recent evidence on the graded nature of the knowledge children use in making cognitive judgments in this task. I also show that the connectionist approach can lead us to understand why there are periods of relative stasis in development, punctuated by periods of relatively rapid change. I discuss how the approach can lead us to understand how readiness to profit from particular experience may change gradually as a child performs overtly at the same developmental level over an extended period of time. The choice of the balance scale task allows us to compare the connectionist approach to the symbolic approach taken in work by Siegler (Klahr & Siegler, 1978; Siegler, 1976, 1981; Siegler & Klahr, 1982) and to the algebraic approach taken by Wilkening and Anderson (1991). Some of the connectionist simulation work reviewed here was reported in McClelland (1989) and

McClelland and Jenkins (1991). However, I extend the previous simulations to address the torque difference effect of Ferretti and Butterfield (1986) and to examine factors that influence ease of mastery of the weight and distance cues that must be used to perform correctly in the balance scale task.

THE BALANCE SCALE TASK

The balance scale task was introduced by Inhelder and Piaget (1958) and studied extensively by Siegler (1976, 1981) and many others. In the standard version of the task, which is the main focus here, the child is presented with a balance scale like the one in Fig. 4.1. Some number of weights are placed on one peg on the left of the fulcrum, and some number of weights are placed on one peg on the right. The child's task is to predict which side would go down if the scale were free to move. Typically a series of trials is given with different numbers of weights on different pegs, and there is no feedback; that is, the scale is imobile so that the child does not learn whether the prediction is right or wrong.

Siegler's Rules

Siegler (1976) developed a set of possible rules that children might use in the balance scale task, and a procedure for determining which of the rules the child was using. The rules, taken from Siegler (1976), are presented in Fig. 4.2. A quick summary can be given as follows: Children who use Rule 1 attend to the number of weights on each side, but not the the distance from the fulcrum. Thus, they say the sides balance if the weights are the same on both sides; otherwise, they say the side with the greater weight will go down. Children who use Rule 2 are like children who use Rule 1, except that they take distance into account if the weights are the same on both sides; in this case they say the side where the weights are the furthest from the fulcrum will go down. Children who use Rule 3 appreciate that both weight and distance matter. For these children, if the number of weights is greater on one side and the distance is greater on the other, the child will be uncertain

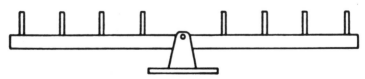

FIG. 4.1. A balance scale of the type used by Siegler (1976, 1981). Reprinted from Figure 1 of Siegler (1976), with permission.

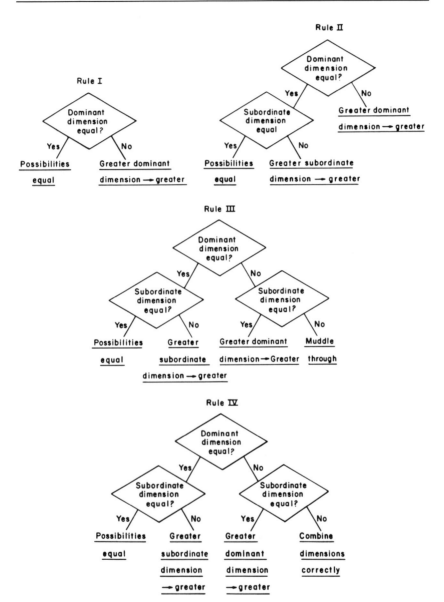

FIG. 4.2.   The four Rules identified by Siegler (1976). Reprinted from Figure 1 of Siegler (1981), with permission.

what to do; operationally, the assumption is that the child simply guesses, distributing the guesses evenly between saying (a) the side with the greater weight goes down, (b) the side with the greater distance goes down, or (c) the sides balance. Children who use Rule 4 appreciate that both cues matter, as well; they differ from children who use Rule 3 in that they understand the physical torque principle that governs which side will go down. This principle implies that the side where the product of weight times distance is greater will go down, and they use this rule in case the cues are in conflict. This allows correct performance in every case.

To assess conformity to these rules, Siegler developed a test consisting of four examples of each of six problem types (Fig. 4.3). In *balance* problems, the weight and the distance were the same on both sides. In *weight* problems, only the weight differed. In *distance* problems, only the distance differed. In the remaining three problem types, both weight and distance differed, and both cues were always in conflict, so that the distance was greater on one side but the weight was greater on the other. For *conflict-weight* problems, the torque was greater on the side with the greater weight; for the *conflict-distance* problems, the torque was greater on the side with the greater distance; and for the *conflict-balance* problems, the torque was the same on both sides. Fig. 4.3 indicates the pattern of responding predicted from each rule for each problem type.

PREDICTIONS FOR PERCENTAGE OF CORRECT ANSWERS AND ERROR PATTERNS
ON POSTTEST FOR CHILDREN USING DIFFERENT RULES

Problem type	Rules				Predicted developmental trend
	I	II	III	IV	
Balance	100	100	100	100	No change-allchildren at high level
Weight	100	100	100	100	No change-all children at high level
Distance	0 (Should say "balance")	100	100	100	Dramatic improvement with age
Conflict-weight	100	100	33 (Chance responding)	100	Decline with age Possible upturn in oldest group
Conflict-distance	0 (Should say "right down")	0 (Should say "right down")	33 (Chance responding)	100	Improvement with age
Conflict-balance	0 (Should say "right down")	0 (Should say "right down")	33 (Chance responding)	100	Improvement with age

FIG. 4.3. Examples of each of the six problem types and patterns of performance that would be predicted by each of the six rules. Reprinted from Table 1 of Siegler (1976), with permission.

Siegler's Findings

Over a series of studies, Siegler (1976, 1981) found that the behavior of about 93% of the subjects aged 5 and up conformed to the predictions of one of the four rules. Scoring was fairly strict, but not absolutely so: 20 out of 24 of the subject's responses had to correspond to a rule before the child was said to conform to it, but this meant that up to 4 responses could be deviant. Fig. 4.4 presents the actual profiles of children who were said to conform to each rule, together with the predicted pattern based on the rule. (Also shown are the predictions of the model to be described later.) There is a fairly close correspondence between the rules and children's behavior, but there are discrepancies that may be at least somewhat systematic; I shall have more to say about these when I consider the predictions of the connectionist model. In one study, children were tested twice to assess the reliability of the rule assessment procedure. In general, consistency was high, although it was not perfect; in particular, children scored as using Rule 2 at the first test showed considerable variability at the subsequent test.

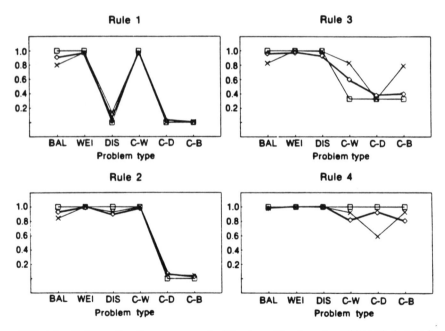

FIG. 4.4.   Patterns of performance on each of the six problem types by children (circles), and the McClelland (1989) balance scale model (Xs) averaged over children or networks satisfying Siegler's (1981) criteria for use of each rule. Also shown is the pattern of performance corresponding to exact adherence to each of Siegler's rules (squares). Reprinted from Figure 2.10 of McClelland (1989), with permission.

Considering developmental trends, there was a strong trend for young children (ages 5–7) to conform to Rule 1 and for children beyond the age of 10 or so to conform to Rule 3 or 4. Rule 2 was used by the fewest children, mostly around the age of 7 to 9 years old. Note that not all young adults use Rule 4; even in groups of college undergraduates, the rate of use of Rule 4 was far from perfect. Also, if the results for so-called Rule 4 subjects shown in Fig. 4.4 indicate that these subjects were not completely consistent in their handling of Rule 4.

To summarize these results, there appears at first glance to be a striking conformity between children's behavior and Siegler's rules, and a clear developmental trend to progress from Rule 1 to Rule 3 and sometimes to Rule 4, with Rule 2 serving as a (possibly optional) transitional rule between Rules 1 and 3. Yet, throughout the data, we see some discrepancies. Not all children score in accordance with any rule (and it seems doubtful that their responses were random). Of those who do score in accordance with a rule, it is clear that frequently not all of their responses match.

Underlying Continuity?

Several other researchers have studied the balance scale task or variants of it and have obtained additional results that suggest that the picture painted by the rule assessment method may not capture all aspects of the relevant knowledge possessed by children. There are two main discoveries. First, the rule that best fits a particular child depends on details of the problems used to assess the rules (Ferretti & Butterfield, 1986; Ferretti, Butterfield, Cahn, & Kerkman, 1986). Second, there are alternative rules or procedures that children might use that could yield data that masquarade as one of Siegler's rules (Wilkening & Anderson, 1982, 1991). Wilkening and Anderson (1991), using a functional measurement approach, and Ferretti et al., using the rule assessment method but with a wider range of problems of each type to permit a more detailed examination, suggested that response patterns that show up on Siegler's test as indicative of the use of any of Rules 1 to 4 sometimes reflect the use of an algebraic rule that incorporates graded influences of weight and distance.

Following their lead, one can construct a decision procedure in which one computes a "psychological torque" T (this need not correspond to true physical torque) for each side of the scale:

$$T_s = \chi \Omega_s + \gamma \Lambda_s + \varsigma \Omega_s \Lambda_s \tag{1}$$

where subscript s indexes the two sides of the scale (l and r), Ω_s and Λ_s are psychological weight and distance variables, and χ γ, and ς are parameters of the child's knowledge. One then chooses a response by computing the difference between T_l and T_r, choosing the side with greater T if the absolute value of the difference is greater than or equal to some criterion C, and choosing *balance* as the response, otherwise. If we make the simplifying assumption that Ω_s is proportional to the actual number of unit weights W_s and Λ_s is proportional to the actual number of units of distance D_s as defined by the experimenter, then the equation can be rewritten:

$$T_s = xW_s + yD_s + zW_sD_s \qquad (2)$$

where x, y, and z are proportional to χ, γ and $\digamma$.

Particular choices of x, y, z, and C now allow us to mimick all of Siegler's rules:

Rule 1.   We get exact equivalence to Rule 1 if $y = z = 0$, $C > 0$, and $x \geq C$. For example, suppose we choose $x = 1$ and $C = 0.5$. Then Equation 2 reduces to:

$$T_s = W_s \qquad (3)$$

So, if the weights are the same on both sides, the child will say balance (the difference is equal to 0, therefore less than C), but if the number of weights differs, the criterion will be exceeded (minimum difference given unit weights is 1, which is greater than C), and the child will say that the side with the greater weight goes down.

Rule 4.   We get equivalence to Rule 4 if $x = y = 0$, $C > 0$, and $z \geq C$. For example, $z = 1$ and $C = 0.5$ produces exact conformity to Rule 4.

Rule 2.   We can produce conformity to Rule 2 under Equation 2 only if we restrict the range of possible differences in distance. Suppose that the maximum difference in distance between the two sides is M. Then we can implement Rule 2 by choosing $z = 0$, $x > My$, and $y > C$. For example, if the maximum difference in distance is 5, we can choose $x = 6$, $y = 1$, and $C = 0.5$. What this amounts to is the assumption that the weight cue is much stronger than the distance cue, and so, if there is any difference in weight it "outweighs" the largest possible difference in distance. Of course, if children who match Rule 2 were really using Equation 2 with these parameters, then there would be some difference-of-distances that would lead them to choose the side with greater distance, even if there is a slight asymmetry of weight.

Rule 3. Note that Rule 3 as defined by Siegler is meant to encompass any strategy in which both weight and distance influence performance but a strict computation of torque is not used. Given the particular problems used by Siegler (1981), kindly provided to me by Siegler (personal communication, October, 1993), it turns out that the simple rule of choosing the side with the greater sum of weight and distance ($x = y = 1$, $z = 0$, $C = 0.5$) results in a pattern of 2 errors out of the 4 conflict problems of each type. This pattern is categorized as an example of the Rule 3 pattern. Likewise, many other additive or mixed additive and multiplicative compensatory strategies will produce Rule 3 behavior.

Matters become even more complex when we consider the fact that there are broad ranges of the space of possible values of the parameters x, y, z, and C that would produce approximate adherence to one or another of Siegler's rules for a particular set of problems. Points in the parameter space that are outside the regions that allow pure rule emulation often allow an adequate approximation to the rule to be categorized under it, given the leniency of the scoring procedure and the restricted range of examples used in particular cases.

The Torque Difference Effect

The algebraic model's use of graded parameters allows it to address the torque difference findings of Ferretti and Butterfield (1986). These investigators constructed sets of problems of the same six types as those used by Siegler, but they explicitly varied the magnitude of the difference in torque between the two sides of the balance scale. There were four levels, where level 1 corresponded to the most minimal torque difference possible between the two sides of the scale, and level 4 corresponded to the largest difference possible within the confines of the problem space (one to six weights on one peg on each side of a fulcrum, with pegs located from one to six distance units from the fulcrum). Each subject was tested with four weight, distance, conflict–weight, and conflict–distance problems at each level of torque difference, as well as a common set of balance and conflict–balance problems (for these two types of problems, torque difference is fixed at 0). This allowed them to examine both the effect of the torque difference variable on children's performance on problems of particular types, and to score children's adherence to each of Siegler's rules separately for each level of torque difference. There were two principal findings. First, the probability of responding correctly was strongly influenced by torque difference, particularly for distance and conflict–distance problems. In both cases, the probability of correct responding increased substantially as torque difference increased. There were slight effects on probability of correct responses for weight and conflict–weight problems, but performance on problems of these types was quite good (85% correct) even at the lowest level of torque difference, and there was a more limited range available for improvement.

The second finding was that apparent adherence to Siegler's rules differed at different levels of torque difference. The data are shown in Table 4.1. As torque difference increased, the percentage of children classified as using Rule 1 decreased, and the percentage classified as Rule 4 increased. The percentage of children classified as using Rule 2 increased and then decreased, and there was a similar, but weaker trend for Rule 3.

These results must be interpreted cautiously, because at the larger torque differences used in this study, a variety of different strategies would allow correct responding on conflict–weight and conflict–difference problems. This means, for example, that the subject may be able to get all of the large torque-difference problems correct without actually multiplying weight times distance and comparing torques, as Seigler's Rule 4 requires (in Siegler, 1976, 1981, care was taken in constructing the conflict problems to prevent apparent success for children using some possible nonmultiplicative strategies). Other aspects of the data are not susceptible to this particular problem, however. If a child were really using Rule 1 or Rule 2 as stated by Siegler, that child's classification would not be affected by torque difference, and yet there were substantial effects of that variable on the probability that children were classified as using either of these two rules.

The torque difference effect is consistent with the idea that the underlying procedures used by children may make use of graded information, in accordance with the algebraic model previously given. The algebraic model, however, has some limitations. It can describe a child's developmental state in terms of the values of a few parameters, but it provides no mechanism for change. What is needed is a model that not only captures the developmental state of a child, but at the same time allows us to account for the process of change of state. We now consider one important and interesting aspect of this process: differential readiness to profit from experience at different points in development.

TABLE 4.1
Percentage of Rule Classifications at Different Torque-Difference (TD) Levels
(Ferretti & Butterfield, 1986)

TD Level	1	2	3	4
1	.29	.19	.17	.05
2	.24	.34	.14	.08
3	.22	.31	.22	.10
4	.19	.15	.15	.37

Readiness

Differential readiness was exhibited in Siegler's work on the balance scale in a series of studies contrasting 5- and 8-year-olds who both scored as Rule 1 users (Siegler, 1976).

In the study of greatest interest here, groups of 5- and 8-year-old Rule 1 users were given a series of 16 conflict problems, with feedback. The children were shown the problem, with the two sides of the scale immobilized. They were then asked to predict which side would go down, and after their prediction the scale was freed so that they could see the actual outcome. The results were quite different for the two groups: Most of the 8-year-olds advanced from use of Rule 1 to a more sophisticated rule (Rule 2 or 3). However, none of the 5-year-olds advanced; half continued to perform at the Rule 1 level, and the other half became unclassifiable, failing to conform to any of the rules (Table 4.2).

Follow up experiments by Siegler (1976) suggested a difference between 5- and 8-year-old children that could account for the difference between the two groups. He asked 5- and 8-year-old children to reproduce balance scale configurations provided by an experimenter. Although 8-year-olds reproduced weight and distance from the fulcrum equally well, 5-year-olds failed to reproduce the distance cue. Through several studies, Siegler established that 5-year-olds cannot encode distance when explicitly instructed to do so; for them to encode distance reliably, they must be given explicit instruction in how to encode it. This strongly suggests that one of the developmental differences between 5- and 8-year-olds is that the 5-year-olds lack not just the inclination, but the ability to encode distance from the fulcrum.

Within the context of the symbolic rule approach, Siegler's results suggest that 8-year-olds do spontaneously encode distance; but those 8-year-olds

TABLE 4.2
Conformity to Siegler's Rules by 5- and 8-year-old Subjects Initially Conforming to Rule 1
After Exposure to Conflict Problems

Age	*1. Children not given explicit training in encoding distance*			
	1	*2*	*3*	*Unclass.*
5	5	0	0	5
8	0	2	5	3

Age	*2. Children who were given pretraining in encoding distance*			
	1	*2*	*3*	*Unclass.*
5	1	3	4	2
8	0	3	7	0

Note. All subjects were scored as conforming to Siegler's Rule I before training.

who adopt Rule 1 in the balance scale task do not spontaneously use this cue in making judgments. However, they can be induced to use it if given feedback indicating that predictions made simply from the weight cue are incorrect. A further study demonstrated that if 5-year-olds are explicitly instructed in how to encode distance, they can do so. Furthermore, the training was sufficient to allow these children to then profit from exposure to a series of conflict problems.

These results suggest that the tendency to spontaneously encode the distance cue accounts for the difference between early (5-year-old) and late (8-year-old) Rule 1 children. But a question arises: Why, if 8-year-olds are spontaneously encoding this cue, do so many of them not spontaneously use it?

Analogous questions can be posed for the weight cue. In another paper, Siegler and Klahr (1982) established that a difference in the tendency to encode the weight cue accounts for a corresponding difference between 3- and 4-year-old children who are able to profit from feedback to make the transition from random responding to Rule 1. Yet, the same 4-year-olds who spontaneously encode weight, do not spontaneously use weight as the basis for their predictions.

To summarize, the readiness studies raise two questions:

1. Why do children of one age spontaneously encode a cue that children at a younger age do not encode? Eight-year-olds spontaneously encode weight and distance; 4- and 5-year-olds spontaneously encode weight but not distance; and 3-year-olds spontaneously encode neither.

2. Why do some children who spontaneously encode a cue fail to use it, whereas others who are just a little older both use and encode the cue?

To my knowledge, no fully adequate answer to these questions was given within the context of a system of rules. Klahr and Siegler (1978) discussed the use of production system models to capture these rules, and they stated that these models can provide adequate descriptions of the state of knoweldge, if they are supplemented by further assumptions about different *encoding operators*. Thus, the difference between the 3-year-old and the 4-year-old is the encode weight operator; the difference between the 4- and 5-year-old is the availability of productions that implement Rule 1; the difference between the 5-year-old and the Rule 1 8-year-old is the encode distance operator; and so on. But little was said in any of these papers about what leads to these differences. The rule approach describes the different states of knowledge, but does little to explain the transitions between these different states.

Siegler (1983) recognized these limitations, and called for increased emphasis on mechanisms of transition. In several recent writings (Siegler, in preparation; Siegler & Munakata, 1993), he suggested that one source of transitions may be change in the probability with which children use different *strategies* (rules and operators, in the earlier terminology of Siegler, 1976, and Klahr & Siegler, 1978). But little was said in what has been written to date about where wholly new rules and operators come from, and it is unattractive to assume that all of developmental change can be adequately understood as a change in probability of selection of pre-existing elements, even if we allow that some of the work will need to be done by combinations of elements, as Siegler and Munakata (1993) suggested.

A CONNECTIONIST APPROACH

The connectionist approach, sketched at the beginning of this chapter, provides a different view of the developmental process. The key difference is that the knowledge underlying performance is not represented in terms of the presence or absence of particular rules, operators, or productions, but in terms of graded connection strengths that may be approximately describable in terms of such symbolic constructs. The approximate descriptions may be useful for providing characterizations of performance (for example, Siegler's Rule 1 is accurate in describing the balance scale performance of many 5–8-year-olds), but do not give insight into the fuzzy edges of performance demonstrated by the torque difference effect or to the developmental progression that underlies the transition from performance characterizable by one rule to performance characterizable by another. Here I show how the connectionist system accounts for much of the same data and provides a way of understanding both the fuzzy edges that we see in many cases and the apparent transitions between discrete states.

Before describing the connectionist system, I stress that there are some findings in the balance scale domain that suggest that the connectionist models do not provide the full story. One example arises in the case of subjects who meet Siegler's criteria for Rule 4, when stringently tested with problem sets like the ones used by Siegler (1976, 1981) that cannot be passed using other compensatory strategies. Data from Wilkening and Anderson (1991), using the functional measurement approach, indicate that most adult subjects use a combination rule that is more additive than multiplicative when adjusting weight or distance on one side of a scale to balance a weight–distance configuration on the other. Assuming (as I do) that this task taps subjects implicit rules rather than explicit strategies, the Wilkening and Anderson data suggest that subjects would not adhere to Rule 4 unless they were actually explicitly multiplying. It is clear from several aspects of

Siegler's data that many of the subjects in his experiments who conform to the Rule 4 pattern actually multiply weight times distance to compute a torque for each side, and then decide which side will go down by comparing the numerical values of these torques through explicit, verbally reportable, arithmetic operations. Among the relevant evidence is the fact that college students and 8th graders can be taught to follow this procedure. Even though few such students spontaneously conform to Rule 4, they can come to do so if given an explicit record of the problems or hints to formulate an explicit rule that considers the number of weights on each side, and their distances from the fulcrum (Siegler & Klahr, 1982). This is not to say that successful navigation of many sets of conflict problems requires explicit use of Rule 4; some sets of such problems can be solved by additive or mixed combinations of weight and distance of the kind I believe characterize intuitive judgments. My claim is that subjects' implicit judgments do not closely mimic a strict multiplicative integration rule, and in cases where great care has been taken to make it difficult to succeed using anything other than strict multiplication of weight times distance, few subjects succeed unless they do use explicit multiplication. People can and do use explicit strategies in some tasks and under some circumstances, and the balance scale task is one that appears to elicit explicit strategies under some conditions.

The main interest of this chapter is in the earlier stages of development that lead up to the Rule 3 stage, where the subject takes both weight and distance into account, but does not know explicitly how to combine them to perform at the Rule 4 level. I claim that performance up to this stage (which characterizes most adults, unless specific emphasis and coaching is given, leading to discovering and articulating the rule) can be based on implicit, graded (connectionist) knowledge, and progress through the stages is based on implicit, incremental learning. There is a role for (conscious, explicit) symbolic rules. In the discussion at the end of this chapter, I examine the role such rules might play and consider how they might interact with connectionist forms of knowledge representation.

The Connectionist Model of McClelland (1989)

The connectionist model is based on the learning principle previously stated: The model is trained on examples of balance scale problems. First, the problem is presented (some number of weights on each side of the scale, placed some distance from the fulcrum on each side). The model must try to predict which side will go down. After the prediction, the network is given feedback in the form of the correct outcome for the problem. Then, the weights are adjusted in accordance with the principle previously stated: Adjust each weight in proportion to the extent that its adjustment will reduce the discrepancy between the model's output (the prediction) and the observed output (the correct response).

To turn this abstract principle into an explicit model, we must make several additional stipulations. First, we must specify a format for representing the problem, both for the input and the outcome. Second, we must specify a network architecture in terms of units and their activation function. Third, we must specify a training regime. The bulk of the work reported here is based on the approach I used in earlier simulations (McClelland, 1989), but in a later section of the chapter, I consider an alternative approach.

In my 1989 work, following up on an earlier model by Jenkins (1989), I chose a way of representing the information needed to solve the problem that was, on the one hand sufficient to distinguish the different possible problem configurations but that, on the other hand, left the network with a substantial task to solve in determining how to interpret the weight and distance information (Fig. 4.5). To allow the network to handle problems involving one to five wieghts on pegs spaced one to five steps from the fulcrum on either side, I provided a total of 20 input units, one to represent

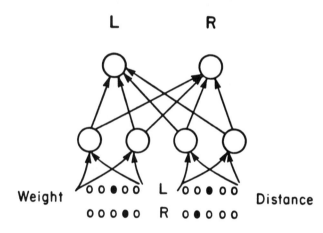

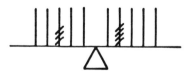

FIG. 4.5. Connectionist network used in the McClelland (1989) balance scale model. Reprinted from Figure 2.7 of McClelland (1989), with permission.

each of the distinct numbers of weights (1-5) on each side, and one to represent each of the distinct distances from the fulcrum of each side. In the figure, the units are arranged into four groups of five, with the two groups on the left representing weight, and the two groups on the right representing distance. With this input representation, a problem can be presented by turning on just the four input units representing the number of weights on each side and their distances from the fulcrum. Note, though, that the input representation only treats the different numbers of weights and the different distances as cardinal numbers; although the units are arranged in increasing order for our convenience, the network has no access to this arrangement, and as far as it is concerned they could be arranged in any other way. At the output level, there were two units. The outcome *left side down* is represented by an activation of 1 on the left unit and 0 on the right; *right side down* is represented by 0 on the left and 1 on the right; and balance is represented by an activation of .5 on both output units. This choice does constrain the network to treat balance as intermediate between the two other alternatives, and injects prior knoweldge of the semantics of the domain into the network.

The network architecture had two other important features: First, it introduced a layer of hidden unit between input and output; and second, it organized these into separate modules, one for encoding the weight information and one for encoding distance. The two-layer structure of the network was imposed to capture the idea that the child must do two things with the information about each dimension: encode that information, and then use the information to predict which side will go down. To be sure, the weight and distance information are encoded in the input to the model. But we can treat this input as corresponding as far as the model is concerned to something akin to the percept in children. Surely, even the youngest children in any of the studies we are considering see—in some sense encode—both the magnitude of the weight (or at least the height of the stack of weights) and its location within the balance scale. We could demonstate this by asking them to point to the top of the stack of weights on each side of the scale. The input representation is intended to capture this level of encoding. But Siegler's (1976, 1981) studies suggest that children differ in the extent to which they encode the relevant dimensions in a form that makes them suitable for predicting the outcome of the balance scale or even for reproducing this information in a copy of a presented balance scale configuration. The intermediate layer of units in the model provides a level that will correspond to this recoding of the perceptual information. The modular organization was imposed to constrain the kinds of solutions the model can find, but as I discuss later, work by Schmidt and Shultz (1991) suggests that imposing this constraint is not crucial.

So far, I have not provided the model with any basis for earlier mastery of the use of weight as a cue as opposed to distance. A definitive treatment of this issue will require a fuller psychological investigation. It is not immediately clear why the weight cue is noticed and used at an earlier age than the distance cue. One possibility is that children have more relevant experiences with variations in weight than they have with variations in distance. It is a widely accepted principle of language acquisition that children learn to use first those cues that are most available as predictors of the correct interpretation (Bates & MacWhinney, 1987). It is likely that the same principle holds in other domains, as well, and the earlier mastery of weight as opposed to distance may be a case in point. One possible relevant source of experience is see-saws, because see-saws are generally set up with a seat equidistant from the fulcrum on either side. Thus, every child will have had experience with the effects of weight differences, but they may have had considerably less experience with effects of differences in distance from the fulcrum. In accordance with this possiblity, the training regime used in the McClelland (1989) simulations involved presenting the network with training cases that contained many more instances of problems where weight varied but distance stayed the same than of any other type. The exact training regimen consisted of creating a corpus of examples consisting of all possible combinations of one of five weights with one of five distances on the left and the right. This yielded 625 distinct problems. The list was augmented with additional copies of each problem involving weights placed the same distance from the fulcrum on both sides. In two runs, there were five copies of each problem of this type; in two other runs there were ten.

In each run, the network was initialized with small, random connection weights. A series of training epochs was then constructed. In each epoch, 100 patterns were chosen at random from the corpus just described. After the presentation of each pattern, the correct answer was presented, and the weights were adjusted a small amount according to the gradient descent learning rule (see McClelland, 1989, for further details). At the end of each epoch, the network was tested on a set of 24 problems modeled after the 24-problem test set used in Siegler (1981), including 4 problems of each type. On each problem, the activation of the two outputs units was compared. If they were within .33 of each other, then response was taken to be balance; otherwise, the network was taken to have predicted that the side corresponding to the unit with the greater activation should go down. This thresholding corresponds to an assumption that the discrete responses in Siegler's task actually reflected an underlying continuity in the internal psychological states.

Basic Simulation Results

The simulation results were presented in McClelland (1989), so I give a brief summary of the main points so that we can focus on some details not emphasized in that paper, and on new simulations. First, the model's performance corresponded to one of Seigler's rules about 85% of the time, not counting an initial phase of about 10 epochs. This 85% conformity figure is less than is typically found in subjects, though not by much. Second, the model exhibits good fidelity to the developmental trends seen in human subjects: All four runs of the model showed a plausible developmental progression, starting with no rule at all, and progressing through relatively stable performance on Rule 1 to Rule 2, to a period of vacillation between fitting the criteria for Rule 3 and Rule 4. Thus, the model captures the expected developmental progression of children, at least at a coarse grain of analysis.

An examination of the connection weights in the model provides some

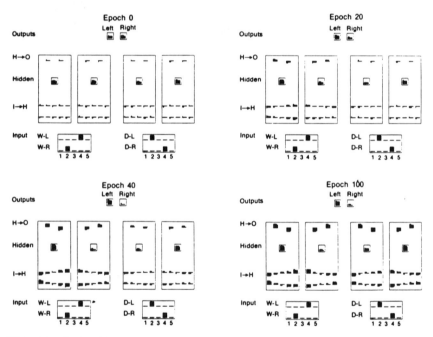

FIG. 4.6.   Connection strengths in the McClelland (1989) balance scale network after different amounts of training, and activations produced by an input consisting of four weights two pegs from the fulcrum on the left and two weights four pegs from the fulcrum on the right. The inputs are shown in the lower part of each of the four panels of the figure. The four large rectangles in each panel display the input and output connections and the activations of each of the four hidden units; activations of the two output units are shown at the top. Activations range from 0 (a horizontal line with nothing over it) to 1.0 (a horizontal line with a solid square block over it), with intermediate values represented by partial blocks. Connection weights range from about −6 to about +6; the sign of each weight is indicated by placing the block above or below the horizontal line, and the magnitude is represented by the size of the block. Reprinted from Figure 2.11 of McClelland (1989), with permission.

insight into how it has learned to perform the balance scale task. Figure 4.6 shows the weights in the network from one run, tested before the beginning of training and then after 20, 40, and 100 epochs. For this run, these points correspond to the beginning of the Rule 1 phase; the end of this phase as the model is about to progress to Rule 2; and the end of the training regime, where it is vaccillating between conformity to Rules 3 and 4.

Initially, the model knows nothing about the task. The connection strengths are small and random and the activations of both output units are near .5 for all inputs. (In this part of the chapter, I use the word *strength* to refer to the magnitude of connections; the word *weight* is reserved for use in reference to the weight variable in the balance scale problems.) Gradually, over the course of training, the connection strengths become organized. We will consider the time course in more detail later. For now, we note that by 20 epochs, this organization has begun for the connections that process the weight cue; but at this point, the network has not reached the point where there is any discernable organization in the connections that process distance. This difference is due to the fact that the network receives considerably more experience with cases in which weight varies as a cue than with cases in which distance varies.

Let us examine the way in which the network has leared to encode the weight dimension. The two representational units have organized themselves so that the activation of one ranges from 0 to 1, as the disparity in number of weights between the two sides (number of weights on the left minus number of weights on the right) varies from − 4 to + 4; the other unit varies from 0 to 1 as the weight disparity varies from + 4 to − 4. This happens as a result of the connection strengths that the network has learned from the input to the hidden units. These place the different numbers of weights on a continuum, with 1 weight and 5 weights having relatively extreme influences (excitatory or inhibitory), and 3 weights having nearly no influence. In the case of the input given in the figure (weight disparity of 2) the first unit takes an activation of about .7, and the second of about .3. In short, the connections from the input units to the hidden units encode the disparity of weight between the two sides of the scale. The connections from these units to the response units then implement the rule: *The side with the greater weight goes down.* The hidden unit whose activation increases as the weight disparity varies from − 4 to + 4 tends to excite the left output unit and inhibit the right output unit, whereas the other hidden unit has opposite influences. Thus, when the disparity is 0, the influences on the output units are in balance, but when the disparity favors one side or the other, this is reflected in a disparity in the activation of the output units. At this point, the network has just reached the point where its behavior corresponds to Rule 1.

Considering the connection strengths at 40 epochs, we see that the pattern in the connections encoding the number of weights has become stronger, and a similar pattern has begun to emerge in the connections that encode distance. At this point, this latter pattern is still too weak (and the connection strengths from the hidden units for distance to the output units are still to weak) for the distance information to affect the choice of responses, except in cases of extreme distance disparity and little or no disparity in weight. However, the connections encoding distance and the connections that use this encoding to influence the predicted outcome have built up to the point where slight further increases will now produce sufficient disparities in the activation at the output level to allow the distance cue to influence responses when the weight is the same on both sides. Yet the connections in the distance pathway are too weak to counteract even small disparities in weight. Consequently, the network's behavior will conform to Rule 2 after these slight further increases. Disparity in distance influences the behavior of the network only when there is no disparity in weight.

Considering the connection weights at 100 epochs, we see that they are equally strong on both sides of the network. This may seem surprising, because the network experiences far more cases where the weights differ but the distances are the same, than cases in which the distances are the same throughout training. The reason things level off eventually is that they reach a point where further increases in connection strength on the weight dimension do not lead to further improvements in performance. At this point, the network's output does not match the exact target values, but the slight changes to the connection strengths that occur as a result of these discrepancies cancel out, because they help with some patterns, but not with others. Meanwhile, there is continuing improvement in encoding and use of information about the distance cue. At this point in training, there is still a slight advantage for the weight dimension relative to the distance dimension, which is why the output shown in the figure shows a slight difference favoring the side where there are more weights. The exact outcome depends on the exact input configuration. The network tends to prefer the side with more weight to the side where the weights are a greater distance from the fulcrum, but there can still be cases in which this slight preference is reversed or neutralized, so the network's behavior over a set of problems is somewhat unsystematic, and therefore appears to conform to Siegler's Rule 3.

Sources of Variability in the Network's Behavior

The network can, if trained very gradually, find a set of connection weights that will allow it to perfectly simulate Rule 4 for the range of values of weight and distance used in these simulations. This behavior is fragile, however, and depends on exact values of connection strengths that are difficult to maintain. The variability introduced by the random sequence to training trails tends to disrupt Rule 4-like performance. In other studies (McClelland, 1991, 1993), I argued that human information processing is intrinsically variable or noisy. Although the present model is deterministic in the sense that the output it generates is a deterministic function of the input and the connection strengths, there is one source of variability from epoch to epoch, namely the random sample of training examples. This, together with use of a learning rate constant large enough so that the random sample of training cases in each epoch exerts a marked enough effect on the connections, introduces fluctuations in the connection strengths from epoch to epoch that produce some inconsistency. This inconsistancy affects different problems of the same type as well as performance on the same problem when the network is tested after different epochs. Although a fully realistic model would, I believe, incorporate processing variability (McClelland, 1993), the variability introduced by the random sequence of training trials has similar effects. Note that the variablity actually affects the activations of the units in the network for all problems, but only affects the actual overt choice of response on some problems. The activations have more of a margin for error in some cases, so they are robust against the amount of variability that arises from the training regime used in this model. The presence of this variability does prevent the model from strictly capturing Rule 4, but this is as it should be, given the evidence previously discussed that exact adherence to Rule 4 depends on use of an explicit multiplicition of numerical quantities.

Discrepancies Between the Connectionist Model and Use of Siegler's Rules

Thus far, we have seen how the model can be used to produce behavior that conforms to Rules 1, 2, and 3, and can occasionally approximately conform to Rule 4, depending on the pattern of connection strengths. If we look at a finer grain, we see that the model does not conform exactly to the pattern of responses predicted by any of the rules. In fact, the model and human subjects deviate from the rules in similar ways, as can be seen by comparing the pattern of performance exhibited by the children and the model to the patterns predicted by Siegler's Rules, in Fig. 4.4. For example, we see in the first panel of this figure that when the model conforms to Rule 1 by Siegler's criteria, it nevertheless occasionally fails on balance problems and occasionally succeeds on distance problems; a similar pattern occurs with human subjects. Similarly, with Rule 2, the model and subjects both tend to make errors on balance and distance problems, and occasionally to get conflict-distance problems correct. With Rule 3, both the model and human subjects make more correct responses on conflict-weight problems than on other types of conflict problems. Finally, with Rule 4, both the model and human subjects err on the conflict problems, not on problems of other types.

There is one place where the model's behavior deviates from the rules in a way that children's behavior does not. This occurs on conflict-balance problems when overall performance conforms to Rule 3. There is a tendency in the same direction under Rule 4, and in a recent replication with a refined version of the 24-item rule-assessment test, a similar deviation occurs under Rule 2. The discrepancy is due to the fact that human subjects tend not to use the balance response unless the scale is symmetrical (same number of weights, same distance from fulcrum, as in the case of balance problems). When it is asymmetrical, as in all types of conflict problems, they appear to adopt a relatively stringent criterion for the balance response. The model does not have the perceptual capacity to detect symmetry, so it cannot apply a different criterion to the two different kinds of cases. I leave it to further research to explore incorporating some form of symmetry detection capability into the model.

For the cases where the model and the children differ from Siegler's rules in similar ways, we might ask what causes these differences. In the case of the model, they arise from two sources. First, the variablity previously discussed introduces some errors; as already stated, these tend to come at places where correct performance depends on exact numerical values of connection strengths. In addition, some discrepancies also arise from the continuous nature of the model's representations. This means, for example, that large discrepancies tend to produce bigger activation differences than smaller ones, as in algebraic models such as the one described by Equations 1 and 2. Because of the graded connection weights, the connection strengths in one of the pathways can be strong enough to make a difference in extreme cases, but not strong enough to do so in subtler cases. So, for example, just before the model makes the transition to full conformity to Rule 2, it performs correctly on extreme disparities in distance but not on small disparities. Similarly, near the end of training, the model can get some conflict-distance problems right if the disparity on distance is much greater than the (conflicting) disparity in weight; and it can get some conflict-weight problems wrong (giving occasionally the balance response) when the disparity in weight only slightly outweighs the disparity in distance. This occasionally leads to cases where the model approximately corresponds to Rule 4, even though it is not in strict correspondence on every problem.

Overlay of Explicit Rules?

The fact that children deviate from Siegler's rules in most of the same places as the model provides further support for the idea that for children there is an underlying continuous representation that varies in strength and is best thought of as approximately captured by Siegler's rules. However, although the discrepancies from the rules tend to occur in the same places in the model as in children, the model deviates more strongly from the rules than children do in almost every case. Indeed, quite often the children fall close to the midpoint between the model's performance and the performance predicted by Siegler's rules. The question arises, then, why it is that the children's behavior comes closer to Siegler's rules than the model's does. One answer may lie in the possibility that children do sometimes use such rules. Perhaps the patterns we see with children reflect a mixture of cases of explicit use of rules combined with other cases in which an implicit, activation-based strategy is used.

Children's tendency to use explicit rules may vary with details of the experimental situation. Some aspects of Siegler's methods may have influenced some children's tendency to use explicit rules in his experiments. In Siegler (1976), some subgroups of subjects in Experiment 1 were explicitly instructed to try to discover the rule that governs the behavior of the balance scale. In Siegler (1981), all subjects were run on three different problems with the same formal structure as the balance scale task, and after each task, each subject was asked to describe how he or she solved the problems on which he or she had just been tested. Because order of tasks was counterbalanced, two thirds of the subjects in the balance scale task would have the expectation that they would be asked to explain the basis of their categorization performance. The need to produce an explicit verbal statement of the procedure they used may have influenced subjects to formulate and use such rules in both of these experiments. Interestingly, the likelihood that a subject's behavior would conform to one of Siegler's rules was higher in his experiments than in experiments by Ferretti et al. (1985) or Ferretti and Butterfield (1986), in which subjects were tested in groups, used paper and pencil to indicate their response, and were not asked to describe how they solved the problems.

Even in cases where there is no explicit expectation that they will have to explain their behavior, subjects may sometimes formulate explicit rules; Karmiloff-Smith (1986) argued that childen may have a natural tendency to try to find a rational basis for their responding in the form of an explicit rule that seems at least approximately right in that it comforms to their implicit response tendencies. Indeed, they may then use the Rule, as opposed to the implicit response tendency, to actually determine their responses. The fact remains, however, that there are discrepancies between subject's responses and the explanations they give of their own behavior. That these discrepancies often accord with the connectionist model's predictions for where such deviations should occur, supports the view that the rules by themselves do not tell the whole story.

Torque Difference Effects

As previously noted, the torque-difference effect of Ferretti and Butterfield (1986) is another phenomenon that strains the notion that children's balance scale responses can be fully understood in terms of the consistent use of a simple explicit rule like Siegler's Rules 1–4. Connectionist models and others that use graded activations and connection weights provide a natural framework for capturing these phenomena. Indeed, Schmidt and Shultz (1991; Shultz, Mareschal, & Schmidt, in press) have shown that both the McClelland (1989) model and their own connectionist model predict torque difference effects. In this section, I explore whether this sensitivity, at least as exhibited in the McClelland (1989) model, permits a good fit to the Ferretti and Butterfield data.

I consider both the influence of torque difference on probability correct responses to different problem types, and the effects of torque difference on the apparent use of Rules 1–4. To do this, I constructed a new test set for the 1989 balance scale model following as closely as possible the procedure Ferretti and Butterfield used to construct their test. Slight differences arose because Ferretti and Butterfield used a scale with six pegs on each side and up to six weights on a peg, but the McClelland (1989) model used only five pegs on a side and up to five weights on a peg. Thus, for simple weight and distance problems, Ferretti and Butterfield used product differences of 1, 3, 12 and 24–30 for the four different levels; I was able to match the first three values but had to use a smaller range, 16–20, for the fourth level. For conflict–weight and conflict–distance problems, Ferretti and Butterfield used differences of 1, 3, 5, and 18–24 units; again, I was able to match the first three values, but had to use a smaller range, 11–15, for the fourth level. The simulation was run just as in McClelland (1989), with the only differences being: (a) the new Ferretti and Butterfield test was given along with a test based on the one used by Siegler (1976) at the end of every epoch, (b) results were based on eight simulation runs of 70 epochs, rather than the four runs of 100 epochs used in McClelland (1989). The simulation was cut off at 70 epochs because of the young age range of Ferretti and Butterfield's subjects (5–11, compared with 5–20 in Siegler, 1981). Because Ferretti and Butterfield's youngest subjects were first graders who performed at the Rule 1 level in Siegler's test, the results presented were taken only from epochs after the network reached the Rule 1 level—this meant that the earliest 10 to 15 epochs of each run were discarded.

The new simulation captures many aspects of the Ferretti and Butterfield (1986) findings on the effects of torque difference. Consider first, the accuracy data as a function of torque difference (Fig. 4.7). As in the Ferretti and Butterfield study, performance on simple weight problems is highly accurate at all levels of torque difference, and so is relatively unaffected

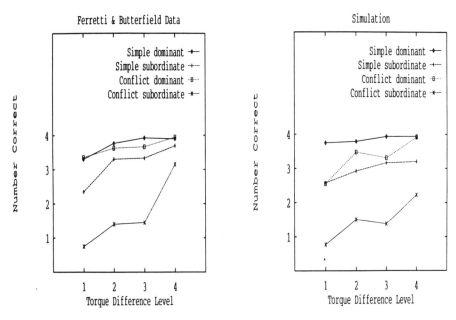

FIG. 4.7.   Average number of responses correct on problems of each of four different types, as a function of level of torque difference. Left panel, human subject data redrawn from Ferretti and Butterfield (1986). Right panel, new simulation results based on the McClelland (1989) balance scale network.

by variations in torque difference, but performance on simple distance and conflict-distance problems improves across levels of product difference. The simulation shows a wider variation on conflict–weight problems over torque difference than is seen in the children's data. Also, the simulation shows less improvement than the children on simple distance and conflict--distance problems at the highest torque difference level. This may be due to the fact that the largest torque differences are less extreme in the simulation than in the actual experiment.

Considering the rule classifications shown in Table 4.3, again the patterns seen in the simulation are similar to the patterns seen in children's responses. As in the experiment, the percentage of Rule 1 designations goes down and the percentage of Rule 4 classifications goes up as torque difference goes up, and both the children and the model show inconsistent trends with Rules 2 and 3. The correspondence to the data is good, with the one discrepancy that the simulation shows more Rule 3 classifications at the lowest level of torque difference than the subjects do.

Although the correspondence between the model and the Ferretti and Butterfield (1986) data is not perfect, it is close enough in several respects to suggest that the mechanisms used in the model and the mechanisms used by children have something in common. Ferretti and Butterfield suggested that

TABLE 4.3
Percentage of Rule Classifications at Different Levels of Torque Difference

TD Level	*1. Ferretti & Butterfield Data*			
	1	2	3	4
1	0.29	0.19	0.17	0.05
2	0.24	0.34	0.14	0.08
3	0.22	0.31	0.22	0.10
4	0.19	0.15	0.15	0.37
TD Level	*2. Simulation*			
	1	2	3	4
1	0.23	0.16	0.37	0.01
2	0.19	0.15	0.22	0.20
3	0.13	0.22	0.29	0.12
4	0.13	0.18	0.10	0.37

children may use rules but ignore small differences. The model provides an alternative interpretation: It suggests that children may rely on the same kind of graded, activation-based process that underlies the model's performance.

Readiness

We now turn to the findings that are of most interest from the point of view of mechanisms of development, namely the findings on the readiness to progress from stage to stage. In McClelland (1989), I simulated Siegler's (1976) experiments on readiness by examining the effect of training on conflict problems using two different networks. The first was a network just entering the Rule 1 phase, and the other was a network that was just about the exit the Rule 1 phase. These are the networks whose weights are shown at Epoch 20 and Epoch 40 in Fig. 4.6. Each network was trained with 16 examples of conflict problems chosen according to the procedures described by Siegler (1976). Siegler's subjects saw the training examples only once, but just to see what would happen, I presented the 16 examples several times, testing on the 24-item rule assessment test after each presentation of the 16-item training set. Performance profiles for the two networks over problem types, after each set of presentations of the conflict problems, are shown in Fig. 4.8. The results are quite dramatic: The network trained with conflict problems just as it is entering the Rule 1 phase regresses, whereas the network trained with conflict problems just as it is exiting this phase moves forward to Rule 2 after the first exposure to the training problems.

The reasons for these different patterns can be found by examining the connections in the network at the time when the conflict training trials are

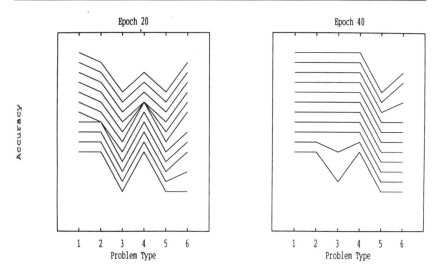

FIG. 4.8. Performance profiles on the rule assessment test after 0 through 10 exposures to a set of conflict problems, after 20 (left) or 40 (right) epochs of training. The figures present successive profiles proceeding back in depth, with the lowest (frontmost) profile in each figure representing performance before the first exposure to the conflict training patterns. Problem type 1 = balance, 2 = weight, 3 = distance, 4 = conflict–weight, 5 = conflict–distance, 6 = conflict–balance as in Figure 4.4. The frontmost profile for the 20-epoch network corresponds exactly to the pure Rule 1 pattern, but with exposure to the conflict problems this profile deteriorates and becomes unclassifiable after the fourth exposure. The frontmost profile for the 40-epoch network corresponds to the Rule 1 pattern with one deviation in the form of one correct response out of four on distance problems. With just one exposure to the conflict problems, the pattern switches over the Rule 2 pattern with one deviation, and even this deviation disappears with just one more exposure.

introduced. In the 20-epoch network considering first the connections from the input units to the internal representation units, there is a definite but still weak (compared to later stages) representation of weight on the two sides of the scale, and virtually no representation of distance. Similarly, considering the connection weights from the internal representation units to the output units, the connections in the pathway that deal with weight encode the fact that the side with the greater weight goes down. For example, the internal representation unit on the left, whose activation varies positively with relative weight to the left, activates the left side down output unit. Again, though, the connections involved are weak at this stage compared to Epochs 40 and 100. Finally, on the distance side of the network, neither unit has significant strength to either output unit. In summary, this network has connections that allow a definite but still weak encoding of relative weight, and a definite but still weak use of this encoding to influence its prediction as to which side will go down. However, it has no encoding of relative distance or of how to use it to influence its predictions as to which side will go down.

Given this situation, consider how the conflict training problems influence the connections in the network. The set of conflict problems present inconsistent feedback with respect to usefulness of the weight cue to predict which side will go down. Indeed, on half of these trials, the side with greater weight goes down; but on the other half, the side with greater weight goes up. Thus, to a network encoding and predicting based on the weight cue, its predictions are in error on one half of the conflict–weight training items. The network makes adjustments to the connections to reduce this error, and in so doing, it reduces the strengths of the connections it uses to encode and use the weight cue. The result in gradual deterioration of performance.

Although the connections are eroding on the weight side of the network, little is happening to the connections on the distance side. Changes to these connections cannot help the network very much. For one thing, as with the weight cue, the feedback is inconsistent. But there is another reason why changes to these connections cannot help. The problem can be seen most easily in considering the connections from the internal representation units to the output units. Changes in these connections do not help performance overall, because the activations of these units do not meaningfully reflect relative distance from the fulcrum on the two sides of the scale. The learning algorithm will increase the strength of the connection from the left-hand distance representation unit to the left side down output unit on a trial where the left side should go down, and will decrease the strength of this connection on a trial where the right side should go down. These influences have no net effect because the activation of the left-hand distance representation unit does not covary with relative distance. So, even if relative distance covaried perfectly with which side goes down, the connections from the distance representation units to the output units would bounce back and forth and little net progress would ensue. A similar problem arises for the connections from the distance input units to the distance hidden units. Given that the connections from the distance representation units to the distance output units are weak, changes in the connection from distance input units to distance representation units have no effect on the predictions of the network. In back propragation, connections are adjusted in proportion to the extent that their adjustment reduces the discrepancy between predicted and observed outcomes, and changes in these connections do not much affect this discrepancy, so the weights are not changed very much.

In summary, conflict training erodes the connections on the weight side of the Epoch 20 network and has little influence on the connections on the distance side. Therefore, this network gradually regresses with repeated presentations of the conflict feedback problems.

Now let us consider the 40-epoch network, also shown in Fig. 4.6. This network differs from the 20-epoch network in two ways. First, the connections on the weight side encode relative weight more strongly and use this cue more forcefully to influence predictions than in the 20-epoch network. Second, the connections on the distance side of the network now encode and use the distance cue, albeit weakly. At this point, the network's profile on the 24-item test shows that it gets one of the four distance problems correct, indicating partial sensitivity to distance cue.

In this case, training with the conflict problems turns out differently. First, consider conflict–weight problems. In these cases, the weight cue dominates and there is little error, and therefore, little change to the connections. Now consider conflict–distance problems. In these cases, the weight cue tends to dominate the output, too, and so there is error—the network makes the wrong prediction. On these trials, the connections on the weight side of the network will be eroded somewhat, but because they are stronger than at 20 epochs, this does not readily reduce the network's use of relative weight to predict which side will go down. This time, the connection weights on the distance side of the network are not eroded; they tend to be strengthened. There is now a basis in the existing connection weights on the distance side of the network on which to build. The distance representation units now represent relative distance. For example, the left distance representation unit's activation increases to the extent that the differences between the distances on the two sides is greater on the left. This unit tends to be active on conflict–distance trials when the left side should go down. On these trials, an increase in the weight from this unit to the left side down output unit will substantially reduce the error, as will a negative increment to the connection from this unit to the right side down output unit. Therefore, relatively large changes are made to these connections. In contrast, the right distance representation unit tends to be relatively inactive on conflict distance trials where the left side should go down. An increase in the strength of the connection from this unit to the left side down output unit will, therefore, have a small effect on the error, as will a negative increment to the connection from this unit to the right side down output unit. Therefore, only small changes are made to these connections. The result is that larger changes are made in the right places. Corresponding changes occur on conflict–distance problems where the distance is greater on the right. Between these two kinds of cases, there is a resulting increase in the extent to which the distance representation units exert the correct influences on the output units, thereby increasing the network's sensitivity to differences in distance. Similar influences also occur in the connections between the distance input units and the distance representation units, so both the encoding and use of the distance cue are strengthened.

Accelerations and Decelerations in Developmental Change

I hope that the previous discussion allows an intuitive understanding of the process whereby the network can exhibit differential readiness to learn at different points in its development. But this discussion, posed as it has been in nonmathematical form, may tend to give more of an "all-or-nothing" flavor to the effects of connection changes at different points in time than is really correct. Specifically, in describing the effects of conflict training on the connections on the distance side of the Epoch 20 network, the description given makes it sound as though it would be impossible for the network ever to learn to make use of the distance cue, even with a totally consistent relationship between relative distance and outcome in terms of which side goes down. Indeed, the same would apply just as well to the connections in the weight side of the network: Initially, the network has no meaningful representation of relative weight or of how to use relative weight, and therefore changes to the connections in the weight side of the network will have no beneficial effect. How then does the network ever learn? It seems that we are in the same place we were when considering models based on learning rules. In these models, the transition suddenly happens at some point, with no suggestion of why it happens then or why it takes so long within a stage if a single discrete change (adding a new production) is required to get from A to B. In the connectionist system, although the transition itself is not instantaneous, it seems as though it must at least *begin* to happen suddenly at some point. Otherwise, how would we progress from the initial state of meaningless connections and null or canceling changes, to the state where the connections have started to become meaningful and the changes begin to cumulate? Are we again faced with some sort of "immaculate transition," as Siegler and Munakata (1993) put it?

No, there is no immaculate transition. Recall that the network is initialized, not with 0 connections, but with very small random values. This means that, due to the random initial values, one of the two hidden units in the weight side of the network will be slightly more strongly activated than the other in those cases where the preponderence of the weight is to the right. The effect can be slight and initially not consistent over different instances in which the proponderence of the weight is to the right, but there will inevitably be a slight relative advantage. This advantage does not represent prior knoweldge about the problem; it only represents the fact that in the presence of random initial connections, some units will naturally tend to be more suitable for some tasks than others. The gradient descent learning procedure exploits these random initial differences. Connection changes that initially almost cancel do not quite cancel completely, and gradually, differences build up. As they do, structure emerges. There is no point at which one could say, "now the network is encoding relative weight and before this it was not," but there are accelerations and decelerations. As structure gradually emerges, changes to particular connections can have large effects on the error. According to the learning rule, larger changes are made to these weights, and there is a double benefit because the changes are larger than they would have been earlier, and at the same time, they have larger effects. Accelerations of this sort, both for the weight cue and for the distance cue, are visible in Fig. 4.9. The acceleration in the connections that process the weight cue mark the onset of the Rule 1 phase, and the acceleration in the connections that process the distance cue mark the transition from the Rule 1 phase on to Rule 2 and then Rule 3.

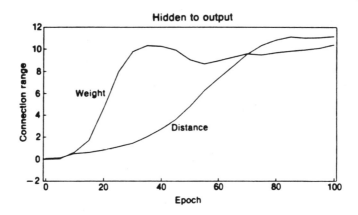

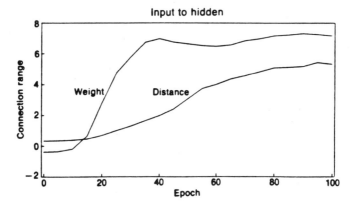

FIG. 4.9.   Relative magnitude of connection weights for processing weight and distance as a function of training. Weights for encoding weight and distance (input to hidden units) are shown in the lower panel. Weights for using the results of these encodings to determine which side of the scale will go down are shown in the top panel. Reprinted from Figure 2.12 of McClelland (1989), with permission.

Must We Assume a Biased Environment?

Before turning to a consideration of the implications of connectionist learning for conceptions of developmental change, I would like to reconsider one of the assumptions of the 1989 model. In that model, I assumed that weight is mastered before distance because of differential relative frequency of experience with weight and distance as cues. In terms of the accelerations seen in Fig. 4.9, we see the same phenomenon played out on slightly different time scales, due to the differential frequency of exposure of the model to each of the two dimensions of the problem. Certainly differences in frequency, if they do exist, would tend to influence the time course of developmental change in the use of different cues, but there are other factors that may also be relevant in this and other problem domains.

One such factor is the relative complexity of the cues to weight and distance. Weight is a stable property of an individual object, whereas distance is inherently a relation between a pair of objects. In the case of the balance scale, the second object is the fulcrum. Perhaps the differential difficulty of encoding weight and distance may turn out to depend not on relative frequency but on this difference in complexity of the two cues.

To illustrate this general point, and to show that connectionist models provide a way of addressing it, I carried out one further simulation using the same way of representing weight information as in the earlier simulation, but a different way of representing distance information. Distance is no longer represented explicitly, but instead, the positions of three things — the two weights and the fulcrum — are all represented. A row of units is used to represent the position of the left weight, another row to represent the position of the right weight, and a third row to represent the position of the fulcrum. To ensure that the model actually computes distance, each problem could be presented in any of a number of positions, with the correct response depending not on the absolute positions of the weights but on their relative positions with respect to the fulcrum.

The new network was trained without any bias in the training set at all; each of the 625 different problems that can be made from a random combination of 1-5 weights on either side of the fulcrum at distances 1-5 units from the fulcrum on either side had an equal chance of being presented in each training epoch. Actual location of the weights and the fulcrum varied randomly from trial to trial, so that the network had to take the relative positions of the weights and the fulcrum into account. As before, each epoch consisted of 100 training examples selected at random, followed by rule assessment using Siegler's test. The results, in the form of the best fitting rule at each epoch, are shown in Fig. 4.10. The results demonstrate an obvious advantage for weight over distance as a cue, in that the model exhibits a very extended Rule 1 phase in which distance has no

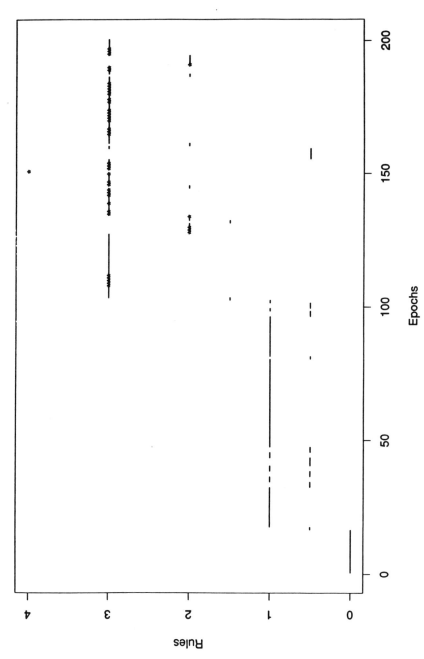

FIG. 4.10. Best fitting rule after each epoch in the new network in which the distance to the weight on each side must be computed based on information about the position of the fulcrum and of the weights on each side of the balance scale. When a dash is used, the best fitting rule fits well enough to satisfy Seigler's (1981) scoring criteria; when a "*" is used there are too many deviations from the ideal pattern to satisfy the criteria, and so the pattern would be unclassifiable.

impact on performance. The results do not provide a perfect fit to all aspects of the developmental data, in that the model never exhibits Rule 2 and there is considerable inconsistency in its performance once it exits the Rule 1 phase. But the results do indicate that connectionist models can easily capture differences in cue complexity, and illustrates how these differences provide another possible basis for developmental differences in the use of different cues.

GENERAL DISCUSSION

This chapter has reviewed earlier work (McClelland, 1989) demonstrating the applicability of a connectionist approach to the apparently rulelike progression of behavior seen in tasks like the balance scale task, and has extended this work in several ways. This work is part of a growing body of connectionist work examining various aspects of development, including research on language development (Elman, 1991; MacWhinney, Leinbach, Taraban, & McDonald, 1989; Plunkett & Marchman, 1989; Rumelhart & McClelland, 1987), conceptual development (Chauvin, 1989, Schyns, 1991), seriation (Mareschal & Shultz, 1993), and other models of performance in the balance scale task (Shultz, Mareschal, & Schmidt, in press). Taken together, these papers provide a growing body of simulation studies suggesting that development may not be a matter of changing systems of rules, but of changing systems of knowledge stored in the form of graded connections. Drawing on these studies, both Karmiloff-Smith (1992) and Halford (1993) have proposed general frameworks for cognitive development that incorporate connectionist principles as the substrate for acquisition of implicit knowledge. Both authors argued that implicit knowledge is only one form of children's knowledge. As I discuss later, I share with these authors the view that implicit knowledge coexists with more explicit knowledge — knowledge that is often verbally reportable and that often corresponds to a system of explicit rules and propositions.

The set of simulations reported in this chapter, taken together with insights arising from the other work just cited, make several important points about the representations that may underlie implicit, intuitive knowledge and the mechanisms through whgich these representations change in response to experience. I summarize the main points arising from the present simulations, discuss how they relate to basic characteristics of connectionist models, and consider some of the broader implications for understanding aspects of cognition and cognitive development.

Sensitivity to Cue Magnitude

First, the simulations provide an account for the sensitivity of performace in tasks like the balance scale task to the magnitudes of the various cues —

in the balance scale task, the magnitude of the disparity in weight and/or distance from the fulcrum on the two sides of the balance scale. These effects, clearly documented by Ferretti et al. (1985) and by Ferretti and Butterfield (1986), as well as other evidence fo the use of algebraic rules in some variants of the balance scale task (Wilkening & Anderson, 1991), indicate that simple rules of the form first proposed by Siegler do not fully characterize children's knowledge of the balance scale in all cases.

This aspect of the model's performance derives from its use of graded connections, rather than all or nothing rules, to capture its relevant knowledge. Of course, this assumption is one the connectionist approach shares with other approaches, such as the *cognitive algebra* approach of Anderson (1991), and other approaches to knowledge representation based on fuzzy logic. It is an assumption that is helpful in providing an account of certain important aspects of the relevant developmental data.

Stagelike Developmental Progressions

Secondly, the simulations account for the general form of the developmental progression seen in the balance scale and many other similar domains. Most importantly, these simulations have shown how stagelike progressions can emerge from incremental, continual change. In this respect, the simulations can be seen as providing an explicit mechanistic basis for one of the main tenets of Piagetian developmental theory. Piaget believed that the process of equilibration produced small changes that accumulated to yield apparently qualitative developmental change, but never showed in detail how this might occur (see Flavell, 1963, for a discussion). The balance scale model reviewed here illustrates how such qualitative changes — apparent stagelike progression — could arise from the accumulation of small incremental changes. In the model, acquisition of the use of each of the two cues begins with an initial phase in which the effects of experience accumulate gradually, followed by a more rapid acceleration. This basic property of connectionist networks, coupled with some basis for easier mastery of one cue than another, is sufficient to account for the developmental progression from initial failure to use either cue, to virtually exclusive reliance on one cue, to a transitional period where both cues are taken into account but one strongly dominates, to a final phase that can be characterized by an approximately additive combination of cues. In other work, examples of this kind of progression toward a fuller implicit grasp of the structure of the domain can be seen. For example, Cleeremans, Servan-Schreiber, and McClelland (1989) trained a simple recurrent connectionist network to anticipate the next element of a sequence based on prior elements. The model shows what I call *progressive penetration* into the structure of the sequence (borrowing a felicitious phrase from Flavell,

1963), in that its performance first corresponds to optimal predictions based only on the preceding element, then progresses successively through phases in which it takes successively more and more elements into account.

Differential Readiness

Third, the simulations account for differential readiness to profit from experience as a function of current developmental state. Although rule-based approaches (Klahr & Siegler, 1978; Siegler, 1976) can characterize the differences as well, they do so in a way that begs the fundamental developmental question, namely, how does the child get to the state of readiness from the state of unreadiness? As previously noted, this is described by Siegler and Munakata (1993) as the problem of the immaculate transition.

These aspects of the model's performance derive from what Elman (1991) called the incremental character of the learning process in connectionist networks. As in Piaget's conception of development, each new accommodation and assimilation builds upon the accumulated residue of past accommodations and assimilations. I tried to make clear how this process works in some detail, both in describing how accelerations occur and in discussing why the network progresses from conflict training at one point in development but not at an earlier point. The essential observation is that the error-correcting learning process relies on the propagation of signals in much the same way that the forward-going activation process does. When connections in the network are random, little is propagated in either direction; but once the connections have begun to capture the structure in the domain, both activation and error signals can propagate effectively.

It has often been observed that back propagation learning is biologically implausible (e.g., Grossberg, 1987). The implication is that models that rely on it use a method that is computationally infeasible for the nervous system, and therefore of little relevance to understanding human cognitive processes. I believe this argument is shortsighted. It is now understood that the computational equivalent of back propagation of error can be implemented in connectionist networks using only the bidirectional propagation of activation (Hinton, 1989; Hinton & McClelland, 1988; Peterson, 1991). As with back propagation, the propagation of information both forward and back depends on the knowledge stored in the connections.

Basis for Differential Use of Cues

Finally, the simulations provide a demonstration of the point that connectionist models provide a natural framework within which to explore the possible basis of developmental differences in the representation and use of various cues. In a wide range of domains, children tend to focus on one cue when there are two or more that are of equal importance from the point of view of the physical processes in play in the domain. Even if we accept the frequently held view that the tendency to focus on a single dimension across a wide range of tasks reflects capacity limits, one of two dimensions will reliably dominate the other, supporting the notion that there are differences in the strength of the child's sensitivity to the dimensions. The connectionist approach allows us to see how both frequency of exposure and complexity of a cue could play a central role in determining which cue will dominate. Other researchers, particularly Bates and MacWhinney, have stressed the importance of cue frequency (what they call *availability*) in development, and MacWhinney et al. (1989) and MacWhinney and Leinbach (1991) have noted that connectionist models capture the effects of availability (as well as validity and conflict validity) in development of use of articles and inflections during language acquisition.

The present simulations are the first to stress the possible developmental implications of the role of cue complexity in multilayer connectionist networks. In fact, the factor I call *complexity*—specifically, the need to take account of higher order relational information to accurately perform some task—is understood to be of central impoprtance in connectionist networks. Perceptrons (networks with one layer of modifiable weights) are not capable of learning to exploit higher order relational information (Minsky & Papert, 1969). Although multilayer perceptrons trained with back propagation can learn to use relational cues, they learn lower order relationships much more easily; the simulation I reported here (of the relative difficulty of learning to extract the higher order distance cue from position information) is one of many cases in point. Although all the reasons why networks have an easier time with simpler cues have not been fully determined, several contributing factors can be identified. Perhaps the fundamental one is the fact that correlations between input and output become contingent on other input variables. The problem, as the network sees it, is one of learning several such conditional contingencies instead of just one.

To make this concrete, consider a network that is learning a relationship between two binary input variables (x_1, x_2) and a single output variable (y), and consider two relationships: $y = x_1$, and $y = (x_1? = x_2)$. (The second function has value 1 if x_1 and x_2 are identical, value 0 otherwise.) The truth tables for these two relationships are shown in Table 4.4. There is a simple noncontingent correlation between x_1 and y in the first case, but no correlation between either x_1 or x_2 and y in the second case. However, in the second case, there is a correlation between x and y that changes sign depending on the value of x_2. A back propagation network of the kind used in this chapter essentially handles this relation in just this sort of way.

TABLE 4.4
Truth Tables for Two Relations

$y = x_1$			$y = (x_1? = x_2)$		
x_1	x_2	y	x_1	x_2	y
0	0	0	0	0	1
0	1	0	0	1	0
1	0	1	1	0	0
1	1	1	1	1	1

Different runs with different random starting connections find slightly different specific solutions, but they all involve at least one hidden unit that learns a contingent correlation. In one typical solution, the network that results from training has one hidden unit that handles the cases where $x_2 = 1$, in which case there is a positive correlation between x_1 and y, and it has another unit that handles cases in which $x_2 = 0$, in which case there is a negative correlation betwen x_1 and y. The learning is much slower in this case than in the case of the simple function $y = x_1$, for several reasons. One is that each of the contingent correlations is only exhibited by a subset of the training cases. A second problem is that the units must learn to specialize; at first, both units are affected by all of the cases and so (in a process we saw in action at other places in this chapter) the changes to the connection weights nearly cancel each other out. As a result, there is a long initial phase where little learning takes place in the relational case.

Halford (1993; Halford et al., in press) has stressed the importance of complexity, measured in terms of the number of interacting problem dimensions that must be considered for adequate performance. Halford proposed the use of Smolensky's (1990) tensor networks to capture complex higher order relations, and specifically proposed a mapping of the balance scale problem onto the tensor product representation. In these representations, each problem dimension is represented by a pattern of activation consisting of a set of elements. Combinations of elements from different dimensions are represented by assigning one connectionist unit to represent every possible N-tuple consisting of one element from each dimension. Obviously on this approach, higher order relations require extremely complex representations. Tensor product representations were used in a wide range of connectionist models (e.g., Rumelhart & McClelland, 1986; Touretzky & Hinton, 1988) but they suffered from combinatorial explosion and from a dispersion of the regularities that must be learned for mastery of the content of particular domains (Plaut & McClelland, 1993; St. John & McClelland, 1987).

The preceding discussion suggests that the use of tensor product representations may not be necessary to capture within a connectionist framework at least some aspects of the empirical findings that suggest that higher order relations are harder to learn. Tensor product networks provide a full set of units, one for every possible conjunction of one element from each dimension. Back propagation networks instead provide a smaller number of units that are assigned by the learning process to capture conjunctions that are necessary to perform a particular task. In both cases, there is an inherent capacity to capture higher order relations, and in both cases, higher order relations are more difficult to capture than simpler ones are.

Is the Feedforward Nature of the Present Model an Inherent Limitation?

Another reason why Halford proposed tensor product representations is the fact that they provide a framework within which knowledge can be flexibly accessed. Tensor product representations treat all dimensions of the problem equivalently, so that any can be used as either input or output. Thus, for example, a tensor product model of the balance scale having separate dimensions for each of the input variables and another dimension for the outcome would allow one to specify all but one input and the outcome, and the model would fill in the missing values. Given the complexities of using tensor product representations, this same flexibility should be possible in connectionist networks that are slight variations on the network used in the simulations reported here. Networks with bidirectional connections can be trained with a variety of learning rules, and there are several extant examples of networks that can take inputs from a subset of the input dimensions and complete the remaining dimensions (given that the subset of dimensions provided in the input provides sufficient constraint on the unspecified dimensions; Hinton, 1981; Movellan & McClelland, in press).

Open Questions for Connectionist Approaches to Cognitive Development

Several fundamental questions remain open at this stage. In concluding, I consider two: The nature of the initial structure that must be built into a network to allow it to learn and to account for the developmental patterns seen in a particular domain, and the relation between what is learned in connectionist networks and explicit knowledge that can be articulated in verbal form.

Nature of the Initial Structure.   The McClelland (1989) network built in considerable initial structure by assuming separate input representations for weight and distance cues and separate internal representation units for learning to represent each of these two cues. To what extent do the results reported here depend on these assumptions? Work by Schmidt and Shultz (1991) cast considerable light on these matters. In one study, Schmidt and Shultz examined the adequacy of a number of variants of my 1989 model, in terms of the extent to which the model would exhibit (a) a high probability of adhering to one of Siegler's four rules after each epoch of training (excluding a few initial epochs), and (b) sequential progression through all four rules. They varied the learning rate, whether or not the hidden units were presegregated, and the degree of bias in the training set favoring exposure to problems in which weight varied but distance was the same on both sides of the scale. Presegregation of the hidden units was not a major factor in determining the adequacy. Although both the learning rate and the degree of bias mattered (generally, more adequate models were obtained with slower learning rates and greater bias), presegregation of the internal units did not. Furthermore, Shultz et al. (in press) showed that adequate simulations are possible using a variant connectionist network that employs a learning algorithm called *cascade correlation,* in which there are no initial hidden units at all, and hidden units are added one at a time to capture error in the network's predictions that it misses without the hidden units.

Although prestructuring the internals of the network is not necessary, all of the networks under consideration—those used by Schultz's group, and those used in my simulations—do assume that the input and output representations are highly structured. It is hardly the case that any of the networks see raw, unencoded perceptual input and extract from this weight and distance. I imagine that the perceptual processes that extract the visual concomitants of these variables from the raw perceptual input draw on hard-wired perceptual mechanisms as well as experience-based learning processes. It is not clear exactly what form these perceptual representations take or what form they need to take to be useful in systems that gradually learn from experience. This is a matter that could be fruitfully explored in future research. Shultz et al. represented different amounts of weight or distance on each side of the balance scale by different degrees of activation of separate units for each weight and each distance, and obtained good simulations of the main phenomena, but other than this variation and the new representation I used in the final simulation reported here, there has not been much work on what aspects of the input (or output) representations are crucial. Input and output representations make a big difference in some cases (Plaut & McClelland, 1993), so it will be important to explore this matter further. The simulations I have reported here say little about the extent of prior constraints that must be built in to allow development to successfully proceed. This is obviously an important issue for future research, but it is not the burden of the present work to address this issue. Rather, the point is to show how experience may be that engine that drives development, through channels determined by initial structure and by the nature of the input and output representations that are used.

Relation of Implicit Connectionist Knowledge to Explicit and Implicit Rules. One of the cornerstones of Siegler's rule assessment approach is the finding that there is a fairly close correspondence between children's verbal reports about how they do the balance scale task and their performance as measured by the rule assessment method. All of the balance scale models, and indeed all of the other extant connectionist models of other developmental phenomena, have nothing to say about this explicit knowledge. Therefore, it is worth considering the status of these explicit reports and their relevance to accounting for subject's behavior.

First of all, both adults and children can and do use explicit rules to govern their behavior some of the time. The connectionist models I have explored here, as well as most other connectionist models, leave out such explicit rules and are obviously missing an important aspect of human cognition. Within the balance scale task, some children use very explicit procedures, at least some of the time. There is good evidence from a variety of sources that older children can and will use Rule 4 if instructed in its use, and can discover this rule for themselves. Although connectionist networks can mimic Rule 4 (or any other deterministic function relating inputs to outputs) arbitrarily closely, implicit knowledge does not generally reach this level of sophistication. In Wilkening and Anderson's functional measurement study, where explicit numerical calculation is not possible due to the use of continuous stimulus and/or response variables, the data indicate that the combination rule is more additive than multiplicative. Thus, subjects who pass Siegler's version of the Rule 4 test, in which the questions were chosen so that the test cannot be passed with a simple additive rule, probably are explicitly multiplying weight times distance.

Although explicit rules are used in some cases, it seems equally clear that they are not used in every case. We know that children and adults will often say one thing and do another, and the verbal reports are incomplete (they do not, for example, encompass small systematic deviations from the rules nor do they accomodate the torque-difference effect). The possibility remains that children (and adults) use implicit rules of the kind that linguists have long believed to underlie the use of natural language.

What connectionist models contribute here is the observation that there is a continuous space of cognitive states, only some of which correspond to what could felicitously be called an implicit rule. Connectionist models can implement rules to any arbitrary desired degree of precision, and when such models are trained in pure environments (i.e., on environments in which the stimuli all embody some system of rules, with no exceptions), they often learn to implement these rules sufficiently precisely that it makes perfectly good sense to describe their behavior in terms of the rules they have learned to implement. For example, Cleeremans et al. (1991) trained a connnectionist network on strings generated by a simple finite-state grammar and found that the network learned to mimic the predictions of the rules of the grammar. With sufficient training, networks can sometimes converge as closely as desired to the exact predictions of various grammars. Crucially, though, connectionist models can also implement input–output mappings that occupy many other points in a continuous state space of input–output mappings. As a result, such models are capable of making smooth transitions from conforming to one rule to conforming to another.

To summarize the discussion thus far: Implicit knowledge embedded in connectionist networks may correspond very closely to some specified system of rules, but need not, and overt behaivor can be guided either by implicit or explicit knowledge, or perhaps by some weighted combination of the two.

Much more could be said about the exact circumstances under which implicit or explicit knowledge will be used, to what extent these different kinds of knowledge will be blended in different task situations, and to what extent implicit knowledge is profitably describable as capturing some implicit rule. There is another issue, however, that lies closer to the heart of the matter and divides connectionist and nonconnectionist approaches to cognitive development. Explicit knowledge does appear to develop, and in the balance scale arena, Siegler's (1976) data show that it develops in some approximate correspondence with the actual ability to use weight and distance information to predict which side of the scale will go down. Connectionist models may provide a way of accounting for the development of this ability as an implicit skill, but still leave many developmentalists unsatisfied because they say relatively little about why it is that explicit knowledge develops. Why, for example, do 6-year-olds report that they choose the side with the greater weight? Why do 9-year-olds report that they take both weight and distance into account?

It may seem at first sight that the connectionist approach fails to provide any basis for understanding these developments in explicit cognition. However, we have seen that connectionist models of the kind discussed here are actually learning, not just how to predict which side will go down in the balance scale task, but how to represent the relevant dimensions at some internal, cognitive level. Karmiloff-Smith (personal communication, 1992) is exploring the idea that those parts of our cognitive systems that formulate and test explicit rules and generate explicit verbal reports might "see" these representations as inputs. Before the ability to form these representations develops, there would be nothing for explicit cognitive processes to build on, but once the ability to represent some information is learned, it would be available for incorporation into verbal reports and for use in the formulation of explicit rules. Verbal communication would ensure that different individuals observing the same events would describe them in similar ways, thereby contributing to the development of the ability to translate the represented information into explicit verbal form. In any case, the development of such representations would be a necessary condition for the incorporation of the information they capture into explicit rules, and we would be part of the way toward an understanding of where explicit representations come from.

Obviously, the preceeding paragraph offers only the faintest glimpse of a possible future rapprochement between theories of implicit and explicit cognition. Karmiloff-Smith and Halford are exploring ways to characterize the linkage between implicit and explicit cognitive processes, but this work is in the early stages of development.

CONCLUSION

For the time being, the fact remains that connectionist models have the most to say about implicit rather than explicit forms of cognition. Within this domain, they provide the prospect of allowing us to begin to understand how cognitive change may arise through the gradual cumulating effects of experience. At the same time, their ability to capture many of the main findings from domains that were once thought to lie in the heart of symbolic cognition suggests that the domain of implicit knowledge, and therefore the potential domain of application of connectionist models, may be broad. Surely humans have explicit knowledge and reason with it, but how much of their reasoning is of this explicit form, and how much this explicit form of reasoning depends on underlying implicit knowledge, remains to be seen. Whatever the final resolution of these issues, it seems likely that connectionist models will contribute to their ongoing exploration.

ACKNOWLEDGMENTS

Preparation of this chapter was supported by grants MH-00385 and MH-47566. I thank Robert Siegler and Graeme Halford for useful input.

REFERENCES

Anderson, N. H. (1991). *Contributions to integration theory. Vol. III: Developmental.* Hillsdale, NJ: Lawrence Erlbaum Associates.
Bates, E., & MacWhinney, B. (1987). Competition, variation, and language learning. In B. MacWhinney (Ed.), *Mechanisms of language acquisition* (pp. 157-193). Hillsdale, NJ: Lawrence Erlbaum Associates.
Chauvin, Y. (1989). Toward a connectionist model of symbolic emergence. In *Proceedings of the Eleventh Annual Conference of the Cognitive Science Society* (pp. 580-587). Hillsdale, NJ: Lawrence Erlbaum Associates.

Cleeremans, A., Servan-Schreiber, D., & McClelland, J. (1991). Finite state automata and simple recurrent networks. *Neural Computation, 1,* 372–381.

Elman, J. (1991). Incremental learning, or the importance of starting small. In *Proceedings of the Thirteenth Annual Conference of the Cognitive Science Society* (pp. 443–448). Hillsdale, NJ: Lawrence Erlbaum Associates.

Ferretti, R. P., & Butterfield, E. C. (1986). Are children's rule-assessment classifications invariant across instances of problem types? *Child Development, 57,* 1419–1428.

Ferretti, R. P., Butterfield, E. C., Cahn, A., & Kerkman, D. (1985). The classification of children's knowledge: Development on the balance scale and included plane tasks. *Journal of Experimental Child Psychology, 39,* 131–160.

Flavell, J. H. (1963)., *The developmental psychology of Jean Piaget.* Princeton, NJ: Van Nostrand.

Grossberg, S. (1987). Competitive learning: From interactive activation to adaptive resonance. *Cognitive Science, 11,* 23–64.

Halford, G. S. (1993). *Children's understanding: The development of mental models.* Hillsdale, NJ: Lawrence Erlbaum Associates.

Halford, G. S., Wilson, W. H., Guo, J., Gayler, R. W., Wiles, J., & Stewart, J. E. M. (1994). Connectionist implications for processing capacity limitations in analogies. In K. J. Holyoak & J. Barnden (Eds.), *Advances in connectionist and neural computation theory. Vol. 2: Analogical connections* (pp. 363–415). Norwood, NJ: Ablex.

Hinton, G. E. (1981). Implementing semantic networks in parallel hardware. In G. E. Hinton & J. A. Anderson (Eds.), *Parallel models of associative memory* (pp. 161–188). Hillsdale, NJ: Lawrence Erlbaum Associates.

Hinton, G. E. (1989). Deterministic Boltzmann learning performs steepest descent in weight-space. *Neural Computation, I,* 153.

Hinton, G. E., & McClelland, J. L. (1988). Learning representations by recirculation. In D. Z. Anderson (Ed.), *Neural information processing systems* (pp. 358–366). New York: American Institute of Physics.

Inhelder, B., & Piaget, J. (1958). *The growth of logical thinking from childhood to adolescence* (A. Parsons & S. Milgram, Trans.). New York: Basic Books. (Original work published 1955)

Jenkins, E. A. (1989). Knowledge restructuring and cognitive development: A parallel distributed processing approach. In M. A. Luszcz & T. Nettelbeck (Eds.), *Psychological development: Perspectives across the life-span* (pp. 205–216). Amsterdam: North-Holland.

Karmiloff-Smith, A. (1986). From megaprocesses to conscious access: Evidence from children's metalinguistic and repair data. *Cognition, 23,* 95–147.

Karmiloff-Smith, A. (1992). *Beyond modularity: A developmental perspective on cognitive science.* Cambridge, MA: MIT Press.

Klahr, D., & Siegler, R. S. (1978)., The representation of children's knowledge. In H. W. Reese & L. W. Lipsitt (Eds.), *Advances in child development* (Vol. *12,* pp. 61–116). New York: Academic Press.

MacWhinney, B., & Leinbach, J. (1991). Implementations are not conceptualizations:Revising the verb learning model. *Cognition, 40,* 121–157.

MacWhinney, B., Leinbach, J., Taraban, R., & McDonald, J. (1989). Language learning: Cues or rules? *Journal of Memory and Language, 28,* 255–277.

Mareschal, D., & Shultz, T. R. (1993). A connectionist model of the development of seriation. In *Proceedings of the 15th Annual Conference of the Cognitive Science Society* (pp. 676–681). Hillsdale, NJ: Lawrence Erlbaum Associates.

McClelland, J. L. (1989). Parallel distributed processing: Implications for cognition and development. In R. Morris (Ed.), *Parallel distributed processing: Implications for psychology and neurobiology* (pp. 9–45). New York: Oxford University Press.

McClelland, J. L. (1991)., Stochastic interactive processes and the effect of context on perception. *Cognitive Psychology, 23,* 1–44.

McClelland, J. L. (1993). Toward a theoryi of information processing in graded, random, interactive networks. In D. E. Meyer & S. Kornblum (Eds.), *Attention & Performance XIV: Synergies in experimental psychology, artificial intelligence and cognitive neuroscience* (pp. 655–668). Cambridge, MA: MIT Press.

McClelland, J. L., & Jenkins, E., (1991). *Nature, nurture, and connections: Implications of connectionist models for cognitive development.* In K. Van Lehn (Ed.), *Architectures for intelligence* (pp. 41–73). Hillsdale, NJ: Lawrence Erlbaum Associates.

Minsky, M., & Papert, S. (1969). *Perceptrons: An introduction to computational geometry.* Cambridge, MA: MIT Press.

Movellan, J. R., & McClelland, J. L. (in press). Learning continuous probability distributions with symmetric diffusion networks. *Cognitive Science.*

Peterson, C. (1991). Mean field theory neural networks for feature recognition, content addressable memory and optimization. *Connection Science, 3,* 3–33.

Pinker, S. (1991). Rules of language. *Science, 253,* 530–535.

Plaut, D., & McClelland, J. (1993). Generalization and componential attractors: Word and nonword reading in an attractor network. In *Proceedings of the 15th Annual Conference of the Cognitive Science Society* (pp. 824–829). Hillsdale, NJ: Lawrence Erlbaum Associates.

Plunkett, K., & Marchman, V. (1989). *Pattern association in a back propagation network: Implications for child language acquisition* (Tech. Rep. No. 8902). San Diego: University of California, Center for Research in Language.

Rescorla, R. A., & Wagner, A. R. (1972). A theory of Pavlovian conditioning: Variations in the effectiveness of reinforcement and non-reinforcement. In A. H. Black & W. F. Prokasy (Eds.), *Classical conditioning 2: Current research and theory* (pp. 64–99). New York: Appleton-Century-Crofts.

Rosenblatt, F. (1959). Two theorems of statistical separability in the perceptron. In *Mechanisation of Thought Processes: Proceedings of a Symposium Held at the National Physical Laboratory, November 1958: Vol. 1* (pp. 421–456). London: HM Stationery Office.

Rumelhart, D. E., Hinton, G. E., & Williams, R. J. (1986). Learning internal representations by error propagation. In J. L. McClelland, D. E. Rumelhart, & the PDP Research Group (Eds.), *Parallel distributed processing: Explorations in the microstructure of cognition: Vol. I* (pp. 318–362). Cambridge, MA: MIT Press.

Rumelhart, D. E., & McClelland, J. L. (1986). PDP models and general issues in cognitive science. In D. E. Rumelhart, J. L. McClelland, & the PDP Research Group (Eds.), *Parallel distributed processing: Explorations in the microstructure of cognition: Vol. 1* (pp. 110–146). Cambridge, MA: MIT Press.

Rumelhart, D. E., & McClelland, J. L. (1987). Learning the past tenses of English verbs: Implicit rules or parallel distributed processing? In B. MacWhinney (Ed.), *Mechanisms of language acquisition* (pp. 157–193). Hillsdale, NJ: Lawrence Erlbaum Associates.

Rumelhart, D. E., McClelland, J. L., & the PDP Research Group. (1986). *Parallel distributed processing: Explorations in the microstructure of cognition: Vols. 1 & 2.* Cambridge, MA: MIT Press.

Schmidt, W. C., & Shultz, T. R. (1991). An investigation of balance scale success. In *Proceedings of the Fourteenth Annual Conference of the Cognitive Science Society* (pp. 72–77). Hillsdale, NJ: Lawrence Erlbaum Associates.

Schyns, P. (1991). A modular neural network model of concept acquisition. *Cognitive Science, 15,* 461–508.

Shultz, T. R., Mareschal, D., & Schmidt, W. C. (in press). Modeling cognitive development on balance scale phenomena. *Machine Learning.*

Siegler, R. S. (1976). Three aspects of cognitive development. *Cognitive Psychology, 4,* 481–520.

Siegler, R. S. (1981). Developmental sequences within and between concepts. *Monographs of the Society for Research in Child Development, 46*(2, Serial No. 189).

Siegler, R. S. (1983). Five generalizations about cognitive development. *American Psychologist, 38,* 263–277.

Siegler, R. S. (in preparation). *Beyond the immaculate transition: Variability, choice, and cognitive development.* New York: Oxford University Press.

Siegler, R. S., & Klahr, D. (1982). When do children learn? The relationship between existing knowledge and the acquisition of new knowledge. In R. Glaser (Ed.), *Advances in instructional psychology: Vol. 2* (pp. 121–211). Hillsdale, NJ: Lawrence Erlbaum Associates.

Siegler, R. S., & Munakata, Y. (1993, Winter). Beyond the immaculate transition: Advances in the understanding of change. *SRCD Newsletter* pp. 3, 10, 11, 13.

Smolensky, P. (1990). Tensor product variable bginding and the representation of symbolic structyures in connectionist systems. *Artificial Intelligence, 46*(1-2), 159–216.

Spelke, E. S., Breinlinger, K., McComber, J., & Jacobsen, K. (1992). Origins of knowledge. *Psychological Review, 99,* 605–632.

St. John, M. F., & McClelland, J. L. (1987). Reconstructive memory for sentences: A PDP approach. *Proceedings of the Ohio University Inference Conference, 1986* (pp. 270–279). Athens: University of Ohio.

Touretzky, D. S., & Hinton, G. E. (1988). A distributed connectionist production system. *Cognitive Science, 12,* 423–466.

White, H. (in press). Parametric statistical estimation with artificial neural networks. In Y., Chauvin & D. E. Rumelhart (Eds.), *Back-propagation theory, architectures, and applications.* Hillsdale, NJ: Lawrence Erlbaum Associates.

Widrow, G., & Hoff, M. E. (1960). Adaptive switching circuits. *Institute of Radio Engineers, Western Electronic Show and Convention, Convention Record, Part 4,* 96–104.

Wilkening, F., & Anderson, N. H. (1982). Comparison of two rule-assessment methodologies for studying cognitive development and knowledge structure. *Psychological Bulletin, 92,* 215–237.

Wilkening, F., & Anderson, N. H. (1991). Representation and diagnosis of knowledge structures in developmental psychology. In N. H. Anderson (Ed.), *Contributions to integration theory. Vol. 3: Developmental* (pp. 45–80). Hillsdale, NJ: Lawrence Erlbaum Associates.

5

Modeling Cognitive Development With a Generative Connectionist Algorithm

Thomas R. Shultz
William C. Schmidt
David Buckingham
Denis Mareschal
McGill University

One of the key unsolved problems in cognitive development is the precise specification of developmental transition mechanisms. As the work in this volume attests, it is clear that computational modeling can provide insights into this problem. In this chapter, we focus on the applicability of a specific generative connectionist algorithm, cascade-correlation (Fahlman & Lebiere, 1990), as a process model of transition mechanisms. Generative connectionist algorithms build their own network topologies as they learn, allowing them to simulate both qualitative and quantitative developmental changes. We compare and contrast cascade-correlation, Piaget's notions of assimilation and accommodation, Papert's little known but historically relevant *genetron* model, conventional back-propagation networks, and rule-based models.

Specific cascade-correlation models of a wide range of developmental phenomena are presented. These include the balance scale task; concepts of potency and resistance in causal reasoning; seriation; integration of the concepts of distance, time, and velocity; and personal pronouns. Descriptions of these simulations stress the degree to which the models capture the essential known psychological phenomena, generate new testable predictions, and provide explanatory insights. In several cases, the simulation results underscore clear advantages of connectionist modeling techniques. Abstraction across the various models yields a set of domain-general constraints for cognitive development. Particular domain-specific constraints are identified. Finally, the models demonstrate that connectionist approaches can be successful even on relatively high-level cognitive tasks.

TRANSITION AS A MAJOR UNSOLVED PROBLEM

Although researchers have come some distance in understanding the development of children's thinking, much of the research has been directed toward a structural analysis of the relevant thought processes. Mechanisms governing developmental transitions were often neglected as this issue was typically viewed as too complex to fathom. Nevertheless, it has also been argued that such structural descriptions do not suffice (Boden, 1982). To fully understand cognitive development, one also needs a theory of the various transformations that structures undergo. Moreover, even when transition mechanisms were tentatively proposed, they tended to account for only qualitative transitions (van Geert, 1991).

Piaget's theory of cognitive development is a prime example of a theory that fails to specify transition mechanisms with sufficient precision (Bates & Elman, 1993; Boden, 1982). The proposed motors of development in Piagetian theory are assimilation, accommodation, and equilibration (Piaget, 1972). Assimilation consists in the child modifying the incoming environmental information to allow it to fit within the child's existing structures. Accommodation occurs when the child modifies existing mental structures under environmental pressures. Finally, equilibration consists in the coordination of assimilation and accommodation so as to achieve optimal harmony between the environment and mental structures. Assimilation and accommodation always occur together, although phases of predominant assimilation or predominant accommodation also occur.

Piaget struggled throughout his career to precisely formulate these ideas (Piaget, 1977). Yet many contemporary researchers feel that Piaget fell short of this goal (Boden, 1982). Piaget was criticized for assuming what he was trying to explain (Macnamara, 1976), as well as for not analyzing critical presuppositions (Ninio, 1979). The issue of how newly created structures are integrated with older structures, without completely disrupting the child's existing reasoning abilities, is not resolved (Boden, 1982). Piaget's concepts are not constrained enough to carry over into the computational domain.

Although we have focused on Piaget's work to illustrate our point, he is not the only theorist who faltered when faced with the problem of transition mechanisms. Indeed, when reviewing a number of proposed transition mechanisms, Flavell (1984) found fault with all of them. The criteria he suggested for evaluating theories of transition are as follows. First and foremost, a good theory should propose clearly defined mechanisms. All modes of operation should be described precisely and in great detail. Second, the theories should suggest empirical studies that would allow evaluation of the plausibility of the models as accounts of how cognitive development proceeds. Thus, the ultimate value of a theory is related to its ability to account for existing observations and to suggest new studies that lead to the discovery of novel phenomena.

A COMPUTATIONAL APPROACH
IS THE REQUIRED SOLUTION

One solution to the lack of precision in transition mechanisms is to use a formal language such as mathematics to describe the processes involved. The consistency of the proposed mechanisms could then be tested through computer simulations. Simulation is an ideal medium for exploring the implications of a complex model and can result in the prediction of seemingly counterintuitive findings (Lewandowsky, 1993). It provides a formal framework that can disambiguate verbal formulations.

The connectionist models we present here make use of both the mathematical and computational levels. The dynamics of a network are specified by activation functions, learning rules, training regimes, and so on. The legitimacy of the proposed model is then evaluated through explicit comparisons of computer simulations with observed psychological data.

The complimentarity of computational modeling and traditional developmental theorizing promises to be fruitful. If modelers can take account of the empirical data provided by traditional psychological accounts, then crucial questions may be answerable (Boden, 1980). The promise of the computational approach is that it naturally satisfies Flavell's (1984) methodological criteria because it is precise and generates novel predictions.

With these goals in mind, early modelers of cognitive development often adopted a production system approach (Boden, 1988). Initially these rule-based models were static descriptions of performance during a particular stage of development. More recently though, developmental researchers are exploring the utility of self-modifying production systems (Klahr, Langley, & Neches, 1987; Newell, 1990). The adequacy of these models, however, was challenged by the application of connectionist models.

Attempts to provide a formal analysis and implementation of Piagetian development within a connectionist framework can be traced to the early 1960s. Papert (1963) tried to build an automated equilibratory system that he called the genetron. He argued that behavioristic learning theorists were correct in claiming that the underlying mechanisms of intelligence are simple if considered independently, but that they unfortunately ignored the interactive complexity of the ensemble. Papert argued that models that relied on progressive and hierarchical acquisition of functions would evolve in a stagelike manner. He hypothesized that such models would develop through alternating periods of first lowering variability in the system, and then constructing new functions. The genetron was largely hand constructed from a collection of elementary perceptrons (two-layered networks). Although an attempt was made to simulate children's developing integration of information in a length comparison task, no tangible empirical results were provided and the project was apparently dropped. Presumably, the technical limitations of perceptrons (Minsky & Papert, 1969) outweighed the potential benefits of this type of model.

APPROPRIATENESS OF CONNECTIONIST APPROACHES

Modern connectionist methods offer a number of potential advantages for the creation of process models of cognition, including the ability of these nets to learn procedural and declarative knowledge, generalize to novel situations, and derive coherent solutions despite variable environmental input. Because of these strengths, connectionist simulations are now starting to illuminate several aspects of cognitive, perceptual, and language development.

Harnad, Hanson, and Lubin (1994) showed how categorical perception might arise as a natural side effect of back-propagation learning. Several psychological phenomena in concept acquisition and semantic development were addressed within the connectionist framework, including prototype and typicality effects, semantic over- and underextension, the mutual exclusivity constraint, vocabulary explosion, and the emergence of comprehension before production (Chauvin, 1989; Schyns, 1991).

Several other aspects of language development were also simulated with connectionist techniques, including the formation of the English past tense (Hare & Elman, 1992; Marchman, 1992; Plunkett & Marchman, 1991), article choice for German nouns (MacWhinney, Leinbach, Taraban, & McDonald, 1989), word recognition and naming (Seidenberg & McClelland, 1989), and syntactic development (Elman, 1993).

The pioneering attempt to apply modern connectionist techniques to developmental problem solving tasks was McClelland's (1989) model of balance scale stages, a task that we discuss in detail later.

Taken together, this research suggests that a connectionist approach to cognitive development cannot be easily dismissed. The models yielded qualitatively accurate simulations of a variety of different phenomena, and provided a number of explanatory insights. Recent theoretical papers argued that the application of connectionist techniques to cognitive development is fostering a needed return to the traditional issues of change and transition (Bates & Elman, 1993; Plunkett & Sinha, 1992; Shultz, 1991). For the aforementioned reasons of difficulty, developmental psychologists have tended to ignore issues of change and transition in favor of diagnostic concerns. Connectionist networks provide a precise and concrete way to think about developmental change.

All of the foregoing models had static network processing structures that were hand designed by the researchers. Further, all of the learning was accomplished solely by small adjustments in network weights over many epochs. For our simulations of cognitive development, we opted instead for a generative algorithm, in which small quantitative changes in connection weights are augmented by qualitative changes in network topology as learning progresses. A number of generative connectionist learning frameworks exist (Alpaydin, 1991; Hertz, Krogh, & Palmer, 1991). We focus on one, cascade-correlation (Fahlman & Lebiere, 1990), that is particularly suitable for modeling cognitive development.

Continuous small weight changes can sometimes produce qualitative behavioral shifts, even in static networks. Such outcomes were described in terms of mathematical catastrophe theory (Pollack, 1990; van der Maas & Molenaar, 1992). A traditional view of cognitive development is that qualitative behavioral changes arise instead from a major restructuring of cognitive processing (Piaget & Inhelder, 1969). A possible advantage of using generative network models is that both types of transition mechanisms can be examined simultaneously. Some qualitative behavioral changes may result from continuous quantitative adjustments alone, whereas others may also require qualitative changes in network topology. Research with static networks does not facilitate the study of interactions between underlying quantitative and qualitative changes.

THE CASCADE-CORRELATION LEARNING ALGORITHM

Cascade-correlation begins with a minimal network topology consisting of a single layer of input units fully connected to a single layer of output units (Fahlman & Lebiere, 1990; Fig. 5.1a). The algorithm then designs and recruits its own hidden units as and when it needs them. Cascade-correlation operates in two alternating phases: an output phase in which weights leading to output units are modified (Figs. 5.1a, 5.1c) and an input phase in which candidate hidden units are trained for installation in the network (Fig. 5.1b). The name *cascade-correlation* presumably derives from the way that hidden units are recruited into the network. In each input phase, the candidate hidden unit whose activations correlate maximally with the network's existing error is selected for installation. Hidden units are arranged in a sort of cascade, so that each new hidden unit receives input from all of the previous hidden units.

Learning proceeds in batch mode, that is, all weight modifications occur

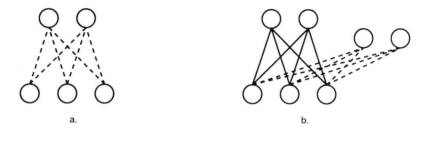

a.   b.

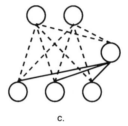

c.

FIG. 5.1.   Training in cascade-correlation. Modifiable connections are represented by dashed lines and nonmodifiable connections are represented by solid lines. (1a) and (1c) refer to output phases, (1b) to an input phase. Adapted with permission from Shultz, Mareschal, and Schmidt (1994).

after a complete blocked presentation of all of the input–output pattern pairs. This is a requirement of the quickprop weight adjustment algorithm that is used within cascade-correlation (Fahlman, 1988). Such a complete presentation of the training patterns is called an *epoch*. *Victory* is achieved when all output activations are within a small threshold of their target values.

There is considerable psychological (Oden, 1987) and physiological (Dudai, 1989; Squire, 1987) evidence for batch learning. For example, the hippocampus processes information in batch mode in order to relay its information to relevant cortical areas at some later time. Batch learning is potentially more computationally efficient than pattern learning because it requires fewer weight updates for the same number of patterns.[1] Batch learning also avoids making and unmaking redundant weight changes that might result from the purely local evaluations of error signals in pattern learning. Even in batch learning, however, outputs are compared to their targets independently of other patterns. Thus, the system never has to process more than one pattern at a time although it does keep a running sum of the error that is eventually used to adjust the weights.

---

[1]In pattern learning, weights are adjusted after every training pattern.

Output Training

During the output training phase, weights leading to the output units are modified so as to minimize the sum of squared error (E):

$$E = \sum_o \sum_p (A_{op} - T_{op})^2 \tag{1}$$

where o indexes the output units, p indexes the input-output pairs, A is the actual activation of an output unit, and T is the target activation for that output unit. If E stagnates (i.e., ceases to change by more than a specified amount for a certain number of epochs) or a specified maximum number of epochs elapses, the algorithm changes to the input phase.

Input Training

During the input training phase, weights leading to the output units are frozen, meaning that they are no longer allowed to change. A number of candidate hidden units are connected with random weights from all input units and existing hidden units. The weights leading to each candidate unit are then adjusted to maximize the absolute value of the correlation (C) between the activation of that unit and the residual error at the output units, across all patterns.

$$C = \frac{\sum_o \sum_p |(h_p - <h>)(e_{op} - <e_o>)|}{\sum_o \sum_p (e_{op} - <e_o>)^2} \tag{2}$$

where h_p is the activation of the candidate hidden unit for pattern p, $<h>$ is the mean activation of the candidate hidden unit for all patterns, e_{op} is the residual error at output o for pattern p, and $<e_o>$ is the mean residual error at output o for all the patterns.

  Training continues until C stagnates or a prespecified maximum number of epochs has elapsed as described earlier. At this point, the candidate unit with the largest C is retained and all other candidate units are discarded. The input weights to the newly installed hidden units are then frozen and the unit is allowed to send output to all of the output units. The algorithm returns to the output training phase with the added power of the new hidden unit that is particularly adept at detecting the residual error that the network was encountering.

The Quickprop Algorithm

Rather than using the usual back-propagation algorithm (Rumelhart, Hinton, & Williams, 1986) to modify weights, cascade-correlation uses a second-order algorithm developed by Fahlman (1988) called *quickprop*. Quickprop was inspired by Newton's minimization methods and incorporates curvature information into the optimization process. It is based on two assumptions: that weights contribute independently to the function being optimized, and that the function is locally quadratic. The value of the function and its slope at the current and previous points are used to uniquely define a parabola. The weight that minimizes this parabola is then selected as the next weight for that connection in the network. Although this is the mechanism at the heart of the quickprop algorithm, under some conditions modifications occur so as to bootstrap the process and avoid certain computational pitfalls (for a detailed description and justification of these modifications see Mareschal, 1992). The actual update rules in Fahlman's code are:

$$w_3 - w_2 = \epsilon f(w_2) \text{ if } w_2 - w_1 = 0$$

$$w_3 - w_2 = \frac{f(w_2)}{f(w_1) - f(w_2)} (w_2 - w_1) \text{ if } w_2 - w_1 \neq 0 \text{ and}$$

$$\left| \frac{f(w_1)}{f(w_1) - f(w_2)} \right| < \mu \tag{3}$$

$$w_3 - w_2 = \mu(w_2 - w_1) \text{ otherwise}$$

where the indices 1, 2, 3, represent three consecutive time steps, f is the derivative of the function being optimized (E in the case of the output phase, C for the input phase), ϵ is a parameter controlling the amount of gradient descent, and m is a parameter controlling the maximum step size. The product $\epsilon f(w_2)$ is added to the weight update even when the previous weight change is nonzero, that is, in lines 2 and 3 of Equation 3, except when the current slope is of opposite sign from the previous slope. This detail is not presented in Equation 3 in order to keep this equation legible.

Activation Functions

Three types of activation functions are available for hidden units in cascade-correlation: *linear*, *sigmoid*, and *gaussian*. Throughout all of the present models, we used sigmoid activation functions, symmetrical around 0 and ranging from -0.5 to +0.5.

$$y_i = \frac{1}{1 + \exp\left(-\sum_j w_{ij}x_j\right)} - 0.5 \qquad (4)$$

where y is the resulting activation of the receiving unit indexed by i, x is the activation of a sending unit indexed by j, and w is the weight connecting those two units. Our input units typically have linear activation functions, meaning that they sum all input into them and output that sum.

Developmental Implications

Papert's (1963) genetron, developed specifically to model Piagetian phenomena, is a historical precedent for cascade-correlation. The genetron consisted of hierarchically ordered and recurrently connected perceptron units. Papert gave several mathematical arguments for why this model should develop through alternate phases of noise reduction and internal function construction, thereby giving rise to stagelike development.

Mareschal (1991) identified similarities between the genetron and cascade-correlation. Both can be expressed within the Piagetian framework. For Piaget, equilibration consisted of alternating periods of accommodation to new information followed by assimilation of familiar information. In connectionist models, the knowledge structure of a domain is embodied in the nodal architecture and the knowledge content is embodied in the weights linking those nodes. The period of error reduction can be viewed as the assimilation (or partial assimilation) of information into previously existing knowledge structures. Only the weights (i.e., the content of the knowledge) are being modified. The period of hidden unit recruitment can be seen as the accommodation of knowledge structures to unassimilated information. As with the child, assimilation corresponds to a period in which new information can be integrated within existing knowledge structures, whereas accommodation corresponds to a period in which genuinely new structures are created out of older ones without functional impairment of the system as a whole.[2]

We now turn to a review of some of our cascade-correlation models of developmental phenomena. These include models of balance scale phenomena; concepts of potency and resistance in causal reasoning; seriation; integration of the dimensions of distance, time, and velocity; and acquisition of personal pronouns. All of these simulations, except for pronouns, involve reasoning about aspects of the physical world. As noted earlier,

---

[2]We extend this interpretation of cascade-correlation in terms of assimilation and accommodation in the General Conclusions and Discussion section.

most developmental connectionist work concerned concept or language acquisition. The simulation choices reflect a smattering of a benchmark modeling problem (balance scale), topics we worked on and thus were interested in and knew well (potency and resistance; pronouns), and basic well-known developmental phenomena (seriation; distance, time, velocity).

THE BALANCE SCALE

The balance scale task is an appealing candidate for cognitive develop-mental computational modeling. The task combines an explicit and well-defined methodology with detailed human observations. The clarity and replicability of balance scale phenomena with humans, coupled with the classical developmental appeal of its stagelike character, led to both connectionist (McClelland, 1989; Shultz & Schmidt, 1991) and rule-based models (Langley, 1987; Newell, 1990).

We used cascade-correlation as a transition mechanism to create two general types of working models of developmental balance scale phenom-ena, each embodying different sets of theoretical assumptions. One type of model adopted the assumption of a biased training environment, after McClelland (1989). A second type of model investigated the effect that prestructuring the network's starting state had on development of behavior on the balance scale. After reviewing the task's psychological background, an evaluation of existing balance scale models is presented, and then we report on the two cascade-correlation models.

Psychology of the Balance Scale

The balance scale task was developed by Inhelder and Piaget (1958) for their studies of proportionality concepts. Examples of the balance scale appa-ratus appear on the left side of Fig. 5.2. The child is shown a balance scale supported by blocks so that the scale stays in the balanced position. Next, a number of weights are placed around one of a number of evenly spaced pegs on either side of the fulcrum, and it becomes the child's task to predict which arm will go down, or whether the scale will balance, once supporting blocks are removed. For perfect responding, the task requires that the child integrate information from the two dimensions of weight and distance. Perfect performance on this task can be calculated via multiplication. Torques can be calculated for both the left and right arms by multiplying weight by distance; the side with the larger torque will go down. If the torques are equal, then the scale will balance.

Siegler (1976, 1981) operationalized Inhelder and Piaget's (1958) obser-vations with a rule assessment methodology, proposing that development

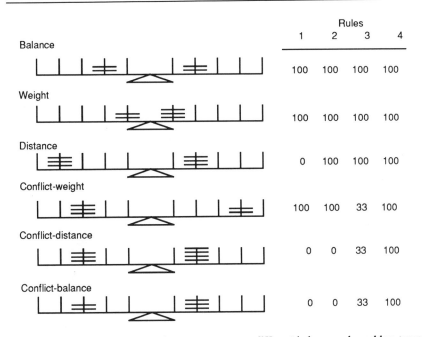

FIG. 5.2.   Predicted percentage of correct answers on different balance scale problem types for children responding in accordance with different rules. Adapted with permission from Shultz, Mareschal, and Schmidt (1994).

on the balance scale task is characterized by the use of four increasingly powerful rules. Children diagnosed as using a given rule are classified as being in the corresponding stage of development. Stage 1 performers use only weight information to determine if the scale will balance. Stage 2 subjects emphasize weight information but consider distance if weights on either side of the fulcrum are equal. Stage 3 subjects correctly integrate both weight and distance information for simple problems, but respond indecisively when one arm has greater weight and the other greater distance. Stage 4 subjects correctly integrate weight and distance information for near perfect performance, suggesting but not requiring that they explicitly understand and use torques. There is some debate concerning the proportion of the population that reaches Stage 4, yet it is clear that some individuals do so (Siegler, 1981). Because very few studies have assessed adult competencies, there remains the possibility that Stage 4 performance may be achieved given a high degree of experience, perhaps even without explicit knowledge of torque (Shultz, Mareschal, & Schmidt, 1994).

In order to assess children's stages of development, Siegler partitioned the entire set of balance scale problems into six different problem types, and used performance on a subset of these problems to classify subjects as conforming to a particular rule. *Balance* problems have equal numbers of weights placed at equal distances from the fulcrum. In *weight* problems, distances on either side of the fulcrum are equal so the side with more weights goes down. In *distance* problems, the arm with greater distance goes down because the two sides have equal weights. *Conflict* problems have greater weight on one arm and greater distance on the other. The correct response to a conflict problem determines its classification as a *conflict-weight*, *conflict-distance*, or *conflict-balance* problem. A child's performance was classified by the pattern of successes and errors observed when tested with 24 problems, 4 from each of the 6 problem types. Siegler's four rules, as they appear on the right side of Fig. 5.2, define the expected percentages of correct responses across the six problem types.

A number of basic observations emerged from balance scale research using both Piagetian style observation and Siegler's rule assessment methodology. First, as children get older, they appear to progress systematically through rule-based stages as described earlier. A second developmental observation is a pattern of U-shaped performance between Stages 2 and 4 for conflict–weight problems. Children predict correct outcomes for these problems during Stages 1 and 2, lose this ability during Stage 3, and regain it in Stage 4. A third balance scale regularity is that the greater the difference in torque between the two sides of a balance scale, the more likely it is that a child will respond correctly (Ferretti & Butterfield, 1986). This torque difference effect makes it possible for the same child to be classified at different stages by Siegler's rule assessment procedure depending on the test problems' differences in torque.

A Review of Previous Balance Scale Models

There are three symbolic models and two connectionist models of the balance scale task published to date. Klahr and Siegler (1978) modeled each of the four stages of balance scale development as production rules. This work is descriptive of the child's performance, but no attempt was made to provide a mechanism for stage transitions. Langley (1987) expanded upon Klahr and Siegler's (1978) findings by adding a transition mechanism. Langley's model started with a set of rules that made random predictions. The system would then learn from its errors on specific problems and improve with experience. The transition mechanism was a discrimination process that looked for differences between cases in which correct predictions were made and cases in which errors were made.

Langley (1987) reported that the system learned to perform at Stage 3, but never reached Stage 4. Moreover, it did not appear to move through Stages 1 and 2 on its way to Stage 3. The model's responses were not tested for the torque difference effect or for U-shaped development on conflict-weight problems.

Newell (1990) reported on a model of the balance scale task using the

Soar architecture, which creates rules by chunking the results of search-based problem solving. This model learned to correctly respond to just four balance scale problems, moving through Stages 1, 2, and 3 in the process, although Stage 4 was never achieved. The model's responses were not tested using Siegler's rule assessment methodology, and no attempt was made to test for the torque difference effect or for U-shaped development on conflict–weight problems. There was no comparison of the model's output to human data, except for an overall qualitative judgment of stage transition. The psychological realism of this Soar model is questionable. First, stage transition apparently occurred from processing a single exemplar, whereas children have years of experience lifting and holding objects before they make the same transition. Second, it is unclear how dependent the Soar model was on observing specific exemplars in a certain order (Shultz & Schmidt, 1991). Finally, as mentioned, the Soar model failed to reach the level of Stage 4 responding.

McClelland (1989) used a back-propagation network that assumed separate processing of weight and distance information, implemented by having two hidden units receive only weight input and two others receive only distance input. A subset of all the possible training patterns was randomly selected each epoch with a strong bias in favor of equal distance problems. It was suggested that this bias, responsible for the appearance of the first two stages, reflects children's extensive experiences picking up differing numbers of objects and their limited experience at placing such objects at various distances from a fulcrum. Recent extensions to this model (McClelland & Jenkins, 1991) also demonstrated a differential readiness to learn, behaviorally similar to children in Siegler's (1976) experiments.

McClelland's model successfully captured many of the details found in the human balance scale literature, including orderly stage progression. It can also capture the torque difference effect (Schmidt & Shultz, 1991). However, this model failed to achieve a consistent level of Stage 4 performance. Of notable merit, McClelland's was the first balance scale model subjected to the rigorous rule assessment methodology used with humans and the first to demonstrate that progression through rule-based stages could be accomplished by connectionist learning.

The Environmental Bias Model

We have previously reported on a cascade-correlation model of development on a 10-peg, 10-weight balance scale task (Shultz, Mareschal, & Schmidt, 1994; Shultz & Schmidt, 1991). This model incorporated the assumption of an environmental training bias (after McClelland, 1989), where equal-distance problems (problems in which the distance of weights on either side of the balance scale are equal) were much more frequent than other types of problems in the training corpus. This training bias makes it difficult for the network to extract information contributed by the distance dimension, but allows the network to rely on weight information, thus encouraging initial performance at Stages 1 and 2. Coupled with this environmental bias was a training method that gradually introduced new patterns for the network to learn from. This training method is called *expansion training* and it conforms to the authors' assumption that the child's environment changes gradually as the child is exposed to more and more instances of lifting and holding objects.

The initial network topology of the environmental bias model appears in Fig. 5.3. The input encoding of both distance and weight information was implemented using integers in the range of 1 to 5. The activation values of the outputs (2 real numbers between -0.5 and $+0.5$) are interpreted to transform the network's output into one of three possible predictions. A prediction of *left side down* was conveyed by excitation of the first output unit and inhibition of the second output, whereas a prediction of *right side down* was conveyed by the reverse pattern. A *balance* prediction was conveyed by neutral (i.e., 0) values on both outputs.

The environmental bias model's initial training corpus was composed of 100 training patterns randomly selected without replacement from the entire set of 625 possible training instances (1 to 5 weights per peg, crossed with 1 to 5 regularly spaced pegs on either arm). Of these initial patterns, approximately 90% had weights placed equally distant from the fulcrum. On each subsequent epoch, another training pattern was randomly drawn

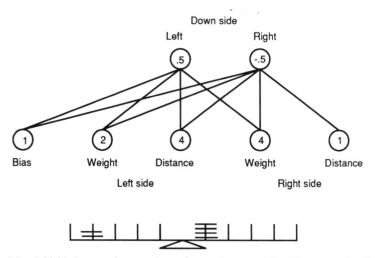

FIG. 5.3.   Initial balance scale network topology and an example of input encoding for the environmental bias balance scale network.

with replacement (also subject to the same bias) and added to the set of instances from which the network learned.

After each output epoch, the network's performance was evaluated using Siegler's rule assessment methodology. Twenty-four testing instances balanced for torque difference (four from each of the six different problem types, and of those four, one from each of four different torque difference levels) were randomly chosen at the beginning of each simulation run for use in assessing the network. All 16 runs of the model demonstrated orderly longitudinal stage progression as scored according to the criteria used in human studies (Siegler, 1976). Transitions between stages were typically soft, with a good deal of going back and forth between stages before settling into the higher stage. There were also observations of stage skipping and regression back to earlier stages (Shultz, Mareschal, & Schmidt, 1994; Shultz & Schmidt, 1991). A limited amount of stage skipping and regression is characteristic of human data as well (Chletsos, De Lisi, Turner, & McGillicuddy-De Lisi, 1989; Siegler, 1981).

Also congruent with human data, less error was observed in network responses to testing problems with larger torque differences. Recall that torque difference is the absolute difference between the torques on each arm of the balance scale.

The environmental bias model was also capable of strong Stage 4 performance, a quality missing in all previous balance scale modeling efforts (Langley, 1987; McClelland, 1989; Newell, 1990). Furthermore, the model captured all of these phenomena without having to separate the internal representations of weight and distance, as were required in previous connectionist models of the task (McClelland, 1989).

The Prestructured Weight Dimension Model

A second modeling attempt investigated whether a cascade-correlation model would naturally pass through all of the stages witnessed with humans if it were to start off focusing on weight information. This simulation tested the merits of a nativist position that sees evolution as having innately specified some initial state, as well as the initial structure, of the computational apparatus. This is similar in spirit to Spelke's (1990) suggestion that infants have implicit assumptions about their world that organize their sensory inputs.

Just as the evolutionary medium consists of an infinitely large space of possible tokens, so too does the connectionist medium. The entire space of possible models for a given network topology is delimited by a separate dimension for each degree of freedom in the model (each network connection, or weight), and the starting point of the model within this connection space constrains the form that the token model can take on the basis of new experiences. Evolution can be viewed in this light, as a coarse search through a space of possible organism types. Learning can be described as the further investigation of the local connection space around a token individual (Nolfi, Elman, & Parisi, 1990).

The current simulation investigated whether or not a connectionist model possessing, from the outset, a structure for assimilating weight but not distance information would produce the developmental sequence observed in children's balance scale performance. Another way of phrasing this is to ask whether domain-specific knowledge, as part of the network's starting state, can produce a realistic developmental sequence as domain-general learning procedures are applied. Whereas the environmental model discussed earlier places domain-specific constraints in the environment, this model internalizes such constraints.

There are several ways of placing a network into a particular region of connection space. One could supply initial connection weight values by hand, arrange for them to be inherited by natural selection (Belew, McInery, & Schraudolph, 1990), or pretrain the network with equal distance problems.

We adopted the last of these approaches for ease of implementation, creating a model in which networks were first placed in a region of connection space such that they performed at the level of stage 1, before being exposed to a corpus of unbiased training instances. The initial prestructured network topology appears in Fig. 5.4. Ten inputs and an obligatory bias unit were fully connected to each of two output units. Of the 10 inputs, 5 represented the left arm of the balance scale, and 5 represented

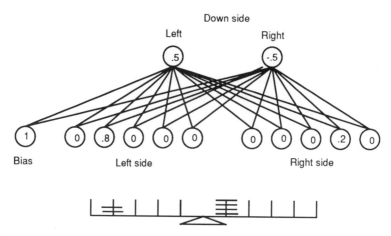

FIG. 5.4. Initial network topology and an example of input encoding for the prestructured weight balance scale network.

the right arm. Distance for either arm was encoded by a real valued number in the range of 0.0 to 1.0 that was proportional to the distance at which weights were placed on the arm. The weight dimension was represented locally with each unit of a given arm corresponding to the number of weights placed on that arm. For a given balance scale problem, the distance input value was entered as input to the corresponding weight input unit. This input encoding provides a compact representation of balance scale problems, yet does not produce a significantly different style of learning from locally encoded networks (Schmidt, 1991). The method of interpreting the outputs used in the environmental bias model was retained for use in the current model.

Network weights were randomly initialized in the range of -1.0 to $+1.0$ before pretraining began. During pretraining, the networks were exposed to a corpus consisting only of weight problems, until a proficient level of performance was reached, thereby endowing the network with a structure capable of processing weight problems. At this point, the network's connection weights were preserved and the training set was switched to include all 625 possible training instances. This second phase of training continued until the network had learned all of the training patterns.

After each output epoch during the second training phase, the responses of 96 networks to a set of 88 different testing problems were recorded. The testing problems included the 24 testing problems used by McClelland (1989) to diagnose network performance, and 4 problems from each of the four nonbalance problem types at four different torque difference levels. This collection of testing problems provided enough information to classify the networks' responses at four different levels of torque difference, as well as in the conventional manner in which problem type is confounded with torque-difference level.

Longitudinally, of the 96 networks, 83 (86%) were classified by one of Siegler's four rules at some point in development. Eighty nets (83%) demonstrated all four rules in the idealized sequence (1, 2, 3, 4). Sixty-eight nets (71%) displayed temporary regressions from Rule 4 to Rule 3. No other substantial regressions occurred. Thirteen nets (14%) skipped a stage at some point in development.

All of the networks performed well on the weight problems without requiring hidden units, and each required the addition of a single hidden unit in order to accommodate distance information. In all cases, the addition of this unit propelled them from Stage 1 into subsequent stages. This transition demonstrates that at least some qualitative changes in behavior (the use of distance information) require qualitative changes in network structure. However, we also observe qualitative behavioral changes (conforming to increasingly sophisticated rules) from the less drastic quantitative adjustment of connection weights.

Next, a cross-sectional analysis of rule use was carried out according to the method detailed by Schmidt (1991; Schmidt & Shultz, 1991). The 86% of networks that were classified by one of Siegler's four rules was fairly close to the human figure of 78%. If one drops the youngest age group from this calculation, as Siegler (1981) did, then 84% of nets were classified, compared with 91% of children. Fig. 5.5 plots the percentage of errors made on Siegler's six problem types at each of the four stages for Siegler's rules, children's data, and our network simulations. The epochs chosen for network results were those that most closely matched the children's data. In Fig. 5.5 there is a close correspondence between human and network responses for Rules 1 and 2. Rule 3 network performance deviated from the children's data in a number of ways, with poorer performance on weight and distance problems and better performance on conflict–balance prob-

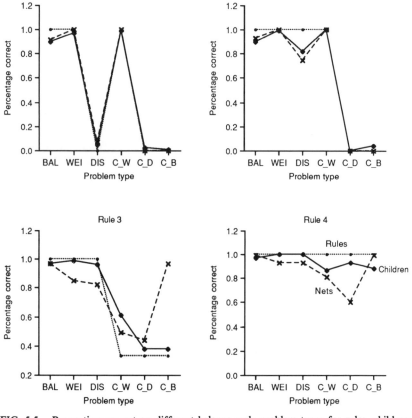

FIG. 5.5.   Proportion correct on different balance scale problem types for rules, children, and networks with early weight experience.

lems. Network Rule 4 performance was also generally worse than that of the children, with a notable difference on conflict–distance problems. Fig. 5.5 also depicts a U-shaped developmental trend in network performance on conflict–weight problems across Stages 2 through 4, similar to that observed with children.

Two different analyses for detecting the torque difference effect were performed on these networks. First, a cross-sectional analysis classified the network with four different testing sets, each containing problems of differing magnitudes of torque difference. Classifications of network performance improved with torque difference. As depicted in Fig. 5.6, the model's mean number of problems correct for each of the problem types increased with torque difference, except at torque difference level 4 for weight problems. The human data show similar trends, with children more frequently solving problems correctly from larger torque difference levels (Ferretti & Butterfield, 1986).

The second analysis used to assess the torque difference effect contrasted a network's total sum of squared error scores (*tss*) collected at each level of torque difference midway (output epoch 40) and late (output epoch 80) in training. Networks were tested with each of the four distinct testing sets,

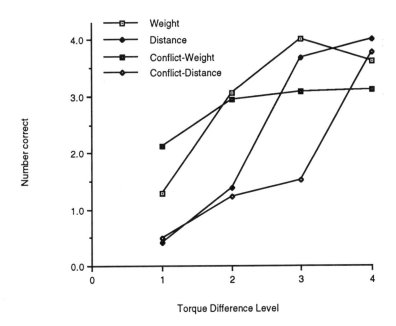

FIG. 5.6.   Differences in accuracy for balance scale problem types at different levels of torque difference for networks with prestructured weight experience.

consisting of problems chosen from a unique torque difference level, that were used in the cross-sectional analysis of the torque difference effect. At each of the four levels of torque difference, there were four problems representing each of Siegler's six problem types. The *tss* error scores from each output epoch sampling demonstrated strong negative linear trends. Although a measure of this sort is not strictly applicable to human data, this trend demonstrated that the larger the problem's torque difference, the smaller the error observed.

In summary, the prestructured weight dimension model demonstrated that all four of Siegler's rules do indeed fall naturally out of a cascade-correlation network that starts off from an initial state structured to specifically process weight but not distance information. Moreover, networks in the current simulation demonstrated some of the finer subtleties of human performance such as U-shaped development curves on conflict–weight problems and the torque difference effect.

Balance Scale Conclusions

The cascade-correlation balance scale models reported in this chapter capture the phenomena in children's balance scale data, including orderly stage progression and the torque difference effect. Both cascade-correlation models achieved a consistent level of Stage 4 performance, and at least one of the models also demonstrated U-shaped error performance for conflict–weight problems. Furthermore, both models accomplished their successes without the need to prespecify the network topology, or to assume separate processing structures for the weight and distance dimensions. It would appear that a generative connectionist learning algorithm is not only capable of implementing successful models of cognitive development on the balance scale task, but does so with fewer assumptions and a greater level of success than do previous methods. Although the use of a domain-general learning algorithm was crucial, both models required domain-specific constraints in terms of either the structure of the environment or the initial placement of the network in connection space. There is not yet definitive evidence for differentiating the better set of modeling assumptions, although both models do make predictions about the learning environment. One model predicts that there is an environmental bias, whereas the other does not. Both models predict that Stage 4 performance does not necessarily require explicit knowledge of the torque rule, and that this competence can be achieved by adequate exposure to the problem domain.

The cascade-correlation learning architecture (and connectionism in general) greatly constrains the range of successful implementations of the balance scale task. Only a few specific sets of underlying assumptions yield the desired longitudinal performance. It will be of telling interest, for purposes of model and theory building, to discover what characteristics of successful connectionist implementations correspond with human data. Our modeling efforts have captured a number of key phenomena observed in the human cross-sectional data, including some aspects of performance that other models failed to achieve. Accurate models of this nature can provide a means of investigating longitudinal properties that are difficult to reveal solely via the typical cross-sectional investigations of children.

CONCEPTS OF POTENCY AND RESISTANCE
IN CAUSAL PREDICTION

Accurately predicting the magnitude of a physical effect requires the integration of information regarding potency of the cause and resistance to the effect's occurrence. In some physical systems, potency and resistance are combined in a subtractive manner $(p - r)$ to produce the effect, whereas in others, they are combined by division $(p \div r)$.

Psychology of Potency and Resistance

Past research on the development of these concepts revealed a number of psychological regularities. Zelazo and Shultz (1989) conducted a study with two pieces of physical apparatus, one of which combined potency and resistance using a subtraction rule (a two-tray balance scale) and the other combining potency and resistance using a division rule (a ramp). From 1 to 6 equal weights of identical appearance could be placed on the *potency* tray of the balance, and from 1 to 6 identical weights could be placed on the *resistance* tray of the balance. The magnitude of effect was indicated by the degree of deflection of a dial on the face of the scale. The six levels of potency and six levels of resistance generated 36 possible patterns. In an analogous way, from one to six wooden blocks of identical appearance could be placed at the top or bottom of the ramp. The number of blocks placed at the top constituted the manipulation of potency; the number of blocks placed at the bottom constituted the manipulation of resistance. Magnitude of effect was the distance traveled by the leading edge of the leading block at the bottom of the ramp after the collision caused by the release of the blocks at the top. The six levels of potency and six of resistance for the ramp generated 36 effect size patterns.

With increasing age, children showed an increase in the number of levels of potency and resistance used and gradual convergence on the correct rule. The subtraction rule was acquired earlier than the division rule, and there was temporary overgeneralization of subtraction to division problems.

Potency and Resistance Simulations

We were able to simulate these psychological regularities in cascade-correlation networks (Shultz, Zelazo, & Strigler, 1991). As in the psychological research, 72 problems were created by combining six levels of potency and six levels of resistance with two different combination rules, subtraction and division. These problems were the training patterns for some of the network simulations. Potency and resistance were coded in a variety of different ways in different simulations, but we focus here on what we called *Gaussian* coding. The six amounts of potency or resistance were coded over six input units such that the *nth* unit received an input value of 3 and the two surrounding units an input value of 1 each. Other input units in the same bank received an input of 0. Thus, the input unit activations approximated a Gaussian distribution. There were six such units for potency and six for resistance. In addition, there was an apparatus unit that was coded as 0 for subtraction and 1 for division. All inputs and the bias unit were fully connected to a single output with a linear activation function that represented the magnitude of effect, scaled to fall between 0 and 1.

Before each epoch of training, the network was tested with the 36 subtraction training patterns, the 36 division training patterns, and 36 non-trained patterns in which the subtraction outputs were associated with an apparatus unit coded for division. Comparing error scores on the first two sets of patterns provided a measure of how well the network was learning the correct subtraction and division rules, respectively. Comparing error scores on the second and third pattern sets enabled an assessment of whether or not the network might be using subtraction to solve the division problems.

Learning and overgeneralization effects in one network are portrayed in Figs. 5.7 and 5.8, respectively. Fig. 5.7 shows earlier and deeper learning of subtraction than of division. Fig. 5.8 shows a sizable overgeneralization effect in which, just prior to asymptotic performance, the error for a subtraction rule on the division problems is lower than that for a division rule on five epochs. All of the Gaussian coded networks showed these general patterns, although not at precisely the same epochs.

To examine the ability of these networks to simulate the gradual increase in levels of potency and resistance, a separate simulation was run in which network predictions were generated every fourth epoch (up to 20 epochs) for all of the 72 training patterns. These predictions were analyzed in the same manner as for human subjects to obtain the number of levels of potency and resistance employed on both subtraction and division problems (Zelazo & Shultz, 1989). The results, plotted in Fig. 9 for each of four apparatus and potency versus resistance combinations, reveal a steady increase in the numbers of levels used. For comparison, the mean numbers of levels used by human subjects are listed in the upper left corner of Fig. 5.9.

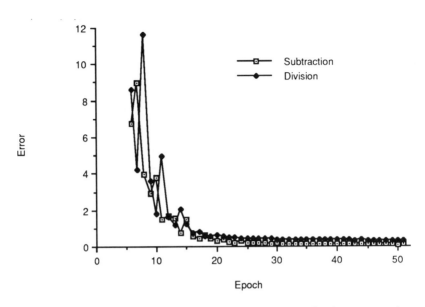

FIG. 5.7.   Learning of subtraction and division in a potency and resistance network.

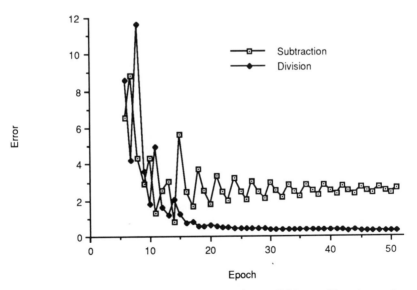

FIG. 5.8.   Temporary overgeneralization of subtraction to division problems in a potency and resistance network.

227

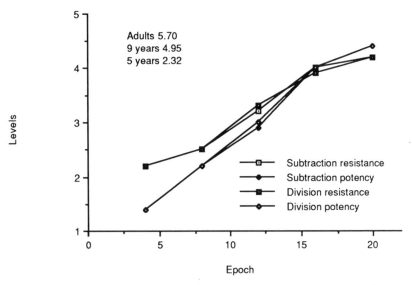

FIG. 5.9.   Mean numbers of levels of potency and resistance used over epochs.

One concern with networks that use distributed binary input codings is that, because they employ so many input units and consequently have so many weights, they might be memorizing the training patterns rather than abstracting useful generalizations about them. Generalization ability was assessed by training the networks with a randomly selected two thirds of the training patterns and testing on both the training patterns and the one third nontrained patterns at each epoch. Mean error for 10 networks at each epoch for training and test patterns is presented in Fig. 5.10. The results reveal that error for the test patterns decreases with that for the training patterns, indicating good generalization.

All of these results held up with a variety of different input coding techniques, except that coding potency and resistance with integer values precluded a gradual construction of these dimensions. All of the cascade-correlation networks we tried reached an asymptote error close to the adult error of 1.08, computed in the same way as network error. None of the networks recruited any hidden units to reach this level of performance.

We had more difficulty simulating these effects with back-propagation networks, whether or not they were equipped with hidden units. This is probably due to the fact that units with sigmoid (S-shaped) activation functions are somewhat unstable in their middle range in that a small change in net input can produce a large change in activation. Using linear output units was avoided because excessive positive feedback can occasionally lead to diverging output activations. Because cascade-correlation switches to a hidden unit recruitment mode if a fixed number of epochs has

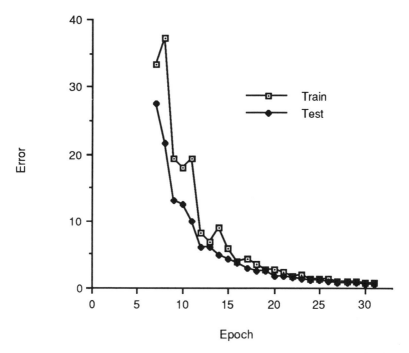

FIG. 5.10.   Mean error at each epoch for training and test patterns on potency and resistance problems.

passed, it can escape from such cases. Thus, it is relatively safe to use linear output units in the cascade-correlation architecture. The option of linear output units in cascade-correlation thus provided an unexpected advantage. Further experimentation revealed that it was possible to simulate the human regularities with nonlinear output units, but these effects are more robust with linear outputs.

Potency and Resistance Conclusions

Network simulations of the concepts of potency and resistance covered all of the phenomena found in the effect size predictions of children. These included an increase in the number of levels of potency and resistance used and convergence on the correct rules as learning progressed, early acquisition of the subtraction rule, and temporary overgeneralization of subtraction to division problems. All but the first of these phenomena would appear to be due to the domain-general characteristics of cascade-correlation learning, particularly to the use of an activation function that sums the inputs to a receiving unit. An additive activation function makes it easier to learn subtraction than division. Visual inspection of network weights indicated the networks were using the apparatus unit to dampen down predictions for division problems. Because the networks were using the same set of weights to solve both subtraction and division problems, the subtraction rule emerged first and temporarily generalized to division before the weights were sufficiently adjusted to lower the division errors.

The gradual increase in the number of levels of potency and resistance used to predict effect size is due to a domain-specific constraint of input encoding that does not inherently represent quantitative dimensions. The Gaussian coding technique used here is one of a number of coding techniques that fail to provide quantitative dimensionality. Initially, the network knows nothing about the relations among adjacent input units. As learning progresses, the network constructs the dimensions of potency and resistance. In contrast, coding inputs as integers on single units fails to generate an increase in levels used, because the quantitative dimensions are explicitly provided to the network.

SERIATION

Piaget and his colleagues (Piaget, 1965; Piaget & Inhelder, 1973) developed the seriation task in order to demonstrate the presence of developmental stages in children's transitive reasoning. Because the results initially seemed clear and replicable, a number of production rule models of children's seriation were published (Baylor, Gascon, Lemoyne, & Pothier, 1973; Young, 1976). However, these models remained structural descriptions in the sense that they depicted behaviors at particular stages and did not implement any transition mechanisms.

In this section we describe a cascade-correlation model of the development of children's seriation abilities. A more detailed account can be found in Mareschal and Shultz (1993). We begin with a brief review of the relevant psychological literature. Then, the network architecture is described. Finally, the model's performance is presented and evaluated.

Psychology of Seriation

Piaget (1965) reported that children's ability to seriate (sort) a set of objects along a specified dimension evolved through four successive stages of performance. Children in the first stage made no real effort to order the objects and either moved them around at random or presented the objects in the same order as they had found them. Children in the second stage were able to correctly order subsets of the set of objects, but did not extend this order over the whole set. Hence, they would construct successive ordered subsets of two, three, or four objects. This led to a variety of characteristic outcomes including ordered pairs of triplets, a series that first rises then falls off, and correct seriation of the first few elements followed by inability to continue the series appropriately. Children in the third stage sorted the complete set of items, but only by using an empirical trial and error method with many self-corrections. Finally, children classified as being in the fourth stage constructed an ordered set quickly and efficiently by applying what appeared to be a systematic strategy. Piaget labeled this strategy the *operational method*. It consisted in selecting the smallest, as yet unordered, element and moving it into its correct place in the series.

Rule-based models (Baylor et al., 1973; Young, 1976) succeeded in capturing the systematicity of performance at each of these four stages. However, in depth protocol analyses revealed that seriation was far more flexible than Piaget suggested (Young, 1976). Random selection strategies were observed in children of all ages, including those well into the fourth, operational stage (Kingma, 1982).

Moreover, perceptual factors were found to influence children's perfor-mance. Piaget (1965) noticed that if the differences between elements were too large, then Stage 3 seriators would artificially be promoted to Stage 4 because the empirical method they use would be efficient given the high perceptual salience of the dimension generating the order. Conversely, if differences between objects become sufficiently small, seriation perfor-mance deteriorates (Elkind, 1964; Kingma, 1984). Also, Koslowski (1980) showed that Stage 1 seriators could be made to seriate at a Stage 4 level if given an abbreviated task with few items. She suggested that these children possessed the requisite seriation skills and that there is development in the precision with which these skills are applied.

The production rule models not only fail to capture stage transitions but do not address the perceptual saliency issues. A connectionist approach suggests an alternative modeling solution because (as illustrated throughout this chapter) it can capture rulelike behavior and perceptual effects without sacrificing flexibility.

The Seriation Model

We adopted an approach first suggested by Young (1976), who decomposed seriation into a succession of independent moves based on immediate perceptual features. Similarly, our cascade-correlation model is designed to respond to independent arrays with an appropriate move. Once a move has been computed by the network model, it is carried out by supporting software, and the network is then presented with the resulting array. Iterating this procedure may ultimately produce an ordered array.

The network was given the dual task of identifying which item should be moved and where it should be moved, according to Piaget's operational method. We opted for a modular solution because simulations using a single homogeneous network failed to demonstrate psychologically realistic performance. A number of researchers argued for modular task decomposition (Jacobs, Jordan, & Barto, 1991; Minsky, 1986). Modular architectures were claimed to increase both learning speed and generalizability (Jacobs et al., 1991).

The two modules consist of two simultaneously but independently trained networks, as shown in Fig. 5.11. The *which* network is trained to identify which item should be moved when presented with an array. The *where* network is trained to identify where an item should be moved to when presented with the same array. In both cases, targets are defined as the move dictated by Piaget's operational method. As noted earlier, this involved selecting the smallest unordered stick and placing it in its correct position. The modules are independent because the weight updates within each network are based solely on the error arising within that network. Each network has no information concerning the performance of its counterpart. Because each move requires integrating responses across modules, the macroscopic behavior of the model as a whole results from the interaction of the developmental states of each independent module. Thus, systematic errors may arise when one module lags behind the other in performance.

The model was trained to seriate an array of six items as follows. Each item had a unique value determined by an integer ranging from 1 to 6. The location of the item was spatially coded on a bank of six linear input units. Thus, a completely ordered array was coded by a 1 in the first unit, a 2 in the second unit, and so forth, with a 6 in the sixth unit. The output (whether *which* or *where*) was coded on a bank of six sigmoid units in which the unit coding the correct position is turned on and all others are turned off. The actual response was determined by selecting the output unit with the highest activation.

Pilot studies revealed that the model was sensitive to the disorder of the arrays presented. Disorder was quantified as the sum squared distance (d^2) from the target ordered array. Input patterns were classed as being distant from the solution if d^2 was greater than 20 and near to the solution if d^2 was less than or equal to 20. Of the total 720 possible six-element patterns, 79% are distant patterns and 21% are near patterns. A biased training set was constructed by randomly sampling 50 distant and 50 near patterns. In order to capture the fact that even very young children can successfully order sets of 3 elements, we included 20 3-element series in the training set.

The model's performance was evaluated in two ways. Generalization was tested by evaluating whether or not the model produced the correct move for all of the possible six-element series. Its seriation stage performance was

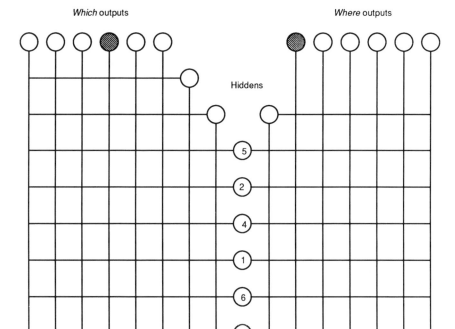

Which outputs   Where outputs

Hiddens

5
2
4
1
6
3

Array inputs

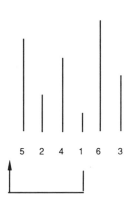

5 2 4 1 6 3

FIG. 5.11.   Modularized seriation networks. The row of vertical units contains the input units on which is represented the current status of the array to be seriated. The input feeds independently to the left-hand and the right-hand modules. The left-hand side is devoted to computing which item in the array should be moved, and the right-hand side is devoted to computing where the item should be moved to. In this case, the *which* module has two hidden units and the *where* module has one hidden unit. Inputs and target outputs are shown for the array {5 2 4 1 6 3}. The stick in the fourth position should be moved to the first position of the array.

evaluated by presenting a test pattern to the network.[3] The state resulting from each move was cycled back as the next input. The cycling process continued until the presence of a loop was detected. From the resulting trace of arrays, the model was then classified as being in one of the four developmental stages.

Stage classification can be somewhat of a problem, not just for networks, but also for children (Kingma, 1982). In particular, it is not always clear how to differentiate between Stage 3 and Stage 4 seriators. In our simulations, Stages 1 and 2 are diagnosed as described by Piaget. To distinguish between Stage 3 (empirical) and Stage 4 (operational) seriators, both the procedure used and the number of self-corrections criteria are simultaneously applied. A network is classified as Stage 4 if it correctly constructs a series according to the operational method with at most one error from which it continues using the same operational method, or if it seriates in the same or fewer moves than required by the operational method. It is classified as Stage 3 if it constructs a completed series in any other way. Under these conditions, networks typically exhibited a succession of all four stages in the correct order.

To test whether or not these networks responded to perceptual variations in the same way as children do, we ran three additional conditions. In these, the training set consisted only of the 100 6-element arrays. The three conditions differed only in the size of differences between successive elements of the ordered set: 1.0, 0.5, 0.25. The proportions out of 20 models able to complete a full sort by the end of training were 0.85, 0.55, 0.15 respectively. Thus, as with the children, the more easily the stick sizes can be distinguished, the better the seriation performance. Furthermore, 85% of the models trained with 1.0 size differences were diagnosed at Stage 4, as compared to only 25% of the nets trained with 0.5 size differences. This supports Piaget's (1965) claim that Stage 3 performers would be classed at Stage 4 as size differences between sticks increase.

Inspection of Hinton diagrams generated at epochs representing consistent stage behavior revealed no drastic differences in weights between adjacent stages. Instead, stage differences were marked by rather small modifications in the size of weights. The Hinton diagrams also revealed that the development of seriation ability began by adjusting weights leading to those units dealing with the short end of the series and was progressively extended along the length of the series until appropriate weights were found for the larger end of the series.

Finally, the disorder of the array positively predicted the model's ability to identify the correct move in the generalization test. In a study carried out on children aged 4 to 7 years, we found that disorder was similarly related

---

[3]Following Retschitzki (1978), we used the {5 2 4 1 6 3} array.

to children's decisions as to whether a series was completed, or still needed some sorting (Mareschal, 1992).

Seriation Conclusions

Cascade-correlation nets captured progression through the four seriation stages, as well as a perceptual effect based on the differential sizes of the items to be sorted. Another perceptual effect on array disorder was noted, and some supporting psychological evidence was provided by studies of children who showed more difficulty with less disordered arrays.

A number of domain-specific constraints were required to capture seriation stages, including a modularization of the task into *which* and *where* subnets and a slight environmental bias in favor of smaller and less disordered arrays. Both of these biases seem reasonable. Smaller arrays are probably more common to the young child's experience than large ones, and less disordered arrays are more likely to function as a cue to sorting attempts than are highly disordered arrays. In any case, these biases could be considered as predictions for the young child's environment. Task modularity could also conceivably be assessed through psychological research that concentrated on possible dissociations between selection and insertion abilities.

Perceptual effects in seriation can be attributed to the domain-general characteristics of the learning algorithm. As with the balance scale task, more distinctive quantitative inputs naturally result in clearer activation signals downstream and more decisive moves; inputs to hidden and output units are a function of the activation values of sending units.[4]

DISTANCE, TIME, AND VELOCITY

Recently we began to extend our research from tasks that involve the integration of two physical dimensions (e.g., weight and distance in the

---

[4]In chapter 8 (this volume), Klahr critizes our seriation model for not exhibiting the multiple strategies typical of children. However, our model is motivated by the fact that it is the rule-based models that are too rigid to account for both individual variation among children and the variation across seriation problems due to perceptual effects on the seriation task (as their authors freely admit). In contrast, even though we constructed our training patterns with the single rule specified by Piaget (move the smallest unordered stick to its correct position), we found considerable variation in performance among nets and problems (Mareschal, 1992). A variety of behaviors fell under various stage diagnoses, and there was sufficient variation to account for the various perceptual effects. This is the only existing seriation model to spontaneously generate variation, and much of that variation does correspond to variation in children.

balance scale task, and potency and resistance in causal prediction) to those involving three dimensions. The example we cover here is the integration of distance, time, and velocity concepts. In classical physics, distance is defined as $d = t \times v$, time as $t = d \div v$, and velocity as $v = d \div t$, where d is distance, t is time, and v is velocity.

Psychology of Distance, Time, and Velocity Concepts

Piaget (1969, 1970) investigated the development of these concepts after Einstein had inquired about the nature of children's understanding of time and velocity. Piaget's research led him to conclude that the acquisition of these concepts occurred in three stages. At 4 or 5 years of age, intuitive notions emerge. For example, children's early concept of distance traveled is in terms of the stopping point of an object rather than the interval between starting and stopping points. These early intuitions are followed by an intermediary stage and finally, the adultlike concepts emerge at approximately 8 or 9 years of age. In response to Einstein's inquiry, Piaget concluded that although an intuitive notion of velocity existed independent of time, the notion of time was dependent on the child's notion of velocity at most ages. Thus, children's early understanding was more akin to relativistic concepts of time and velocity.

Siegler and Richards (1979) addressed several methodological difficulties in Piaget's work, including the use of tasks that were not necessarily comparable across concepts. Siegler and Richards presented children with two toy trains running along parallel tracks and asked them to judge which train either traveled for the longer time, the greater distance, or faster. They hypothesized three rules based on Piaget's work. Children using Rule 1 would make their judgments based on the stopping points of the trains. Those using Rule 2 would also consider starting points when the trains stopped at the same point. Finally, children using Rule 3 would solve the problems correctly.

Siegler and Richards used a rule assessment methodology similar to that employed with the balance scale. Their results indicated that 5-year-old children used Rule 1 on all three tasks, whereas adults used Rule 3. In between these two age groups, children often confused velocity and distance, distance and time, and time and velocity. In addition, children understood distance and velocity concepts before time concepts.

Levin (1977) examined children's understanding of time and argued that in tasks used by Piaget and Siegler and Richards, distance and velocity information served as interfering cues with children's understanding of time. Moreover, Levin (1979) argued that cues logically unrelated to time interfere in a similar manner.

Wilkening (1981) made a similar argument, suggesting that research by Piaget and others appeared to have tested the child's ability to ignore rather than integrate dimensional cues. For example, to judge which train traveled the greater distance, the child simply had to compare the distance of the two trains and ignore their times and velocities.

Within the framework of Anderson's (1974, 1991) Information Integration Theory, and its assessment methodology, *functional measurement*, Wilkening (1981) designed new tasks in which values on two dimensions were given and the value of the third dimension had to be inferred by the child. For example, in a distance-inference task, children were shown an apparatus that had, at one end of a footbridge, a dog and several other animals that were said to be frightened of the dog. The children were told that the other animals would run along the bridge as soon as the dog began to bark and would stop when the barking ceased. The task involved determining how far each animal would run. Thus, the children were given the characteristic velocity of the animals and the time they ran (the duration of barking), and asked to infer the distance they would run.

Wilkening studied the performance of three age groups: 5-year-olds, 10-year-olds, and adults. The findings included the following: (a) in the distance-inference task, all age groups used the correct multiplication rule; (b) in a time-inference task, 10-year-olds and adults employed the correct division rule, whereas 5-year-olds used a subtraction rule, $t = d - v$; (c) in a velocity-inference task, the two older age groups used a subtraction rule, $v = d - t$, and the 5-year-olds used an identity rule, $v = d$.

Wilkening concluded that young children did have the ability to integrate these dimensions. However, he was unwilling to make comparative claims about the developmental rates of the three concepts because it appeared that the subjects had differing memory demands across the three tasks. For example, in the distance task, subjects of all age groups used an eye-movement strategy in which they appeared to "follow" the imaginary animal as it ran across the footbridge.

In a follow-up study, Wilkening (1982) attempted to increase the memory demands of the distance task by presenting the time information (barking) before the velocity information (animal identity) and lessen the memory demands of the velocity task by visually presenting the time information. The modifications partially supported his hypothesis in that 5-year-olds were observed to use an additive rule ($d = t + v$) in the distance task. However, the results of the velocity task remained unchanged. Thus, it remains to be seen whether or not the mastery of time before velocity concepts is an accurate description of the developmental course or a memory artifact of Wilkening's tasks.

Simulating the Acquisition of Distance, Time, and Velocity Concepts

We followed Wilkening's example by creating input patterns that included information about two dimensions and having the network predict, as output, the value of the third dimension. We chose dimensional values ranging from 1 to 5 as our input values. The dimension that was to be predicted received an input of 0. We crossed five levels of distance, time, and velocity respectively to obtain 75 input patterns. There were 25 instances of each of the three inference pattern types: distance, time, and velocity.

The initial network topology consisted of three banks of input units, one bank each for distance, time, and velocity information, connected to one linear output unit. We used what we call *nth* encoding for the dimensional values on the input units. In *nth* encoding, a value *n* is represented by assigning an input value of 1 to the *nth* input unit and 0 to all other units. Thus, to encode the 3 dimensional values having a range of 1 to 5, a total of 15 input units were used—5 units for each dimension. For a given inference pattern, one input bank would receive activations of 0 on all five of its inputs, indicating it was unknown. With respect to the other two input banks, the appropriate unit would receive an activation of 1 corresponding to its dimensional value and 0 on the other units within the bank.

Training And Testing.   At each epoch of training, all 75 inference problems were presented to the network. Thirty networks were trained for a maximum of 1,500 epochs. Every fifth epoch, the net was tested to obtain the relevant information necessary to assess its performance.

In analyzing a network's performance, we are not so much interested in whether or not the network can accurately predict, for example, a given velocity from time and distance information. Rather, we are interested in what sort of rule best captures the network's predictions over each of the three problem types. Thus, we look at correlations between the network's responses and those predicted by various plausible rules such as identity ($v = d$, or $v = t$), addition ($v = d + t$, or $v = d - t$), or multiplication ($v = d \times t$, $v = t \div d$, or $v = d \div t$) rules. In this way, we investigated networks' ability to capture the stage progressions observed by Wilkening with children. In order to capture consistent network performance, a given rule had to correlate positively with network responses, account for more than 50% of the variance in network responses, and account for more of that variance than other rules did.

Results.   A stage-by-epoch plot of a typical network based on stage onset and offset and hidden unit recruitment is shown in Fig. 5.12. All 30 networks demonstrated a similar developmental sequence. As can be seen, early in training, before the recruitment of any hidden units, time and velocity identity stages ($t = d$ and $v = d$) were observed. On average, these identity stages began together and lasted for the same length of time. The time and velocity identity rules were strong predictors of the networks' responses, accounting for over 90% of the variance in predictions. During

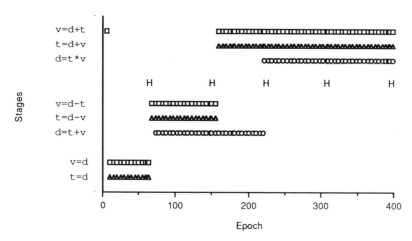

FIG. 5.12.   Rule diagnosis results for one network showing the progression of stages over epochs for distance, time, and velocity inferences. Each *H* marks the recruitment of a hidden unit.

this same period, the networks' responses to distance-inference patterns was not captured by any of the rules that were tested.

After the first hidden unit had been recruited, additive stages were observed with respect to all three inference types. Distance, time, and velocity inferences were captured by the additive rules $d = t + v$, $t = d - v$, and $v = d - t$, respectively. Although all three of these stages began at approximately the same epoch, the distance additive stage was typically longer. These 3 additive rules were good predictors of the networks' responses, accounting for over 80% of the variance in predictions.

Multiplicative stages of time ($t = d \div v$) and velocity ($v = d \div t$) inferences began just after the second hidden unit was recruited. On average, the multiplicative stage of distance inferences ($d = t \times v$) began after the third hidden unit was recruited. All three defining multiplicative rules of the stages eventually reached a maximum r^2 of 1.00. This occurred earlier for time and velocity inference patterns than for distance inferences. See Buckingham and Shultz (1994) for a more detailed presentation of these results.

Analysis of Hinton diagrams revealed that the first hidden unit distinguished distance inference patterns from time and velocity inference patterns. Typically, weights from the time and velocity input banks were of the same sign and opposite in sign to weights from the distance input bank. As a result, when a distance inference pattern was presented, the time and velocity inputs augmented each other. In contrast, when a time or velocity inference pattern was presented, the distance input was counteracted by the velocity or time input. Unfortunately, Hinton analysis of the second and third hidden units were less revealing. However, given the relatively abrupt transition after the installation of these hidden units to multiplicative stages, the need for increased nonlinearity seems evident.

Conclusions on Distance, Time, and Velocity

Our simulation results differ only marginally from Wilkening's (1981) human results. The distance developmental sequence observed in network performance is the same as the one found by Wilkening—a progression from an additive rule to correct integration based on multiplication. With respect to the time and velocity developmental sequences, the networks began with an identity rule, progressed to an additive rule, and then finished with a correct multiplicative rule. Wilkening's human subjects did the same, except that they showed no identity rule for time inferences and failed to reach the correct multiplicative rule for velocity inferences. Our network results predict these "missing" stages for younger and older (more experienced) subjects than those used by Wilkening.

Identity, additive, and multiplicative stages in network performance emerged from the domain-general constraints of the cascade-correlation learning algorithm. That is, identity rules arise from the limited computational abilities of cascade-correlation's initial perceptron topology. Although simple weight adjustment is sufficient to decrease a substantial proportion of the sum of squared error of the various inference patterns, it is insufficient to allow the emergence of performance characterized by more advanced rules. After the recruitment of a single hidden unit, more complex performance emerges that can be characterized by additive rules in which two known values are added or subtracted to predict a third value. Finally, performance characterized by the correct multiplicative rules requires further computational nonlinearity provided by the recruitment of additional hidden units.

Developmental performance, characterized by specific algebraic rules, can be simulated in a network that learns by simple weight adjustment and hidden unit recruitment. The progression from linear to nonlinear rules parallels the potency and resistance simulations presented earlier. Such progressions occur naturally in cascade-correlation nets because they employ units with an additive activation function.

ACQUISITION OF PERSONAL PRONOUNS

Consider the following interchange:

Father (to daughter): "OK, Jane, let's practice our pronouns."
Jane (enthusiastically): "Okay, dad."

Father (pointing to himself): "Me" (and then to daughter): "You!"
Jane (pointing to herself gleefully): "You!"
Father (pointing to himself): "No, no. Me!"
Jane (confused, points to father): "Me!"
Father (frustrated after several failed attempts): "OK, me Daddy, you Jane."

This fictional dialogue between a father and his young daughter is meant to illustrate two problems a child faces when trying to learn the correct use of personal pronouns such as *me* and *you*. First, the referent of *me* and *you* is not fixed but shifts with conversational role. For example, when a child's father and mother talk to each other, both refer to themselves as *me* and to the other as *you*. Thus, the referent of *me* and *you* depends on who is speaking and who is being addressed. Second, the model for correct use of personal pronouns is not ordinarily given in speech addressed directly to the child. As just demonstrated, when a father addresses his child, he refers to himself as *me* and to the child as *you*. If Jane were to imitate what she heard, she would incorrectly refer to herself as *you* and to her father as *me*. Such errors have been called *reversal errors* because the child reverses the correct use of the pronouns.

Psychology of Personal Pronouns

Given that the task of learning personal pronouns is so complex, it is remarkable that most children master their correct use by 3 years of age (Clark, 1978). Perhaps even more remarkable is the fact that the majority of children do so without reversal errors (Charney, 1980b; Chiat, 1981). However, some children, like the fictional Jane, do make reversal errors, and such errors can often persist for months (Clark, 1978; Oshima-Takane, 1992; Schiff-Meyers, 1983).

Theories of personal pronoun acquisition can be placed in one of two categories: those focusing on children's correct performance, and those focusing on the errors children make. Within the former category, research focused on speech roles (Shipley & Shipley, 1969) and imitation without understanding (Charney, 1980b). Examples of theories focusing on errors include children's inability to distinguish self from other (Bettleheim, 1967; Charney, 1980a) and the interpretation of pronouns as names, in which the first person pronoun equals the name of the parent and the second person pronoun equals the name of the child (Clark, 1978). Regardless of the focus, these theories can account for only part of the picture. Focusing on errors does not explain how the majority of children master personal pronouns without error, and focusing on correctness fails to explain why some children make persistent reversal errors.

In an attempt to understand the variation in children's pronoun errors, Oshima-Takane (1988) hypothesized that the nature of the speech that a child hears plays a critical role. Although some researchers have argued that nonaddressed speech (in which the child is not being talked to) is unimportant in language acquisition (de Paulo & Bonvillian, 1978; Ervin-Tripp, 1971), Oshima-Takane maintained that it is this type of speech that enables the child to acquire the correct semantic rules for pronouns. The correct semantic rules specify that the first person pronoun refers to the person using it and the second person pronoun refers to the person who is addressed.

The importance of nonaddressed speech in acquiring personal pronouns was shown in both a training experiment (Oshima-Takane, 1988) and an observational study (Oshima-Takane & Derevensky, 1990). In the training experiment, 18 English-speaking, 19-month-old children and their parents participated in a pronoun game. In the nonaddressee condition, the game had two parts. In the first part, the mother pointed to herself and said *me*. Then the father said *me* pointing to himself, after which the mother pointed to the father and said "Yes, you." Immediately following this exchange, the second part of the game began. Here the mother pointed to herself and said *me* once again and then waited for the child to say *me* pointing to himself or herself. If the child said *me* the mother responded "Yes, you." If the child did not respond, the mother simply pointed to the child and said *you*. In any event, the game was then replayed.

In the addressee condition, the game involved only the second part of the nonaddressee game, except that both mother and father took turns addressing the child. The results of this experiment indicated that only the children who heard nonaddressee speech were able to use the pronouns without error. In contrast, reversal errors were common among children in the addressee condition.

In the observational study, 16 first- and secondborn children who had a sibling 1 to 4 years older were observed during free-play sessions (Oshima-Takane & Derevensky, 1990). Although the two groups did not differ on general language measures such as mean length of utterance, the secondborn children acquired personal pronouns earlier than the firstborn children. This result was predicted from the fact that secondborn children have more opportunities to hear speech not addressed to them because they hear conversations between the parent and older sibling.

We attempted to model the learning of personal pronouns in English. We used extreme versions of Oshima-Takane's (1988) training experiment, as illustrated in Fig. 5.13. In this figure, the arrows originate from the speaker, start out in the direction of the addressee, and end up pointing to the referent. We trained the network in two phases. During Phase 1, the network was trained on only parent speaking patterns, illustrated in the top

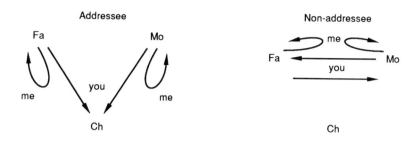

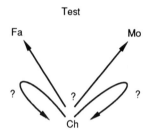

FIG. 5.13. Training patterns for the pronoun simulations. Adapted with permission from Shultz, Buckingham, and Oshima-Takane (1994).

half of Fig. 5.13, simulating the early period in which children listen to conversations without participating. In Phase 2, the network was trained on child speaking patterns, illustrated in the bottom half of Fig. 5.13, simulating the later period when children join in conversation. The critical question was how long it would take the network to learn the child speaking patterns in Phase 2 given the type of Phase 1 training it had received.

Pure Condition Simulations

In our first set of simulations (Shultz, Buckingham, & Oshima-Takane, 1994), we examined two idealized situations: one in which a child only hears speech addressed to him or her (addressee condition), and the opposite situation in which he or she only hears speech between his or her parents (nonaddressee condition).

We used four patterns in each condition. In the addressee condition, shown in the top left of Fig. 5.13, the patterns corresponded to both the mother and the father addressing the child and saying *me* and *you* appropriately. In the nonaddressee condition, shown in the top right of Fig. 5.13, the patterns corresponded to one parent addressing the other parent and referring to the self or the other. In Phase 2, the network was trained on child speaking patterns, shown at the bottom of Fig. 5.13. There were four such patterns corresponding to the child speaking to each parent and saying *me* or *you*. Again, the critical question was how long it would take the network to learn the child speaking patterns in Phase 2 given the type of Phase 1 training it had received.

The initial network topology consisted of six input units and a bias unit fully connected to two output units (Fig. 5.14). The six input units were comprised of three pairs of units corresponding to speaker, addressee, and referent, respectively. The identities of the participants in the conversation were distributed across a pair of units as follows: 1 0 for father, 0 1 for mother, and 1 1 for child. The target values on the output units were $+0.5$ -0.5 for *me* responses and -0.5 $+0.5$ for *you* responses.

We discovered that addressee training during Phase 1 was easy for our networks. On average, the networks required only 14 epochs to reach victory. This contrasted sharply with the length of time needed to master nonaddressee patterns, where the mean number of epochs to victory was 47 epochs. Moreover, only within the nonaddressee condition was it necessary to recruit a hidden unit. The extra computational power provided by the hidden unit was necessary to encode the shifting pronominal reference found in the nonaddressee patterns. That is, in the addressee patterns, *you* always referred to the child and *me* always referred to the mother or the father. Conversely, in nonaddressee training, the referent of *me* and *you* could be either *mother* or *father*.

Training times required for Phase 2 patterns revealed the opposite tendency. That is, networks that had received nonaddressee Phase 1 training were able to learn Phase 2 patterns very quickly ($M = 14$ epochs),

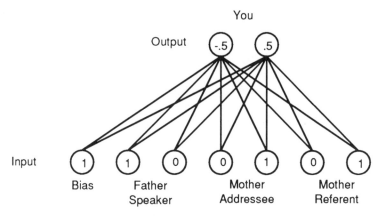

FIG. 5.14. Initial network topography and an example of input and output coding for the situation in which the father speaks, points to the mother, and says *you*.

whereas those that had received addressee training in Phase 1 required 111 Phase 2 epochs, on average. In addition, the networks in the latter condition needed to recruit a hidden unit, whereas the nonaddressee networks did not. Again, we took this as evidence that nonlinear computational power was needed to encode pronominal shifts. Because the networks that received nonaddressee training had already compensated for these shifts, they could more easily learn the child speaking patterns.

Networks in the addressee condition showed persistent reversal errors before performing correctly. Fig. 5.15 shows a plot of the output activations for a typical run in the addressee condition. The dashed lines indicate the score thresholds for positive and negative targets. For the network to be considered as using a particular pronoun, the two outputs have to be on opposite sides of these dashed lines. This network initially says *you* when it should be saying *me*: The network begins by making a reversal error. In contrast, networks in the nonaddressee condition often showed rapid correct generalization, as can be seen in Fig. 5.16. Thus, rapidly correct generalization was associated with nonaddressee training, and persistent reversal errors were associated with addressee training.

Mixed Condition Simulations

Our second pronoun simulation (Shultz, Buckingham, & Oshima-Takane, 1994) examined a more realistic learning environment. By using five

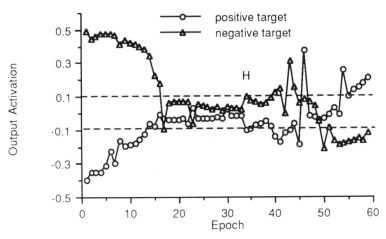

FIG. 5.15.   Results for one pronoun network in the addressee condition. Output activations are plotted across epochs for the pattern in which the child is speaking to the mother and referring to self. After making persistent reversal errors, the mistake is eventually overcome following the recruitment of a hidden unit, marked by an *H*. Adapted with permission from Shultz, Buckingham, and Oshima-Takane (1994).

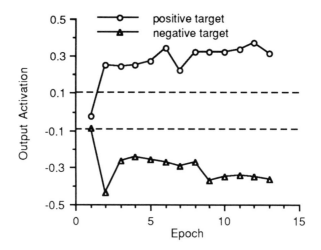

FIG. 5.16.   Results for one pronoun network in the nonaddressee condition. Output activations are plotted across epochs for the pattern in which the child is addressing the father referring
to self. Adapted with permission from Shultz, Buckingham, and Oshima-Takane (1994).

conditions with frequency multiples of addressee:nonaddressee patterns of
9:1, 7:3, 5:5, 3:7, and 1:9, we examined the effects of various hybrid
learning environments. The 9:1 and 5:5 conditions might correspond to the
linguistic environments of first- and secondborns, respectively. A firstborn
is likely to hear addressee speech during the day, while one parent is away
at work, and a bit of nonaddressee speech in the evening, when the working
parent returns. A secondborn, in contrast, is likely to receive about equal
measures of addressee and nonaddressee speech all day. The extra nonaddressee speech is provided by conversations between the caretaking parent
and the older sibling.

The same network topography and training patterns used in the first
experiment were used in this simulation. The only difference was in the
number of exposures of a given pattern during an epoch. After the network
had learned the 40 patterns of Phase 1, it was trained on the four child
speaking patterns as in the previous simulation.

At first we were surprised to find that networks having more addressee
than nonaddressee patterns took longer to learn the Phase 1 patterns, as is
illustrated in Fig. 5.17. This was the opposite of what happened in our
previous simulation. However, upon reflection, this might also be explained
in terms of shifting pronominal reference. The need to encode such a shift
could be temporarily masked by the frequency of addressee patterns.

The time required to learn the child speaking patterns in Phase 2 reflects
what was found in the earlier simulation. As can be seen in Fig. 5.18, there
is a negative linear trend associated with increased frequency of non-

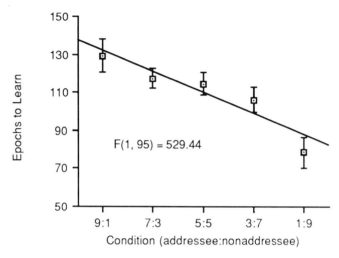

FIG. 5.17. Mean number of epochs needed to reach victory on pronouns in Phase 1 with standard deviation error bars. Adapted with permission from Shultz, Buckingham, and Oshima-Takane (1994).

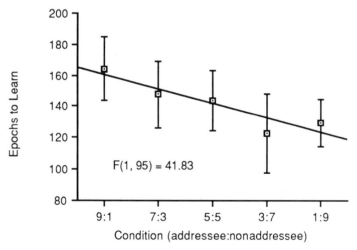

FIG. 5.18. Mean number of epochs needed to reach victory on pronouns in Phase 2 with standard deviation error bars. Adapted with permission from Shultz, Buckingham, and Oshima-Takane (1994).

addressee patterns. In other words, networks receiving more nonaddressee training learned more rapidly than networks receiving more addressee training. This supports the notion that secondborn children learn personal pronouns earlier than firstborn children because of their opportunity to hear speech not addressed to them (Oshima-Takane & Derevensky, 1990).

Adding a Self/Other Input Unit

It occurred to us that the task presented to our networks might be difficult because we assumed the network was the child, but were in no way telling it so. That is, the input patterns only indicated the identity of the individuals with respect to linguistic role (i.e., speaker, addressee, or referent). We did not tell the network that in the addressee situation the network was being talked to, and that in the nonaddressee situation it was merely listening to two other speakers. In order to be more realistic, we decided to make this information explicit to the network.

To code the identity of the network, we added a third input unit to each of the three input unit pairs. This additional unit indicated whether the individual being encoded was the child (self) or one of the parents (other). An activation of 1 was used to indicate *other*, whereas 0 indicated *self*. Otherwise, the architecture and training patterns were the same as in the first pronoun simulation.

Compared to networks in the first pronoun simulation, the self/other unit increased the rate of learning by six epochs on average in the addressee condition but had no influence on the nonaddressee condition. This latter finding was not surprising because the self/other input unit should not contribute to understanding, as it had a constant value of 1 across patterns (i.e., the parents occupied all speech roles). In the addressee condition, the added salience that parents and child were different made learning easier than the already simple addressee task.

Of more interest was whether or not the explicit information about self or other would benefit the network in Phase 2, where the child speaking patterns had to be learned. The number of epochs needed to learn in the addressee condition was cut to about one half (60 epochs) the original time. In the nonaddressee condition, there was a increase of approximately 4 epochs.

Thus, the time required for the net to learn the proper use of personal pronouns was substantially reduced in the addressee condition by the addition of self/other information. This did not alter the basic finding that nonaddressee training aided the acquisition of child speaking patterns as compared to addressee training. Moreover, error patterns found in the first simulation were unchanged in the current simulation. That is, reversal errors were still associated with addressee training, and fast and accurate generalization still reflected nonaddressee training. Thus, it appears that the findings in the previous simulations were not due to our having made the task confusing by not explicitly telling the network that it was playing the role of the child.

Pronoun Conclusions

By manipulating domain-specific constraints regarding how much addressee versus nonaddressee speech to which the network was exposed, we simulated children's performance that is marked by persistent reversal errors and correct performance. The more nonaddressee speech to which the network is exposed, the less time is required for the network to learn the correct semantic rules. An interaction between domain-specific and general constraints is responsible for correct rule use. We found that hidden units are necessary to encode pronominal shifts. In order for the networks to detect these shifts, some nonaddressee speech has to be processed and hidden units must be in place.

Use of computer simulations enabled us to look at idealized learning environments that would have been impossible to find in a child's world or to replicate within a laboratory setting. For example, we were able to have a purely nonaddressee environment where the network's attention was guaranteed without the need for participation in conversations.

The use of connectionist architectures allowed us to examine some realistic effects with respect to the frequency with which children were exposed to nonaddressee and addressee input. For example, we were able to examine the differing expected environments of first- and secondborn children. Within a symbolic framework such as Soar (Newell, 1990) such frequency effects would be difficult to obtain. For Soar, presentation of a single instance of a given type of linguistic input would typically be sufficient to create a rule to account for it. Yet, it is obvious that children hear many instances of personal pronouns as they discover the correct semantic rules for pronoun use.

We showed that prior knowledge attained from addressee and nonaddressee speech greatly affects the ability to generalize to a new situation in which the network begins to use pronouns. Our simulations, along with Oshima-Takane's (1988) findings, suggest that children acquire the correct use of personal pronouns by attending to speech that is not addressed to them. Also, it is likely that persistent reversal errors are due to children attending to speech addressed to them without having much opportunity to hear nonaddressee speech.

GENERAL CONCLUSIONS AND DISCUSSION

We reported on successful cascade-correlation simulations in several different domains of cognitive development. Most of these domains deal with the child's understanding of aspects of the physical world. In the case of a noted benchmark task for developmental simulations, the balance scale, our network models captured the progression through four rule-based stages and the torque difference effect. The latter is a perceptual salience effect wherein problems with large absolute torque differences between one side of the balance scale and the other are easier to solve than problems with small torque differences. Our network models also captured all major psychological regularities regarding the prediction of effect magnitude from information on causal potency and causal resistance, including the correct order of rule emergence, temporary overgeneralization of an early rule, and increasing levels of potency and resistance. In the realm of seriation, the networks mimicked the development of four rule-based stages and a well-documented perceptual effect on differential stick sizes. Networks also predicted a new perceptual effect based on array disorder, for which some confirming evidence has been found. In the case of integration of time, distance, and velocity cues, the networks captured known rule-based stages and predicted reasonable new ones. In the one area of language development we simulated, acquisition of personal pronouns, network models simulated the beneficial effect of listening to overheard speech, as opposed to speech addressed to the child. This entailed a stage transition from persistent reversal errors to correct usage in the case of children exposed to a large proportion of directly addressed speech, and nearly errorless performance in the case of children exposed to a large proportion of overheard speech.

To appreciate the relations among the different simulation topics, it is useful to note that they can be classified in terms of whether the inputs and outputs are quantitative or qualitative in nature. All of the simulations require the integration of two or more distinct sources of input information to predict some result or action. The balance scale task requires integration of quantitative information on the weight and distance of objects on two sides of the scale to produce a qualitative prediction of which side of the scale will tip down. The causal prediction task requires integration of quantitative information on causal potency and causal resistance to quantitatively predict effect size. Seriation requires integration of quantitative information on the size and position of each of a number of sticks to yield a qualitative move: which stick to move and where to move it. The time–distance–velocity task requires integration of quantitative information on two dimensions to predict the quantitative value of a third dimension. Use of the personal pronouns *me* and *you* requires integration of qualitative information on the identities of speaker, addressee, and referent to yield a qualitative selection of the correct pronoun. This classification of tasks can be useful in interpreting perceptual effects. We now turn to a discussion of key features that can be abstracted from the various simulations.

Rule Learning

As noted in the review of previous work, connectionist learning has been demonstrated to generate rulelike behavior without explicit representation of rules. All of the present simulations show such rulelike behavior: the four balance scale rules; the two rules for predicting effect size from causal potency and resistance; the four seriation rules; the numerous normative and primitive rules for integrating time, distance, and velocity cues; and the semantic rules governing the use of English personal pronouns. In none of these cases were the relevant rules explicitly represented in the networks. Rather, rule use had to be diagnosed from systematic behavior just as is commonly done in psychological research with children. Explicit in the networks are units and their interconnections and activations. Patterns of network activity, after appropriate changes in network topology and weights, are capable of causing the network to behave as if it were following rules. Of course, the same might be true of children.

The basis for rulelike behavior in connectionist models is the ability of these networks to extract statistical regularities in the learning environment. In some cases, these regularities are simple linear relationships, but in the more interesting cases the regularities are subtle nonlinear relationships. In both cases, the network learns to similarly treat similar input–output pairs. But in the nonlinear cases, signaled in cascade-correlation nets by the recruitment of hidden units, the network must learn an underlying similarity structure that is not evident from examining the input patterns alone. Rather, the net's ability to represent abstract nonlinear similarity structures is developed through learning.

Unlike most previous models in cognitive development, the rulelike behavior of connectionist networks is learned, rather than hand designed by the modeler.[5] Several previous models of the balance scale and seriation, for example, were characterized by hand-designed explicit rules that captured particular stages but failed to develop in the sense of moving naturally from one set of rules to the next.

Does rulelike behavior in connectionist networks mean that the networks are merely different implementations of symbolic rule-based systems (Fodor & Pylyshyn, 1988)? Not if the implementation differences make a difference in terms of ability to predict and interpret psychological phenomena. For example, one advantage of a connectionist implementation of rulelike behavior is that the "rules" are less brittle, in the sense of being more tolerant of input coding error, and more likely to generalize appro-

---

[5]A notable exception among explicit rule-based systems is Soar (Newell, 1990), a production system that learns its own rules through look-ahead search.

priately to novel patterns. Both minor deviations from trained inputs and novel, but similar, inputs would be handled in a mostly correct fashion by connectionist nets that have not simply memorized the training patterns. Simple memorization of training patterns can occur if the network has excess computational power (not likely in cascade-correlation nets because they recruit only the power they need) and is trained too deeply. Appropriate generalization to novelty was demonstrated in all of the present simulations. Other "implementational" advantages of connectionist nets are discussed later.

Stages

Not only do cascade-correlation nets learn appropriate rulelike behaviors, they can also learn them in psychologically realistic sequences. Such invariant sequences are a hallmark of stages of cognitive development (Flavell, 1971). Getting stages in the correct developmental order is not easy for computational modelers. For the domains treated here, even those previous models with a transition mechanism (all on the balance scale) failed to capture all of the stages in the correct order. Langley's (1987) rule-based model of the balance scale captured only Stage 3, ignoring Stages 1 and 2, and failing to reach Stage 4. The Soar model of the balance scale failed to progress past Stage 3 (Newell, 1990). The back-propagation model of the balance scale did reach Stage 4, but failed to stay there (McClelland, 1989). Reaching and staying in the final stage on the balance scale is partly a matter of learning the problem sufficiently deeply, but it is also a matter of being able to construct new representational power, something with which rule-based models and static connectionist networks have had considerable difficulty. Both the Langley model and the Soar model lacked the ability to represent torques and could not apparently develop this ability. The static back-propagation network model of the balance scale could not reach and stay in Stage 4 without sacrificing Stages 1 and 2.

Cascade-correlation nets captured the correct stage progressions in all five domains that were studied here, and did so with a variety of desirable psychological properties, including soft transitions, some stage skipping, and a limited amount of regression to early stages. Again, one notices less brittleness than is common in explicit rule-based models. With network models, transition to a higher level stage is typically soft and tentative, occasionally a stage is skipped altogether, and sometimes the net reverts back to an earlier stage at least temporarily. These tendencies reflect the dynamic, chaotic quality of connectionist networks. Due to the randomness inherent to starting configurations and other vagaries of travel through weight space and topology space, network behaviors are not entirely clear-cut and uniform.

It was argued elsewhere that connectionist models tend to produce those aspects of stages that are supported by psychological data (qualitative change, ordinality, and organization), and avoid producing those aspects of stages that are inconsistent with psychological data (abruptness and concurrence; Shultz, 1991). Networks do undergo qualitative changes in their behavior, capture invariant sequences of behavior, and exhibit a good deal of organization; but they change stages somewhat gradually and, because they are typically task specific, do not change stages all at once across domains.

The ability of cascade-correlation nets to capture correct stage sequences was due to a variety of factors. In the case of the balance scale, it was critical for the net to be in a particular region of connection weight space early in its developmental history and to recruit a small number of hidden units. The critical region of connection weight space is characterized by an emphasis on how much things weigh, as opposed to where they are placed on the balance scale, and could be managed either by environmental bias in favor of equal distance problems or by prestructuring network connections. With the current focus in the connectionist literature on determining what can be accomplished by learning from scratch, innate ideas are not much explored. But the potential for such investigation exists. Some connectionist researchers are beginning to study the breeding of connectionist networks through genetic algorithms (Belew et al., 1990) and the interaction of evolutionary processes with learning (Nolfi et al., 1990).

Stage sequences on the potency and resistance task and the time-distance-velocity task were the result of a network activation rule that sums its inputs. Hidden unit recruitment was also required for the achievement of higher level stages in the integration of time, distance, and velocity cues. Seriation stages resulted from a modularization of the task into selecting versus moving a stick and slight environmental biases in favor of smaller, less disordered arrays. The sequence of stages in the acquisition of personal pronouns (persistent reversal errors followed by correct usage) was due to an environmental bias for hearing directly addressed speech and the recruitment of a small number of hidden units.

Perceptual Effects

Connectionist techniques can also capture a variety of perceptual effects on cognitive developmental tasks. In the present work, these include the torque difference effect on the balance scale and the stick size effect in seriation. Such perceptual effects can be expected to occur whenever two or more items, quantitatively described, are being mapped onto a qualitative comparison. In contrast, no such effects can be expected on tasks like potency and resistance or time-distance-velocity, where quantitative inputs predict a quantitative output. No matter how distinctive the input values are for these quantitative to quantitative tasks, the idea is to predict the output value as precisely as possible.

Such perceptual effects are pervasive in cognitive developmental research, but no theoretical account integrates them with the cognitive features of the task. Perceptual effects appear to be particularly immune to symbolic rule-based accounts because rules are typically sensitive only to the direction of input differences, not to the amount of such differences. For example, a balance scale rule might be sensitive to whether one side of the scale had more weights than the other side, but it would not typically be sensitive to how much more. In contrast, the naturalness of the emergence of these perceptual effects from connectionist models is worth noting. Perceptual effects are a natural result of the continuous nature of network computations. Larger differences in inputs produce clearer activation patterns on hidden units and more decisive qualitative decisions on output units. Connectionist accounts hold the promise of a much tighter theoretical integration of perceptual and cognitive factors than was previously possible. This is another case of where connectionist implementations have a decided implementational and explanatory advantage over rule-based implementations.

Theoretical Issues

Connectionist models are not psychological theories. Rather, they are powerful tools that may, along with more conventional empirical and theoretical work, help us to develop coherent psychological theories (Mc-Closkey, 1991). Good theories explain phenomena in terms of independently motivated principles and show how previously unrelated phenomena derive from common underlying principles. Theoretical ideas emanating from successful connectionist models often satisfy these criteria (Seidenberg, 1993). Here, the explanatory principles are constraints on cognitive development — some, domain-general and others, domain-specific.

Among the domain-general constraints: (a) Cognitive judgments, decisions, and actions result from brain-style computation, in which excitation or inhibition is passed among simple processing units that vary in their temporary level of activity; and (b) Cognitive developmental transitions occur through the dual techniques of connection weight adjustments between existing units and recruitment of new hidden units, both of which serve to reduce the discrepancy between expectations and results. In the present models, these domain-general constraints are formally specified by the cascade-correlation algorithm.

Among the domain-specific constraints: (a) Some problems are too difficult to solve in a single homogenous network. Such problems require modularity in network organization, such that different networks solve different aspects of the overall problem. (b) Different problems require different coding schemes for inputs and outputs in the training and generalization patterns. Although many phenomena appear to be robust against considerable variation in coding techniques, different problems do require particular input data and output actions. (c) Some phenomena require bias in either the training environment or the initial weight structure.

These domain-specific constraints can be taken as testable predictions whenever they are not yet empirically documented. Such constraints are similar to Gelman's (1990) *first principles* that, to enable learning, focus the child's attention on the relevant features of the environment. This type of constraint does not force the child to attend to particular data, but it does provide a filter for data relevance.

We differ from the more extreme nativist positions in the belief that our particular input representations are not necessarily innate. We do not claim that children are born with knowledge representations innately adapted for tasks such as seriation or balance scales, but rather, their performance on these tasks results from a process that incorporates these types of input constraints. That is, when children become able to learn about tasks like seriation or the balance scale, they do so under the kinds of input constraints described by our models. We leave open the question of whether these specified input configurations result from a maturational process or from earlier learning (e.g., during infancy) that itself might have been highly constrained.

Weight adjustment is suited to modeling underlying quantitative changes, whereas hidden unit recruitment is suited to modeling qualitative ones. This allows a novel and computationally precise reformulation of Piaget's useful, but vague, notions of assimilation and accommodation. Indeed, we can now go one step farther than did Piaget, because he had no way of describing learning without accommodation, that is, without qualitative change.

Using Piaget's terms, one can conceptualize three general types of cognitive encounters in cascade-correlation nets: assimilation, assimilative learning, and accommodation. Pure assimilation occurs without learning. It is represented in cascade-correlation by correct generalization to novel problems without either weight changes or hidden unit recruitment. Assimilative learning occurs by weight adjustment, but without hidden unit recruitment. Here, the network learns new patterns that do not require nonlinear changes in representational power. Accommodation occurs via hidden unit recruitment when new patterns cannot be learned without nonlinear increases in computational power.

In cascade-correlation, these three types of encounter are all driven by the same process—adaptation via error reduction. Although these three possibilities can be conceptualized as qualitatively different from each other, it is perhaps more useful to view them quantitatively, on a dimension of learning difficulty. Pure assimilation is easiest because it requires little or no learning, whereas accommodation is relatively difficult, as assessed by metrics such as epochs to learn.

Adaptation through assimilation and accommodation can also be reinterpreted through rule-based and back-propagation perspectives, but with less satisfactory results. In a rule-based learning system like Soar, assimilation could be construed as rule-firing, and accommodation, as chunking new rules through impasse-driven search (Newell, 1990). In back-propagation learning, accommodation could be viewed in terms of weight adjustment and assimilation as the absence of such adjustment (McClelland, 1989). There is room for assimilative learning in neither of these frameworks. All learning in rule-based systems seems to create qualitatively different structures. Each new rule adds qualitatively different structure (van Geert, 1991). Conversely, no learning in static back-propagation nets creates qualitatively different structures because the network topology never changes. Yet, psychologically, some learning requires small quantitative adjustments (e.g., learning a new phone number), whereas other learning requires more substantial qualitative changes in representation and processing (e.g., learning to use personal pronouns or learning to integrate time, distance, and velocity information).[6]

Thus, on theoretical grounds, cascade-correlation is a particularly promising tool for modeling and eventually explaining cognitive development. The simulations reported here suggest that cascade-correlation networks can capture a wide range of developmental phenomena. Such successful applications could lead to new explanatory theories of cognitive development, although these new theories might look rather different than do classical information processing accounts (Seidenberg, 1993).

In broad outline, such a connectionist-inspired theory views the child as being equipped with powerful, general purpose learning techniques, based primarily on pattern association, but capable of constructing new represen-

---

[6]Klahr's chapter 8 (this volume) suggests that computational analysis of Piaget's notions of assimilation and accommodation is uninformative. Our motivation for this analysis is to show that the mathematics of cascade-correlation can be related to some traditional, albeit vague ideas about transition in cognitive development. This might enhance the relevance of our simulations for traditional developmentalists, but more significantly it underscores the importance of having a transition rule that incorporates both qualitative and quantitative change. Also, the mapping of computational models to assimilation and accommodation is not as unconstrained as Klahr suggests. The developmental models presented throughout this volume are each sufficiently specified to determine whether they incorporate qualitative or quantitative change.

tations and thus, greater computational power. Knowledge is represented by patterns of activation across many simple processing units, not by explicitly formulated symbolic rules. Cognitive processing occurs according to basic principles of neuronal functioning (excitation and inhibition) rather than by the matching and firing of rules. Rather than an artificial separation between perceptual and cognitive processes, there is a tight theoretical integration of perception and cognition. Such a system can be innately structured in certain ways and learns from environmental feedback, based primarily on correlations among events and instances, with sensitivity to biases afforded by the learning environment. Qualitatively new representational skills emerge as required to reduce error. When new representational structures do emerge, they elaborate on the results of earlier computations. Learning is the primary engine of cognitive transitions, yielding the many qualitative and quantitative changes one sees in cognitive development.

ACKNOWLEDGMENTS

This work was supported by grants from the Natural Science and Engineering Research Council of Canada and the Fonds pour la Formation de Chercheurs et l'Aide à la Recherche du Québec.

REFERENCES

Alpaydin, E. (1991). *GAL: Networks that grow when they learn and shrink when they forget* (Tech. Rep. No. 91–032). Berkeley, CA: International Computer Science Institute.

Anderson, N. H. (1974). Information integration theory: A brief survey. In D. H. Krantz, R. C. Atkinson, R. D. Luce, & P. Suppes (Eds.), *Contemporary developments in mathematical psychology* (Vol. 2, pp. 236–305). San Francisco: Freeman.

Anderson, N. H. (1991). Functional memory in person cognition. In N. H. Anderson (Ed.), *Contributions to information integration theory: Vol. 1. Cognition* (pp. 1–55). Hillsdale, NJ: Lawrence Erlbaum Associates.

Bates, E. A., & Elman, J. L. (1993). Connectionism and the study of change. In M. H. Johnson (Ed.), *Brain development and cognition* (pp. 623–642). Oxford, England: Blackwell.

Baylor, G. W., Gascon, J., Lemoyne G., & Pothier N. (1973). An information-processing model of some seriation tasks. *Canadian Psychologist, 14*, 167–196.

Belew, R., McInery, J., & Schraudolph, N. N. (1990). *Evolving networks: Using the genetic algorithm with connectionist learning* (Tech. Rep. No. CS90–174). San Diego: University of California, Cognitive Computer Science Research Group, Computer Science and Engineering Department.

Bettleheim, B. (1967). *The empty fortress: Infantile autism and the birth of the self*. New York: The Free Press.

Boden, M. A. (1980). Artificial intelligence and Piagetian theory. In M. Boden (Ed.), *Minds*

258   SHULTZ ET AL.

and mechanisms: Philosophical psychology and computational models (pp. 236–261). Ithaca, NY: Cornell University Press.

Boden, M. A. (1982). Is equilibration important? A view from artificial intelligence. *British Journal of Psychology, 73,* 65–173.

Boden, M. A. (1988). *Computer models of mind.* New York: Cambridge University Press.

Buckingham, D., & Shultz, T. R. (1994). A connectionist model of the development of velocity, time, and distance concepts. In *Proceedings of the Sixteenth Annual Conference of the Cognitive Science Society* (pp. 72–77). Hillsdale, NJ: Lawrence Erlbaum Associates.

Charney, R. (1980a). Pronoun errors in Autistic children: Support for a social explanation. *British Journal of Disorders of Communication, 15,* 39–43.

Charney, R. (1980b). Speech roles and the development of personal pronouns. *Journal of Child Language, 7,* 509–528.

Chauvin, Y. (1989). Toward a connectionist model of symbolic emergence. In *Proceedings of the Eleventh Annual Conference of the Cognitive Science Society* (pp. 580–587). Hillsdale, NJ: Lawrence Erlbaum Associates.

Chiat, S. (1981). Context-specificity and generalization in the acquisition of pronominal distinctions. *Journal of Child Language, 8,* 75–91.

Chletsos, P. N., De Lisi, R., Turner, G., & McGillicuddy-De Lisi, A. V. (1989). Cognitive assessment of proportional reasoning strategies. *Journal of Research and Development in Education, 22,* 18–27.

Clark, E. V. (1978). From gesture to word: On the natural history of deixis in language acquisition. In J. S. Bruner & A. Garton (Eds.), *Human growth and development* (pp. 85–120). Oxford, England: Oxford University Press.

de Paulo, B. M., & Bonvillian, J. D. (1978). The effect on language development of the special characteristics of speech addressed to children. *Journal of Psycholinguistic Research, 7,* 189–211.

Dudai, Y. (1989). *The neurobiology of memory: Concepts, findings, and trends.* Oxford, England: Oxford University Press.

Elkind, D. (1964). Discrimination, seriation, and numeration of size and dimensional differences in young children: Piaget replication study VI. *Journal of Genetic Psychology, 104,* 276–296.

Elman, J. (1993). Learning and development in neural networks: The importance of starting small. *Cognition, 48,* 71–99.

Ervin-Tripp, S. (1971). An overview of theories of grammatical development. In D. I. Slobin (Ed.), *The ontogenesis of grammar: A theoretical symposium* (pp. 189–212). New York: Academic Press.

Fahlman, S. E. (1988). Faster-learning variations on back-propagation: An empirical study. In D. S. Touretzky, G. E. Hinton, and T. J. Sejnowski (Eds.), *Proceedings of the 1988 Connectionist Models Summer School* (pp. 38–51). Los Altos, CA: Morgan Kaufmanm.

Fahlman, S. E., & Lebiere C. (1990). The cascade-correlation learning architecture. In D. S. Touretzky (Ed.), *Advances in neural information processing systems 2* (pp. 524–532). Los Altos, CA: Morgan Kaufmann.

Ferretti, R. P., & Butterfield, E. C. (1986). Are children's rule assessment classifications invariant across instances of problem types? *Child Development, 57,* 1419–1428.

Flavell, J. H. (1971). Stage-related properties of cognitive development. *Cognitive Psychology, 2,* 421–453.

Flavell, J. H. (1984). Discussion. In R. J. Sternberg (Ed.), *Mechanisms of cognitive development* (pp. 187–209). New York: Freeman.

Fodor, J. A., & Pylyshyn, Z. W. (1988). Connectionism and cognitive architecture: A critical analysis. *Cognition, 28,* 3–71.

Gelman, R. (1990). First principles organize attention to and learning about relevant data: Number and the animate–inanimate distinction as examples. *Cognitive Science, 14,* 79–106.

Hare, M., & Elman, J. L. (1992). A connectionist account of English inflectional morphology: Evidence from language change. In *Proceedings of the Fourteenth Annual Conference of the Cognitive Science Society* (pp. 265–270). Hillsdale, NJ: Lawrence Erlbaum Associates.

Harnad, S. Hanson, S.J., & Lubin, J. (1994). Learned categorical perception in neural nets: Implications for symbol grounding. In V. Honavar & L. Uhr (Eds.), *Artificial intelligence and neural networks: Steps toward principled integration* (pp. 191–206). New York: Academic Press.

Hertz, J., Krogh, A., & Palmer, R. G. (1991). *Introduction to the theory of neural computation.* New York: Addison-Wesley.

Inhelder, B., & Piaget, J. (1958). *The growth of logical thinking from childhood to adolescence.* New York: Basic Books.

Jacobs, R. A., Jordan, M. I., & Barto, A. G. (1991). Task decomposition through competition in a modular connectionist architecture: The what and where vision tasks. *Cognitive Science, 15,* 219–250.

Kingma, J. (1982). A criterion problem: The use of different operationalizations in seriation research. *Perceptual and Motor Skills, 55,* 1303–1316.

Kingma, J. (1984). The influence of task variations in seriation research: Adding irrelevant cues to the stimulus materials. *Journal of Genetic Psychology, 144,* 241–253.

Klahr, D., Langley, P., & Neches R. (Eds.). (1987). *Production system models of learning and development.* Cambridge, MA: MIT Press.

Klahr, D., & Siegler, R. S. (1978). The representation of children's knowledge. In H. W. Reese & L. P. Lipsitt (Eds.), *Advances in child development and behavior* (pp. 61–116). New York: Academic Press.

Koslowski, B. (1980). Quantitative and qualitative changes in the development of seriation. *Merrill-Palmer Quarterly, 26,* 391–405.

Langley, P. (1987). A general theory of discrimination learning. In D. Klahr, P. Langley, & R. Neches (Eds.), *Production system models of learning and development* (pp. 99–161). Cambridge, MA: MIT Press.

Levin, I. (1977). The development of time concepts in young children: Reasoning about duration. *Child Development, 48,* 435–444.

Levin, I. (1979). Interference of time-related and unrelated cues with duration comparisons of young children: Analysis of Piaget's formulation of the relation of time and speed. *Child Development, 50,* 469–477.

Lewandowsky, S. (1993). The rewards and hazards of computer simulations. *Psychological Science, 4,* 236–243.

Macnamara, J. (1976). Stomachs assimilate and accommodate, don't they? *Canadian Psychological Review, 3,* 67–173.

MacWhinney, B., Leinbach, J., Taraban, R., & McDonald, J. (1989). Language learning: Cues or rules? *Journal of Memory and Language, 28,* 255–277.

Marchman, V. A. (1992). *Language learning in children and neural networks: Plasticity, capacity, and the critical period* (Tech. Rep. No. 9201). San Diego: University of California, Center for Research in Language.

Mareschal, D. (1991). *Cascade-correlation and the genetron: Possible implementations of equilibration* (Tech. Rep. 91-10-17). Montréal: McGill University, McGill Cognitive Science Centre.

Mareschal, D. (1992). *A connectionist model of the development of children's seriation abilities.* Unpublished master's thesis. McGill University, Montréal, Canada.

Mareschal, D., & Shultz, T. R. (1993). A connectionist model of the development of seriation. In *Proceedings of the Fifteenth Annual Conference of the Cognitive Science Society* (pp. 676–681). Hillsdale, NJ: Lawrence Erlbaum Associates.

McClelland, J. L. (1989). Parallel distributed processing: Implications for cognition and development. In R. G. M. Morris (Ed.), *Parallel distributed processing: Implications for psychology and neurobiology* (pp. 8–45). Oxford, England: Oxford University Press.

McClelland, J. L., & Jenkins, E. (1991). Nature, nurture, and connections: Implications of connectionist models for cognitive development. In K. VanLehn (Ed.), *Architectures for intelligence* (pp. 41–73). Hillsdale, NJ: Lawrence Erlbaum Associates.

McCloskey, M. (1991). Networks and theories: The place of connectionism in cognitive science. *Psychological Science, 2*, 387–395.

Minsky, M. (1986). *The society of mind.* New York: Simon & Schuster.

Minsky, M., & Papert, S. (1969). *Perceptrons.* Cambridge, MA: MIT Press.

Newell, A. (1990). *Unified theories of cognition.* Cambridge, MA: Harvard University Press.

Ninio, A. (1979). Piaget's theory of space perception in infancy. *Cognition, 7*, 125–144.

Nolfi, S., Elman, J. L., & Parisi, D. (1990). *Learning and evolution in neural networks* (Tech. Rep. No. 9019). San Diego: University of California, Center for Research in Language.

Oden, G. C. (1987). Concept, knowledge, and thought. *Annual Review of Psychology, 38*, 203–227.

Oshima-Takane, Y. (1988). Children learn from speech not addressed to them: The case of personal pronouns. *Journal of Child Language, 15*, 95–108.

Oshima-Takane, Y. (1992). Analysis of pronominal errors: A case study. *Journal of Child Language, 19*, 111–131.

Oshima-Takane, Y., & Derevensky, J. L. (1990, April). *Do later-born children delay in early language development?* Paper presented at the International Conference on Infant Studies, Montréal, Canada.

Papert, S. (1963). *Intelligence chez l'enfant et chez le robot.* [Intelligence in the child and the robot.] In L. Apostel, J. Grize, S. Papert, & J. Piaget. La filiation des structures. *Etudes D'Epistemologie Genetique, 15*, 131–194.

Piaget, J. (1965). *The child's concept of number.* New York: Norton.

Piaget, J. (1969). *The child's conception of time.* London: Routledge & Kegan Paul.

Piaget, J. (1970). *The child's conception of movement and speed.* London: Routledge & Kegan Paul.

Piaget, J. (1972). *Problèmes de psychologie génétique.* [Problems of genetic psychology.] Paris: Denoel/Gontier.

Piaget, J. (1977). *The development of thought: Equilibration of cognitive structures.* Oxford, England: Blackwell.

Piaget, J., & Inhelder, B. (1969). *The psychology of the child.* New York: Basic Books.

Piaget, J., & Inhelder, B. (1973). *Memory and intelligence.* London: Routledge & Kegan Paul.

Plunkett, K., & Marchman, V. (1991). U-shaped learning and frequency effects in a multi-layered perceptron: Implications for child language acquisition. *Cognition, 38*, 43–102.

Plunkett, K., & Sinha, C. (1992). Connectionism and developmental theory. *British Journal of Developmental Psychology, 10*, 209–254.

Pollack, J. B. (1990). Language acquisition via strange automata. In *Proceedings of the Twelfth Annual Conference of the Cognitive Science Society* (pp. 678–685). Hillsdale, NJ: Lawrence Erlbaum Associates.

Retschitzki, J. (1978). L'évolution des procédures de sériation: Étude génétique et simulation. [Evolution of seriation procedures: Developmental study and simulation.] *Archives de Psychologie, 46*, Monographie 5.

Rumelhart, D. E., Hinton, G. E., & Williams, R. J. (1986). Learning internal representations by error propagation. In D. E. Rumelhart & J. L. McClelland (Eds.), *Parallel distributed processing: Explorations in the microstructure of cognition* (Vol. 1, pp. 318–362). Cambridge, MA: MIT Press.

Schiff-Meyers, N. (1983). From pronoun reversals to correct pronoun usage: A case study of a normally developing child. *Journal of Speech and Hearing Disorders, 48*, 385–394.

Schmidt, W. C. (1991). Connectionist models of balance scale phenomena. Unpublished honours thesis, McGill University, Montréal, Canada.

Schmidt, W. C., & Shultz, T. R. (1991). *A replication and extension of McClelland's balance scale model* (Tech. Rep. No. 91-10-18). Montréal: McGill University, McGill Cognitive Science Centre.

Schyns, P. (1991). A modular neural network model of concept acquisition. *Cognitive Science, 15*, 461–508.

Seidenberg, M. S. (1993). Connectionist models and cognitive theory. *Psychological Science, 4*, 228–235.

Seidenberg, M. S., & McClelland, J. L. (1989). A distributed, developmental model of word recognition and naming. *Psychological Review, 96*, 523–568.

Shipley, E. F., & Shipley, T. E. (1969). Quaker children's use of *Thee*: A relational analysis. *Journal of Verbal Learning and Verbal Behavior, 8*, 112–117.

Shultz, T. R. (1991). Simulating stages of human cognitive development with connectionist models. In L. Birnbaum & G. Collins (Eds.), *Machine learning: Proceedings of the Eighth International Workshop* (pp. 105–109). San Mateo, CA: Morgan Kaufman.

Shultz, T. R., Buckingham, D., & Oshima-Takane, Y. (1994). A connectionist model of the learning of personal pronouns in English. In S. J. Hanson, T. Petsche, M. Kearns, & R. L. Rivest (Eds.), *Computational learning theory and natural learning systems: Intersection between theory and experiment* (Vol. 2, pp. 347–362). Cambridge, MA: MIT Press.

Shultz, T R., Mareschal, D., & Schmidt, W. C. (1994). Modeling cognitive development on balance scale phenomena. *Machine Learning, 16*, 57–86.

Shultz, T. R. & Schmidt, W. C. (1991). A cascade-correlation model of balance scale phenomena. In *Proceedings of the Thirteenth Annual Conference of the Cognitive Science Society* (pp. 635–640). Hillsdale, NJ: Lawrence Erlbaum Associates.

Shultz, T. R., Zelazo, P. R., & Strigler, D. (1991, April). *Connectionist modeling of the development of the concepts of potency and resistance in causal prediction.* Paper presented at the meeting of the Society for Research in Child Development, Seattle, WA.

Siegler, R. S. (1976). Three aspects of cognitive development. *Cognitive Psychology, 8*, 481–520.

Siegler, R. S. (1981). Developmental sequences between and within concepts. *Monographs of the Society for Research in Child Development, 46* (Whole No. 189).

Siegler, R. S., & Richards, D. D. (1979). Development of time, speed, and distance concepts. *Developmental Psychology, 15*, 288–298.

Spelke, E. (1990). Principles of object perception. *Cognitive Science, 14*, 29–56.

Squire, L. (1987). *Memory and brain.* Oxford, England: Oxford University Press.

van der Maas, H. L. J., & Molenaar, P. C. M. (1992). Stagewise cognitive development: An application of catastrophe theory. *Psychological Review, 99*, 395–417.

van Geert, P. (1991). A dynamic systems model of cognitive and language growth. *Psychological Review, 98*, 3–53.

Wilkening, F. (1981). Integrating velocity, time, and distance information: A developmental study. *Cognitive Psychology, 13*, 231–247.

Wilkening, F. (1982). Children's knowledge about time, distance, and velocity interrelations. In W. J. Friedman (Ed.), *The developmental psychology of time* (pp. 87–112). New York: Academic Press.

Young, R. (1976). *Seriation by children: An artificial intelligence analysis of a Piagetian task.* Basel, Switzerland: Birkhauser.

Zelazo, P. D., & Shultz, T. R. (1989). Concepts of potency and resistance in causal prediction. *Child Development, 60*, 1307–1315.

6

Two Forces in the Development of Relational Similarity

Dedre Gentner
Northwestern University

Mary Jo Rattermann
Hampshire College

Arthur Markman
Columbia University

Laura Kotovsky
University of California at Los Angeles

Analogy commands the attention of developmental psychologists, first, because like grammar and mathematics, analogy is a supremely elegant form of thought; and, second, because of its importance in cognitive development. An appreciation of relational similarity is fundamental to learning beyond the basic level — to grasping theory-laden concepts that must be defined relationally, such as *predator* in biology and *limiting case* in mathematics. In this chapter, we explore two forces that promote the development of relational similarity. Our goal is to illuminate both the nature of the similarity mechanism and its role in experiential learning.

Despite the attention given to how and when children acquire the ability to process relational similarity — to carry out analogies — a number of important issues remain unresolved. Most researchers agree that there is a relational shift from early reliance on either holistic or object-level similarities to the possibility of purely relational similarities (Gentner, 1988; Gentner & Rattermann, 1991). However, there is disagreement as to the nature of the shift. Is it governed by cognitive stage or by degree of domain knowledge; is it maturational or the product of learning; is it an all-or-none shift from object similarity to relational similarity; and finally, when does it occur, with nominations ranging from *during infancy* through *at formal operations*?

A precise model of the comparison process is needed to clarify the question of what changes with development. Our account is based on modeling the comparison process as one of alignment and mapping of representations. We make three chief points. First, we argue that analogical development is primarily a matter of changes in knowledge, rather than changes in global competence or processing capacity. Our second claim is that language learning — specifically, the acquisition of relational terms — is crucial in the development of relational comparison. Our third claim is that *the process of similarity comparison* is instrumental in the development of analogy. We present evidence that the comparison process itself invites attention to relational structure and that it can promote the acquisition of portable relational knowledge. We conjecture that the acquisition of relational language and the process of relational comparison provide mutual bootstrapping that drives representational change.

We begin with a review of the research and theoretical issues. Then, we outline the structure-mapping approach and present the Structure-mapping Engine (SME), our simulation of similarity and analogy comparison, along with some adult findings that illustrate the computational principles. Next, we present two studies of children's acquisition of relational comparisons and model these developmental studies using SME. Our results suggest that the basic similarity process is the same for children as it is for adults. What varies is the knowledge representations this process acts on.

THE DEVELOPMENT OF RELATIONAL SIMILARITY

There is considerable evidence for a relational shift in development of similarity (Gentner, 1988). After reviewing a large number of studies, Gentner and Rattermann (1991) proposed the following account of the *career of similarity*. Young infants tend to respond to overall (literal) similarity and identity between scenes, such as the similarity between a red ball rolling and another red ball rolling. The earliest partial matches are based on *object similarity*: direct resemblances between objects, such as the similarity between a round red ball and a round red apple. With increasing knowledge, children come to make single-attribute matches such as the similarity between a red ball and a red car, and finally, *relational similarity* matches, such as the similarity between a ball *rolling on* a table and a toy car *rolling on* the floor. For example, when asked to interpret metaphors like *A tape recorder is like a camera*, 6-year-olds produced object-based interpretations such as *Both are metal and black*, whereas 9-year-olds and adults focused chiefly on common relational structure (e.g., *Both can record something for later*; Gentner, 1988). Billow (1975) reported that metaphors based on object similarity could be correctly interpreted by children of about 5 or 6 years of age, but that relational metaphors were not correctly interpreted until around 10 to 13 years of age. Gentner and Toupin (1986) contrasted the effects of object similarities and relational structure. Children were shown a simple story acted out by toy characters, and then asked to re-enact the story with a new group of characters. For some stories, the new characters were similar to their corresponding original characters; in others, the characters were different; and in the worst case, the *cross-mapped analogy* condition, similar characters played different roles across the two stories, so that object similarities interfered with the best plot mapping. Both 6- and 9-year-olds were highly sensitive to object similarity: They were most accurate at re-enacting the story in the high-similarity condition and least accurate in the cross-mapped condition. For half the children, the relational structure was augmented by adding an explicit causal or moral summary statement. Under these conditions, 9-year-olds were nearly perfect even on the cross-mapped condition. However, 6-year-olds showed no improvement. Thus, both groups benefited from object commonalities that supported the structural mapping, but, in accord with the relational shift hypothesis, only the older group benefited from the presence of higher- order relational structure.

Global Competence Views of Relational Development

Explanations for the relational shift fall into two main classes: those that posit a global change in cognitive competence, and those that posit domain specific shifts driven by change of knowledge.

Piaget linked the development of higher order relational similarity to global shifts in competence — specifically, the acquisition of formal operations at around 11 or 12 years of age (Inhelder & Piaget, 1958; Piaget, Montangero, & Billeter, 1977). Piaget, Montangero, and Billeter presented children with pictures forming A:B::C:? analogies such as *Bicycle:Handlebars::Ship:?* and asked them to choose the best completing picture. Although older children (9-year-olds) were able to choose the correct relational response (here, a *rudder*), young children (5-year-olds) often responded with thematic associates (e.g., *seagull*). This shift from thematic to relational responding was also found by Sternberg and his colleagues using materials such as A:B::C:D analogies constructed from pictures of human forms (Sternberg & Downing, 1982; Sternberg & Nigro, 1980; Sternberg & Rifkin, 1979).

The idea that perception of relational similarity must await formal operations has few current adherents, because of the many studies demonstrating earlier abilities. However, it is still possible to maintain that there is a global cognitive shift that permits relational mapping, but that it occurs well before the formal operations stage. Halford and his colleagues have explored this position. They provide an elegant and precise account of the relational shift based largely on developmental increases in processing capacity (Halford, 1987, 1992, chap. 3, this volume). On their view, young children's cognitive capacity is insufficient to process the information needed to find relational similarities. Over the course of development, processing capacity increases (Halford, Mayberry, & Bain, 1986) permitting the child to perform increasingly more complex analogical mappings (Halford, 1992). Halford proposed that children go through four stages of analogical ability: (a) *element mappings*, in which element correspondences are based on matching common attributes; (b) *relation mappings* (at around 2 years), in which simple binary relations are placed in correspondence, along with the elements associated with these relations; (c) *system mappings* (at around 4 or 5 years), in which systems of two relations are placed in correspondence; and (d) *multiple-system mappings* (at around 11 years), in which systems of three or more relations are placed in correspondence. Although Halford (chap. 3, this volume) also allows for knowledge effects, such as chunking of information, his account of the relational shift emphasizes global change and a maturational increase in processing capacity.

Knowledge-Change Views of Relational Development

Knowledge-based accounts assume that the relational shift results from changes in knowledge, not from global and/or maturational changes (Brown, 1989; Brown & DeLoache, 1978; Brown & Kane, 1988; Chen & Daehler, 1989; Crisafi & Brown, 1986; Gentner, 1977a, 1977b, 1988; Gentner & Rattermann, 1991; Ortony, Reynolds, & Arter, 1978; Vosniadou, 1987, 1989). On this view, the chief predictor of whether a child can carry out a comparison is his or her knowledge of the two domains.

One line of evidence for the knowledge-change view is that even very young children can show considerable analogical ability provided the domains are familiar. For example, Gentner (1977a, 1977b) demonstrated that preschool children can perform a spatial analogy between the familiar base domain of the human body and simple pictured objects, such as trees and mountains. When asked, "If the tree had a knee, where would it be?," 4-year-olds (as well as 6- and 8-year-olds) were as accurate as adults in performing the mapping of the human body to the tree, even when the orientation of the tree was changed or when confusing surface attributes were added to the pictures. Ann Brown has conducted a number of ingenious experiments demonstrating early transfer abilities. In one study, she found that after one experience using a tool to pull a desirable toy closer, 20- to 30-month-old children would transfer the notion of *pulling tool* to a new situation and choose an appropriate tool from a new set of transfer objects (Brown, 1989, 1990). In other studies, Brown and Kane (1988) taught 4-year-olds about biological mechanisms such as mimicry and camouflage and found that children could map from a base scenario of *using ladybugs to control aphids* to propose the solution *use purple martins to control mosquitoes*. It is probably true that in both these tasks the relational mapping was supported by some object-level similarity. For example, both the pulling tools had to be long with hooklike protuberances, resulting in some common shape. In the second study, the similarity between aphids and mosquitoes may have contributed to children's performance. It is notoriously difficult to control object similarity in designing naturalistic analogical materials, partly because real causal scenarios often involve similar objects in similar relations (See Gentner, Rattermann, & Campbell, 1994). However, although these results do not provide evidence for purely relational transfer, they do support the claim that greater knowledge permits greater degrees of structure-sensitive mapping.

A second line of evidence for the claim that the relational shift is a knowledge-driven shift rather than a global cognitive shift is that it occurs at different ages for different domains and tasks. Gentner and Rattermann (1991) came to this conclusion on the basis of a survey of developmental findings. For example, in the story-mapping task discussed in the preceding section, Gentner and Toupin (1986) found a shift between 6 years and 9 years: Only the older children benefited from the presence of higher-order relational structure. Yet 4-year-olds show some ability to perform relational mappings in Brown and Kane's biological mechanisms task and on Gentner's body parts mapping task. There is even evidence that a relational shift can occur during infancy. Kolstad and Baillargeon (1991) showed babies repeated events of salt being poured into and out of containers, first showing the infants the container, including its sides and bottom. After the babies were familiarized to this event of filling and pouring out salt, they were shown a transfer event: the same pouring event with one of two new objects. One of the transfer objects was perceptually different from the training objects, but was otherwise a perfectly normal container. The other object was perceptually similar to the original, but appeared to have no bottom. Kolstad and Baillargeon found that 5.5-month-old infants looked reliably longer (indicating surprise) at the perceptually dissimilar event, but not at the "bottomless" container. In contrast, 10.5-month-old infants looked reliably longer at the causally different event, the "bottomless" container. Their encoding of the first event apparently included the notion that the bottom of the container had supported the salt. Their surprise reaction occurred in response to causally relevant relational commonalities and not to overall similarity. This suggests that during their first year of life, babies may undergo a small but distinctive relational shift within the highly familiar arena of *containment*.

The evidence summarized suggests that the shift occurs at different times for different domains because of differential knowledge: the deeper the child's domain knowledge, the earlier the relational shift. This provides support for a relational shift based on change in knowledge. But by itself it cannot be conclusive, for a global change of competence could also account for this decallage if we assume that the relations vary in complexity across domains. In this chapter, we pursue two lines of inquiry that can provide firmer support for the knowledge-change account. First, we show that children who initially fail to perform a relational mapping can show a pronounced gain in performance when given more knowledge. Second, we simulate the process of similarity matching, varying the degrees of knowledge assumed. We show that, using the same process, the model shifts from performing nonrelationally to performing relationally when given more knowledge.

STRUCTURE-MAPPING AND STRUCTURAL ALIGNMENT

To sort out these issues requires a theory of how analogy and similarity are processed. We propose that both children and adults compare mental representations via a structure-mapping process of alignment of conceptual representations (Falkenhainer, Forbus, & Gentner, 1989; Gentner, 1982, 1983, 1989). According to this view, the commonalities and differences between two situations are found by determining the maximal structurally consistent match between the representations of the two situations (Gentner, 1983, 1989; Gentner & Markman, 1994; Goldstone, 1994; Goldstone & Medin, 1994; Markman & Gentner, 1990, 1993; Medin, Goldstone, & Gentner, 1993). A *structurally consistent* match conforms to the *one-to-one mapping* constraint (i.e., an element in one representation corresponds to at most one element in the other representation) and to the *parallel connectivity* constraint (i.e., if elements correspond across the two representations, then the elements that are linked to them must correspond as well). When more than one structurally consistent match exists between two representations, contextual relevance and the relative systematicity of the competing interpretations are used. All else being equal, the match with the richest and deepest relational match is preferred (the *systematicity* principle).

Arriving at a maximally deep structural alignment might seem to require an implausibly discerning process, or even advance knowledge of the point of the comparison. But in fact, as the SME simulation makes clear, structural alignment can be realized with a process that moves from a rather blind stage of forming local (often inconsistent) matches to a stage in which deep, structurally consistent alignments are formed by capitalizing on connections between predicates (Falkenhainer, Forbus, & Gentner, 1986, 1989) . We describe SME in detail later; for now a sketch of the general process is sufficient.

SME takes as input propositional representations that consist of entities, attributes, functions and relations.[1] *Entities* are simply the objects in the domain and *attributes* are used to describe these objects. *Functions* are used to describe dimensional properties such as size and position. *Relations* are predicates that represent links between entities, attributes, functions, or other relations. Given two representations, SME operates in a local-to-global manner to find one or a few structurally consistent matches.[2] In the first stage, SME proposes matches between all identical predicates at any level (attribute, relation, higher-order relation, etc.) in the two representations. At this stage, there may be many mutually inconsistent matches. In the next stage, these local correspondences are coalesced into larger mappings by enforcing structural consistency: *one-to-one mapping* (each object in one representation is constrained to match to at most one object in the other representation) and *parallel connectivity* (matching predicates are constrained to have matching arguments). Although relations must match identically, SME allows correspondences between nonidentical functions or objects if they are arguments of matching relations. This allows a structural match to be made across nonidentical objects. It also permits a match across nonidentical dimensions (because dimensions are represented as functions). This is a way of capturing a psychological claim that dimensionalized attributes—that is, attributes such as size, weight, and brightness—that have been extracted as dimensions of a domain are particularly likely to participate in cross-dimensional mappings. (We return to the issue of dimensionalization in development later.)

SME then gathers these structurally consistent clusters into one or two global interpretations (called *GMAPS*). It then makes candidate inferences in the target. It does this by adding to the target representation any predicates that currently belong to the common structure in the base that are not yet present in the target. These function as possible new inferences imported from the base representation to the target representation. Finally,

---

[1]Relations and attributes are predicates taking truth-values, whereas functions instead map objects or sets of objects onto objects or values. However, for brevity we sometimes use the term *predicate* to refer to all three categories—relations, attributes, and functions.

[2]In this chapter, we describe SME in its Literal Similarity mode that allows attributes, functions, and relations to determine the best match between two representations. In order to model other tasks, SME can also be run in Analogy mode (relations only) and Mere Appearance (attributes only) modes. We think that the all-purpose Literal-similarity matcher is the better model of the normal similarity process.

the interpretations are given a structural evaluation. This evaluation is calculated by giving each matching predicate an evidence score. Predicates then
pass a portion of their evidence to their arguments in a cascadelike fashion
that implements a preference for systematicity (Forbus & Gentner, 1989). All
else being equal, SME prefers a deep system of matches to a collection of
isolated matches (even given the same number of correspondences). Thus,
the process begins with local matches, but the final interpretation of a
comparison is a global match that preserves large-scale structures.

Two immediate predictions arise from this model. First, carrying out a
comparison process should promote a structural alignment. Second, the
interpretation of a comparison emerges from the interaction of relational
and object-based matches. A study by Markman and Gentner (1990, 1993)
with adults illustrates these phenomena. We presented subjects with pairs of
scenes like those displaying the *monotonic decrease* relation, as shown in
Fig. 6.1. (Similar materials are used in the developmental studies presented
later in this chapter.) The pairs were designed to contain cross-mapped
objects—perceptually similar objects that play different roles in the relational structure of the two scenes (Gentner & Toupin, 1986). The task was
a simple *one-shot mapping task*. We pointed to the cross-mapped object in
one scene (e.g., Circle B on the left side of Fig. 6.1) and asked subjects to
select the object in the other scene that best went with that object. They
generally selected the perceptually similar object (Circle AA in the right
hand configuration, which is the same size as Circle B). In the key
experimental manipulation, other subjects were asked to rate the similarity
of all the pairs of pictures prior to performing the mapping task. These
subjects were significantly more likely to place the cross-mapped object in
correspondence with the object playing the same relational role (e.g., Circle
BB, the middle circle in the right-hand configuration) than the subjects who
only performed a one-shot mapping. It seems that the simple act of carrying
out a similarity comparison promotes a structural alignment.

The second prediction, that the winning alignment is a function of both

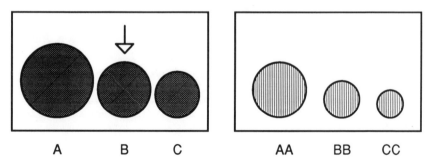

A   B   C   AA   BB   CC

FIG. 6.1. Sample stimuli displaying the monotonic change in size relation like those used by
Markman and Gentner (1990, 1993).

object similarity and relational similarity, was tested in a second study. This study made use of the fact that in a cross-mapping, the object-based interpretation and the relational interpretation are incompatible. Thus, increasing the similarity of the objects should increase the likelihood that the preferred match will be based on object similarities. Similarly, increasing the depth and strength of the relational match should increase the likelihood that the relational match will be the winner.

Subjects were again given pairs of pictures in patterns such as monotonic decrease (Fig. 6.1). For half the subjects, the pairs contained simple objects like circles and squares. The results were as given: Those subjects who rated similarity prior to making a mapping made more relational responses than subjects who simply did the mapping task. The other half of the subjects received richer, more complex objects, such as globes, scales, and faces, for which the pairwise object similarity was high. These subjects tended to make object-based mappings, even when they rated similarity prior to making their mapping. Although carrying out a comparison tends to induce a structural alignment, when object similarities are high relative to the degree of relational overlap, then object matches still may dominate the interpretation. This pattern is evidence that, even for adults, the process of interpreting a comparison involves both object matches and relational matches.

Simulating the Comparison Process

When we simulated these comparisons using SME, the results were consistent with subjects' performance. Before discussing the results, we describe SME's representational format. Although the specific details of a given representation are not crucial, the general assumptions are psychologically important. As stated previously, the model takes as input two propositional representations constructed from entities, attributes, functions, and relations. Within SME, these representational elements have strict definitions:

- *Entities* correspond to the objects in a domain.
- *Attributes* are unary predicates and are used primarily to describe independent descriptive properties of objects such as *thin*(Mary) or *short*(John).
- *Functions* (which unlike attributes and relations, do not take truth values, but rather, map objects onto objects or values) are used primarily to state dimensional properties like *size*(Mary) or *weight-*(John).
- *Relations* are multi-place predicates that represent links between two or more entities, attributes, functions, or relations. We distinguish between *first-order relations*, which link objects (e.g., above[circle, triangle]) or their attributes (e.g., greater(*height*[Mary], *height*[John]) from *higher-order relations*, which link other relations (e.g., cause(buy[Mary, ball], possess[Mary, ball]).

Two points must be made about these representations. First, they are assumed to be *conceptual structures*, not verbal formulas, although for convenience words are used to label the nodes and predicates. For example, synonymous words typically have nearly identical representations. Second, these representations are intended as *psychological construals*. We are not aiming to capture the best, most complete, or most logical description of a situation, even if such a thing were possible. On the contrary, we assume that the same person may have alternate construals on different occasions, and that which comparisons are made and how they are interpreted depends on the person's current representation. The idea is to capture the processes of comparison between two situations as currently represented.

To simulate the Markman and Gentner results, we gave SME structural representations of two same-dimension monotonic-decrease stimuli (Fig. 6.2). These representations embodied four additional assumptions. Of these, the final two are of special interest, because later in this chapter we make different representational assumptions for children.

1. Similar objects are represented by nodes with similar sets of attributes. Thus, the cross-mapped objects in these scenes had identical size and shape attributes.

2. Complex objects have more attributes than simple objects. Thus, the object match between cross-mapped objects is stronger the richer and more complex the matching objects (Tversky, 1977).

3. We assume that adults conceive of certain attribute types such as size, darkness, and spatial position as dimensions, and we represent these as functions. (We suggest later that the extraction of dimensions is an important representational change during development.)

4. Finally, we assume that the adult notion of *monotonic decrease* can be represented as a higher-order relation connecting first-order pairwise comparisons (represented as greater-than relations) along dimensions. The higher-order relation expresses a coordination between monotonic change along two dimensions: for example, left–right position and size.

Representations for these stimuli were submitted to SME, run in general similarity mode as already described. All possible interpretations (GMAPS) were generated.[3] When the stimuli contained sparse objects, the winning GMAP — that is, the interpretation that received the highest evaluation of all those generated for this pair (evaluation score = 16.50) — corresponded to the relational match between scenes, as shown in Fig. 6.3a. In this

---

[3]In SME's normal (and most plausible) simulation mode, it produces only one or two best matches for a comparison (Forbus & Oblinger, 1990). However, SME can be run in exhaustive mode when, as here, one wishes to see all possible interpretations of a comparison and their evaluations.

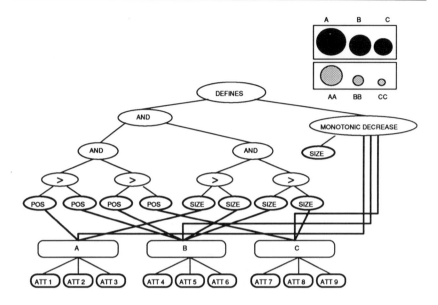

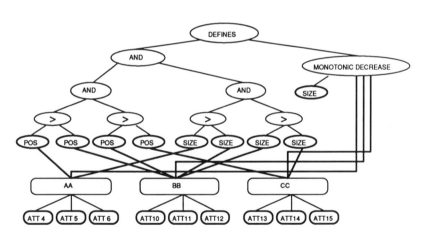

FIG. 6.2. Sample propositional representations from the simulation of the study by Markman and Gentner (1990, 1993). The representations shown here depict the adult representation of monotonic decrease.

interpretation the matching relational structure has been preserved: The objects have been placed in correspondence based on the similarity in their relational roles. Figure 6.3b shows the best ranked object interpretation for this pair. This interpretation aligns the matching attributes of the cross-mapped objects (Circle B with Circle AA), but shows very little matching relational structure. In the sparse-object simulation, the evaluation score for this object-based interpretation (evaluation score = 11.50), lagged

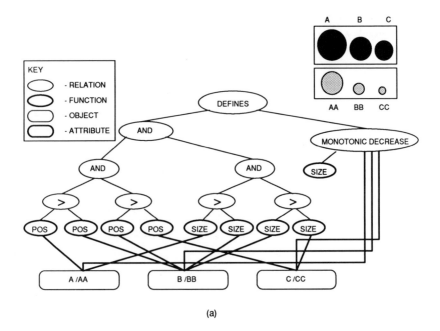

(a)

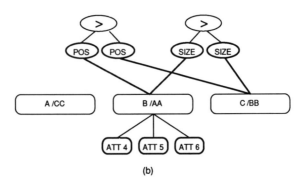

(b)

FIG. 6.3. Relation-based (a) and object-based (b) interpretations generated by SME when presented with the representations in Fig. 6.2. The relational interpretation received a higher evaluation score than the object interpretation.

behind that of the relational alignment shown in Fig. 6.3a. However, when the simulation was given richer object representations with greater object-matching potential, the cross-mapped-object-based interpretation overcame the relational match. This fits with the psychological findings concerning cross-mapped pairs: First, the comparison process induced a relational alignment in our subjects, which prevailed when the objects were sparse;

and, second, as object richness increased, so did the probability that the object match would win over the relational alignment. If the cross-mapping is removed, so that we have a simple analogy with dissimilar objects in the base and target, then SME, like adult subjects, readily makes the structural alignment.

STRUCTURAL ALIGNMENT AND THE RELATIONAL SHIFT

Now let us apply these ideas to development. We suggest that for children as well as for adults, similarity and analogy involve aligning two representations. When the object matches and the relational alignment are correlated, as in literal similarity, they are mutually supporting and there is one dominant interpretation. But when there is conflict, as in a cross-mapping, then whether the relational match or the object match will prevail depends on several factors. As with adults, the richer the object match, the more likely it is to prevail, and the larger and deeper the relational match, the more likely it is to prevail. Developmentally, these assumptions interact with considerations of change of knowledge. When children's domain theories are weak, their representations of the objects are likely to be much richer than their representations of the relations. As their knowledge of domain relations increases, children's relational representations become richer and deeper, increasing the likelihood that their comparisons will focus on matching relations. Thus, there occurs a relational shift: Children become able to carry out primarily relational matches. But, as evidenced in the adult results, the relational shift does not imply the disappearance of object similarity as a psychological factor. Rather, it refers to the *possibility* of making purely relational matches.

We have suggested that changes in knowledge drive the relational shift. In the following section, we consider two kinds of evidence for this claim. Our first line of evidence is a set of experiments that ask whether children who initially fail a relational mapping task are better able make a relational mapping after learning about the domain relations. If giving children knowledge of the relevant relational structure improves their performanceon a relational mapping task, then this constitutes an in principle demonstration that changes in domain knowledge, rather than maturation, are sufficient to account for the normally observed improvements.

A second way to gain insight into this phenomenon is to make use of a computer simulation of similarity processing. If we can simulate both younger and older children using the same processes and changing only the knowledge representations, this will support the change-of-knowledge account of the relational shift. The simulation allows us to ask what we never could about a real human: What would happen if we changed only the knowledge and not the processing?

We present two studies of mapping in children. Both use simple analogies based on perceptual relations such as monotonicity. This was done so that the relational structure could be grasped without presupposing extensive conceptual knowledge. Both studies follow the same logic. We first devise a task sufficiently difficult that young children normally fail to make a relational mapping. Then we try to create a change in their knowledge and ask whether they are then able to see the relational mapping. We consider two kinds of knowledge change: *structural enrichment* — adding higher order relational knowledge to initially shallow representations; and *re-representation* of initially holistic representations in a way that permits relational commonalities to be extracted. The first is a special case of *enrichment*, the second, of *restructuring* (Carey, 1985, 1991; Chi, 1981; Karmiloff-Smith, 1991, 1992; Norman & Bobrow, 1979). The studies we now describe provide evidence for both possibilities.

Finally, in addition to testing whether change of knowledge occurs, we wished to investigate how it occurs. Our studies further suggest two mechanisms or promoters of knowledge change: structural alignment and acquisition of relational language. We defer discussion of these until after we describe the results. For now, we list five predictions:

1. There will be a relational shift: Older children will perform more relationally than younger children.
2. Because the shift arises from knowledge, not age *per se*, giving children additional domain knowledge will lead to earlier relational mappings.
3. (Mechanism 1) The use of relational language can promote relational mapping.
4. (Mechanism 2) Because structural alignment induces attention to relational structure, the comparison process itself can promote relational mapping.
5. Because the comparison process is multiply constrained, both object similarity and relational similarity will affect performance.

If these five empirical predictions are borne out, this will support the claim that the relational shift is governed by changes in knowledge rather than changes in processing.

INVESTIGATING CHILDREN'S ACQUISITION OF RELATIONAL COMPARISON

Investigation 1: Solving Cross-Mappings

In these studies, we assessed children's ability to make relational mappings that varied in their predicted difficulty (Rattermann & Gentner, 1990;

Stimulus Sets

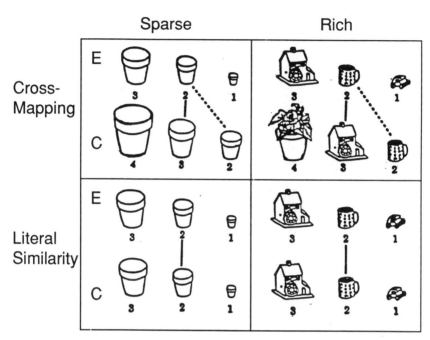

FIG. 6.4. Sample stimuli displaying the monotonic change relation from the mapping studies (Gentner & Rattermann, 1991; Rattermann & Gentner, 1990; Rattermann et al., 1994). Two of the objects are cross-mapped for both the (a) sparse and (b) rich pairs.

Rattermann, Gentner, & DeLoache, 1994). The easy pairs were literal similarity pairs, in which the object similarities supported the required relational alignment; the difficult pairs were cross-mapped pairs, in which the object similarities opposed the relational alignment (Gentner & Toupin, 1986). As in the study by Markman and Gentner described earlier, we varied the richness of the objects so that the interplay between object similarities and relational similarities could be examined.

Children were presented with two configurations of objects, each arranged according to the *monotonic increase (or decrease) in size* relation, operationalized as three objects in a row, increasing in size from left to right or right to left (see Fig. 6.4). One set of objects was designated as the child's (C) set, the other as the experimenter's (E). The child was asked to close his eyes while the experimenter hid stickers under one object in each set.[4] Then

---

[4]For clarity of presentation, we assume a male subject and a female experimenter, although in fact, roughly equal numbers of boys and girls participated.

the child opened his eyes and watched as the experimenter lifted one of her objects to reveal where the sticker was located in her set. The child was told that if he watched carefully, he could figure out where the sticker was hidden in his set. The rule was always the same: The child's sticker was hidden under the object that had the same relative size and position as the chosen object in the experimenter's set. To succeed, the child had to focus on common relational roles (e.g., the largest and leftmost object in both sets). If the child found the sticker on the first attempt, he was allowed to keep it. If not, he was shown where it was but was not allowed to keep it.

Within this basic task, two variables were manipulated: the richness and complexity of the objects and the mapping type (cross-mapping vs. literal similarity). Richness was manipulated by using either sparse objects, such as clay pots and blue plastic boxes, or rich objects, such as a pot of brightly colored silk flowers, a toy house, a colorful mug, and a toy car (see Fig. 6.4 for examples of rich and sparse stimuli.). The second variable was mapping type. Half of the subjects received literal similarity mappings, in which the object similarities suggested the same correspondences as the relational mapping. The other half received cross-mappings, in which the object similarities suggested different correspondences than did the relational mapping. Using a between-subjects design, we tested twelve 3-year-olds and twelve 4-year-olds in each of the four possible conditions formed by crossing stimulus richness (sparse vs. rich) with task type (literal similarity vs. cross-mapping). Additionally, twelve 5-year-olds were tested in each of the two richness conditions of the cross-mapping task.[5]

The predictions for the basic task were as follows. First, children in the literal similarity condition should perform better (i.e., should make more relational responses) than those in the cross-mapping condition, because in literal similarity, the object matches draw the children toward the correct relational alignment. We also expected an interaction between object richness and mapping type. In the literal similarity task, for which the object similarities supported the relational interpretation, we expected children to perform better on the rich stimuli than on the sparse stimuli. The reverse pattern should be found in the cross-mapping task, for which object similarity was in conflict with the relational interpretation. Because the rich object match should provide a more tempting competitor to the relational mapping than the sparse object match, children should perform worse on this relational task with the rich stimuli than with the sparse stimuli.

Figure 6.5 presents the proportion of correct responses across age in the literal similarity and cross-mapped conditions. Not surprisingly, the 4-year-olds were nearly perfect on literal similarity mappings (top graph), whether

---

[5] Because of the overall high performance of the 3- and 4-year-olds in the literal similarity task, the 5-year-olds were tested only in the two cross-mapping conditions.

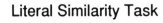

Literal Similarity Task

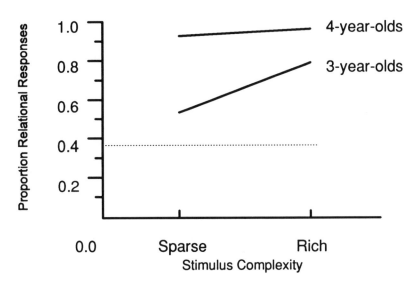

Cross-Mapping Task

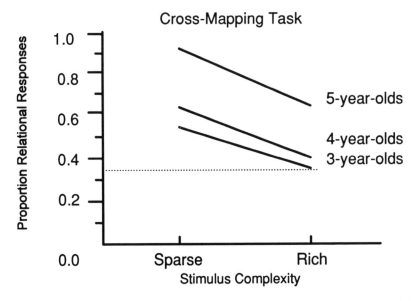

FIG. 6.5. Proportion of relational responses for different age groups in each condition of the mapping study (Gentner & Rattermann, 1991; Rattermann & Gentner, 1990; Rattermann et al., 1990).

279

they had rich stimuli (89% correct) or sparse stimuli (94% correct). However, the 3-year-olds benefited from object similarity, even in this "easy" condition. They made significantly more relational responses to the rich stimuli (85% correct) than to the sparse stimuli (55% correct). This pattern is striking, because even 3-year-olds might have been expected to find the literal similarity task easy even with sparse objects.

As predicted, the cross-mapped condition was harder (bottom graph). Also as predicted, the effects of object similarity in cross-mapped pairs were opposite to those in literal similarity. Both 3- and 4-year-old children had difficulty producing relational responses and the difficulty was greater for rich stimuli than for sparse stimuli. The results bear out the prediction that children should have trouble focusing on the matching relational structure in the face of competing object similarities. This conclusion is reinforced by the finding that children selected the identical object (rather than the object playing the same relational role) more often for the rich stimuli (42% for the 3-year-olds, 32% for the 4-year-olds) than for the sparse stimuli (23% for the 3-year-olds, 23% for the 4-year-olds). Consistent with the relational shift predictions, 5-year-olds were considerably better at maintaining a relational mapping despite cross-mapped objects, although they showed the same pattern of greater difficulty with rich objects (68% correct for rich as compared to 95% correct for sparse stimuli).

These orderly results underscore the joint contribution of object similarities and relational commonalities to the comparison process. Rich object similarities make relational responding easy for children when they suggest the same correspondences as the relational mapping (as occurs in the literal similarity condition), and hard for children when they suggest different correspondences from the relational mapping (as occurs in the cross-mapped condition). Sparse object similarities have weaker effects, giving mild support in literal similarity mappings and having mild negative effects on relational mappings for cross-mappings.

Parenthetically, the object richness effect here is a particularly clear instance of Tversky's (1977) self-similarity effect, whereby rich objects are more similar to themselves than are sparse objects. Self-similarity is theoretically important because it is counterevidence to a mental distance account of similarity, in which all identical pairs are at distance = 0. Because much of the prior evidence for self-similarity comes from perceptual confusion patterns in speeded tasks, the present evidence constitutes a significant broadening of the evidential basis for self-similarity effects, and hence, for a componential account of similarity over a mental distance account.

These results are consistent with the predictions of the structural alignment framework. Alignment and mapping involve interplay between local object similarities and global relational similarity. The more compelling the local similarities, the more they influence the overall relational mapping for better or worse. Furthermore, consistent with the relational shift hypothesis, with increasing age and experience, children become better able to focus on relational commonalities across a range of object similarities.

Can It Be Taught? The Effect Of Relational Language. The next study has two purposes. The first is to shed light on whether the improvement in relational performance across age is due to increases in knowledge, as we have suggested, or to maturational increases in processing capacity, as Halford's framework would predict. The second is to explore a more specific hypothesis, namely, our third prediction, that the acquisition of relational language contributes to the relational shift.

In this study, we again gave children the cross-mapping task, but this time we gave them labels for the higher-order relational pattern of *monotonic decrease*. In the previous study, some children had spontaneously applied the labels *Daddy, Mommy, Baby* to the objects (see also Smith, 1989). Because these terms seemed to apply to the monotonic decrease pattern, in this next study we taught twenty-four 3-year-olds to use these labels. We gave them "families" in which the largest object was labeled *Daddy*, the middle, *Mommy* and the smallest, *Baby*. The children received explicit training trials with labeled families of penguins and bears. For example, the experimenter pointed and said, "This is my Daddy, this is my Mommy, and this is my Baby. This is your Daddy, this is your Mommy, and this is your Baby. If my sticker is under my Daddy, then your sticker is under your Daddy." Then the children were tested on the same stimul—boxes and baskets in the sparse condition and houses, cars, and so on, in the rich condition—as in the first experiment. We had previously ascertained that children understood all the first-order relations between objects (the pairwise size comparisons); the question was whether the family labels would increase children's ability to appreciate the higher-order pattern by inviting them to import a familiar relational schema. If so, this would increase the level of relational responding.

The results of the labeling manipulation were dramatic: The 3-year-olds' performance in the cross-mapping task improved on both the sparse (89% relational responding) and rich (79% relational responding) stimuli. This is a substantial gain over their performance in Experiment 1 (54% and 32% correct, respectively). In fact, the 3-year-olds in this study performed at a level comparable to that of 5-year-olds, as though the children had gained 2 years of insight (see Fig. 6.5).

We might worry that this impressive performance depended on maintaining an artificially high level of explicit labeling. However, in a subsequent study we found that 3-year-olds given the label training could successfully maintain their performance without continued use of labels by the experimenters. In this test, after the first transfer trial, we gave children new stimuli and told them to arrange them "as they should be" so that we could play the game. Then we conducted the transfer task as in the original experiments, with no mention of the labels by the experimenter. We found that children who had received the label training did well. Of the 3-year-olds who had received training, 81% reached criterion with the sparse stimuli and 50% with the rich stimuli, as compared with the control (no training) group, of which 50% reached criterion with sparse stimuli and 12% with rich stimuli.[6] Interestingly, sparse objects remained easier than rich objects even under training. That the adverse effects of object richness persisted is consistent with our view that the relational shift is not all or none.

A second objection might be that *Daddy, Mommy,* and *Baby* do not name relational roles, but instead serve as a set of three object names. This interpretation contrasts with our suggestion that the task improvement stemmed from the fact that *Daddy-Mommy-Baby* labeled a higher-order relational schema for monotonic decrease. This possibility was tested in another study in which we taught children nonsense labels (such as *jiggy, gimli,* and *fantan*) that could only serve as pure object names. Their performance was not improved over the nonlabeled condition; in fact there was a tendency toward *worse* performance (Rattermann & Gentner, 1990; Rattermann, Gentner, & DeLoache, 1994). Thus, we suggest that the use of relational labels invited attention to the relation of monotonic change, making it more likely that young children would notice the matching relational structure. These results suggest the importance of possessing compact labels for relational patterns.

Finally, we note that we did not provide children with entirely new knowledge in this study. Rather, we invited an analogy that suggested that the stimuli could be viewed in terms of a relational structure the children already knew. We suspect this kind of cross-domain analogizing is a powerful force in development, and that it is often promoted by the use of common labels.

Overall, these findings are consistent with the view that representational change is the underlying mechanism of the relational shift. These data do not fit well with maturational stage theories. The children succeeded in a higher-order mapping at a mean age of 3 years, 6 months, slightly below Halford's hypothesized transition age of 4 years for multiple relation mappings, and far before Piaget would have granted the capacity for higher order relational mapping. More fundamentally, it is hard to see how any maturational theory could account for the radically different performance that occurred between two groups of the same age as a function of training.

---

[6]The dependent measure for this study was the number of children (out of 12 per group) who reached a criterion of four consecutive correct trials within the training set of 10 trials.

Yet the relational shift is not all or none. Rather, there is an interplay between the richness of the object matches and the depth of the relational matches. In cross-mapped trials, young children performed worse with rich object matches than with sparse object matches, and the reverse was true for literal similarity trials (for the same reason — namely, that the rich object matches were more alluring than the sparse object matches). Just as increasing object richness increased the strength of object-based interpretations, so increasing the amount and depth of the matching relational structure (by using relational labels) increased the likelihood of a relational interpretation. By the age of 5 years, the necessary relational knowledge was firmly in place, and this structure could be used as the basis of a mapping, even in the presence of a competing rich object match. However, even 5-year-olds performed better with sparse objects than with rich objects in cross-mapping trials. This pattern argues against the suggestion that "children would only solve analogies on the basis of object similarities when they were ignorant of the relations on which the analogy was based" (Goswami, 1992, p. 92). Rich object matches are perennially attractive.

These studies exemplify *structural augmentation* or *enrichment* of knowledge. Via the analogy with family relations, a higher-order pattern was added to the children's representation. We do not rule out the possibility that more radical restructuring may have taken place for some children; but this assumption is not necessary to account for the shift. We return to these findings later in this chapter, when we present a simulation of this comparison process.

Overall, these studies are consistent with the hypothesis that increases in children's relational knowledge play a significant role in their developing ability to match on the basis of relations. However, if our assumptions are correct, these results bear chiefly on augmentation or enrichment, albeit structural augmentation. We turn now to a set of studies that addresses the issue of *re-representation of knowledge*.

**Investigation 2: Development of
Cross-Dimensional Similarity**

The previous section examined how adding higher-order relations to children's representations can increase their ability to make relational mappings within a domain. We now describe a series of studies that examine how re-representing the components of a domain can ease the determination of cross-dimensional similarities (Kotovsky & Gentner, 1990, 1994). In these studies, the difficulty for children lay in seeing patterns across different dimensions. We first describe the basic task and demonstrate an age shift in performance. Then we describe two manipulations that increase young children's ability to make these mappings.

We showed 4-, 6-, and 8-year-old children (12 children at each age) triads of figures and asked them to say which of two alternatives was most similar to the standard. The figures were sets of squares or circles differing in size and darkness. The standard was always constructed to fit one of two higher order perceptual relations: either monotonic change or symmetry. *Monotonic change* was operationalized as three objects in a line, identical except for the dimension of interest—either size or darkness—that increased (or decreased) steadily across the three objects. *Symmetry* was operationalized as three objects in a line with a central object flanked on either side by objects that were identical to each other. The middle object and the outer objects differed only along the dimension of interest—either size or darkness (see Fig. 6.6).

Although the child could select either response—there was no feedback—one of the two choices was always clearly more similar to the standard from the adult point of view. This alternative, the *relational choice,* depicted the same relational structure as the standard, but contained different objects. The other comparison figure (the *foil* or *nonrelational choice*) used the same objects as the relational choice, but these objects were haphazardly arranged so that there was no good higher-order relational structure. Thus, both alternatives matched the standard equally well at the object level, and the relational alternative matched better at the relational level, making the relational match preferable to anyone who recognized the matching rela-

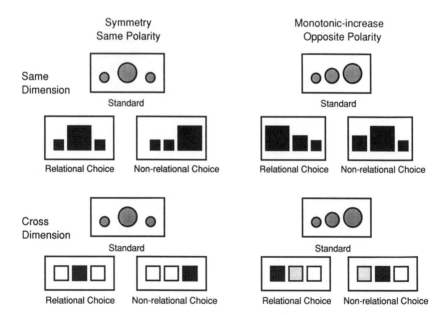

FIG. 6.6.   Sample stimuli from the similarity triads task (Kotovsky & Gentner, 1990).

tional structure. (Adult subjects showed virtually 100% relational respond-ing.) Thus, we can refer to the relational alternative as the *correct choice*, even though children were allowed to make whichever choice they liked.

The key manipulation was to vary the transparency of the mapping. The standard and the relational choice could match either within (e.g., size to size) or across (e.g., size to darkness) dimensions, and could either have the same or opposite direction of increase (polarity). That is, the design varied whether the polarity and dimension of variation matched between the standard and comparison figures. In *same-polarity trials*, first-order in-creases in the standard figure mapped to first-order increases in the correct figure (e.g., xXx and oOo). In *opposite-polarity* trials, first-order increases in the standard figure mapped to first-order decreases in the correct figure (e.g., xXx and OoO). In *same-dimension* trials, the comparison figures and standard both varied along the same dimension (e.g., size). In *cross-dimension* trials, the comparison figures varied along a different dimension than did the standard (e.g., darkness vs. size).

This design gave rise to four different types of trials: same polarity/same dimension, different polarity/same dimension, same polarity/different dimension and different polarity/different dimension (see Fig. 6.6 for a sample of each type). Let us consider the choice difficulty from the child's point of view. First, object matches were never of any use to the child, for in all the triads (even on the same-dimension trials) the correct response and the foil were equally similar (or dissimilar) to the standard at the level of objects. However, the four trial types varied in whether they could only be solved at a highly abstract level, or whether they could also be solved (that is, a choice could be made) on the basis of shared lower-order relations. The easiest trial type was the same polarity/same dimension type, for it could be solved with no recourse to higher-order structure. The child only needed to recognize the matching first-order relations to find the relational choice. For example, in the stimulus in Fig. 6.6, the second object is bigger than the first and the third objects for both the standard and the correct choice. Because these *bigger-than* relations are scrambled in the foil, the relational choice could be selected simply by matching the specific first-order rela-tions. Knowledge of the higher-order symmetry relation was not needed.

The task was more difficult for opposite-polarity and cross-dimensional trials, where these low level relational matches were no longer available. For opposite-polarity trials, the child had to notice that the same overall pattern held in both items, even though increases in size or darkness in one array corresponded to decreases in size or darkness in the other array. Similarly, to make the relational response on cross-dimensional trials, children had to recognize that the overarching symmetry or monotonic-change relation dictated placing *bigger-than* relations in correspondence with *darker-than* relations. Because a deeper understanding of the relational systems was

TABLE 6. 1
Mean Proportion of Relational Responses by Age and Condition

	Same-Polarity		Opposite-Polarity	
Age	Same-Dimension	Cross-Dimension	Same-Dimension	Cross-Dimension
4	0.68	0.49	0.49	0.48
6	0.90	0.75	0.77	0.72
8	0.96	0.90	0.93	0.80

required to solve the opposite-polarity and cross-dimensional trials, we expected that children would make fewer relational choices on these stimuli than on same-polarity, same-dimension items.

In the first experiment, polarity match was a between-subjects factor and dimension match was a within-subjects factor (Kotovsky & Gentner, 1994, Experiment 1). Each child received 16 same-polarity trials or 16 opposite-polarity trials.[7] Table 6.1 shows the proportion of times children of different ages selected the (correct) relational alternative. The results support the predictions just described. The 4-year-olds seemed to choose randomly in all but the most concrete condition: They were reliably above chance only for the same-polarity, same-dimension stimuli. The 6-year-olds were above chance in all conditions, but, like the 4-year-olds, selected the relational choice more often on same-polarity, same-dimension trials than on any other type of trial. Finally, the 8-year-olds performed well in all conditions, although they too tended to make the fewest correct responses in the condition predicted to be the most difficult: the opposite-polarity, cross-dimension condition. These results are consistent with Chipman (1977) and Chipman and Mendelson's (1979) findings that perception of higher-order visual structure increases developmentally. These findings provide evidence for the predicted relational shift.

The Effect of Relational Labels. So far, we have evidence for a relational shift with age. As before, the central question is whether changes in knowledge and experience underlie the apparent age shift. In subsequent studies, we used only 4-year-olds and investigated whether training on the higher-order perceptual structure of these stimuli would improve their cross-dimension performance. We used only same-polarity triads. (Recall that 4-year-olds had performed at chance on even the same-polarity

---

[7]In a subsequent session children were shifted to the opposite-polarity condition (Kotovsky & Gentner, 1994, Experiment 1b). Children performed better on the second day when the task order was same-polarity to opposite-polarity than in the reverse order, consistent with our thesis here.

cross-dimensional triads.)[8] The first training task involved teaching labels for the relations (*more-and-more* for monotonic change, and *even* for symmetry). During the training task, children learned (with feedback) to classify the stimuli, one at a time, as to whether they were *more-and-more* or *even*.

After training, the children were given the eight cross-dimensional (same-polarity) triads, with the same similarity choice task as in Experiment 1. The 5 (out of 12) 4-year-olds who scored above criterion in the labeling and sorting task (75% correct categorizations and/or four productions of the labels) were well above chance on cross-dimensional trials (72% relational responding).[9] As in the Rattermann, Gentner and DeLoache (1990, 1994) studies, the use of relational labels increased children's attention to common relational structure. But whereas the children in the Rattermann et al. studies were given *Daddy, Mommy,* and *Baby* labels that could tap their existing schemas, the kind of training provided in the Kotovsky and Gentner (1990, 1994) task allowed children to build up the higher-order relational patterns for *more and more* and *even* over the course of the experiment. These newly reified relational patterns could then be more readily noticed and used.

In the Rattermann et al. task, the alignment is one of matching identical relational structure. The difficulty, of course, lay in ignoring the misleading cross-mapped object. The Kotovsky and Gentner task posed a different difficulty: namely, that of perceiving cross-dimensional commonality. To see the cross-dimensional similarity, children must align representations containing different first-order relations. For example, they must match monotonic change across *darker-than* relations with monotonic change across *bigger-than* relations. From the previous study, we know that common labels are one impetus to such a creative alignment. In the next study we investigated a different mechanism of change: repeated alignment itself. We have evidence from the Markman and Gentner (1993) studies that similarity comparisons promote structural alignment. We asked now

---

[8]In this and all subsequent studies, only the 16 same-polarity triads were used. Half were same-dimension (four size, four darkness) and half cross-dimension. All subsequent studies use 4-year-olds only (see Kotovsky & Gentner, 1994 Experiments 3–5). To avoid identity between the standard and the relational alternative, half of the darkness-change stimuli were blue circles, and the other half pink squares. For size-change, half were black-and-white patterned circles and half black squares.

[9]The results across all twelve 4-year-olds were weaker: 59% correct, only marginally significantly different from chance. However, we suspect that the children would have done better with more experience in the labeling and sorting task. (They were given only one pass through the cards.) A later training study with a more extended training regime produced strong results (Kotovsky & Gentner, 1994, Experiment 5).

whether prior experience in aligning same-dimension comparisons (which we know are accessible to 4-year-olds) would help them to see the relational structure necessary to align cross-dimensional comparisons.

Progressive Alignment. In this experiment, a simple change was made. The same set of triads was presented as in the first study, but the order was changed. Trials were blocked so that same-dimension trials were seen before cross-dimensional trials. Thus, children saw the easier trials before the more difficult ones. This blocking improved 4-year-olds' performance to 60% correct on the cross-dimension trials, marginally above chance. In comparison, 4-year-olds had achieved only 49% matching choices (chance performance) on cross-dimension trials when the trials were randomly mixed in Experiment 1. The difference becomes striking if we consider only the children who understood the same-dimension trials. When the same-dimension and cross-dimension trials were mixed in Experiment 1, even children who performed above the 75% criterion on the same-dimension trials were correct on only 48% of the cross-dimension trials (chance performance). In contrast, when the same-dimension trials were blocked initially, children who were at least 75% correct on the same-dimension trials ($n = 5$) went on to choose correctly on 80% of the cross-dimensional trials (significantly above chance).

This finding suggests that there is transfer from the easier same-dimension trials to the cross-dimensional trials when the same-dimensional trials are massed together. From other studies we have evidence that this is not a mere effect of task practice, for doubling the number of trials with size alone is not enough. Children must have concentrated experience in alignment within each of the two dimensions, size and darkness. Such repeated within-dimension alignments apparently potentiate subsequent cross-dimensional alignment.

How might this happen? The fact that young children initially fail to see the similarity among cross-dimensional comparisons suggests that such nonmatching relations are hard for them to align. We assume that the relations here are initially representing domain-specific manner (e.g., *darker than* and *bigger than*). Given two different domain-specific relations, some kind of re-representation is required in order to see these patterns as alike. The notion of re-representation to improve alignment is important in theories of analogy and case-based reasoning (Burstein, 1983; Falkenhainer, 1988; Gentner & Rattermann, 1991; Kass, 1989; Keane & Brayshaw, 1988) as well as in theories of conceptual development (Karmiloff-Smith, 1991).

What kind of re-representation might apply here? We speculate that children may initially view dimensional relations in a holistic manner. Specifically, we suggest that their representation of a difference in magnitude is typically conflated with the dimension of difference: for example, *darker*(a, b). Later, they re-represent these differences in a manner that separates the comparison and the dimension: for example, *greater*[*darkness*(a), *darkness*(b)]. Such a re-representation would make it possible to notice that there is some commonality between change in size and change in darkness. The idea is that extracting the specific dimensions from the relation of change along a dimension permits flexible cross-dimensional alignment. We examine this claim in more detail in the simulations to follow (see Fig. 6.8).

This proposal is in the spirit of the research of Smith, Kemler and their colleagues, who have demonstrated that the acquisition of adult dimensional structures is a lengthy process involving a shift from holistic to analytic processing (Smith, 1989; Smith & Kemler, 1977). Our claim is that repeated alignments, sometimes abetted by relational labels, help the child extract common structure. On this account, similarity comparisons contribute to the child's gradual disembedding (or decontextualizing, or desituating) of initially fused knowledge into separable representations (see Nunes, Schliemann, & Carraher, 1993). Also in accord with our thesis, Smith and Sera (1992) provided persuasive evidence that language learning contributes to children's learning to dimensionalize the world.

Children must not only separate perceptual knowledge into dimensions, but must come to see them as dimensions, as possessing a unified (often ordinal) structure. Once dimensions are extracted and represented, it becomes possible to grasp analogous structure across different dimensions. It is this kind of dimensionalization and alignment that permits humans to deal fluently with cross-domain metaphoric systems such as *up/down* → *good/bad* and the others discussed by Lakoff and his colleagues (Gibbs & O'Brien, 1990; Lakoff & Johnson, 1980; Turner, 1987, 1991).

All this suggests that children's early perceptual representations are conservative and context-specific and that they gradually develop dimensionally separated representations. The process of disembedding or desituating dimensions is promoted when children receive repeated opportunities to align the embedded dimensional structure; it is also promoted by learning common language that invites the extraction of dimensional commonalities. As the child gradually extracts the dimensions that apply within and across domains, cross-dimensional alignments become increasingly available. The child can see consistent mappings between structures across different dimensions.

This process of extracting dimensions is not smooth, as the work of Smith, Kemler, and Shepp showed convincingly (Shepp, 1978; Smith, 1984, 1989; Smith & Kemler, 1977). Smith (1989) showed that 2-year-olds do not possess anything like the adult notion of uniform dimensions within and across domains. For example, they fail to group according to like dimensions, and they fail to attend to dimensional identity in classification (Smith & Kemler, 1977). When asked to order three objects, a 2-year-old may be as pleased with *little, medium-sized, dark* as with *little, medium-sized, big.* Smith theorized that to the 2-year-old, *bigger* and *darker* both count as *more.* Overall, the picture that emerges from these studies, as well as from our own, is that between the ages of 2 and 5 years of age children come to see perceptual similarity in terms of what adults consider *like* dimensions. Clearly, children's ability to extract and attend to the dimension of variation in a given event is a necessary aspect of learning to group on the basis of like dimensions.

MODELING THE EFFECTS OF KNOWLEDGE CHANGE USING SME

The data from the developmental studies described suggest that knowledge change plays a crucial role in the development of relational sensitivity. In the studies by Rattermann, Gentner, and DeLoache (1990, 1994), the knowledge change seems to be an augmentation of children's domain knowledge, whereas in the studies by Kotovsky and Gentner (1990, 1994), the knowledge change seems to be a re-representation of existing knowledge structures. In this section we present simulations of the effects of both kinds of changes. The idea is to use SME to keep the process of comparison fixed and then vary the knowledge representation on which it operates. If the postulated changes in knowledge representation produce the observed changes in children's similarity performance, then we have evidence that change of knowledge could provide a sufficient explanation for the observed effects. Note that we are not simulating the re-representation process itself here, although such re-representation during analogy is an important aspect of our ongoing research (e.g., Falkenhainer, 1988). As earlier, we use the Structure-mapping Engine (SME; Falkenhainer, Forbus, & Gentner, 1986, 1989) in literal similarity mode to simulate the process of structural alignment and mapping. (The section surrounding Figs. 6.1–6.3 describes the simulation.) Our goals are, first, to achieve greater specificity in our discussion of representational change, and second, to discover whether change of knowledge is sufficient to produce the observed changes in children's performance.

Simulating Investigation 1: Structural Augmentation

In the Rattermann, Gentner, and DeLoache (1990, 1994) study, children saw two sets of objects and were asked to map from one set to the other.

There was a marked shift toward more relational mappings with age (and, in the later studies, with training).

Representational Assumptions. We made the assumption that the 3- and 5-year-olds differed primarily in whether their representations included the higher-order relational structure of monotonic change in size. The 3-year-olds were assumed to lack this higher-order relational pattern unless given training with relational labels. Thus, the following assumptions were made in the representations given to SME:

1. 1.For 5-year-olds, we assumed that the representations included higher-order relations of *monotonic change*: for example, *monotonic decrease in size*, as shown in Fig. 6.7.
2. For 3-year-olds prior to training, we assumed knowledge of only the first-order relations between objects, as shown in the dotted box in Fig. 6.7.

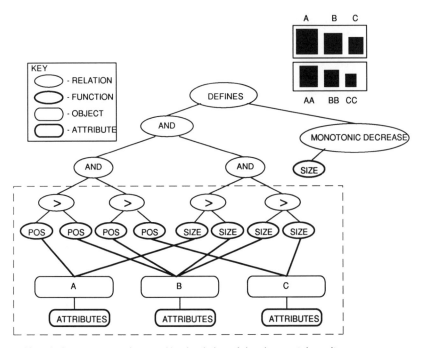

Knowledge representation used in simulation of developmental results.
(Area within the dashed box is the novice representation.)

FIG. 6.7. Representations assumed for the older children (full representation) and the younger children (boxed section of representation) in the mapping study (Gentner & Rattermann, 1991; Rattermann & Gentner, 1990; Rattermann et al., 1994).

3. We assumed that 3-year-olds after training with relational labels have augmented their representations to include monotonic decrease, so that their representations are equivalent to those of older children.

Further Representational Assumptions. As in our simulations of the Markman and Gentner adult studies, we modeled the sparse and rich stimuli by varying the number of attributes each object possessed (its intrinsic richness) as well as the number of its attributes not shared by the other objects in its stimulus set (its distinctiveness).

4. Sparse objects were modeled with three attributes: two shared in common with the other objects in its set, and one that was distinctive.
5. Rich objects each possessed five attributes, none shared with any of the objects in its set (to capture the distinctiveness of the rich objects).
6. Literal similarity was modeled by placing object similarity and relational structure in synchrony in two representations. Objects playing the same relational role in the two representations were described by the same attributes.
7. The cross-mapping condition was modeled by placing object similarity and relational similarity in conflict. Thus the objects in matching relational roles were described by different attributes. The cross-mapped objects (which played different relational rules in the two representations) had identical attribute sets.

Simulation Results. The results of the computational simulation are comparable to the results found in the empirical work, as shown in Table 6.2. For *literal similarity* pairs, when the representations were local, a higher evaluation score was given to the relational mapping with the rich objects (15.5) than with the sparse objects (12.5). This result corresponds to the performance of the 3-year-olds, who made more relational responses to the literal similarity materials for rich stimuli than for sparse stimuli. When the representations included the higher-order relation of monotonic decrease, SME's evaluation scores for the relational mapping were higher than for the shallow representation, although the evaluation was still higher for the rich pairs (19.0) than for the sparse pairs (16.0). This result is consistent with the performance of the 4-year-olds, who responded relationally to the literal similarity stimuli, but still performed better with the rich items than with the sparse items.

For the *cross-mapping* task, the results of the simulation also paralleled the performance of the children in the experiments. For these pairs, SME

TABLE 6.2
Results of Simulation of Rattermann, Gentner and DeLoache Task

| | | Representation Type | | | |
| | | Local Representation | | Higher-Order Relations | |
	Richness	Object GMAP[a]	Relational GMAP	Object GMAP	Relational GMAP
Literal Similarity	Sparse	12.50[b]	(same)	16.00	(same)
	Rich	15.50	(same)	19.00	(same)
Cross-mapping	Sparse	10.00	9.00	10.00	13.00
	Rich	11.50	8.00	11.50	11.50

[a]All values are GMAP evaluation scores generated by SME. [b]In Literal Similarity simulations, the object and relational GMAPs are the same.

generated both an object similarity interpretation and a relational similarity interpretation. When local relational structure was used (to simulate younger children), for sparse sets, the relational similarity mapping (evaluation = 13.0) received a higher evaluation score than the object similarity match (evaluation = 10.0). In contrast, for rich stimulus sets the object interpretation (evaluation = 16.5) received a higher evaluation score than the relational interpretation (evaluation = 8.0). This result corresponds to the empirical finding that 3-year-olds (and 4-year-olds) could make relational mappings for sparse stimuli, but not for rich stimuli.

When SME was given representations with higher-order relational structure for the sparse stimuli (simulating 5-year-olds and the 3-year-olds who were given familiar labels), the relational interpretation received a higher evaluation score than the object interpretation. For the rich stimuli, the relational interpretation and the object interpretation received the same evaluation score. This pattern is consistent with the behavior of 5-year-olds (and 3-year-olds given relational labels). On sparse object sets the deep relational mapping is clearly preferred, whereas on rich object sets there is a mixture of relational and object-based alignments.

The major conclusion from these simulations is that change of knowledge is sufficient to account for the relational shift. The same process model running on two different knowledge representations can simulate older children and younger children. When higher-order relational structure is included, SME's performance is like that of the older children, who readily master the relational mapping task. When the higher-order relational structure is removed, SME resembles the younger children, who fall prey to object matches and fail to master the task.

The simulations lend concrete support to our claim that the comparison process is an interaction of object matches and relational matches. In our simulations, as in the children's performance, object commonalities could either increase the likelihood of a relational response (in the literal similarity case, in which object commonalities supported the relational interpretation) or decrease the likelihood of a relational match (in cross-mapped pairs, for which object commonalities and relational commonalities were in competition). Only with deep relational representations did the relational interpretations prevail over rich cross-mapped objects. These simulations suggest that the relational shift need not involve a casting aside of objects. It results not from neglect of objects in the child's representations, but rather from an increase in the amount and depth of relational knowledge represented.

Investigation 2: Dimension-Specific and Dimension-General Representations

The results to be simulated from the Kotovsky and Gentner (1990, 1994) task are that (a) both younger and older children respond to within-dimension relational matches such as monotonic decrease in size, (b) older (but not younger) children spontaneously respond to cross-dimensional relational matches, and (c) younger children can be brought to notice the higher order cross-dimensional commonality if they are first given concentrated experience on both of the within-dimension comparisons.

Representational Assumptions. The ability to notice cross-dimensional commonality results from the recognition that dimensions like *bigger* and *darker* share some underlying similarity: They state that one value is somehow "more" than another along their respective dimensions. We speculate that the younger children represented magnitude difference in a dimension-specific way—roughly, *x is bigger than y*—whereas the older children represented magnitude difference in a dimension-general manner. Their encoding, we assumed, separates the specific dimension out of the magnitude comparison: *x's size is greater than y's size.* Note that the same information is encoded in both representations; the difference is in how analytical the representation is. The dimension-embedded encoding bigger(square1, square2) could be described as contextually embedded, conservative, or situated. The dimension-general encoding of the same relation greater[size(square1), size(square2)]. is more analytic than the first. It requires that the dimension of size has been extracted. This way, which dimension is affected can be separated from how it is affected (increase, decrease, and so on). We represent such extracted dimensions as functions: for example, *size*(x).[10]

SME treats these representations differently. Because SME matches

---

[10]In showing SME's representations, we represent relations in boldface and functions in boldface italics.

relations only if they are identical, it would see no correspondence between, say, bigger(x, y) and darker (a, b). In contrast, when given the second, more analytic encoding:

greater[*size*(a), *size*(b)]
greater[*darkness*(x), *darkness*(y)],

SME can readily perform a cross-dimensional alignment. Because SME allows nonidentical functions to correspond, two representations with identical relations over different dimensions can match. Thus, the second, more analytic encoding permits cross-dimensional alignment in SME, because the match between the two magnitude relations is then apparent.

Our representational assumptions in simulating the developmental change were as follows:

1. We assumed that 4-year-olds encoded the arrays in terms of dimension-specific relations (embedded relations) as shown in Fig. 6.8a, such as bigger(square1, square2) and darker(square1, square2).
2. We assumed that 4-year-olds encoded a dimensionally embedded change-in-size relation across the three objects (monotonic-decrease-in-size in Fig. 6.8a).
3. We assumed that 8-year-olds (and 4-year-olds after training) encoded the arrays in terms of dimension-general representations as shown in Fig. 6.8b, such as:

   greater[*size*(square1), *size*(square2)] and
   greater[*darkness*(square1), *darkness*(square2)],

   (where *size*(x) and *darkness*(x) are functions).
4. We assumed that 8-year-olds (and 4-year-olds after training) encoded a dimension-general relation of change (monotonic-decrease in Fig. 6.8b).
5. The objects were simulated in the same way as the sparse objects in the prior studies: namely, as having a few attributes shared with other objects in the figure, and one distinctive attribute (because only one dimension varied within each figure; see Fig. 6.8).

Simulation Results.   When embedded relations were used, the relational interpretation received a much higher evaluation for the same-dimensional comparison (evaluation score = 11. 50) than for the cross-dimensional comparison (evaluation score = 7.50). This result is consistent with the finding that 4-year-olds performed significantly better on same-dimension trials than on cross-dimension trials. In contrast, when monotonic decrease

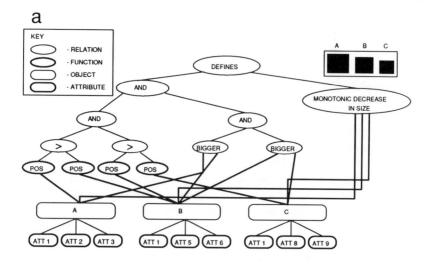

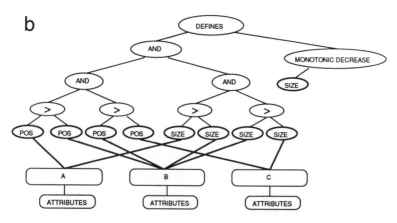

FIG. 6.8. Relational structures corresponding to the younger (a) and older (b) children in the triads study (Kotovsky & Gentner, 1990). The main difference between these representations lies in whether decrease along a dimension is represented holistically or analytically.

was represented using dimension-general encoding, the relational interpretation was preferred in both the same-dimensional comparison (evaluation score = 16.50) and the cross-dimensional comparison (evaluation score = 16.50). This result is consistent with the finding that 8-year-olds could spontaneously notice cross-dimensional comparisons.

The results of this simulation show that representational change alone is sufficient to account for the results presented here. The development of cross-dimensional comparisons can be modeled by assuming that children initially represent comparisons between values in a dimension-dependent fashion, but later re-represent these comparisons in a dimension-independent way. The simulation suggests that the dimensionalization of domains may be a key factor in acquiring the adult arsenal of reasoning tools. We return to this point later.

GENERAL DISCUSSION

The research summarized here suggests several conclusions. First, it supports the *career of similarity* thesis: Children begin with highly concrete similarity matches and gradually become able to appreciate partial matches. Second, among partial matches we see a relational shift from early focus on object-based matches to a later ability to perceive purely relational commonalities. Third, this development is driven by changes in domain knowledge. Fourth, we found support for several specific claims of the structure-mapping theory of the comparison process. On this account, the ability to make a purely relational alignment — an alignment not supported by, or even inconsistent with, the object similarities — requires that the structural alignment be rich enough and deep enough to prevail given the pressures from object similarity. We found that relational matches could be promoted in several ways predicted by the theory: (a) by diminishing the salience of competing object similarities (e.g., by using sparse objects in the Rattermann, Gentner, & DeLoache mapping studies); (b) by augmenting the salience of supporting object similarities (as in the rich-object literal similarity matches in the mapping studies); (c) by augmenting the depth of the matching relational structure (e.g., by adding higher-order relations, as in the mapping studies); (d) by highlighting the matching relational structure, as occurred in both studies; and (e) by re-representing two mismatching concrete relational structures so that they become instead two partially matching structures, as in the cross-dimensional task. We also considered two experiential forces that promote highlighting and re-representation: First, the acquisition of relational language and second, the progressive alignment of a series of cases so as to reveal common relations.

Language and Representational Change

These studies suggest that learning relational language fosters relational insight in several ways (see Gentner & Rattermann, 1991, for a review). One contribution of language is to allow children to transfer familiar relations to a new domain, as in the *Daddy, Mommy, Baby* studies. Another way is by reifying relational patterns, thus making them more salient, as we suggest occurred when the children in the Kotovsky and Gentner series learned *even* and *more-and-more*. A third way that language may promote relational learning is that the use of a common label may lead children to search for relational similarities between two different situations, despite the presence of dissimilar perceptual attributes. That is, we suggest that alignment and re-representation can be invited through common language. Language may provide a kind of conceptual juxtaposition that is perhaps more powerful than the temporal juxtaposition that led to alignment in the within-to-cross-dimensional transfer studies.

Research on word learning has shown that words have the power to focus children's attention on commonalties among objects (Gelman & Markman, 1987; Gentner, 1978; Landau, Smith, & Jones, 1988; Markman, 1989; Markman & Hutchinson, 1984; Waxman, 1991; Waxman & Senghas, 1992). This research has demonstrated the powerful effect of labels on children's acquisition of concepts. For example, Markman and Hutchinson asked 2- and 3-year-old children to select another object that "goes with" a standard object. Given a choice of two objects, the children chose a thematically related choice (e.g., a web for a spider). However, if a novel word was used along with the task (e.g., "This is a dax, show me another dax") then children often selected the taxonomic choice (e.g., a spider for a fly). Thus, the label—even one whose meaning was not known in advance—oriented the child toward some notion of *like kind*. Although most of this research has focused on nouns referring to objects, we believe the same phenomena can occur with relations. That is, we believe that the use of a common term can serve as an invitation to find a common relation, provided the children have already learned names for the objects in the scene (Gentner, 1982; Markman, 1989). There is some preliminary evidence for this claim. Smith and Sera (1992) found evidence that children's acquisition of dimensional language influences their cognitive organization of the dimensions. In some pilot studies, Gentner and Wolff (1994) found that introducing a new relational term helps 5-year-olds solve relational analogies.

Progressive Alignment and Representational Change

Kotovsky and Gentner's results suggest that re-representation is a natural extension of the comparison process. We were able to increase children's performance on cross-dimensional trials simply by blocking the within-dimension trials before the harder cross-dimensional trials, and this despite the fact that children were given no feedback on their responses. We speculate that the within-dimension comparisons, being strong overall matches, are easy for children to perceive. Each time a pair of these dimensionally embedded relational structures is aligned, their common structure is highlighted. Thus, repeated experience on within-dimension pairs permits the child to extract deep common structures, which then form the basis for cross-dimensional alignment and re-representation. When these deep but dimensionally specific structures are juxtaposed in the cross-dimensional trials, the alignment process operates to promote re-representation of the comparison relations into a more domain-general format. We refer to this process as *progressive alignment*.

Our position that re-representation is central is clearly related to Karmiloff-Smith's (1991, 1992) theory of cognitive development, especially to her claim that initially implicit procedural knowledge becomes available explicitly through representational redescription. However, there are some differences between the accounts. First, the scale of the changes discussed here is more local than in Karmiloff-Smith's discussion. Whereas Karmiloff-Smith emphasized metalevel insights into one's own processes, we see a role for re-representation even at the simple content level. Second, our research focuses particularly on *mechanisms* of re-representation. We believe this level of explanation is crucial to understanding the phenomenon. Third, whereas Karmiloff-Smith proposes that redescription processes begin only after behavioral mastery is attained in a given domain, we assume that alignment and re-representation happen from the start. The reason that re-representation does not seem to be occurring in very young children is that their earliest representations are so richly embedded in concrete detail, and so lacking in higher-order abstractions, that only the most conservative similarity matches can be made. These early matches and their resulting inferences may go unnoticed; they are far too simple to be the kind of insights that parents proudly relate. Nonetheless, we suggest that they pave the way for the more dramatic comparisons to come.

The Early Conservativeness Of Similarity

We have stressed that early similarity matches tend to rely on massive overlap between the items, and that only with experience do children become able to appreciate partial similarity and analogy. Our current findings support this conclusion. In both studies, children could respond well to literal similarity before they could take advantage of purely relational commonalities. One implication of the "career of similarity" thesis is that children's earliest similarity matches should be highly conservative; that is, they should rely on extremely large overlap. Our survey of the development of similarity turned up considerable evidence for this claim (Gentner & Rattermann, 1991). For example, Baillargeon found a fascinating ability in infants to perform a rudimentary kind of inferential mapping, but only under conditions of near identity (Baillargeon, 1987, 1990, 1991; Baillargeon, Spelke, & Wasserman, 1985). Normally, 4½-month-old infants who have been habituated to a screen rotating back and forth through an 180° arc show no surprise when a solid box is placed behind the screen and in the path of its trajectory, and is (apparently) crushed into a tiny fraction of its former size. (Note that the apparent crushing of the box takes place behind the screen and out of the infant's line of sight.) However, if another box of the same size and shape is placed next to the to-be-crushed box, the babies show surprise at the crushing event, provided that this second box (which remains visible throughout the event) is identical or highly similar to the first "to-be-crushed" box. For example, given a visible box that was red with white dots, the 4½-month-olds could successfully make the mapping (and thus show surprise) if the "crushed" box was red with green dots, but not if it was yellow with green dots or, worse, yellow with a clown face.

We interpret this finding as suggesting that the babies are doing a kind of similarity-based mapping, using the box that is visible to infer (or remember) the size of the occluded box as it disappears behind the screen (Gentner & Rattermann, 1991). What is striking is the conservativeness of the process. The babies appear to require a strong overall similarity match before they can make the match. Results like these bring home the magnitude of the human achievement in acquiring the kind of flexible, purely relational similarity capability that adults take for granted. Thus, the development of similarity proceeds from the perception of overall similarity between two situations to the ability to perceive partial similarity matches, and among these partial matches, object-matches precede relational matches.

Relation to Other Views

The Primacy of Relations View. We have discussed the positions of Brown and Goswami under the general rubric of the knowledge-based account of the relational shift. However their position is somewhat more complex than this. Goswami and Brown stress the early availability of relational similarity, and at times seem to argue that there is no relational shift: Relational similarity is dominant from the start (Brown, 1989, 1990; Goswami, 1992; Goswami & Brown, 1990). Clearly, our results do not support such a position. The results of both studies show a strong relational shift with experience. In the Rattermann, Gentner, and DeLoache mapping studies, there was a shift from object matches to relational matches in the cross-mapping studies: Children showed increasing dominance of relational similarity with increasing knowledge of relations. Furthermore, children performed better when the object matches were consistent with the relational alignment, and worse when they were inconsistent. In the Kotovsky and Gentner studies, young children needed concrete same-dimension matches; only children with more domain experience (acquired over time or by training) could appreciate cross-dimensional matches sharing purely higher-order relational similarity. These findings, which demonstrate a relational shift in development, are hard to reconcile with the claim that relational mapping behavior is fully present from the start.

However, this apparent disagreement may be partly terminological. Goswami at times seems to adopt a very liberal criterion for the use of the term *relational similarity*. For example, as evidence that infants use relational similarity, Goswami (1992) cited Meltzoff's (1990) finding that 14-month-olds will watch an adult who is imitating their current behavior (e.g., shaking a toy when the infant shakes a similar toy) in preference to one who is imitating their past behavior. Meltzoff's intriguing evidence certainly suggests that babies are aligning their own actions with those of the adult. But to describe this match as relational similarity obscures the fact that the two events—*adult shaking toy* and *baby shaking [similar] toy*—match closely at the object level as well as at the relational level. Such a match fits the description of *overall* or *literal similarity*. Again, in her reanalysis of Baillargeon's occluded box example discussed earlier, Goswami (1992) referred to babies' use of a near-identical standard as a *relational comparison* and cited this study as evidence that even young infants can perceive relational similarity. We would term the likeness between a red box with white dots and a red box with green dots one of literal similarity, and not one of purely relational similarity.

If Goswami is using the term *relational similarity* to subsume both literal similarity and analogy, then there would be no disagreement as to its primacy. The claim that overall similarity can be perceived from the start coincides with the claims of the relational shift hypothesis. However, to equate relational similarity and overall similarity would seem to render discussions of the later development of purely relational similarity rather cumbersome. If, on the other hand, Goswami's claim is that an appreciation of purely relational similarity precedes an appreciation of object-based similarity, then this view is quite distinct from our own, and is countermanded by the results here.

A related but distinct position on early relational similarity is Bryant's (1974) thesis that relational similarity precedes absolute similarity. Bryant pointed out that when young children are given comparisons like "5 is greater than 3," they find it easier to match on the basis of the dimensional relation than on the basis of the absolute values. The results of the Rattermann et al. mapping studies point the way to a reconciliation between Bryant's findings and the relational shift claim. Absolutes are values along one dimension only, and hence are extremes in the direction of sparseness. Thus, for absolutes, as for the sparse objects in our experiment, the pull of object similarity is very low (i.e., self-similarity is very low). For when the objects differ only along one dimension, say size, then in a cross-mapping, say *5 2* and *2 1*, the best object match (*2 → 2*) is only one feature better than the object match (*2 → 1*) required to support the relational mapping.

Thus, even with a beginner's knowledge of relational structure, relational similarity may win out over object similarity when the objects are absolutes. In contrast, rich objects like the ones in our experiment have high self-similarity: This means that the *2 → 2* object match is much stronger than the *2 → 1* object match. Thus, the relational mapping becomes less likely as the richness of the objects (and therefore the degree of object similarity) increases. It becomes more likely either as the objects become less interesting or as the relational structure becomes deeper and more salient. Consistent with this account, when a focus on relations is desired — for example, when teaching mathematics — sparse objects such as x's and y's are often preferred (Uttal & DeLoache, 1994). According to this account, we can expect to see a relational shift in most domains. Relational similarity gains ascendancy with increasing knowledge.

The relational shift is not absolute: It does not represent a shift from using exclusively object similarity to using exclusively relational similarity. Adults can use purely relational matches, and tend to find them more sound and apt than object matches (Gentner & Clement, 1988; Gentner, Rattermann, & Forbus, 1993), but they use overall similarity matches whenever possible. Furthermore, when objects and relations are pitted against one another we find effects of both kinds of similarities in studies of comparison (Gentner & Markman, 1993; Goldstone, 1994; Goldstone & Medin, 1994; Markman & Gentner, 1990, 1993; Medin, Goldstone, & Gentner, 1993), in problem-solving research (Novick, 1988; Ross, 1984, 1989) and in device transfer (Schumacher & Gentner, 1988). The comparison process typically involves both object similarity and relational similarity throughout development.

The Global Change View. These results argue against theories that propose that relational similarity must await some advanced stage of cognitive development (Piaget, Montangero, & Billeter, 1977). They accord with the position that children should be seen as domain novices rather than as underdeveloped information processors (Brown & DeLoache, 1978; Carey, 1985; Chi, 1981).

Our findings are also problematic for Halford's account, according to which children's performance on relational analogies is governed largely by maturational increases in their processing capacity (Halford, 1987, 1992, 1993). Halford's account of the relational shift is that children's ability to perform analogical reasoning tasks depends on whether their processing capacity is equal to the structural complexity of the task. Tasks that require only unary predicates, such as object attributes, make fewer demands than those requiring the mapping of a binary relation. Tasks whose solution requires mapping systems of relations induce an even higher processing load. Halford and his colleagues have carried out many closely reasoned studies of topics such as transitivity and class inclusion that demonstrate the expected shift in performance with age. They have simulated their view in the STAR model, which represents relational structure in a distributed connectionist system using tensor products (Halford, Wilson, Guo, Wiles, & Stewart, in press; Smolensky, 1990).

Halford's emphasis on a maturational increase in processing capacity contrasts with our claim that the relational shift derives from the acquisition of higher-order structure. In part this difference derives from a difference in the ways the two theories represent complex relational structure (Gentner, 1992). Halford models structures such as monotonic increase as consisting of multiple relations between objects. The idea then is that greater processing capacity is required to find correspondences between representations containing multiple relations. In contrast, we represent complex relational patterns in terms of higher-order relations that take lower-order relations or propositions as arguments. Because the human comparison processor (like SME) favors connected systems, resolving a similarity comparison is easier when there are higher-order relations connecting lower-order relations that would otherwise be independent. Simulations using SME bear out this claim. SME is faster and more certain of the best match when given deep representations than when given flat representations. Thus, increases in domain knowledge can actually decrease the processing load associated with relational tasks in that domain. This argument is cousin to the demonstrations of Bower and Winzenz (1969), Bransford and Johnson (1972), Mandler and Mandler (1964) and others to the effect that adding more connecting material can make a task easier.

Our results that children can shift from object-based similarity to relational similarity in the space of a few minutes run contrary to the claim that the relational shift stems from a maturational increase in processing capacity. In particular, the fact that 3-year-olds who are taught higher-order relations can then use them to perceive relational similarity runs against Halford's suggestion that the ability to process relational similarity is acquired at about 3½ or 4 years of age. However, Halford's account also allows for the effects of learning; for example, chunking of relations into larger relations. Although our account stresses learning more and maturation less than his view, there is considerable agreement between the two views.

SME and Re-representation

The SME simulations serve a dual purpose. First, they demonstrate that the observed developmental changes in ability to make relational mappings can be mimicked by holding the similarity process constant and changing the representations it operates over (and, moreover, changing the representations in ways consistent with our task interventions). Second, the simulations suggest that the process of comparison might itself be part of the learning process, in two respects: (a) repeated alignment might focus a learner on large common structures, and (b) finding aligned mismatches provides candidates for re-representation. Structural alignment thus acts as a domain-general process that is sensitive to domain-specific information.

We have discussed re-representation (e.g., decomposing two similar predicates to reveal some identical subpredicates) as a key mechanism in progressive alignment. However, another possibility is suggested by the ACME simulation of Holyoak and Thagard (1989). Rather than requiring identical relations, it uses a similarity table: The more similar two predicates, the better their match.[11] In this approach, learning to make cross-dimensional mappings could be done simply by entering a high similarity for the two relations; the child would just learn that *darker* is similar to *bigger*, and so on. Although this approach seems less cumbersome than the re-representational approach proposed here, we believe it is psychologically incorrect, for two reasons. First, *darker* is not in fact similar to *bigger*. The child would be mistaken to suppose that a dark horse would resemble a big horse, for example. Second, entering a local similarity value for these two predicates misses the fact that they correspond by virtue of a larger domain mapping. If in a given context *darker* corresponds to *bigger*, then *lighter* must correspond to *smaller, pale* to *small, darkening* to *growing*, and so on. All these would have to be given high values in the similarity table. It is difficult to conceive of a mechanism that could accomplish this without losing the simplicity that made the similarity table attractive in the first place. Moreover, if the table could be changed to reflect these domain mappings, we would face an even worse version of the first problem. Our similarity metric would tell us that a big horse is like a dark horse *and* that a pale horse is like a small horse, and so on.

The problem is made more acute by the large number of system-mappings in common use: *dark/light* → *sad/happy, dark/light* → bad/good, dark/ligh → *confusing/clear*, and so on (Lakoff & Johnson, 1980; Turner, 1987, 1991; see also Kittay, 1987). To account for all these mappings within a similarity table would render the table incoherent and factually incorrect. SME's technique avoids these problems. It does not try to capture dimensional mappings by setting the pairwise similarity of individual predicates, but by representing them as system mappings in which nonidentical functions representing dimensions (like *darkness* and *size*) correspond by virtue of their roles in the larger matching structures. Once two dimensions are placed in correspondence, the mapping can readily be extended: *increase*

---

[11]In contrast, SME's decompositional approach captures degree of similarity through the number of overlapping representational components. Later versions of ACME have explored other similarity algorithms.

in darkness (*darkening*) corresponds to *increase in size* (*growing*), and so on. This generativity is a significant advantage of our dimension mapping approach over the use of similarity tables.

In our simulations we did not simulate the re-representation process itself. This is because our aim is to show that change of representation is sufficient to account for the observed developmental changes. However, simulating the re-representation process has been the focus of considerable recent research in analogy (Burstein, 1983; Falkenhainer, 1988; Gentner & Rattermann, 1991; Kass, 1989; Keane & Brayshaw, 1988). Falkenhainer's (1988) Phineas system, which uses contextual structure-mapping to model scientific discovery, re-represents predicates to improve the alignment under carefully specified conditions. For example, it tries to find a common superordinate for two nonmatching antecedents whose match is invited by the overall alignment, provided that their consequents match. Keane's Incremental Analogy Matcher (IAM) models the analogical process as one of iterative mapping, with later mappings incorporating more information (Keane & Brayshaw, 1988). Kass (1989) described a set of "tweaks" by which explanations of prior cases can be adapted to apply to a current situation. A complete model of the developmental changes described here will include the mechanisms of re-representation itself. Once two dimensions are placed in correspondence, the mapping can readily be extended. This extendability and generating is a significant advantage of a dimension-mapping approach over the use of similarity tables.

Although we have emphasized the importance of domain knowledge, other factors may also play a role in the development of comparison ability. As Klahr and Wallace (1976), Siegler (1984), and Sternberg (1984) have emphasized, it is unlikely that one explanation will cover all of cognitive development in an arena this size. One possibility that is consistent with structure-mapping theory is that children do not initially share the adult preference for structurally consistent and systematic mappings. That is, children may only gradually develop the preference for higher-order relational matching. The possibility that a preference for systematicity and structural consistency is culturally influenced is supported by an examination of the writings of medieval alchemists. Their aesthetic was different from the modern one; it encompassed rich, structurally inconsistent analogies and many-to-one mappings (Gentner & Jeziorski, 1989, 1993). Recent connectionist models of analogical mapping also suggest ways to capture a lack of structural consistency. Holyoak and Thagard's (1989) ACME and Goldstone and Medin's (1994) SIAM both use localist connectionist networks to determine the best match between scenes. In both systems, the one-to-one correspondence rule, for example, is a pressure rather than a firm constraint. Thus, another developmental shift worth examining is a potential shift in the firmness of the constraints on alignment and mapping.

Cross-Domain Mappings

We speculate that analogical mapping between domains may be a major
mechanism of learning and discovery in the developing child (see Gentner &
Rattermann, 1991; Halford, 1993; Siegler, 1989) as in the scientist (Gentner, 1982; Gentner & Jeziorski, 1993; Nersessian, 1992). We suggest that
alignments, sometimes abetted by common relational labels, contribute to
the child's gradual analysis (or disembedding, or desituating) of initially
context-bound knowledge into separable representations and help the child
see common structure across different dimensions (see Nunes, Schliemann,
& Carraher, 1993). The gradual dimensionalization of the child's world
brings with it the ability to align structure across different domains. The
ramifications of this representational change are vast. As mentioned earlier,
the mapping of structure across different domains underlies the rich set of
cross-domain metaphoric systems that pervade our language (Carbonell,
1982; Gentner & Boronat, 1992; Gibbs & O'Brien, 1990; Kittay, 1987;
Kittay & Lehrer, 1981; Lakoff & Johnson, 1980; Nagy, 1974; Turner, 1987,
1991). Such cross-domain analogies can occur seemingly unconsciously, as
when Bowerman's (1981, 1982) preschool child asked "May I have some
candy behind dinner?" (a possible time–space analogy). In other cases, the
analogy is noticed, as when a child in our cross-dimensional task announced
with delight, "It's exactly the same, but different."

The discarding of Piaget's global stage system in favor of a domain-
knowledge view of cognitive development threatens to leave us with a
piecemeal account, one that lacks any link between, for example, conservation of volume and conservation of weight. We speculate that analogy
provides that link. The child who has caught on to conservation in one or
two prior domains is more likely to learn the principle in the next domain.
For example, in an intriguing study, Gelman (1969) taught 5-year-olds, who
initially failed to conserve length, number, mass, and liquid, a discrimination learning task with length and number. Their subsequent conservation
performance was near perfect on length and number; but more impres-
sively, the children also improved substantially on conservation of the two
nontrained quantities, mass and liquid amount. In another study, Gelman
(1982) taught children conservation of small numbers and found that they
subsequently improved their performance on tasks involving conservation
of large numbers. Simon and Klahr's (chap. 7, this volume) simulation of
this finding using their Q-Soar simulation further demonstrates how
knowledge of conservation can transfer from small numbers to large
numbers. Consistent with our transfer-of-knowledge account, Simon and
Klahr suggest that an understanding of discrete numbers provides the basis
for learning to reason about continuous quantities.

We suggest that there is a kind of mutual promotion cycle, whereby analogy and similarity act to increase representational uniformity (through re-representation to increase alignment), and are in turn promoted by uniform representations (because the more alignable the representations, the more likely it is that the likeness will be noticed and the comparison made). This positive feedback cycle contributes to what we have called the *gentrification of knowledge* (Gentner & Rattermann, 1991) — to the gradual replacement of the idiosyncratic perceptions of childhood by the sturdy, relatively uniform representations of the adult cultural world view.

SUMMARY AND CONCLUSIONS

We have focused on two ways in which children become fluent at higher-order relational comparison. First, as they gain information about higher-order relations in a domain, they become better able to make complex relational mappings, even in the face of cross-mappings that may distract them from the relational correspondences. Second, information they already possess may be re-represented to determine deeper similarities.

A number of forces drive these representational changes. One force is the comparison process itself. Our results suggest that simply carrying out similarity and analogy comparisons may play a fundamental role in the development of representations. Alignment of structure may focus the child on a limited number of areas where knowledge enrichment or re-representation is likely to be fruitful. Although similarity is often treated rather slightingly in current theories of cognitive development, these results suggest that similarity — even mundane within-dimension similarity — can act as a positive force in learning and development.

A second force is language. Language provides names for abstract relational structures, reifying complex information and making it easier to manipulate. By applying familiar labels in a new domain, children may learn to transfer relational structures learned in one situation to novel circumstances. Finally, language and comparison may act in concert: The conceptual juxtaposition and alignment invited by common language can lead children to form relational categories.

ACKNOWLEDGMENTS

This chapter grew out of a symposium presented by the authors at the third annual Midwestern Artificial Intelligence and Cognitive Science Society conference in Carbondale, IL, 1990. The developmental research was supported by NSF grant BNS-87-20301 and by The Center for the Study of Reading at the University of Illinois at Urbana-Champaign Grant 400-31-0031. The development of the Structure-Mapping Engine was supported by ONR contract N00014-89-J1272. We thank Ken Forbus, Doug Medin, Judy DeLoache, David Uttal, Phil Wolff, and Ron Ferguson for insightful discussions on these issues, and Tony Simon for helpful comments on the manuscript.

REFERENCES

Baillargeon, R. (1987). Object permanence in 3.5- and 4.5-month-old infants. *Developmental Psychology, 23*, 655–664.
Baillargeon, R. (1990). *The role of similarity in infants' use of visible objects as cues for hidden objects.* Unpublished manuscript.
Baillargeon, R. (1991). Reasoning about the height and location of a hidden object in 4.5- and 6.5-month-old infants. *Cognition, 38*, 13–42.
Baillargeon, R., Spelke, E. S., & Wasserman, S. (1985). Object permanence in five-month-old infants. *Cognition, 20*, 191–208.
Billow, R. M. (1975). A cognitive developmental study of metaphor comprehension. *Developmental Psychology, 11*, 415–423.
Bower, G. H., Clark, M. C., Lesgold, A. M., & Winzenz, D. (1969). Hierarchical retrieval schemes in recall of categorized word lists. *Journal of Verbal Learning and Verbal Behavior, 8*, 323–343.
Bower, G. H., & Winzenz, D. (1969). Group structure, coding and memory for digit series. *Journal of Experimental Psychology Monograph, 80*(2, Pt. 2).
Bowerman, M. (1981). The child's expression of meaning: Expanding relationships among lexicon, syntax and morphology. In H. Winitz (Ed.), *Native language and foreign language acquisition* (Vol. 379, pp. 172–189). New York: New York Academy of Sciences.
Bowerman, M. (1982). Starting to talk worse: Clues to language acquisition from children's late speech errors. In S. Strauss (Ed.), *U-shaped behavioral growth* (pp. 101–145). New York: Academic Press.
Bransford, J. D., & Johnson, M. K. (1972). Contextual prerequisites for understanding: Some investigations of comprehension and recall. *Journal of Verbal Learning and Verbal Behavior, 11*, 717–726.
Brown, A. L. (1989). Analogical learning and transfer: What develops? In S. Vosniadou & A. Ortony (Eds.), *Similarity and analogical reasoning* (pp. 369–412). New York: Cambridge University Press.
Brown, A. L. (1990). Domain specific principles affect learning and transfer in children. *Cognitive Science, 14*, 107–134.
Brown, A. L., & DeLoache, J. S. (1978). Skills, plans, and self-regulation. In R. S. Siegler (Ed.), *Children's thinking: What develops?* (pp. 3–35). Hillsdale, NJ: Lawrence Erlbaum Associates.
Brown A. L., & Kane, M. J. (1988). Preschool children can learn to transfer: Learning to learn and learning from example. *Cognitive Psychology, 20*, 493–523.
Bryant, P. E. (1974). *Perception and understanding in young children: An experimental approach.* New York: Basic Books.
Burstein, M. H. (1983). Concept formation by incremental analogical reasoning and debugging. *Proceedings of the International Machine Learning Workshop* (pp. 19–25). Urbana: University of Illinois.

Carbonell, J. G. (1982). Metaphor: An inescapable phenomenon in natural language comprehension. In W. G. Lehnert & M. H. Ringle (Eds.), *Strategies for natural language processing* (pp. 415–435). Hillsdale, NJ: Lawrence Erlbaum Associates.

Carey, S. (1985). *Conceptual change in childhood.* Cambridge, MA: MIT Press.

Carey, S. (1991). Knowledge acquisition: Enrichment or conceptual change? In S. Carey & R. Gelman (Eds.), *The epigenisis of mind: Essays on biology and cognition* (pp. 257–291). Hillsdale, NJ: Lawrence Erlbaum Associates.

Chen, Z., & Daehler, M. W. (1989). Positive and negative transfer in analogical problem solving by 6-year-old children. *Cognitive Development, 4,* 327–344.

Chi, M. T. H. (1981). Knowledge development and memory performance. In M. Friedman, J. P. Das, & N. O'Conner (Eds.), *Intelligence and learning* (pp. 221–230). New York: Plenum.

Chipman, S. F. (1977). Complexity and structure in visual patterns. *Journal of Experimental Psychology: General, 106,* 269–301.

Chipman, S. F., & Mendelson, M. J. (1979). Influence of six types of visual structure on complexity judgments in children and adults. *Journal of Experimental Psychology: Human Perception and Performance, 5,* 365–378.

Crisafi, M. A., & Brown, A. L. (1986). Analogical transfer in very young children: Combining two separately learned solutions to reach a goal. *Child Development, 57,* 953–968.

Falkenhainer, B. (1988). *Learning from physical analogies: A study of analogy and the explanation process* (Tech. Rep. No. UIUCDCS-R-88-1479). Urbana: University of Illinois, Department of Computer Science.

Falkenhainer, B., Forbus, K. D., & Gentner, D. (1986). The structure-mapping engine. In *Proceedings of the Meeting of the American Association for Artificial Intelligence* (pp. 272–277). Los Altos, CA: Morgan Kaufmann.

Falkenhainer, B., Forbus, K. D., & Gentner, D. (1989). The structure-mapping engine: Algorithm and examples. *Artificial Intelligence, 41,* 1–63.

Forbus, K. D., & Gentner, D. (1986). Learning physical domains: Toward a theoretical framework. In R. S. Michalski, J. G. Carbonell, & T. M. Mitchell (Eds.), *Machine learning: An artificial intelligence approach* (Vol. 2, pp. 311–348). Los Altos, CA: Morgan Kaufmann.

Forbus, K. D., & Gentner, D. (1989). Structural evaluation of analogies: What counts? In *Proceedings of the Eleventh Annual Conference of the Cognitive Science Society* (pp. 341–348). Hillsdale, NJ: Lawrence Erlbaum Associates.

Forbus, K. D., & Oblinger, D. (1990). Making SME greedy and pragmatic. In *Proceedings of the Twelfth Annual Conference of the Cognitive Science Society* (pp. 61–68). Hillsdale, NJ: Lawerence Erlbaum Associates.

Gelman, R. (1969). Conservation acquisition: A problem of learning to attend to relevant attributes. *Journal of Experimental Child Psychology, 7,* 167–187.

Gelman, R. (1982). Accessing one-to-one correspondence: Still another paper about conservation. *Journal of Psychology, 73,* 209–220.

Gelman, S. A., & Markman, E. M. (1987). Young children's inductions from natural kinds: The role of categories and appearances. *Child Development, 58,* 1532–1541.

Gentner, D. (1977a). Children's performance on a spatial analogies task. *Child Development, 48,* 1034–1039.

Gentner, D. (1977b). If a tree had a knee, where would it be? Children's performance on simple spatial metaphors. *Papers and Reports on Child Language Development, 13,* 157–164.

Gentner, D. (1978). Testing the psychological reality of a representational model. *Proceedings of Theoretical Issues in Natural Language Processing* (Vol. 2, pp. 1–7). Urbana: University of Illinois, Association for Computing Machinery.

Gentner, D. (1982). Are scientific analogies metaphors? In D. S. Miall (Ed.), *Metaphor: Problems and perspectives* (pp. 106–132). Brighton, England: Harvester.

310   GENTNER ET AL.

Gentner, D. (1983). Structure-mapping: A theoretical framework for analogy. *Cognitive Science, 7*, 155–170.

Gentner, D. (1986). *Evidence for structure-mapping analogy and metaphor* (Tech. Rep. No. UIUCDCS-R-86-1316). Urbana: University of Illinois, Department of Computer Science.

Gentner, D. (1988) Analogical inference and analogical access. In A. Prieditis (Ed.), *Analogica* (pp. 63–88). Los Altos, CA: Morgan Kaufmann.

Gentner, D. (1989). Mechanisms of analogical learning. In S. Vosniadou & A. Ortony (Eds.), *Similarity and analogical reasoning,* (pp. 199–241). London: Cambridge University Press.

Gentner, D. (1990). *Metaphor as structure mapping: The relational shift.* (Tech. Rep. No. 488). Urbana: University of Illinois, Center for the Study of Reading.

Gentner, D. (1992). Commentary on Halford. *Human Development, 35,* 218–221.

Gentner, D., & Boronot, C. B. (1992). *Metaphors are (sometimes) processed as generative domain-mappings.* Unpublished manuscript.

Gentner, D., & Clement, C. (1988). Evidence for relational selectivity in the interpretation of analogy and metaphor. In G. H. Bower (Ed.), *The psychology of learning and motivation* (Vol. 22, pp. 307–358). New York: Academic Press.

Gentner, D., & Jeziorski, M. (1989). Historical shifts in the use of analogy in science. In B. Gholson, A. Houts, R. A. Neimeyer, & W. R. Shadish (Eds.), *The psychology of science and metascience* (pp. 296–325). New York: Cambridge University Press.

Gentner, D., & Jeziorski, M. (1993). The shift from metaphor to analogy in western science. In A. Ortony (Ed.), *Metaphor and thought* (2nd ed., pp. 447–480). Cambridge, England: Cambridge University Press.

Gentner, D., & Markman, A. B. (1994). Similarity is like an analogy: Structural alignment in comparison. In C. Cacciari (Ed.), *Similarity.* Brussels: Brepols.

Gentner, D., & Rattermann, M. J. (1991). Language and the career of similarity. In S. A. Gelman & J. P. Byrnes (Eds.), *Perspectives on language and thought: Interrelations in development* (pp. 225–277). London: Cambridge University Press.

Gentner, D., Rattermann, M. J., & Campbell, R. (1994). *Evidence for a relational shift in the development of analogy.* Unpublished manuscript.

Gentner, D., Rattermann, M. J., & Forbus, K. D. (1993). The roles of similarity in transfer: Separating retrievability and inferential soundness. *Cognitive Psychology, 25,* 524–575.

Gentner, D., & Toupin, C. (1986). Systematicity and surface similarity in the development of analogy. *Cognitive Science, 10,* 277–300.

Gentner, D., & Wolff, P. (in press). Metaphor and knowledge change. In A. Kasher & Y. Shen (Eds.), *Cognitive aspects of metaphor, structure, comprehenson, and use.*

Gibbs, R. W., & O'Brien, J. E. (1990). Idioms and mental imagery: The metaphorical motivation for idiomatic meaning. *Cognition, 36,* 35–68.

Gibbs, R. W., & O'Brien, J. E. (in press). Idioms and mental imagery: The metaphorical motivation for idomatic meaning. *Cognition.*

Goldstone, R. L. (1994). Similarity, interactive activation, and mapping. *Journal of Experimental Psychology: Learning, Memory, and Cognition, 20*(1), 3–28.

Goldstone, R. L., & Medin, D. L. (1994). Time course of comparison. *Journal of Experimental Psychology: Learning, Memory, and Cognition, 20*(1), 29–50.

Goswami, U. (1991). Analogical reasoning: What develops? A review of research and theory. *Child Development, 62,* 1–22.

Goswami, U. (1992). *Analogical reasoning in children.* Hove, UK: Lawrence Erlbaum Associates.

Goswami, U., & Brown, A. L. (1990). Higher-order structure and relational reasoning: Contrasting analogical and thematic relations. *Cognition, 36,* 207–226.

Halford, G. S. (1987). A structure-mapping approach to cognitive development. *International Journal of Psychology, 22,* 609–642.

Halford, G. S. (1992). Analogical reasoning and conceptual complexity in cognitive development. *Human Development*

Halford, G. S. (1993). *Children's understanding: The development of mental models.* Hillsdale, NJ: Lawrence Erlbaum Associates.

Halford, G. S., Maybery, M. T., & Bain, J. D. (1986). Capacity limitations in children's reasoning: A dual task approach. *Child Development, 57,* 616–627.

Halford, G. S., Wilson, W. H., Guo, J., Wiles, J., & Stewart, J. E. M. (in press). Connectionist implications for processing capacity limitations in analogies. In K. J. Holyoak & J. Barnden (Eds.), *Advances in connectionist and neural computation theory, Vol. 2: Analogical connections.* Norwood, NJ: Ablex.

Holyoak, K. J., & Thagard, P. (1989). Analogical mapping by constraint satisfaction. *Cognitive Science, 13,* 295–355.

Inhelder, B., & Piaget, J. (1958). *The growth of logical thinking from childhood to adolescence.* New York: Basic Books.

Karmiloff-Smith, A. (1991). Beyond modularity: Innate constraints and developmental change. In S. Carey & R. Gelman (Eds.), *The epigenesis of mind: Essays on biology and cognition* (pp. 171–197). Hillsdale, NJ: Lawrence Erlbaum Associates.

Karmiloff-Smith, A. (1992). *Beyond modularity: A developmental perspective on cognitive science.* Cambridge, MA: MIT Press.

Kass, A. (1989). Strategies for adapting explanations. In *Proceedings: Case-Based Reasoning Workshop* (pp. 119–123). San Mateo, CA: Morgan Kaufmann.

Keane, M. T., & Brayshaw, M. (1988). The incremental analogical machine: A computational model of analogy. In D. Sleeman (Ed.), *Third European working session on machine learning* (pp. 53–62). San Mateo, CA: Morgan Kaufmann.

Kittay, E. (1987). *Metaphor: Its cognitive force and linguistic structure.* Oxford, England: Clarendon.

Kittay, E., & Lehrer, A. (1981). Semantic fields and the structure of metaphor. *Studies in Language, 5*(1), 31–63.

Klahr, D., & Wallace, J. G. (1976). *Cognitive development: An information processing view.* Hillsdale, NJ: Lawrence Erlbaum Associates.

Kolstad, V., & Baillargeon, R. (1991). *Appearance and knowledge-based responses to containers in infants.* Unpublished manuscript.

Kotovsky, L. & Gentner, D. (1990). Pack light: You will go farther. In *Proceedings of the Second Midwest Artificial Intelligence and Cognitive Science Society Conference* (pp. 60–72). Hillsdale, NJ: Lawrence Erlbaum Associates.

Kotovsky, L., & Gentner, D. (1994). *Progressive alignment: A mechanism for the development of relational similarity.* Unpublished manuscript.

Lakoff, G., & Johnson, M. (1980). The metaphorical structure of the human conceptual system. *Cognitive Science, 4,* 195–208.

Landau, B., Smith, L. B., & Jones, S. S. (1988). The importance of shape in early lexical learning. *Cognitive Development, 3,* 299–321.

Mandler, G. (1967). Organization and memory. In K. W. Spence & J. T. Spence (Eds.), *Psychology of learning and motivation* (Vol. 1, pp. 328–372). New York: Academic Press.

Mandler, J. M., & Mandler, G. (1964). *Thinking: From association to Gestalt.* New York: Wiley.

Markman, A. B., & Gentner, D. (1990). Analogical mapping during similarity judgments. In *Proceedings of the Twelfth Annual Conference of the Cognitive Science Society* (pp. 38–44). Hillsdale, NJ: Lawrence Erlbaum Associates.

Markman, A. B., & Gentner, D. (1993). Structural alignment during similarity comparisons. *Cognitive Psychology, 25,* 431–467.

Markman, E. M. (1989). *Categorization in children: Problems of induction.* Cambridge, MA: MIT Press.

Markman, E. M., & Hutchinson, J. E. (1984). Children's sensitivity to constraints on word meaning: Taxonomic versus thematic relations. *Cognitive Psychology, 16,* 1–27.

Medin, D. L., Goldstone, R. L., & Gentner, D. (1993). Respects for similarity. *Psychological Review, 100*(2), 254–278.

Meltzoff, A. N. (1990). Foundations for developing a concept of self: Role of imitation in relating self to other and the value of social mirroring, social modeling and self-practice in infancy. In D. Cicchetti & M. Beeghly (Eds.), *The self in transition: Infancy to childhood* (pp. 139–164). Chicago: University of Chicago Press.

Miller, G. A. (1956). The magic number seven, plus or minus two: Some limits on our capacity for processing information. *Psychological Review, 63,* 81–93.

Nagy, W. (1974). *Figurative patterns and the redundancy in lexicon.* Unpublished doctoral dissertation, University of California at San Diego.

Nersessian, N. J. (1992). How do scientists think? Capturing the dynamics of conceptual change in science. In R. N. Giere, & H. Feigl (Eds.), *Minnesota studies in the philosophy of science* (pp. 3–44). Minneapolis: University of Minnesota Press.

Norman, D. A., & Bobrow, D. G. (1979). Descriptions: An intermediate stage in memory retrieval. *Cognitive Psychology, 11,* 107–123.

Novick, L. R. (1988). Analogical transfer, problem similarity, and expertise. *Journal of Experimental Psychology: Learning, Memory, and Cognition, 14,* 510–520.

Nunes, T., Schliemann, A. D., & Carraher, D. W. (1993). *Street mathematics and school mathematics.* New York: Cambridge University Press.

Ortony, A., Reynolds, R. E., & Arter, J. A. (1978). Metaphor: Theoretical and empirical research. *Psychological Bulletin, 85,* 919–943.

Piaget, J., Montangero, J., & Billeter, J. (1977). La formation des correlats [The formation of correlations]. In J. Piaget (Ed.), *L'Abstraction reflechissante* (pp. 115–129). Paris: Presses Universitaires de France.

Rattermann, M. J., & Gentner, D. (1990). The development of similarity use: It's what you know, not how you know it. In *Proceedings of the Second Midwest Artificial Intelligence and Cognitive Science Society Conference* (pp. 54–59). Hillsdale, NJ: Lawrence Erlbaum Associates.

Rattermann, M. J., Gentner, D., & DeLoache, J. (1990). Effects of labels on children's use of relational similarity. In *Proceedings of the Twelfth Annual Conference of the Cognitive Science Society* (pp. 22–29). Hillsdale, NJ: Lawrence Erlbaum Associates.

Rattermann, M. J., Gentner, D., & DeLoache, J. (1994). *Effects of relational and object similarity on children's performance in a mapping task.* Unpublished manuscript.

Ross, B. H. (1984). Remindings and their effects in learning a cognitive skill. *Cognitive Psychology, 16,* 371–416.

Ross, B. H. (1989). Some psychological results on case-based reasoning. In *Proceedings: Case-Based Reasoning Workshop* (pp. 144–147). San Mateo, CA: Morgan Kaufmann.

Schumacher, R. M., & Gentner, D. (1988). Remembering causal systems: Effects of systematicity and surface similarity in delayed transfer. *Proceedings of the Human Factors Society 32nd Annual Meeting* (pp. 1271–1275). Santa Monica, CA: Human Factors Society.

Shepp, B. E. (1978). From perceived similarity to dimensional structure: A new hypothesis about perceptual development. In E. Rosch & B. B. Lloyd (Eds.), *Cognition and categorization* (pp. 135–167). Hillsdale, NJ: Lawrence Erlbaum Associates.

Siegler, R. S. (1984). Mechanisms of cognitive growth: Variation and selection. In R. J. Sternberg (Ed.), *Mechanisms of cognitive development* (pp. 141–162). Prospect Heights, IL: Waveland Press.

Siegler, R. S. (1989). Mechanisms of cognitive development. *Annual Review of Psychology, 40,* 353–379.

Smith, L. B. (1984). Young children's understanding of attributes and dimensions: A comparison of conceptual and linguistic measures. *Child Development, 55,* 363–380.

Smith, L. B. (1989). From global similarities to kinds of similarities: The construction of dimensions in development. In S. Vosniadou & A. Ortony (Eds.), *Similarity and analogical reasoning* (pp. 146–178). New York: Cambridge University Press.

Smith, L. B., & Kemler, D. G. (1977). Developmental trends in free classification: Evidence for a new conceptualization of perceptual development. *Journal of Experimental Child Psychology, 24,* 279–298.

Smith, L. B., & Sera, M. D. (1992). A developmental analysis of the polar structure of dimensions. *Cognitive Psychology, 24,* 99–142.

Smolensky, P. (1990). Neural and conceptual interpretation of PDP models. In J. L. McClelland, D. E. Rumelhart, & the PDP Research Group (Eds.), *Parallel distributed processing. Vol. 2: Psychological biological models* (pp. 390–431). Cambridge, MA: MIT Press.

Spinillo, A. G., & Bryant, P. (1991). Children's proportional judgments: The importance of "half." *Child Development, 62,* 427–440.

Sternberg, R. J. (1984). Mechanisms of cognitive development: A componential approach. In R. J. Sternberg (Ed.), *Mechanisms of cognitive development* (pp. 163–186). Prospect Heights, IL: Waveland Press.

Sternberg, R. J., & Downing, C. J. (1982). The development of higher-order reasoning in adolescence. *Child Development, 53,* 209–221.

Sternberg, R. J., & Nigro, G. (1980). Developmental patterns in the solution of verbal analogies. *Child Development, 51,* 27–38.

Sternberg, R. J., & Rifkin, B. (1979). The development of analogical reasoning processes. *Journal of Experimental Child Psychology, 27,* 195–232.

Turner, M. (1987). *Death is the mother of beauty. Mind, metaphor, and criticism.* Chicago, IL: University of Chicago Press.

Turner, M. (1991). *Reading minds: The study of English in the age of cognitive science.* Princeton, NJ: Princeton University Press.

Tversky, A. (1977). Features of similarity. *Psychological Review, 84,* 327–352.

Uttal, D., & DeLoache, J. (1994). *Mapping and symbolization processes in young children.* Paper presented at the meeting of the Piaget Society, Chicago, IL.

Vosniadou, S. (1987). Children and metaphors. *Child Development, 58,* 870–885.

Vosniadou, S. (1989). Analogical reasoning as a mechanism in knowledge acquisition: A developmental perspective. In S. Vosniadou & A. Ortony (Eds.), *Similarity and analogical reasoning* (pp. 413–437). New York: Cambridge University Press.

Waxman, S. (1991). Semantic and conceptual organization in preschoolers. In J. Byrnes & S. Gelman (Eds.), *Perspectives on language and thought* (pp. 107–145). Cambridge, England: Cambridge University Press.

Waxman, S. R., & Senghas, A. (1992). Relations among word meanings in early lexical development. *Developmental Psychology, 28*(5), 862–873.

Wolff, P., & Gentner, D. (1992). The time course of metaphor comprehension. In *Proceedings of the Fourteenth Annual Conference of the Cognitive Science Society* (pp. 504–509). Hillsdale, NJ: Lawrence Erlbaum Associates.

7

A Computational Theory of Children's Learning About Number Conservation

Tony J. Simon
Georgia Institute of Technology

David Klahr
Carnegie Mellon University

Among the child's most important conceptual acquisitions are the information processes that underlie quantification: the knowledge and skills related to the encoding and manipulation of quantitative information. Like the acquisition of another major conceptual system, language, the earliest developments occur long before children enter a classroom, whereas most of the formal aspects of numbers are learned in school. In this chapter, we suggest that the earliest bases for understanding numbers are founded upon innate or early developing perceptual capabilities of the young child. More specifically, we focus on the development of children's understanding of number conservation and the construction of the knowledge required by that transition.

Since Piaget, conservation has been thought to be the first major conceptual advance in children's numerical development. It is not the kind of knowledge that results from what young children learn in school, and yet it appears to be a foundation that must be securely in place before many other concepts of number and arithmetic can be acquired. Although conservation of number is one of the most heavily researched phenomena in cognitive development, a satisfactory theoretical account of its acquisition remains to be formulated. The first computational models of different *states* of conservation knowledge were proposed nearly 20 years ago (Klahr & Wallace, 1976). More recently, Klahr, (1984) sketched a flowchart type model of the *transition processes* but he did not implement it as a computational model. In this chapter, we extend those earlier ideas and integrate them with Soar (Newell, 1990) — a unified theory of cognition — to present a *computation model of conservation acquisition*. The model was first proposed by Simon, Newell and Klahr (1991), and we elaborate that account in this chapter.

Our computational model demonstrates that conservation learning derives from the ability to make accurate measurements and to use them to evaluate the numerical effects of transformations on collections of objects. Our account is the logical inverse of the one presented by Piaget. The difference between our position and the Piagetian one concerns the developmental roles of two central conceptual attainments in the development of quantification abilities. These are *conservation knowledge* (understanding the behavior of quantities under transformation) and *measurement skills* (creating quantitative values for bodies of material).

The Piagetian view (Piaget, Inhelder and Szeminska, 1960) is that conservation is a logical prerequisite to the ability to measure. Piaget reasoned that, without an understanding of the essential nature of quantity, measurements in terms of those quantities would mean nothing and would be of no practical use. The opposing view is that measurement is the necessary precursor of conservation (Klahr & Wallace, 1976; Miller, 1984). Measurement is the empirical tool used to gather information about whether or not some dimension of a transformed entity has remained quantitatively invariant. Miller stated that "practical measurement procedures appear not to be late-developing concomitants of a more general understanding of quantity. Instead, the measurement procedures of children embody their most sophisticated understanding of the domain in question. The limitations of these procedures constitute significant limits on children's understanding of quantity" (p. 221).

Such measurement is not always possible. The limitations Miller spoke of determine what children can learn about quantity. They are responsible for the pattern in the development of conservation. Number, or discrete quantity, conservation is acquired first. Also, preconservers can reason successfully about transformations of small discrete quantities but not about large ones (Cowan, 1979; Fuson, Secada, & Hall 1983; Siegler, 1981). Conservation of continuous quantities such as length, area, and volume is acquired a year or two later (Siegler, 1981).

One type of limitation is on *processes*, that is, to what kinds of things measurement procedures can be applied. As Piaget et al. (1960) stated, "to measure is to take out of a whole, one . . . unit, and to transpose this unit on the remainder of the whole." Thus, any material to be measured must afford the measurer some unit that can be used in that process. This characteristic is not present in continuous quantities. Beakers of water or pieces of string do not exhibit any evident subunits. Only the employment of special tools such as rulers or measuring cylinders (and the knowledge of how to use them) can create subunits that can be used for quantification. On the other hand, discrete quantities are defined by collections of individual subunits of the quantity as a whole. No special tools are needed because quantification abilities are present to some extent in even the youngest children. Young children appear to be particularly sensitive to the fact that unitary objects, and not subparts of those objects, have a special status. In learning language, they choose that level for the assignment of novel word labels (Markman, 1990), and in quantification of collections, they choose that level for the assignment of units (Shipley & Shepperson, 1990) Thus, discrete quantities are clearly easier to identify, and thus, to measure.

A second type of limitation is in the abilities of children who attempt to use measurement procedures. The children that need to carry out measurements to determine quantitative invariance are those below the age of 5. However, their quantification skills are not well developed. They are efficient at *subitizing*: a fast, accurate perceptual quantification mechanism (Chi & Klahr, 1975; Svenson & Sjoberg, 1983). Subitizing, however, has a limit of about four objects (Atkinson, Campbell & Francis, 1976; Simon, Cabrera, & Kliegl, 1993). Young children's counting is only reliable for collections of about the same size (Fuson, 1988).

Therefore, the measurement-before-conservation view predicts the learning events that enable the acquisition of quantitative invariance knowledge. It follows that, if measurement is needed to be able to reason about quantity, learning can occur only when the effects of transformations of small collections of objects are evaluated. These quantities have to be discrete because young children are not capable of creating consistent subunits from continuous quantities. Gelman (1977) showed that 1-year-olds can reason about some transformations when the number of objects involved is very small. The discrete quantity requirement was supported by Piaget et al.'s (1960) and Miller's (1984) findings that, given the task of dividing up an object such as a cookie into equal parts, young children created many arbitrarily sized subunits. These are unsuitable for quantification because counting them fails to produce accurate absolute measures for single entities, or to produce relative measures of multiple entities.

Miller (1989) further demonstrated the interaction between the use of measurement procedures and the acquisition of quantitative knowledge. He tested 3- to 10-year-olds on a modified equivalence-conservation task, where the effect of transforming one of a pair of quantities must be established. A variety of transformations were applied to different materials to test number, length, and area conservation. Miller demonstrated that the effects of transformations are easy to determine when measurement procedures provide good cues to the actual quantity, and vice versa. For example, spreading out a row of objects has no effect if number is the conservation dimension in question, but it does affect length conservation. Therefore, the appropriate measurement tool for this transformation would be enumeration in a number task. However, it would produce no information useful for evaluating length conservation. Thus, Miller predicted that performance would be best where transformations were relevant to the domain: The effects of spreading a row of objects would be easily evaluated in the number task, but the effects of changing their size would not. The results were as predicted, showing that the acquisition of quantitative knowledge depends on the selection and application of appropriate measurement procedures.

Our theory follows that of Klahr (1984) in stating that it is measurement of collections of discrete objects that provides information upon which knowledge about quantitative invariance is built. Conservation knowledge is acquired in situations where invariance can be empirically verified. In other words, learning events occur when the materials allow children to use their measurement capabilities to obtain a numerical measurement for a collection of objects before and after it has been transformed. The two measurements can then be compared and the result attributed to the transformation as its effect. If the results are identical, the quantity is unchanged and the transformation is deemed to have a nonquantitative effect for the dimension in question — it *conserves number*. If some difference is detected, the transformation is found to be nonconserving. Such differences can be simply detected by means of discriminations based on subitizing. With sufficient domain knowledge, the direction and magnitude of the change can also be determined. Thus, we conclude that the initial learning experiences for invariance knowledge are based on measurements of small collections of discrete objects within the subitizing range. Such a view is consistent with Starkey's (1992) conclusion that simple numerical abstraction competence supports numerical reasoning before the emergence of the mature counting skill.

In the following sections of this chapter, we present the various components of our theory of conservation learning and the accompanying computational model. We begin in by examining the phenomenon of conservation in order to establish the learning task that our model will account for. Then, we discuss the particular training study that we used as the vehicle for our demonstration of conservation learning, and present our theory of number conservation learning in more detail. Next, we briefly overview Soar, the computational medium within which our model is constructed, and then present a detailed account of Q-Soar, our computational model of number conservation learning. Finally, we extend the account of conservation beyond the behaviors directly modeled by Q-Soar and draw conclusions.

THE PHENOMENON OF CONSERVATION

A central tenet of Piagetian theory (Piaget, 1952, 1970) is that the acquisition of conservation knowledge is a crucial step in the child's development of mature conceptual capabilities. Piaget (1968, p.978) defined conservation as follows:

> We call "conservation" (and this is generally accepted) the invariance of a characteristic despite transformations of the object or of a collection of objects possessing this characteristic. Concerning number, a collection of objects "conserves" its number when the shape or disposition of the collection is modified, or when it is partitioned into subsets.

As we stated, children's knowledge about the effects of transformations must be empirically derived in the first instance because all transformations have different effects on different physical dimensions of the transformed material. For example, whether or not the pouring transformation conserves quantity depends on what is poured and what is measured:

> If we pour a little sugar into red sugar water, we do not change temperature, amount, height, width, or redness, but we increase sweetness. If we add more of an identical concentration, we do not change temperature, redness or sweetness; however the amount increases, as does liquid height, but not width (in a rigid container). On the other hand, if we add water, we increase two extensive quantities (amount, liquid height), reduce two intensive quantities (redness, sweetness), and leave one unchanged (temperature). (Klahr, 1982, pp. 68–69)

Therefore, a central component of what must be learned, either in training studies or by being naturally acquired by the child outside the laboratory, are the linkages between transformational attributes and their dimensional effects as measured in a variety of contexts.

The centrality of conservation concepts to most theories of cognitive development produced a vast database of empirical results. Nevertheless, a computational model that can account for the regularities has yet to be fully specified. There are structural and processing accounts of the knowledge used by a child who "has" conservation, as well as global characterizations of the acquisition of that knowledge, such as Piaget's assimilation and accommodation processes, Klahr and Wallace's (1976) time-line processing, and Halford's (1982) levels of cognitive systems. However, neither these nor any other accounts completely stated a set of operations and their interaction with a specified learning mechanism and shown this to produce the pattern of behavior observed in children acquiring conservation knowledge.

Q-Soar is a model of the acquisition of conservation knowledge designed to meet several criteria for computational models of developmental phenomena:

1. Such models should be based on a principled cognitive architecture, rather than a set of arbitrary and ad hoc mechanisms. For Q-Soar, the architecture is Soar, to be described in a later section.

2. Computational models should be constrained by the general regularities in the relevant empirical literature. There are a number of such regularities, that is, findings that are consistently reported and for which there is little or no disconfirming evidence. The critical regularities for the construction of Q-Soar are later discussed in detail.

3. Computational models should generate the same behavior as do the children in the specific domain being modeled. More specifically, they should compute an approximation of subjects' final knowledge states, given an approximation of initial states and external inputs like those imposed by experimental and/or natural conditions.

Although more than 20 years have passed since Klahr and Wallace (1970) proposed an information processing approach to cognitive development, there are no computational models of any major developmental transitions that satisfy all of these criteria. The Klahr and Wallace work on the development of quantitative concepts (Klahr, 1973, 1984; Klahr & Wallace, 1973, 1976) consisted of verbal descriptions, flow charts, and production-system models of distinct performance levels in the general domain of quantitative reasoning, including subitizing, counting, estimation, class inclusion, transitive reasoning, and quantity conservation. However, with respect to transition processes, their most fully developed model (Wallace, Klahr, & Bluff, 1987) went only as far as a partially specified architecture for supporting developmental transitions.

More recent computational accounts of developmental phenomena have been of two kinds:

1. One type of account is highly constrained by data from empirical studies of children's acquisition of knowledge in a domain, but the computational model itself is not constrained by any theoretical principles. Instead, it is based on pragmatic decisions about how to implement a set of assumed mechanisms (e.g., Siegler, 1991).

2. The other type of account is based on a broad set of theoretical assumptions that are consistent with a range of specific implementations. Examples include the adaptive production system used by Halford et al. (chap 3., this volume) to model the acquisition of transitive inference, the connectionist model used by McClelland (1989) to model the acquisition of balance scale rules and the concept-formation system used by Jones and

VanLehn (1994) to model the strategy changes in young children's arithmetic. Computational models of this type, although they suggest interesting learning mechanisms, tend to be relatively unconstrained by either any particular empirical results on children's knowledge acquisition or by illustrations that their central constructs are critical in accounting for other aspects of human cognition.

The purpose of our approach is to formulate a model that is tightly constrained by both a general theory of the cognitive architecture and a specific set of empirical results. Q-Soar's challenge is to demonstrate that it can model the learning reported in Gelman's (1982) training study, to be described next. The further issue of explaining general developmental regularities is addressed in the final section of the chapter.

A TRAINING STUDY

Simon and Halford (chap. 1, this volume) discuss simulating the activities of children engaged in a training study as one way to ensure that the model and the child engage in very similar activities while acquiring the knowledge involved in a transition of interest. In constructing our simulation of training studies, we were faced with the choice of modeling either our own arbitrary view of the essential properties of a typical training situation, or one specific training situation chosen from the vast conservation training literature. The problem with the former choice is that there is no typical training study. Detailed examination of the literature on conservation training studies reveals that they vary along so many potentially relevant dimensions that it is impossible to get agreement on even a prototypical training study, let alone a set of defining properties. For example, Field's (1987) review organized a collection of 25 recent conservation training studies with preschoolers along nine dimensions and three theoretical orientations.[1] Without any principled basis on which to construct a typical study, we chose to simulate a specific training study with well-defined procedures and clear quantitative outcomes.

Gelman's Training Procedure

As noted, we chose a training study reported by Gelman (1982) in which 3- and 4-year-olds were trained in a brief session using small collections of

---

[1] The procedural dimensions were design, pretest, training, materials, reinforcements, verbal rule instruction, posttest, justifications, and delayed posttest. The theoretical orientations were specific experience, cognitive readiness, and perceptual readiness. Space does not permit an elaboration of these *guiding models*, as Field (1987) called them, but training studies vary widely along both procedural and theoretical dimensions.

discrete objects (N = 3–4) in both equivalence (two rows of equal number) and inequivalence (two rows of unequal number) relations, and in which the transfer test included both small (N = 4–5) and large (N = 8–10) collections. Gelman trained one group and used two types of control groups. Children in the experimental group were trained with two types of collections in counterbalanced order. Half the children were first shown an equivalence relation (two rows of four items each), and the other half were first shown an inequivalence relation (one row of four and one row of three). In both equivalence and inequivalence collections, the items were initially placed in one-to-one correspondence.

For each type of collection, there were nine steps, as illustrated in Fig. 7.1:

1. The display was presented in one-to-one correspondence and the child was instructed to count the number of items in one of the rows.
2. That row was covered by the experimenter and the child was asked, "How many are under my hands?"
3. The child was instructed to count the number of items in the other row.
4. That row was covered by the experimenter and the child was asked, "How many are under my hands?"
5. The child was asked to judge whether the two uncovered rows contained "the same number or a different number" of items.
6. While the child watched, the length of one of the rows was spread or compressed.
7. The experimenter pointed to the altered (or unaltered) row and asked, "Are there still N here?"
8. The experimenter pointed to the other row and asked the same question.
9. The child was asked whether the pair of rows had the same number or a different number of items, and to explain his or her judgment.

All children answered the questions correctly (except for one 3-year-old who needed a slight extra prompt).

Gelman used two control groups. Children in the cardinal-once group were exposed to only one row (of three or four items). For that one row, they were exposed to Steps 1–2 and 6–7. (Each row was altered four times to provide a comparable number of counting trials between the experimental and control groups.) The other control group (no-cardinal) simply counted single rows of three or four items, but the children in that group were not asked to "indicate the cardinal value rendered by the count."

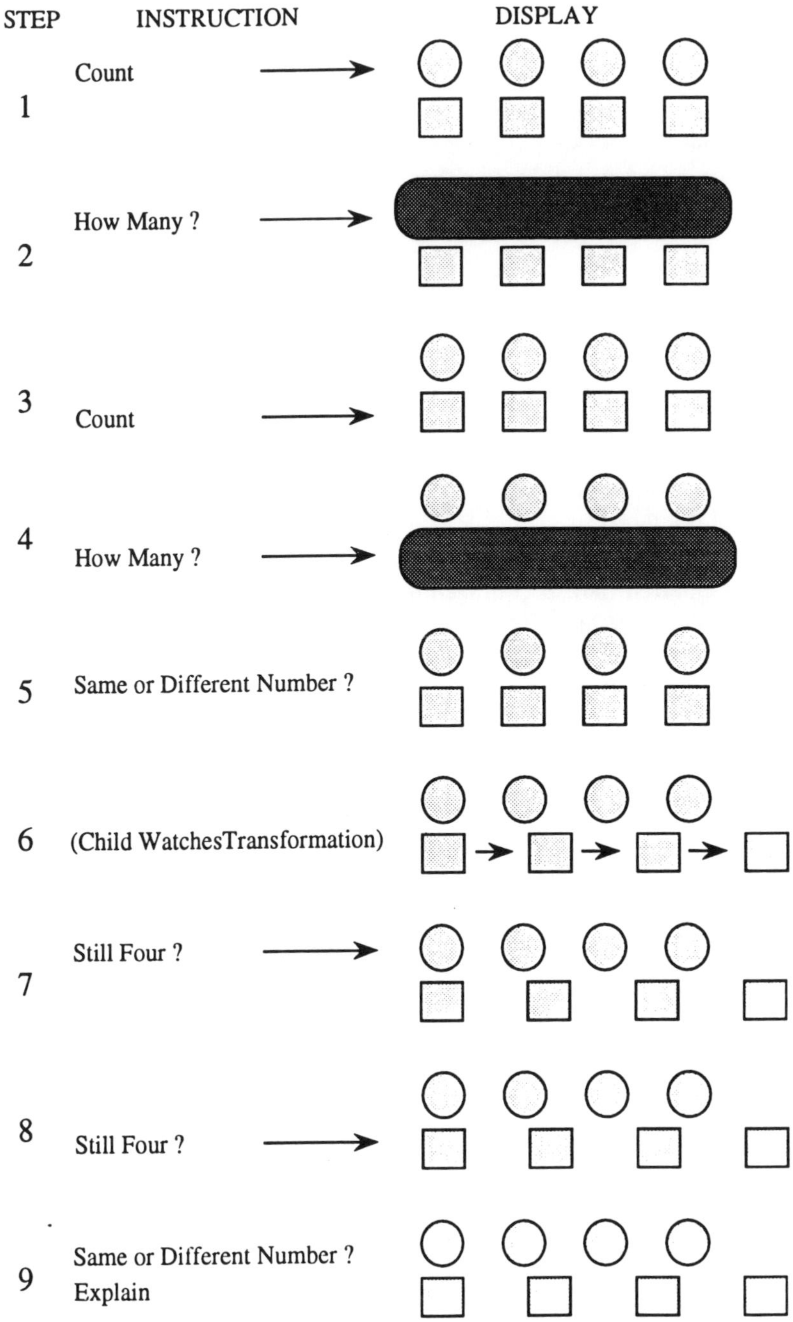

STEP	INSTRUCTION	DISPLAY
1	Count	
2	How Many ?	
3	Count	
4	How Many ?	
5	Same or Different Number ?	
6	(Child Watches Transformation)	
7	Still Four ?	
8	Still Four ?	
9	Same or Different Number ? Explain	

FIG. 7.1. Graphical representation of the experimental procedure.

323

Conservation Test

Immediately following the experimental or other procedures, conservation tests were administered. Each child was given four different conservation tasks (large or small set size, and equal or unequal numbers of items in the two rows). Small sets included either 4 and 5 or 5 and 5 items, and large sets included either 8 and 10 or 10 and 10 items:

> The order of presentation of large and small set sizes was counterbalanced as was the order of conservation of equality and inequality tasks within a set-size range. The equal arrays were equal in length prior to the transformation and unequal in length after being transformed. The reverse was true for the nonequivalent arrays: before being transformed they were unequal in length and then equal in length after the transformation. The conservation trials were run in the standard way older children are tested, and *included requests for explanations.* Likewise, children were discouraged from counting. (Gelman, 1982, p. 213)

Because children were discouraged from counting, and because one or both of the rows had at least five items, and because children of this age do not count beyond three or four items reliably (Fuson, 1988), it is likely that the *pre-transformation* equivalence (or nonequivalence) of both large and small arrays was established by one-to-one correspondence.

Results

For both the large and small sets, there was almost no difference in the equal and unequal set sizes, so those results are collapsed in the following discussion. Table 7.1 shows the overall proportion of correct judgments on conservation tasks. The effect of condition is striking: Overall, the exper-

TABLE 7.1

Proportion of Correct Conservation Judgments (Over all Four Judgments and all Subjects) In Each Condition, Derived From Table 1 in Gelman (1982)

Age & Set Size	Experimental (n = 21)	Cardinal-Once (n = 24)	No-Cardinal (n = 16)
3s on small set size	71	11	13
4s on small set size	75	58	16
3s on large set size	72	8	0
4s on large set size	65	34	13
Overall 3s	71	9	6
Overall 4s	70	46	15

imental groups passed about 70% of the conservation trials, compared to passing rates from 0% to 15% for the "untrained" (no-cardinal) groups. Trained threes and fours did equally well on large and small sets.

The interesting difference between the threes and fours occurred in the cardinal-once groups. For threes, cardinal-once training had no effect, but for fours it had a substantial effect when tested on both small and large set sizes. This is important, because the children in the cardinal-once group were trained only in identity conservation (transforming a single row), rather than equivalence conservation (transforming one of a pair of rows).[2] That is, they were never trained to notice that the relation between two different collections remained the same under a perceptual transformation, nor could they use one-to-one correspondence to reason about the effects of the transformations to which they were exposed. Instead, they could only learn that the initial and final cardinal value of a collection remained unchanged under certain kinds of transformations (i.e., spreading and compressing). Apparently, many 4-year-olds, though few 3-year-olds, were able to learn about transformations without the further help of one-to-one correspondence.

Gelman's categorization of children's explanations for their correct responses are presented in Table 7.2 in terms of (our interpretation of) whether the explanation makes reference to the transformation or to one-to-one correspondence. Gelman gave examples of two categories: *irrelevant transformation* (*They just moved*) and *addition/subtraction* (*You need another one to make them the same*) explanations. Initial equality or inequality of number explanations presumably stated that the original value still held, whereas the content of one-to-one correspondence explanations is obvious. The majority of the children's explanations referred to the transformation and, as can be seen in Table 7.2, there were more of these transformationally referenced explanations than there were explanations in terms of one-to-one correspondence. More specifically, for the experimental threes, experimental fours, and cardinal-once fours, the proportion of transformationally referenced explanations was 61%, 81%, and 65%, respectively, whereas for the same groups, one-to-one correspondence was used for only 21%, 9%, and 15% of the explanations.

Three-year-olds did not benefit from cardinal-once training, and 4-year-olds in the experimental group benefited more than did their agemates in the cardinal-once group. Rather than attribute these differences to the role of one-to-one correspondence, we note that subjects in the experimental group, but not in the cardinal-once group, received repeated exposure to

---

[2]See Klahr (1984) for a full discussion of the difference between identity conservation (IC) and equivalence conservation (EC). Note that Klahr's account of the acquisition of conservation rules is presented entirely in terms of the simple IC situation.

TABLE 7.2
Reference to Transformation or One-To-One Correspondence of Gelman's
Explanation Categories

	Transformation	One-to-One
Irrelevant transformation	X	
Addition/subtraction	X	
Initial equality/inequality	X	
One-to-one correspondence		X

observations of the following transitive relation. When, for example, two rows of objects have the same number, and after spreading the transformed row has the same number as before, then the untouched row and the transformed row still have the same number of objects.

It is not difficult for the child to compute the effect of the transformation. First, each set was counted before and after the transformation for the experimental trials, rendering one-to-one matching redundant. Second, in experimental trials, the pre- and posttransformation information is visible in the form of a transformed and an untransformed row after the transformation has taken place. However, in the cardinal-once trials, memory of the pretransformation information is always required to compute the transformation's effect. All of the 3-year-olds and some of the 4-year-olds apparently needed this additional information (and reduction of processing) that was provided to the experimental group.

A THEORY OF NUMBER CONSERVATION KNOWLEDGE

We summarize our view of the important difference between the experimental group and the cardinal-once group as follows. Subjects in the experimental group were exposed to equivalence (or inequivalence) conservation trials in which they observed and encoded an initial quantitative relation between two collections, and then observed a quantity-preserving transformation on one of the collections. They then requantified both collections and noted that the relation had not changed. In contrast, subjects in the cardinal-once group, because they were dealing with only one collection rather than two, were in an identity conservation situation. That is, they had to judge, after observing a spreading or compressing transformation, whether or not the quantity following the transformation was the same as the quantity preceding it; they could not simply requantify and compare the two rows.

In both situations, acquired knowledge stemmed primarily from the discovery that certain types of transformations have no effect on the numerosity of an object set, even though the transformations may affect other properties, like the spatial density or length of the set. This conclusion is independent of the number of objects in the set that was measured when the new knowledge was created. In other words, what was learned was a characterization of the quantity-preserving aspects of the transformation in question.

Q-Soar was built to model this piece of knowledge acquisition. In order to do this, the system must be able to specify:

1. The knowledge state prior to the training (i.e., a nonconserving child).
2. The encoding of the collection(s) prior to transformation. This includes salient features such as number, length, and density, as well as other features that may be irrelevant for the task at hand.
3. The encoding of the relation between collections (for the experimental group).
4. The encoding of the collection(s) following transformation.
5. The encoding of the physical aspects of the transformation (e.g., salient motion, how objects were moved, how many were moved, direction of movement).
6. New knowledge acquired from repeated trials of the kind presented to both groups.

The model will have two variants, and each will be exposed to the three kinds of stimulus presentations (corresponding to the experimental, cardinal-once, and no-cardinal groups): Q-Soar-4 will model the 4-year-olds, who learn from both the experimental manipulations and the cardinal-once manipulations. Q-Soar-3 will model the 3-year-olds, who learn only from the experimental condition.

This set of general hypotheses about the essential mechanisms involved in the child's acquisition of number conservation can be called *Q Theory*, to distinguish it from Q-Soar, which conjoins Q Theory with the assumptions of a particular cognitive architecture (Soar) to form a more complete operational theory. A full theory of conservation will ultimately contain assumptions about the nature of the environments in which development takes place (see Simon & Halford, chap. 1, this volume). Indeed, it is the lack of justifiable assumptions that can be made about naturally occurring conservation experiences that forces us to focus entirely on training studies.

THE SOAR ARCHITECTURE

This section describes the relevant aspects of the Soar architecture. More detailed accounts exist elsewhere (Laird, Newell, & Rosenbloom, 1987;

Laird, Swedlow, Altmann, & Congdon, 1989; Newell, 1990). Besides being an operational architecture, Soar is also a theory of cognition that explains a variety of psychological phenomena. We make no attempt to describe that wider background here (cf. Lewis et al., 1990; Newell, 1990).

All tasks are formulated in Soar as search in problem spaces, where operators are applied to states in an attempt to attain a goal state. Problem spaces can be thought of as packages of knowledge about different tasks. The operators within a given space (and knowledge about constraints on legal states) define the problem solver's competence for a task. For example, a complete problem space for the Missionaries and Cannibals puzzle contains the necessary operators to carry out moves, knowledge about the goal state, and knowledge about legal and illegal moves. Problem solving proceeds sequentially by decisions that select problem spaces, states, and operators. This processing gathers knowledge from a long-term recognition memory that is implemented as a production system. This memory matches structures in working memory and retrieves knowledge that elaborates the existing state and suggests preferences for the next step to take.

If Soar cannot make a decision, an impasse occurs and Soar automatically generates a subgoal in which a new problem space can be used to find the required knowledge. A major reason that Soar exhibits the impasse and subgoal pattern is that not all of the knowledge required to carry out a task can be searched for within a single problem space. For example, should the goal arise in the Missionaries and Cannibals context to explain why the boat does not sink, there will be no knowledge in the problem space to implement that process. In response, an impasse will arise and in the resulting subgoal, Soar will select a problem space for solving such an explanatory problem, because this is a different task requiring different knowledge. Once that knowledge is found, subgoals are resolved and processing continues where it left off (Newell, 1990).

Soar has a single learning mechanism, called *chunking*, that learns new productions, or chunks, for resolved impasses. When similar situations are encountered, the knowledge generated by the previous subgoal processing is automatically retrieved so that the impasse is not recreated. The chunk will apply in a wider set of circumstances than the exact conditions under which it was created. This is because the chunking mechanism carries out an analysis that is a form of explanation-based learning (DeJong & Mooney, 1986; Mitchell, Keller, & Kedar-Cabelli, 1986; Mooney, 1991; Rosenbloom & Laird, 1986) to determine the critical features of the situation that led to the creation of the new knowledge. In future situations, these act as cues to make the new knowledge available. The behavioral implication of chunking is that Soar exhibits a shift from deliberate to automatic processing as the situations it encounters become increasingly familiar. In other words, knowledge becomes compiled from search-based retrieval to recognition-based retrieval (Anderson, 1987; Rosenbloom & Newell, 1986).

Q-SOAR'S ACQUISITION OF NUMBER CONSERVATION KNOWLEDGE

The knowledge and processes that enable Q-Soar to acquire number conservation knowledge are implemented as a set of problem spaces that are depicted in Fig. 7.2. The figure shows the problem spaces that are selected to carry out processing in response to given deficiencies in available knowledge; these deficiencies are stated as labels on the downward-pointing sides of the arrows. Once sufficient knowledge is returned (as depicted by the upward-pointing side of the arrows), the original processing can continue. The new knowledge becomes immediately accessible on later occasions in the form of chunks. The top panel depicts the knowledge required to interpret task instructions and to establish initial values before a transformation is applied. The lower panel depicts the knowledge involved in determining the quantitative effects of transformations.

The figure also distinguishes between task-motivated problem spaces (unshaded) and theory-motivated problem spaces (shaded). The unshaded spaces contain those operations that any task analysis of the training studies would deem to be necessary for its successful completion. These processes include the ability to understand instructions, create responses, and determine relative or absolute values for the objects used in training and testing. The shaded problem spaces contain operations that we, as theorists, assert are necessary to enable the cognitive architecture, Soar, to achieve the behavior and learning that constitute the attainment of number conservation as shown by children in the 3- to 4-year-old age range.

Q-Soar's design presumes that young children acquire number conservation knowledge by measurement and comparison of values to determine the effects of transformations on small collections of discrete objects. Having been shown a transformation to a set of objects, the child first categorizes the transformation and then initiates a conservation judgment about the transformation's effect. Ideally, categorization will identify the observed transformation as an instance of a larger class, with effects that are known to be associated (through chunking) with this class. If not, then pre- and posttransformation values created by measurement processes are compared to determine the effect of the transformation. The learning over this processing creates new knowledge about this kind of transformation, thatwill become available on future occurrences in similar contexts.[3] Now the transformation's effects can be stated without the need for any empirical processing. In other words, the necessity of the effects is recognized.

---

[3] The notion of similarity involved is the occurrence in the new situation of the same essential features used in the prior situation. There is no similarity metric involved.

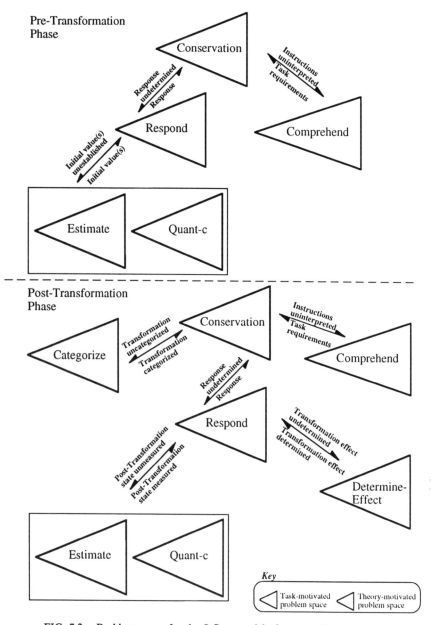

Pre-Transformation
Phase

Conservation

Instructions
uninterpreted
Task
requirements

Response
undetermined
Response

Respond

Comprehend

Initial value(s)
unestablished
Initial value(s)

Estimate   Quant-c

Post-Transformation
Phase

Categorize

Transformation
uncategorized
Transformation
categorized

Conservation

Instructions
uninterpreted
Task
requirements

Comprehend

Response
undetermined
Response

Respond

Transformation effect
undetermined
Transformation effect
determined

Post-Transformation
state unmeasured
Post-Transformation
state measured

Determine-
Effect

Estimate   Quant-c

Key

◁ Task-motivated
problem space   ◁ Theory-motivated
problem space

FIG. 7.2.   Problem spaces for the Q-Soar model of conservation behavior.

Regularities and Theoretical Assumptions

The behavior exhibited by Q-Soar is constrained by a set of regularities in the literature on early numerical abstraction and reasoning. The processes that Q-Soar employs to generate that behavior are determined, in part, by five assumptions we make about the knowledge and strategies used by 3- and 4-year-old children in the context of conservation experiments. These regularities and theoretical assumptions are discussed in detail and are integrated in Table 7.3. The top half of the table relates the regularities (R1 to 6) to 3- and 4-year-olds' abilities and tendencies to quantify, and to their abilities to correctly answer conservation questions about sets of different sizes. The lower half of the table maps the competencies provided for our Q-Soar models of 3- and 4-year-olds onto those abilities and it shows the role played by the theoretical assumptions we made.

Six critical regularities define the requirements for the behavior of Q-Soar:

R1. Young children in the 3- to 4-year age range can consistently obtain accurate specific quantitative values for small sets of objects (up to three or four; cf. Fuson, 1988; Starkey, 1992).

R2. Young children can execute a counting procedure for larger numbers when requested and can accurately monitor the counts of others. However, children below the age of 4 do not spontaneously use counting as an effective method for solving a range of quantitative problems, including comparing the relative numerosity of two sets of objects (Briars & Siegler, 1984; Fuson, 1988; Sophian, 1987; Starkey, 1992; Wynn, 1990).

TABLE 7.3
Regularities and Assumptions Underlying the Construction of Q-Soar

Age	Accurate Quantification?		Count to Quantify or Compare Set Sizes?		Solve Conservation of Discontinuous Quantity?	
	$n < 4$	$4 < n \leq 10$	Spontaneously	On Demand	$n < 4$	$4 < n \leq 10$
3	yes *R1 R3*	no *R2*	no *R2*	yes *R2*	yes *R4 R6*	no *R5*
4	yes *R1 R3*	no *R2*	yes *R2*	yes *R2*	yes *R4 R6*	no *R5*

			Verify Outcome Quantitatively?			
			Spontaneously	Via Conflict		
Q-Soar–3	yes	no	no *A4*	yes *A4*	yes *A1–A5*	no
Q-Soar–4	yes	no	yes *A3*	yes *A3 A4*	yes *A1–A5*	no

R3. children from an early age are able to accurately and rapidly enumerate three or four items by the process of subitizing (Chi & Klahr, 1975; Svenson & Sjoberg, 1983; van Loosbroek & Smitsman, 1990).

R4. Children who have not fully acquired conservation knowledge can still correctly answer conservation questions when they can obtain a specific quantitative value for the objects concerned (cf. Siegler, 1981).

R5. Children who have not fully acquired conservation knowledge do not correctly answer the conservation question when they cannot obtain a specific quantitative value for objects concerned (cf. Halford & Boyle, 1985).

R6. Young children can respond correctly and provide explanations for tests of conservation of quantity when discrete materials are used (such as counters or cookies) before they can do this on tests involving materials with continuous properties, such as columns of water or areas of space (cf. Gelman & Baillargeon, 1983).

There are five assumptions underlying the construction of Q-Soar. The first two concern the typical expectations held by young children about the behavior of sets of objects under transformation in the context of conservation experiments. The remaining three are our modeling assumptions about how these first two are implemented in Q-Soar in terms of knowledge and processes:

A1. Young children assume that the numerical value of a row of objects will not change if the row is not transformed. Gelman (1977) showed in her "magic studies" that children as young as 2 years of age operate with the assumption that the numerical value of a set of objects will remain constant in the absence of any observable manipulation of the set.

A2. Young children assume that the numerical value of a row of objects is likely to change if the row is visibly transformed by an experimenter. Many experiments, notably those of Donaldson (1978), showed that the act of an experimenter making explicit physical changes to a set of objects suggests to young children that some significant change will result from the action.

A3. Four-year-olds know that they can use measurement to verify whether Assumption 2 is true or false. By measuring the numerical value of the objects before and after the transformation, a determination can be made as to whether or not the action changed the number of the objects. Sophian (1987) showed that by this age, children are beginning to spontaneously use counting to solve quantitative problems. However, all 4-year-olds can verify outcomes using subitizing where set sizes are small enough.

A4. Three-year-olds do not typically attempt to verify the effects of a transformation, but they may be motivated to create a measurement if faced with two conflicting sources of evidence. If one source of information suggests that the value of the objects has changed whereas another suggests that it has not, 3-year-olds will attempt to determine the true effect of the transformation where measurement is possible. Sophian (1987) showed little spontaneous use of counting in relevant tasks for children of this age.

A5. Three- and 4-year-olds have the capacity to store and recall pre- and posttransformation values, but only 4-year-olds systematically do so. Four-year-olds have the knowledge that it is important to do this in order to determine the effect of a transformation. There is a sizable literature on young children's strategic use of their mnemonic capacity that indicates that, even if 3-year-olds have the same capacity for remembering as older children and adults, they have little knowledge about how to exploit that capacity and thus, their untutored memory performance is poor (Brown, Bransford, Ferrara, & Campione, 1983).

Q-Soar's behavior in simulating the training study is described in sections that correspond to the problem spaces involved. References are made to the example procedure in Fig. 7.1, so that the reader can keep track of both the current subproblem that Q-Soar is attempting to solve and the arrangement of the objects concerned. The description is presented using the experimental procedure because it is a superset of the other two control conditions. The actual behavior that Q-Soar produces during this procedure, and its subsequent behavior on one of the test conditions, is presented in the Appendix. (Recall that the cardinal-once group only experienced Steps 1–2 and 6–7 and the no-cardinal group experienced only Step 1.)

Conservation Task Operations

To carry out a conservation task, five basic processes are required. These correspond to Soar operators in the CONSERVATION problem space: COMPREHEND-INSTRUCTION, CATEGORIZE-TRANSFORM-ATION, DETERMINE-RESPONSE, RETURN-RESPONSE, and WAIT.

All operators process internal representations in working memory. These representations correspond to aspects of the external situation to which the model is attending. There is a focus of attention, determined partly by external sources, such as the experimenter asking questions or drawing attention to the experimental materials. It can also be determined by internal processing, such as attention to individual items during counting. The internal representations are in the form of *annotated models* (Lewis, Newell, & Polk, 1989) — descriptions of attended aspects of the external situation symbolically expressed as objects with parts, properties, and relations to other objects. These models are manipulated by operators and augmented with knowledge from memory and from the external situation via perception.

Each step in the experimental (and other) procedures is carried out in response to an instruction or request from the experimenter; we refer to these as *instructions*. When an instruction is perceived, its meaning must be represented as an annotated model. This model is constructed by a COMPREHEND-INSTRUCTION operator in the manner of an existing system, called NL-Soar, which is implemented in the COMPREHEND problem space; Lewis et al. (1989) described this process. COMPREHEND-INSTRUCTION operators produce a representation of a request called a *behavior-model object*. In Step 1 of Fig. 7.1, for example, the child is requested to count the row of circles. In this case, the COMPREHEND-INSTRUCTION operator would produce a behavior-model object representing the operation *measure*, the argument *circles*, and the dimension *number*. Thus, a behavior-model object is a child's representation to himself or herself of what behavior should be carried out to achieve the task. In general, the child is perfectly capable of behaving without such a plan, but in the case of an experiment, he or she must represent (and remember) the instruction to be carried out. These representations also play a role in mediating the speed of acquisition of conservation knowledge.

Once the instruction has been comprehended and represented, Q-Soar must still produce a response. To do so, it selects the DETERMINE-RESPONSE operator. Q-Soar implements Steps 1 and 2 (and then Steps 3 and 4) in Fig. 7.1 with a single DETERMINE-RESPONSE operator, that is augmented with the instructions represented on the behavior-model object. If the response is not immediately available, then there will be an impasse and other problem spaces will be selected to compute the response. When the system has created a response that satisfies the instructions (such as the value *four* for Steps 1 and 2), it selects the RETURN-RESPONSE operator to output the answer and then waits for the next instruction by selecting the WAIT operator.

Q-Soar's first response to observing a transformation (Step 6) is to categorize it. This is done before responding to posttransformation questions by selecting the CATEGORIZE-TRANSFORMATION operator. The categorization process is described in a later section.

Response Determination

If the DETERMINE-RESPONSE operator in the CONSERVATION space cannot immediately produce a response to the counting instructions of Steps 1 and 2, there will be an impasse. The RESPOND space will always be selected when the DETERMINE-RESPONSE operator impasses, because it contains the three operators that are required to create responses in the conservation task: MEASURE, COMPARE, and RECALL. In the case where Steps 1 and 2 have been comprehended as requiring a measurement, the MEASUREMENT operator is selected. Depending on the number of objects and their representation, either the QUANT-C or ESTIMATE space is selected to carry out this measurement. That measurement is returned as the result of the MEASURE operator and, in turn, it is also returned as the result of the top-level DETERMINE-RESPONSE operator.

Once Q-Soar has created and returned a measurement for the circles and squares, it perceives and comprehends the question "same or different number?" in Step 5. The resulting DETERMINE-RESPONSE operator will be augmented with the instruction *compare*, the arguments *circles* and *squares*, and the dimension *number*. Because this is the first time the instruction has been encountered, there will be no immediately available response and, in the resulting subgoal, the COMPARE operator will be selected in the RESPOND space. This operator tests whether or not the values for the measurements of the two rows match, because only a *same* or *different* response is required. In the current example, that processing will be carried out in the QUANT-C space if a value for that comparison is not immediately available.

Once the comparison has been created and returned, and the transformation has been observed and categorized (Step 6 and lower panel of Fig. 7.2), the experimenter asks, "Are there still N objects?" for each row (where N is the number of objects in the row). These instructions are treated in a similar way to Steps 2 and 4, by selecting a DETERMINE-RESPONSE operator. However, the operator is now augmented with the operation *recall*. If no answer to the question is immediately available, that operator will impasse and the RECALL operator will be selected in the RESPOND space. The implementation of this operator differs when it is applied to rows that have been transformed. The alternatives depend on the model variant (Q-Soar–3 or Q-Soar–4) and training condition (experimental or cardinal-once), as discussed in the next section. Responses to the "Are there still N?" question with respect to an untransformed row (e.g., Step 7 in Fig. 7.1) are dealt with in the following way. Recall that Assumption 1 stated that the numerical value of a row of objects will not change if the row is not transformed. The value for the row in question is assumed to be the same before and after the transformation of the other row. Q-Soar–4 is able to recall the pretransformation value and return it as the answer to this question. This is not the case for Q-Soar–3 (see Assumption A5). However, even without retrieving the correct value with the RECALL operator, Q-Soar–3 can correctly answer the question by requantifying the objects. This can be done by because because no row has more than four objects.

Effect Determination

The way that Q-Soar responds to the "Are there still *N*?" question for transformed rows is not only to produce a posttransformation value, but to determine the effect of the transformation. The DETERMINE-EFFECT problem space is selected if the RECALL operator impasses, because no effect of the transformation is immediately available. In order to learn about the effect of the transformation, the system must compare the pre- and posttransformation values for the row. Also, some role must be attributed to the transformation for the value of that comparative judgment. This can be as simple as identifying it as the action that created the posttransformation array. In other words, this process creates the knowledge to answer the implicit question, "What change did the transformation make to the number of objects?" This new knowledge states that, whenever such a transformation is applied, the relation between the pre- and posttransformation values that have just been computed will hold for the dimension in question. For example, the response to Step 9 in Fig. 7.1 is that a spreading transformation causes no change because it produces an identical value to the one that existed before it was applied, namely *four squares* in both cases.

Effect Determination in Q-Soar-4. Q-Soar-4 determines the effect of transformations in the same way for both the experimental and cardinal-once conditions. Although Assumption A2 stated that children believe that the value of a row will change when it is transformed, Assumption A3 stated that 4-year-olds have the knowledge that this can be verified when it is possible to measure the materials before and after a transformation is applied. This is the case in both of these conditions because of the small number of discrete objects. Thus, in all cases, Q-Soar-4 makes a pre- and posttransformation value comparison to determine the effects of observed transformations.

Effect Dertermination in Q-Soar-3. Q-Soar-3 behaves differently in the experimental and cardinal-once conditions. In the experimental condition its behavior is like that of Q-Soar-4, due to Assumption A4. This assumption stated that 3-year-olds do not readily engage in verifying a transformation's effect, but may be induced to do so if they are faced with two conflicting sources of evidence. This is always the case with the experimental condition. Before transformations, the two rows are in one-to-one correspondence so equal trials have equal-length rows and unequal trials have unequal-length rows. In other words, perceptual information and quantitative information are not in conflict. However, "transformations on unequal trials yielded rows of the same length; equal trials involved rows of different lengths" (Gelman, 1982, p. 212). After transformation, quantitative information, which was available via subitizing, and perceptual information were in conflict: Unequal rows were the same length and equal rows were different lengths. This conflict leads Q-Soar-3 to recall the pretransformation value it measured and check it against the posttransformation value of the row.

In the cardinal-once condition, no such conflict exists. There is a single row of objects that, when transformed, takes on a new visual appearance. There is nothing in the visual array to suggest that the assumed change in its numerical value should be doubted. Thus, Q-Soar-3 makes no attempt to compare pre- and posttransformation values of rows. As with the untransformed row, it answers the question "Are there still N?" by requantifying. Because no comparison is made to the original value, no learning can take place regarding whether or not the transformation has had any effect on the numerical value of the row.

Effect Determination Operations. There are two operators in the DETERMINE-EFFECT space. The RECALL operator recalls a pretransformation value for comparison to the posttransformation value. The DETERMINE-EFFECT operator matches pre- and posttransformation values for the transformed row as previously described. The process is a simple match that tests whether or not the values are the same. A requested determination of the magnitude or direction of the change will require accessing quantification knowledge. The result of this match is returned by the DETERMINE-EFFECT operator as the effect of the transformation, and the basis of its determination (e.g., that pre- and posttransformation values matched) constitutes an explanation. This will be the result of the RECALL operator in the RESPOND space and, ultimately, the DETERMINE-RESPONSE operator in the CONSERVATION space. The chunks that are built when this new knowledge is returned enable immediate retrieval of the effect of the current transformation. These chunks will fire in response to selection of the DETERMINE-RESPONSE operator, letting Q-Soar immediately return the effect and explanation of the transformation. This demonstrates the shift in conservation performance from empirical examination of materials to direct explanation of the transformation's effects.

Quantification and Estimation

In the preceding sections, we showed how the acquisition of number conservation knowledge in Q-Soar is founded on empirical processing, whose results are then used by the effect determination process. In this section, we examine the quantification and estimation abilities available to Q-Soar that implement the measurement and comparison processes.

Quantification.   The primary measurement capability that is possessed by young children is quantification. This quantification subsystem, which we call *Quant-C,* for "quantification in conservation," includes only capabilities that produce cardinal values for small sets of entities. Thus, it includes subitizing and counting of small sets.

In cases where values are to be determined in terms of number, the QUANT-C problem space may be selected to implement the measurement. Selection of the space depends on two factors. The first is whether the conservation property represented on the MEASURE operator suggests the use of QUANT-C processes (e.g., in the case of discrete objects, but not liquid). The second is the suitability of the representation for the application of operators in the QUANT-C problem space.

Even in cases where the conservation property suggests Quant-C processes for determining equivalence, the problem solver may still be unable to use it. In order to select the QUANT-C space, the representation of objects to be measured must be in the form of symbols representing discrete objects that are in one-*onto*-one mapping (hereafter *onto*) with their external referents. We assume such representations are only possible for set sizes within the range young children can subitize: a limit of four objects. Above this limit, a much looser one-*into*-one mapping (hereafter *into*) is used. The process of subitizing in the QUANT-C space is not controlled by an operator: it is simply that of creating an *onto* representation of up to four external referents. This approach is based on the view that there is a special code for the representation of discrete quantities that is primitive to the architecture and that differs from the formal code used to communicate about numbers with words such as *three* or symbols like *3*. We call this primitive representation the *basic quantitative code* (Newell, 1990) and assume that it provides the agent with an ability to represent quantity in a primitive form.

There are six operators in the QUANT-C space: ATTEND, INITIAL-IZE, FETCH-NEXT, COUNT-NEXT, COMPARE, and MEMORIZE. The ATTEND operator attends to the objects specified in the behavior-model object and sets up an *onto* representation. All of the other operators are involved only if counting and not subitizing is to be carried out. The INITIALIZE operator selects a mark for identifying objects to be counted, selects an initial word from the counting string to be used, and selects an initial object to be processed. The COUNT-NEXT operator assigns a selected count word to a marked object and, where cardinal responses (Fuson, 1988) are to be returned, assigns that label to the cardinality of the set. FETCH-NEXT obtains a next item to be counted, marks it, and obtains a next count word to be assigned. The COMPARE operator can be used to test either the relative similarity or difference of values created by MEASURE operators. The MEMORIZE operator carries out a deliberate act of memorization on the final response to a pretransformation and posttransformation instruction, so that the results are stored in long-term memory and are available for the processes that determine the effect of the transformation.

None of these operations can be directly applied to *into* representations. However, one can count large collections of objects if perceptual and motor operations can be carried out to serially map individual items onto their external referents, thereby creating transitory *onto* representations for up to four items at a time. If this cannot be done or if a decision is made against doing so, the only recourse is to use estimation operations.

Preceptual Estimation. Perceptual estimation in the children modeled by Q-Soar is unidimensional — the relative number of two numerous rows of objects is determined either by length or by density, but not both. Siegler (1981) showed that a child's ability to integrate more than one dimension to solve a range of problems does not develop until around 8 years of age. Thus, estimation in conservation settings is inaccurate, because one dimension is often inadequate for an accurate quantitative judgment.

The ESTIMATION problem space is selected to obtain values for materials under a number of conditions. Q-Soar may be requested to create a relative quantity judgment where there are too many objects to create an *onto* representation. In this case, the model uses perceptual estimation, in which the primary cue as to quantity is the length of the rows. A MATCH operator carries out a type of one-to-one matching called *end matching* (Klahr & Wallace, 1976), that tests whether the end items of each row are above or below the end items of the other row. If this is not the case, the longer row is assumed to be more numerous. A MEMORIZE operator stores the result of this processing, just as in the QUANT-C space.

Categorization

As mentioned earlier, Q-Soar categorizes observed transformations.[4] This means that it identifies critical features that are common to individual transformations, such as that all spreading actions move things further apart irrespective of the objects in question. Chunks created from processing in the DETERMINE-EFFECT problem space associate the new

---

[4] The current version of Q-Soar does not fully implement this process. Instead, the structures that would be created by an existing system called AL-Soar (Miller & Laird, 1990) are fed into working memory.

effect with the category of the transformation, not to the specific instance. As a result, invariance effects will be cued by any new transformation that can be identified as a member of that category. This enables novel situations to cue knowledge acquired about other members of the same category. Thus we assume that all novices, especially young children, form concepts to facilitate plausible generalizations about novel instances. Chunking models this desirable behavior, as do some other methods of explanation-based learning. As noted by Mooney (1991), categorization need not be limited to a single dimension, but it should be sensitive to current goals. For example, when confronted with studies of number conservation like Gelman's, Q-Soar may "CATEGORIZE" spreading, compressing, piling, and distributing together because they have no numeric effect. In contrast, if the concern is with spatial density, then compressing and piling would constitute a category with the opposite effect of spreading and distributing. The imposition of conceptual cohesiveness by goals or effects is related to *ad hoc* categorization introduced by Barsalou (1983).

Q-Soar selects the CATEGORIZE problem space when there is a transformation represented on the state and the CATEGORIZE-TRANSFORMATION operator in the CONSERVATION space cannot retrieve a type for it. The categorization process identifies in the representation of the transformation a set of features that are predictive of a certain classification. It is implemented as a recognition task. If a new instance is not immediately recognized as a member of a known class, features are progressively abstracted out of the instance description until the instance is recognized as a known class member. If no class is retrieved, then a new one is formed using the set of features in the new instance. For example, when all the features common to all spreading transformations are present, and none that are indicative of some other type of action (like compressing) are represented, the transformation will be treated the same way that other spreading transformations would be in the current context.

Learning Conservation Knowledge in Q-Soar

The preceeding subsections presented the problem spaces and operators that comprise Q-Soar. How then do these components combine to create the number conservation knowledge that is the result of the effective training procedures? The answer is that they are called upon to contribute knowledge as Q-Soar experiences impasses during problem solving. These impasses arise dynamically from the particular task that Q-Soar is working on and the knowledge it brings to bear on each task at a given time. Thus, the conservation knowledge that the system has depends on what problems it has tried to solve and what knowledge it had available when it tried to solve them.

For example, if the knowledge required to respond to the question about the relative quantity of the two rows of objects in the initial array is not available, an impasse will arise. Q-Soar will have already quantified the two values, but no comparative value will exist. The resulting series of impasses ground out in the selection of the COMPARE operator in the QUANT-C space. The successful creation of that comparative value resolves the impasse and creates a new piece of information that is available for later instances of the same problem. This kind of processing is repeated for every impasse that the system encounters. Some of these chunks simply reduce the amount of search that Q-Soar engages in on subsequent trials (such as chunks that implement the instruction comprehension operators). Other chunks, such as those that arise from COMPARE operators in the QUANT-C space, not only reduce search but also directly contribute to the ultimate conservation judgments the system makes.

The result of one such impasse is the chunk (hereafter the *conservation* chunk), marked in the Appendix, that produces the conservation response. Due to the explanation-based nature of chunking, some generalization will occur with respect to the applicability of the chunk. Specifically, only features that existed before the impasse arose can become conditions for chunks. This is to ensure that an impasse for the same problem will not recur. However, not all of the preexisting features will become conditions; only those that are used to compute the result in the subgoal will be selected. This means that the chunked result will be retrieved in a wider set of circumstances than the one in which it was formed. However, it does not mean that Q-Soar exhibits conserving responses after one trial. When simulating human cognition, Soar builds chunks only for the results created from the lowest goal in a subgoal stack. This *bottom-up* chunking causes the architecture to exhibit a gradual progression from deliberate (search-based) to automatic (recognition-based) behavior.

In the case of Q-Soar, the conservation chunk at first only implements the response to the DETERMINE-EFFECT operator because that was the operator that led to the final impasse from which the chunk was created. Only after a series of trials is there a single subgoal caused by the top-level DETERMINE-RESPONSE operator. Then the information in the original chunk becomes available to implement that operator and thus enable a recognitional response to the effect of an observed transformation, as in the case of a conserving child.

By acquiring conservation knowledge in this way, Q-Soar does not create any single knowledge structure that represents a *conservation concept*. Instead, it builds a series of chunks that, when appropriately cued, enable the system to exhibit number conservation. In other words, rather than learning concepts that define the features of conserving transformations, Q-Soar acquires generalized knowledge about the effects of observed transformations that is cued by other, similar transformations in similar contexts. As already described, these pieces of knowledge are acquired incrementally as problems are solved by the system with different amounts of available knowledge. In this particular modeling study, Q-Soar was led to acquire its conservation knowledge by the use of a training regime. However, this was not a supervised concept-learning situation in which preclassified examples of concepts are presented for the system to learn. Q-Soar is never presented with the concept of conservation; it is merely asked to solve a series of problems that were experimentally demonstrated to result in the acquisition of conservation knowledge. These kinds of problems can be encountered and solved without supervision and, as can be seen in the next section, we claim that Q-Soar should be capable of learning conservation knowledge without training but at a slower speed than demonstrated here.

TOWARD A FULL THEORY OF CONSERVATION

Q-Soar successfully models the acquisition of conservation knowledge attained by subjects in Gelman's training study in an implementation within Soar's unified cognitive theory. In this final section, we describe the behavior of Q-Soar before and after training. We also describe what we anticipate as the necessary steps toward a full theory of conservation in other domains.

One can evaluate an enterprise such as that presented here in terms of Piaget's (1964) well-known criteria for "real" conservation:

> But when I am faced with these facts [that *learning* of structures seems to obey the same laws as the *natural development* of these structures], I always have three questions which I want to have answered before I am convinced.
>
> The first question is, "Is this learning lasting? What remains two weeks or a month later?" If a structure develops spontaneously, once it has reached a state of equilibrium, it is lasting, it will continue throughout the child's entire life. When you achieve the learning by external reinforcement, is the result lasting or not and what are the conditions for it to be lasting?
>
> The second question is, "How much generalization is possible?" When you have brought about some learning, you can always ask whether this is an isolated piece in the midst of the child's mental life, or if it is really a dynamic structure which can lead to generalizations.
>
> Then there is the third question, "In the case of each learning experience what was the operational level of the subject before the experience and what more complex structures has this learning succeeded in achieving?"

To these three questions, we add a fourth: How can subjects (and Q-Soar) learn so rapidly from a brief training study, when untrained subjects take several years to acquire the same knowledge?

Durability and Robustness of Learning

With respect to Piaget's first question, Q-Soar makes a specific theoretical claim: A chunk, once learned, is always available, and will be evoked whenever the context-specific information that was included in the original chunk is recognized and encoded. For the Soar architecture, chunking is an automatic acquisition mechanism that is applied to all processing that takes place. Thus, by undertaking the processing that is induced by the externally driven training procedure, the learning of conservation knowledge will occur.

The empirical prediction associated with this claim is not straightforward. The general pattern of results with increasingly remote posttests is that, for awhile, performance declines as a function of intervening time between training and testing, but then performance improves as one would expect with the natural acquisition of conservation. At present, we have no principled explanation of this in terms of chunking.

Generalization

The second question refers to the specificity of learning from experience. This is a well-established empirical fact and is predicted by the chunking mechanism (Laird, Rosenbloom, & Newell, 1986). In the context of Q-Soar, chunking predicts little generalization from learning about certain transformations of discrete objects to other transformations of different materials (e.g., the pouring of water). Indeed, this is what one usually finds from conservation training studies: little generalization to other kinds of quantity conservation.

Transfer from small to large number tasks is achieved by the generalization inherent in Soar's chunking mechanism. The actual objects that are measured in determining a conservation judgment are not tested when it is retrieved from memory. There are tests for the kind of transformation and the conservation property (in this case, number) and these delimit the scope of transfer. If that were not so, Q-Soar would predict unrealistically fast learning: to transformations of quantities that are not affected in the same way as the one measured.

In addition, transfer is also limited with respect to continuous quantities, such as volumes of liquid. Acquiring knowledge about continuous quantity is not addressed by Q-Soar. Nevertheless, having acquired conservation knowledge based on small number measurement, a problem solver must come to appreciate what is common to transformations like lengthening and the pouring of liquids. This requires that these transformations be represented as actions that neither add nor remove any of the materials that they manipulate. In other words, this is a problem of representation change. The child must move from domain-specific characterizations of the effects of transformation classes in terms of discrete number to representations where the effect is separated from the dimension that it impacts. This would allow commonalities between transformations that have a "more" or a "same" effect to be noticed, irrespective of what it is that they are affecting. In their account of the development of analogical reasoning, Gentner, Ratterman, Markman, and Kotovsky (chap. 6,this volume) present a transition mechanism that is concerned with precisely this sort of representation change.

Finally, we suggest that the problem solving that enables the identification of the common features of different transformations and materials can best be described as a discovery process. The learner operates with a set of expectations based on current knowledge. This will at some point create a violation of the expected effects of a transformation. The learner's task is to generate a hypothesis of what caused that violation, to devise ways of testing that hypothesis, and to integrate the results either into new hypotheses or modified knowledge. Research on scientific reasoning (Klahr & Dunbar, 1988), instructionless learning (Shrager, 1987), and analogy (Gentner, 1983) provided good explanations of the nature of such processes. Mediating factors in the effectiveness of that problem solving are the selection and combination of features that are considered for inclusion in the analysis (Bransford, Stein, Shelton, & Owings, 1981).

Operational Level and Structural Change

With respect to Piaget's third question, Q-Soar makes explicit statements about the complex structures arising from the training of conservation responses. These can be seen by examinations of Q-Soar–3 and Q-Soar–4 before and after training.

Q-Soar–3 and Q-Soar–4 Before Training.   Before experiencing the three conditions of Gelman's training study, both versions of Q-Soar are able to execute all the steps of the three experimental conditions. The only difference between the two versions is that Q-Soar–3 does not start out with the knowledge that the effects of transformations can be verified by comparing pre- and posttransformation values. Apart from this difference, both versions have all the described capabilities.

However, because neither variant has undergone any training or learned about the effects of any transformations, both versions of Q-Soar fail all of the conservation tests that Gelman used. Neither system can accurately measure the large number of objects in the tests to yield the correct comparative answers. They must use estimation, a process that results in the assertion that a longer row contains more objects than a shorter row. Finally, both untrained variants of Q-Soar–3 and Q-Soar–4 are unable to determine the effects of the transformations and so cannot state an explanation. Before training, then, both are true nonconservers. We now examine their behavior after training. Because the no-cardinal condition is not expected to induce any change in behavior, we discuss only the results of the other two conditions.

Q-Soar-3 After Cardinal-Once Trials. Without employing its memorization capability to recall and compare pre- and posttransformation values, Q-Soar-3 cannot learn anything about the numerical effect of observed transformations. Thus, based on Assumption A2, it always assumes that the value of the row changes. Because this is never the case in the experiment, Q-Soar-3 is always wrong and it fails the conservation tests. As can be seen in Table 7.1, 3-year-olds produced few correct responses.

Q-Soar-3 After Experimental Trials. As explained, the conflicting information in experimental trials after a transformation induces Q-Soar-3 to recall and compare values in the same way as does Q-Soar-4. Thus, Q-Soar-3 can construct a correct comparison and explanation from such trials. These can then be recalled later, enabling it to pass the conservation tests. The behavior of Q-Soar-3 after the experimental condition produces correct responses and explanations, and is thus consistent with the pattern of results in Table 7.1. It seems likely that the experience of this conflict and the resulting recall and comparison of values provide the means by which 3-year-olds acquire the effect-verification knowledge we have assumed to be available to 4-year-olds and that we provided for Q-Soar-4.

Q-Soar-4 After Both Trials. Having produced a quantitative response before a transformation (e.g., Step 4 in Fig. 7.1), Q-Soar-4 selects the MEMORIZE operator to store the computed values in long-term memory. Then, in the DETERMINE-EFFECT problem space, it selects the RECALL operator to enable it to compare pre- and posttransformation values to determine the effect of the transformation and create an explanation. This knowledge can then be recalled in the tests, enabling Q-Soar-4 to pass the conservation tests after experiencing both the experimental and cardinal-once procedures. This pattern of results is also consistent with that in Table 7.1. The higher proportion of correct responses in the experimental group may reflect the fact that not all 4-year-old children had acquired the effect-verification knowledge that we assumed for Q-Soar-4. Those that had not would be expected to perform less well in the cardinal-once condition, just as was the case for 3-year-olds.

Learning Speed

We stated that Q Theory is designed to account for the natural development of conservation, whereas Q-Soar simulates only conservation learning in a single training study. Therefore, we should explain how the same processes can learn quickly under experimental situations, and yet take a few years to reach the same point during natural development. Two obvious factors are the differences in exposure and the availability of feedback. Intensive exposure to important features and informative feedback are characteristic of training studies, but neither of these is the case in unsupervised everyday activity.

However, we suggest that the greatest influence on learning speed is what we call the goal versus encoding interaction. A learner may activate the goal of measuring the effects of transformations. Alternatively, that learner's processing may be in the service of some other goal, such as building towers out of blocks. Even if the measurement goal has been activated, the learner may not attend to a property of the transformed materials that will reveal any number-invariance knowledge, such as the spatial density of a pile of blocks. Only if the child simultaneously has the goal of measurement and the encoding of number as the feature to be measured will he or she acquire number conservation. Well-designed training studies, such as Gelman's, foster just such optimal conditions, and in Q-Soar these aspects are explicit in the representation of comprehended instructions. Similar directiveness appears to be provided for the child in relatively natural mother–child interactions, as set up by Saxe, Gearhart, and Guberman (1984). We know of no evidence to suggest that the goal and property combination optimal for number conservation learning would be chosen by the child any more or less often than any other, although it is evident that children often set themselves the goal of counting things. Thus, three of the four types of opportunities for learning number conservation knowledge would not produce conservation learning in Q-Soar.

CONCLUSION

In this chapter we presented Q-Soar, a computational model of the acquisition of conservation knowledge as reported in a single experimental training study. This is the first such account to present a set of mechanisms, constrained by a unified theory of cognition, that can be shown to acquire conservation knowledge. The central concept in our theory is that conservation learning is premised on young children's ability to make and use measurements. These measurements are used to make conservation *judgments*—evaluations of the quantitative effects of observed transformations. Therefore, the first kinds of conservation processing that children carry out are empirical. Young children's measurement capabilities are limited to small, discrete quantities and so the first kind of quantity for which conservation judgments can be made is number. The results of these number conservation judgments are turned, by a learning mechanism, into new conservation *knowledge*. Due to the nature of the learning mechanism, that new knowledge applies to more cases than just the one it was constructed from. When similar new number conservation problems are attempted, the new knowledge is immediately retrieved and no effect-determination is required.

Thus, we demonstrated a developmental shift where the child moves from empirically determining the effect of transformations via measurement, to making direct inferences about the necessity of conservation based on prior knowledge. This reverses the logical relationship between measurement and conservation that existed in Piaget's theory and now makes measurement a prerequisite for conservation learning. We also identified transformations involving small discrete collections as the learning events that children use to acquire number conservation knowledge. This opposes Piaget's view that conservation is a domain-independent principle that children acquire, by demonstrating that it arises from and initially applies only to domain-specific experiences with transformations relating to number. Furthermore, we demonstrated that Soar's chunking mechanism is sufficient to account for significant developmental transitions, such as the acquisition of number conservation knowledge. This challenges the Piagetian view that developmental change mechanisms are distinct from simple learning mechanisms. Chunking in Soar began as a model of practice effects in human learning and has since been extended to a wide range of cognitive phenomena (Lewis et al., 1990).

Finally, we showed that not only can Q-Soar account for the rapid learning observed in the Gelman (1982) training study, but also, without modification, it may be able to explain the slower, more opportunistic acquisition of invariance knowledge that is characteristic of a young child's everyday unsupervised learning experiences. Much remains to be done before we can claim that Q-Soar gives a complete account of the acquisition of conservation knowledge. There exist many other training studies (Field, 1987) whose results should also be explicable by the mechanisms of Q Theory. The transfer to conservation of continuous quantity remains to be explained, and an account of natural conservation development is still an important goal. Nevertheless, we believe that the work reported in this chapter represents progress in the creation of computational theories of conceptual development.

APPENDIX: SAMPLE Q-SOAR RUN

Here we illustrate how the problem spaces generate behavior when Q-Soar is presented with a task. The following trace is an abstracted version of the steps presented in Fig. 7. 1, which show Q-Soar in operation for the first time. The second trace shows the model's successful performance on a conservation test.

The traces retain only the critical information, showing the problem spaces (denoted by P) and operators (denoted by O) that are selected in response to the impasses that arise. An impasse is shown by processing in a subgoal (G) being indented under the operator that produced the impasse. When an impasse is resolved, processing continues at the highest level at which an operator can be selected. The operators are augmented with the instruction that led to their initiation or by the objects on which they are focused.

External arrays and instructions are depicted to the right of the trace in lower case and Q-Soar's output is given in the center in upper case. The trace is marked with ** at the points in the run where the key conservation chunk is acquired and where it is evoked. Chunks are created continually throughout the run (one or more when returning from each impasse), but these are not shown.

ABSTRACTED RUN OF Q-SOAR DURING ITS FIRST OPERATION

0 0 0 0
0 0 0 0

How many circles?

```
P:      (CONSERVATION)

O:      (COMPREHEND-INSTRUCTIONS)
O:      (DETERMINE-RESPONSE)
= = >G:(OPERATOR NO-CHANGE)
        P:(RESPOND)
        O:(MEASURE)
= = >G:                    (OPERATOR NO-CHANGE)
  P:                       (QUANT-C)
  O: ((CIRCLE) ATTEND)
  O: (INITIALIZE)
  O: ((CIRCLE) COUNT-NEXT) Counting item: ONE
  O: ((CIRCLE) FETCH-NEXT)
  O: ((CIRCLE) COUNT-NEXT) Counting item: TWO
  O: ((CIRCLE) FETCH-NEXT)
  O: ((CIRCLE) COUNT-NEXT) Counting item: THREE
  O: ((CIRCLE) FETCH-NEXT)
  O: ((CIRCLE) COUNT-NEXT) Counting item: FOUR
  O: (MEMORIZE)
O: (RETURN-RESPONSE)      Answer FOUR
```

How many squares?

```
O: (COMPREHEND-INSTRUCTIONS)
O: (DETERMINE-RESPONSE)
= = >G:(OPERATOR NO-CHANGE)
        P:(RESPOND)
        O:(MEASURE)
= = >G:(OPERATOR NO-CHANGE)
```

```
P: (QUANT-C)
O: ((SQUARE) ATTEND)
O: (INITIALIZE)
O: ((SQUARE) COUNT-NEXT) Counting item: ONE
O: ((SQUARE) FETCH-NEXT)
O: ((SQUARE) COUNT-NEXT) Counting item: TWO
O: ((SQUARE) FETCH-NEXT)
O: ((SQUARE) COUNT-NEXT) Counting item: THREE
O: ((SQUARE) FETCH-NEXT)
O: ((SQUARE) COUNT-NEXT) Counting item: FOUR
O: (MEMORIZE)
O: (RETURN-RESPONSE)        Answer FOUR
```

Same or different number?

```
O: (COMPREHEND-INSTRUCTIONS)
O: (DETERMINE-RESPONSE)
= = >G:(OPERATOR NO-CHANGE)
    P:(RESPOND)
    O:(COMPARE)
= = >G:(OPERATOR NO-CHANGE)
    P:(QUANT-C)
    O:(COMPARE)
O: (RETURN-RESPONSE)        Answer SAME
```

O O O O
⊓ ⊓ ⊓ ⊓
Still four circles?

```
O: (CATEGORIZE-TRANSFORMATION)
O: (COMPREHEND-INSTRUCTIONS)
O: (DETERMINE-RESPONSE)
= = >G:(OPERATOR NO-CHANGE)
    P:(RESPOND)
    O:(RECALL)
O: (RETURN-RESPONSE)        Answer FOUR
```

Still four squares?

```
O: (COMPREHEND-INSTRUCTIONS)
O: (DETERMINE-RESPONSE)
= = >G:(OPERATOR NO-CHANGE)
    P:(RESPOND)
    O:(RECALL)
= = >G:(OPERATOR NO-CHANGE)
    P:(DET-EFFECT)
    O:(RECALL)
    O:(DETERMINE-EFFECT)**
O: (RETURN-RESPONSE)        Answer FOUR
```

Same or different number?

```
O: (COMPREHEND-INSTRUCTIONS)
O: (DETERMINE-RESPONSE)
= = >G:(OPERATOR NO-CHANGE)
    P:(RESPOND)
    O:(COMPARE)
O: (RETURN-RESPONSE)        Answer SAME
    VALUES MATCH BEFORE AND AFTER THIS TRANSFORMATION.
End—Explicit Halt
```

The following rule paraphrases the chunk that Q-Soar learns at the point marked ** in this run and that applies at the point marked ** in the following trace. Pattern-match variables are preceded by question marks.

If Goal ?G1 has State ?S1 and Operator ?O1,
  and State ?S1 has Transformation ?T1 marked on it,
  and Transformation ?T1 is Spreading,
  and Operator ?O1 is Determine-Response,
Then mark State ?S1 with Effect ?E1 of Transformation ?T1,
  where ?E1 states that ?T1 has the effect NONE on the property
  Number, because pre- and posttransformation numerical values matched.

Q-SOAR RUN ON A CONSERVATION TEST AFTER LEARNING

```
                                        0 0 0 0 0 0 0
                                        ⊓ ⊓ ⊓ ⊓ ⊓ ⊓ ⊓ ⊓
P: (CONSERVATION)
                                        Same or different number?
O: (COMPREHEND-INSTRUCTIONS)
O: (DETERMINE-RESPONSE)
= = >G:(OPERATOR NO-CHANGE)
    P:(RESPOND)
    O:(COMPARE)
= = >G:(OPERATOR NO-CHANGE)
    P:(ESTIMATE)
    O:(MATCH-1-TO-1)
                        One-to-one end-match: SAME
    O: (MEMORIZE)
O: (RETURN-RESPONSE)          Answer SAME
                                        0 0 0 0 0 0 0 0
                                        ⊓ ⊓ ⊓ ⊓ ⊓ ⊓ ⊓ ⊓
                                        Same or different number?
                                        Explain
O: (CATEGORIZE-TRANSFORM)
O: (COMPREHEND-INSTRUCTIONS)
O: (DETERMINE-RESPONSE)**
O: (RETURN-RESPONSE)          Answer SAME
        VALUES MATCH BEFORE AND AFTER THIS TRANSFORMATION.
End—Explicit Halt
```

ACKNOWLEDGMENTS

This chapter is a minor revision of work completed in collaboration with the late Allen Newell (Simon, Newell, & Klahr, 1991; Simon, Klahr, & Newell, 1992). We acknowledge the profound impact of Allen's intellectual vision on this project, and we are grateful to him for inviting us to explore with him one of the "frontiers" of his unified theory of cognition (Newell, 1990).

We are sure this would have been a better chapter had Allen Newell lived long enough to make a sustained contribution to it.

We thank Robert Siegler for his comments on earlier drafts, as well as for granting us access to his experimental data, and Rochel Gelman for further explication of her experimental procedures. Finally, the first author wishes to thank members of the Soar group for invaluable help, discussions, and support. This work was funded in part by Contract N00014-86-K-0678 from the Computer Science Division of the Office of Naval Research.

REFERENCES

Anderson, J. R. (1987). Skill acquisition: Compiling weak method problem solutions. *Psychological Review, 94,* 194–210.

Atkinson, J., Campbell, F. W., & Francis, M. R. (1976). The magic number 4 plus or minus 0: A new look at visual numerosity judgements. *Perception, 5,* 327–334.

Barsalou, L. W. (1983). Ad hoc categories. *Memory & Cognition, 11, 211–227.*

Briars, D., & Siegler, R. S. (1984). A featural analysis of preschooler's counting knowledge. *Developmental Psychology, 20,* 607–618.

Bransford, J. D., Stein, B. S., Shelton, T. S., & Owings, R. A. (1981). Cognition and adaptation: The importance of learning to learn. In J. Harvey (Ed.), *Cognition, social behavior, and the environment.* Hillsdale, NJ: Lawrence Erlbaum Associates.

Brown, A. L., Bransford, J. D., Ferrara, R. A., & Campione, J. C. (1983). Learning, remembering and understanding. In J. H. Flavell & E. M. Markman (Eds.), *Handbook of child psychology: Cognitive Development* (Vol. 3 pp. 77–166). New York: Wiley.

Chi, M. T. H., & Klahr, D. (1975). Span and rate of apprehension in children and adults. *Journal of Experimental Child Psychology, 19,* 434–439.

Cowan, R. (1979). Performance in number conservation tasks as a function of the number of items. *British Journal of Psychology, 70,* 77–81.

DeJong, G., & Mooney, R. (1986). Explanation-based learning: An alternative view. *Machine Learning, 1,* 145–176.

Donaldson, M. (1978). *Children's Minds.* Glasgow, Scotland: Fontana.

Field, D. (1987). A review of preschool conservation training: An analysis of an analysis. *Developmental Review, 7,* 210–251.

Fuson, K. C. (1988). *Children's counting and concepts of number.* New York: Springer-Verlag.

Fuson, K. C., Secada, W. G., & Hall, J. W. (1983). Matching, counting and conservation of numerical equivalence. *Child Development, 54,* 91–97.

Gelman, R. (1977). How young children reason about small numbers. In N. J. Castellan, D. B. Pisoni, & G. R. Potts (Eds.), *Cognitive theory* (Vol. 2, pp. 219–283). Hillsdale, NJ: Lawrence Erlbaum Associates.

Gelman, R. (1982). Accessing one-to-one correspondence: Still another paper about conservation. *British Journal of Psychology, 73,* 209–220.

Gelman, R., & Baillargeon, R. (1983). A review of some Piagetian concepts. In J. H. Flavell & E. M. Markman (Eds.), *Handbook of child psychology: Cognitive Development* (Vol. 3, pp. 168–230). New York: Wiley.

Gentner, D. (1983). Structure mapping: A theoretical framework for analogy. *Cognitive Science, 7,* 155–170.

Halford, G. S. (1982). *The development of thought.* Hillsdale, NJ: Lawrence Erlbaum Associates.

Halford, G. S., & Boyle, F. M. (1985). Do young children understand conservation of number? *Child Development, 56,* 165-176.

Jones, R. M., & VanLehn, K. (1994). Acquisition of children's addition strategies: A model of impasse-free, knowledge-level learning. *Machine Learning, 16,* 11-30.

Klahr, D. (1973). Quantification processes. In W. Chase (Ed.), *Visual information processing.* (pp. 3-34). New York: Academic Press.

Klahr, D. (1982). Nonmonotone assessment of monotone development: An information processing analysis. In S. Strauss & R. Stavy (Eds.), *U-shaped Behavioral growth.* New York: Academic Press.

Klahr, D. (1984). Transition processes in quantitative development. In R. J. Sternberg (Ed.), *Mechanisms of cognitive development.* New York: Freeman.

Klahr, D., & Dunbar, K. (1988). Dual space search during scientific reasoning. *Cognitive Science, 12,* 1-48.

Klahr, D., & Wallace, J. G. (1970). An information processing analysis of some Piagetian experimental tasks. *Cognitive Psychology, 1,* 358-387.

Klahr, D., & Wallace, J. G. (1973). The role of quantification operators in the development of the conservation of quantity. *Cognitive Psychology, 4,* 301-327.

Klahr, D., & Wallace, J. G. (1976). *Cognitive development: An information processing view.* Hillsdale, NJ: Lawrence Erlbaum Associates.

Laird, J. E., Newell, A., & Rosenbloom, P. S. (1987). Soar: An architecture for general intelligence. *Artificial Intelligence, 33,* 1-64.

Laird, J. E., Rosenbloom, P. S., & Newell, A. (1986). Chunking in Soar: The anatomy of a general learning mechanism. *Machine Learning, 1,* 11-46.

Laird, J. E., Swedlow, K. R., Altmann, E. M., & Congdon, C. B. (1989). *SOAR 5 user's manual* (Tech. Rep.). Ann Arbor: University of Michigan, Department of Electrical Engineering and Computer Science.

Lewis, R. L., Huffman, S. B., John, B. E., Laird, J. E., Lehman, J. F., Newell, A., Rosenbloom, P. S., Simon, T., & Tessler, S. G. (1990). Soar as a unified theory of cognition. *Proceedings of the Twelfth Annual Conference of the Cognitive Science Society* (pp. 1035-1042). Hillsdale, NJ: Lawrence Erlbaum Associates.

Lewis, R. L., Newell, A., & Polk, T. A. (1989). Toward a Soar theory of taking instructions for immediate reasoning tasks. In *Proceedings of the Eleventh Annual Conference of the Cognitive Science Society* (pp. 514-521). Hillsdale, NJ: Lawrence Erlbaum Associates.

Markman, E. M. (1990). Constraints children place on word meanings. *Cognitive Science, 14,* 57-78.

McClelland, J. L. (1989). Parallel distributed processing: Implications for cognition and development. In R.G. Morris (Ed.), *Parallel distributed processing: Implications for psychology and neurobiology* (pp. 8-45). Oxford, England: Clarendon Press.

Miller, C. S., & Laird, J. E. (1990). *A simple, symbolic model for associative learning and retrieval.* Unpublished manuscript, University of Michigan, Ann Arbor, Artificial Intelligence Laboratory,

Miller, K. F. (1984). Child as measurer of all things: Measurement procedures and the development of quantitative concepts. In. C. Sophian (Ed.), *The origin of cognitive skills* (pp. 193-228). Hillsdale, NJ: Lawrence Erlbaum Associates.

Miller, K. F. (1989). Measurement as a tool for thought: The role of measurement procedures in children's understanding of quantitative invariance. *Developmental Psychology, 25,* 589-600.

Mitchell, T. M., Keller, R. M., & Kedar-Cabelli, S. T. (1986). Explanation-based generalization: A unifying view. *Machine Learning, 1,* 47-80.

Mooney, R. (1991). Explanation-based learning as concept formation. In D. Fisher & M. Pazzani (Eds.), *Concept formation: Knowledge and experience in unsupervised learning* (pp. 174-206). San Mateo, CA: Morgan Kaufmann.

Newell, A. (1990). *Unified theories of cognition.* Cambridge, MA: Harvard University Press.

Piaget, J. (1952). *The child's conception of number.* New York: W. W. Norton.

Piaget, J. (1964). Development and learning. In R. E. Ripple & V. N. Rockastle (Eds.), *Piaget rediscovered.* Ithaca, NY: Cornell University Press.

Piaget, J. (1968). Quantification, conservatism and nativism. *Science, 162,* 976–979.

Piaget, J. (1970). *Structuralism.* New York: Basic Books.

Piaget, J., Inhelder, B., & Szeminska, A. (1960). *The child's concept of geometry.* London: Routledge & Kegan Paul.

Rosenbloom, P. S., & Laird, J. E. (1986). Mapping explanation-based generalization into Soar. *Proceedings of the Fifth National Conference on Artificial Intelligence* (pp. 561–567). San Mateo, CA: Morgan Kaufmann.

Rosenbloom, P. S., & Newell, A. (1986). The chunking of goal hierarchies: A generalized theory of practice. In R. S. Michalski, J. G. Carbonell, & T. M. Mitchell (Eds.), *Machine learning: An artifical intelligence approach,*)Vol. 2, pp. 247–288). Palo Alto, CA: Tioga.

Saxe, G. B., Gearhart, M., & Guberman, S. R. (1984). The social organization of early number development. In B. Rogoff & J. V. Wertsch (Eds.), *Children's learning in the zone of proximal development.* (pp. 19–30). San Francisco, CA: Jossey-Bass.

Shipley, E. F. & Shepperson, B. (1990). Countable entities: Developmental changes. *Cognition, 34,* 109–136.

Shrager, J. (1987).Theory change via view application. *Machine Learning, 2,* 1–30.

Siegler, R. S. (1981). Developmental sequences within and between concepts. *Monographs of the Society for Research in Child Development, 46,* 1–74.

Siegler, R. S. (1989). Mechanisms of cognitive development. *Annual Review of Psychology, 40,* 353–379.

Siegler, R. S. (1991, April). *Variation and selection as cognitive transition mechanisms.* Paper presented at the Biennial Meeting of the Society for Research in Child Development, Seattle, WA.

Simon, T., Cabrera, A., & Kliegl, R. (1993). A new approach to the study of subitizing as distinct enumeration processing. *Proceedings of the 15th Annual Meeting of the Cognitive Science Society* (pp. 929–934). Hillsdale, NJ: Lawrence Erlbaum Associates.

Simon, T., Klahr, D., & Newell, A. (1992). The role of measurement in the construction of conservation knowledge. *Proceedings of the 14th Annual Meeting of the Cognitive Science Society* (pp. 66–71). Hillsdale, NJ: Lawrence Erlbaum Associates.

Simon, T., Newell, A., & Klahr, D. (1991). A computational account of children's learning about number conservation. In D. H. Fisher, M. J. Pazzani & P. Langley (Eds.), *Concept formation: Knowledge and experience in unsupervised earning.* (pp. 423–462). San Mateo, CA: Morgan Kaufmann.

Sophian, C. (1987). Early developments in children's use of counting to solve quantitative problems. *Cognition and Instruction, 4,* 61–90.

Starkey, P. (1992). The early development of numerical reasoning. *Cognition, 43,* 93–126.

Svenson, O., & Sjoberg, K. (1983). Speeds of subitizing and counting process in different age groups. *Journal of Genetic Psychology, 142,* 203–211.

van Loosbroek, E., & Smitsman, A. W. (1990). Visual perception of numerosity in infancy. *Developmental Psychology, 26,* 916–922.

Wallace, J. G., Klahr, D., & Bluff, K. (1987). A self-modifying production system model of cognitive development. In D. Klahr, P. Langley, & R. Neches (Eds.), *Production system models of learning and development.* (pp. 359–436). Cambridge, MA: MIT Press.

Wynn, K. (1990). Children's understanding of counting. *Cognition, 36,* 155–193.

8

Computational Models of Cognitive Change: The State of the Art

David Klahr
Carnegie Mellon University

. . . Serious theorizing about basic mechanisms of cognitive growth has actually never been a popular pastime. . . . The reason is not hard to find: Good theorizing about mechanisms is very, very hard to do.

—Flavell (1984, p. 189)

The chapters in this volume demonstrate that good theorizing about developmental mechanisms is very hard indeed, but not impossible. Collectively, they represent the cutting edge of computational models of developmental processes. My assigned task in this chapter is to provide some commentary on the individual chapters and on the modeling enterprise as a whole. However, my ultimate goal is to persuade you that the formulation and evaluation of such models holds extraordinary promise for theorists of cognitive development.

This concluding chapter is intended as a companion piece to Simon and Halford's opening chapter, which treats many of the issues I would otherwise want to address. The chapter is organized as follows. It starts with a brief history of computational models in developmental psychology and their position in the wider context of information processing approaches to cognitive development. Then it describes the three broad classes of computational models represented in this book, and comments on several important and interesting features of individual models described in the previous chapters. Following that, it offers some general observations about various aspects of formulating computational models of developmental processes.

TWENTY-FIVE YEARS OF COMPUTATIONAL MODELS IN
COGNITIVE DEVELOPMENT

Perhaps the first use of a computational model to account for an aspect of children's thinking was the model that Wallace and I proposed for how children induce rules in sequence extrapolation problems (Klahr & Wallace, 1970a). Our model was a simple variant of Simon and Kotovsky's (1963) pioneering[1] computer simulation model of adult performance on letter series completion problems. It was proposed as an account of children's performance on a limited and well-defined problem. It was precise about the induction process, and the mapping between children's performance and the model performance was unambiguously defined.

The model was silent on issues of learning, transition, and change. Nevertheless, our rationale for creating it was the conviction that—as we argued in a related paper (Klahr & Wallace, 1970b, p. 361)—"the criteria that a transition mechanism must fulfill are likely to be much clearer if a sufficient state description is already in existence before the question of self-modification of structure is addressed." Our view at the time echoed the two-step modeling process suggested by Simon (1962) and quoted in the opening chapter of this book. But this view now strikes me as too simple. It is probably not a good research strategy to propose a performance model and then seek an independent set of transition mechanisms that operate on that performance model. Instead, developmentalists need to formulate computational models that are always undergoing self-modification, even as they perform at a given level or stage. In other words, the challenge is not to construct performance systems that can adapt, but rather to construct adaptive systems that can perform. As evidenced by the chapters in this book, both production-system and connectionist approaches now support the creation of such models.

In the 25 years since the publication of our little series-completion simulation, there were substantial advances in the area of computational models of developmental processes. I tracked this history in several other places (Klahr, 1980, 1984, 1992), and I do not repeat it here. A brief history of production systems—both in artificial intelligence and in psychology— was presented in Neches, Langley, and Klahr (1987). In the production system domain, the most important technical developments with respect to cognitive modeling include Newell's first computer implementation of a production system language (Newell, 1973), Waterman's (1975) adaptive production systems, Anderson's ACTF production system for skill acqui-sition (Anderson, Kline, & Beasley, 1978) and Newell's Soar model (Newell, 1990).

---

[1] I say "pioneering" because it was the first description of a computer simulation model that accounted for human performance to be published in a major U. S. psychology journal.

The history of connectionism was summarized in the first chapter of Bechtel and Abrahamsen (1991) and its relevance to cognitive development is summarized by Shultz et al.'s chapter in this volume. Although the topic *cognitive development*, was absent from the landmark Rumelhart and McClelland (1986) volume, it was clearly present in the papers on language development, an area that remains one of the most active for connectionist modeling.

To summarize both of these histories: Production systems did not initially have the capacity for self-modification, but they were soon designed with such capacity, and PDP models are inherently self-modifying systems. At present, both forms of computational modeling provide means for directly dealing with the fundamental issue of cognitive transition and change.

Equally important as the technical development of systems for expressing computational models was the continued interest of many cognitive developmentalists in using such models to better understand the developmental phenomena they were studying. Developmentalists sought an adequate language for expressing the inherent complexity and dynamics of the developmental process. Piaget boldly and creatively attempted to render these processes in terms of the formalisms available to him at the time: in logic, in mathematics, and in analogies to biological processes. But only since the late 1960s have computational languages adequate to the task become available. The chapters in this book provide examples of work by developmentalists who have stayed the course, continually extending their ability to formulate computational models of developmental phenomena. There are other examples, not represented in this book, of a long-term commitment to computational models, particularly in language development (e.g., MacWhinney, 1978; MacWhinney, Leinbach, Taraban, & McDonald, 1989). More recent was the entry into the field of researchers who would not normally be identified as developmentalists but who, upon realizing the relevance of their modeling techniques to questions of cognitive development, began to create models to address some of the longstanding issues in the field. McClelland's chapter in this volume exemplifies this intellectual path.

Thus, what was only promise in 1970 has become reality in recent years: computational models of self-modifying cognitive systems. The models in this book represent some of the most outstanding exemplars of this work. In the next section, I comment on several aspects of the enterprise as instantiated in these models.

VARIETIES OF COMPUTATIONAL MODELS

The six models described in this book fall into three broad categories — ad hoc models, production systems, and connectionist systems — with two examples of each. In this section, I describe the essential features of these forms of modeling, and then comment on the most important or interesting features of the models described in the earlier chapters. The discussion of individual chapters is organized by type of model. Because many of the chapters share features, the discussion is incremental in its treatment of successive chapters. It is also selective and does not exhaust the possible features of interest.

Ad Hoc Models

In many cases, a researcher may have a theory about some phenomenon that is sufficiently complex so that only a computational model will enable one to derive predictions from it. However, the modeler may not be prepared to make a commitment to the theoretical claims of either connectionist or production-system approaches. In such cases, one chooses to focus on the knowledge structures and computational processes, and employs an atheoretical computational architecture in which to formulate and run the model. This approach enables the model builder to focus on the complexities of the domain under consideration without being constrained by global architectures or particular learning algorithms.

Although such models are usually accompanied by further discussion of how the computational part of the model fits into a larger vision of the developmental process, these descriptions of the larger context do not entail computational models as such. For example, in this volume, Siegler and Shipley's discussion of the larger role of variation and selection is not accompanied by a global system architecture that embodies these processes. One advantage of ad hoc systems is that, because they are not constrained by global theoretical concerns, they often achieve precise and fine-grained fits to empirical measures of children's performance (cf. Siegler & Shipley chap. 2, this volume) whereas the production system or connectionist models are typically matched to data at a higher level of aggregation.

Siegler and Shipley first propose an idea that is broad, plausible, and powerful. They propose a kind of "cognitive Darwinism" in which variation and selection are the driving engines of cognitive change. They support this notion with the observation that in the domain of simple addition—as well as many others—there are long periods during which children have access to, and use, not just one, but many strategies. The question then arises as to how children decide which of their multiple strategies to execute on a given problem. Siegler and Shipley then constrain and focus the vague notion of cognitive variation and selection until what remains is a set of mechanisms that they are able to precisely formulate in a computational model.

Siegler and Shipley challenge the notion that metacognitive processes influence strategy choice in this context by proposing a model in which "intelligent strategy choices . . . arise from application of simpler, more basic processes" (p. 46). Without a good computational model, one could argue endlessly about the roles of variation, selection, and metacognition in cognitive development. Siegler and Shipley manage to avoid such a discussion as they describe the development (i.e., the theoretical development by them) of an increasingly precise account of strategy choice. Because the rules and the data structures have complex interactions, it is necessary to formulate a computational model to derive the implications of the rules. The goal of the model is "to show how a simple cognitive process could produce adaptive strategy choices without anything resembling an executive processor" (p. 46). The first model they describe (Siegler and Shrager, 1984) not only demonstrated such an effect, but also it facilitated the derivation of some nonintuitive predictions about the correlation between error rates and strategy selection that were supported by the empirical results.

The model had its shortcomings. But because it was precisely stated, Siegler and Shipley could also precisely analyze its behavior and conclude that "it was too inflexible, too limited in its explicitness, and too dumb" (p. 54). Harsh words, but true. But could one ever assess a verbally based theory with such exactness? Furthermore, would the path to the elimination of such shortcomings be clear? In Siegler and Shipley's case it was, and their final model ASCM embodies a remedy for each of those shortcomings.

Another interesting feature of the Siegler and Shipley chapter is their use of a series of training trials during which the model learned about the domain in which it was to function. In any model that is supposed to learn or develop, the modeler must decide how to represent the model's interaction with the environment. In some cases, one can make reasonable estimates about the type of relevant exposure, whereas in other cases, the plausibility of the training regime is questionable. In the present case, Siegler and Shipley's estimates about young children's exposure to two-digit problems (with feedback) seem to me to be accurate. As we see later, other modelers do not always make such reasonable estimates. The more general point is that the creation of models that cumulatively react to their environments requires the formulation of an explicit theory of what that environment is. Simon and Halford's chapter addresses this issue in the section on *Environmental Input*, and it remains a major area for further research.

Gentner et al. use computational modeling not to explicate the developmental process as such, but rather to explore the potential sources of difference between children's and adults' analogical reasoning. Thus, their research strategy corresponds to the two-stage approach described earlier: First, create explicit characterizations of developmental differences, and then formulate the models that can account for the transition between earlier and later models. As I noted earlier, this no longer strikes me as the optimal way to proceed. However, in domains in which effective models for adult performance have already been established, the "dumbing down" of adult models to capture children's performance remains a useful heuristic for establishing what the challenges will be for a subsequent developmental model.

Verbal discussion of analogy and similarity is fraught with potential ambiguity and inconsistency, but Gentner et al. are able to be quite clear in their assumptions because they must specify specific data structures and processing steps for their Structure Mapping Engine (SME) to do its job. The model also allows them to explore an interesting hypothesis: that adult–child performance differences are due entirely to representation changes and not at all to global capacity changes. Gentner et al. note that computational modeling "allows us to ask what we never could about a real human: what would happen if we changed only the knowledge and not the processing" (p. 275). Here they echo McCloskey's (1991) view that one of the roles of computational modeling is analogous to animal models of human function: "By studying the animal model rather than working directly with the human system, one may be able to carry out manipulations that could not be performed on human subjects" (p. 393).

This chapter exemplifies another aspect of computational modeling: its cumulative nature. The formulation of computational models has been greatly facilitated by improvements in both production systems and connectionist algorithms. These improvements enable a modeler to use computational tools that have been developed and refined over a long period, and that have become increasingly user friendly. There are now at least two volumes describing computational modeling tools that include easy-to-use software (McClelland & Rumelhart, 1988; Anderson, 1993). But Gentner et al. exploit a different aspect of the cumulation of modeling tools. In addition to the global systems, such as Soar, ACT*, or PRISM, and the connectionist systems, there exist families of computational systems that can act as extensions and augmentations to a particular computational model. In the present instance, Gentner et al. exploit these kinds of potential augmentations to their nondevelopmental model of analogy. They refer to a variety of systems that already exist that could, in principle, model the developmental aspects of their domain. This kind of intermodel crosstalk will become increasingly important in the future, as even more powerful and well-defined computational models become available.

Production-System Models

Production systems make a strong set of theoretical claims about the overall cognitive architecture. The argument for them was made most boldly by

Anderson (1993): "Cognitive skills are realized by production rules. This is one of the most astounding and important discoveries in psychology and may provide a base around which to come to a general understanding of human cognition" (p. 1).

The full set of assumptions about production system architectures are extensive (cf. Newell, 1990; Van Lehn, 1991). In the next few paragraphs, I provide only a brief characterization of production systems, and then I comment on the production system models in this book.

Production systems are a class of computer-simulation models stated in terms of condition–action rules. A production system consists of two interacting data structures: (a) a *working memory* consisting of a collection of symbol structures called working memory *elements*; and (b) a *production memory* consisting of condition–action rules called *productions*, the conditions of which describe configurations of working memory elements and the actions of which specify modifications to the contents of working memory. Production memory and working memory are related through the *recognize–act* cycle, comprised of three distinct processes:

1. The *match* process finds productions, the conditions of which match against the current state of working memory. The same rule may match against working memory in different ways, and each such mapping is called an *instantiation*. When a particular production is instantiated, we say that its conditions have been satisfied. In addition to the possibility of a single production being satisfied by several distinct instantiations, several different productions may be satisfied at once. Both of these situations lead to conflict.

2. The *conflict resolution* process selects one or more of the instantiated productions for applications.

3. The *act* process applies the instantiated actions of the selected rules. Actions can include the modification of the contents of working memory, as well as external perceptual-motor acts.

Production systems can be thought of as complex, dynamic stimulus-response pairs in which both the S and the R involve symbolic structures. They provide both a parallel associative recognition memory, on the condition side, and a serial response on the action side. The basic recognize–act process operates in cycles, with one or more rules being selected and applied, the new contents of working memory leading another set of rules to be applied, and so forth.

Halford et al. focus on the development of children's transitive inference strategies. They adopt a production system architecture (PRISM II) that is inspired by a strong theory of cognition (Anderson, 1983) but that they use more in the sense of a general programming language in which some of the implementation details entail theoretical assumptions. Their TRIMM model is an adaptive production system with two types of productions. Domain-general productions take care of the "housekeeping," and are presumed to be part of the child's general cognitive repertoire. They do not undergo any change during the solving of transitive inference problems. Domain-specific productions, on the other hand, are created as the system interacts with problems in the domain.

One interesting feature of this model is the way in which it adapts the classical type of production system architecture to the demands of developmental modeling. Productions have a strength that varies according to their effectiveness, but in addition, production strength undergoes small random perturbations, so that productions may re-enter the active set after being below threshold on earlier cycles. The strength parameter on each production, combined with several others (effort, threshold, and the constants in the delta modification rules) mean that TRIMM operates in a large parameter space, only a bit of which is described here. One task for the future would be to discover the sensitivity of the model's behavior to these parameters, and the extent to which the parameters correspond to theoretically important aspects of the development of transitive inference.

Another important feature of the Halford et al. chapter is its introduction of processing capacity constraints into the model and into its more general theoretical interpretation. One of the longstanding problems with many computational models is that they do not deal effectively with either temporal or spatial capacity limitations. That is, neither production system nor connectionist architectures provide a principled basis for explaining the rate of cognitive development or what appear to be domain-general capacity constraints at different developmental levels.

Simon and Klahr propose a model of cognitive change during a very brief time span. They ask: What changes during conservation training? They offer an answer in the form of a computational model. The history of their model is of interest because it reflects the maturing of the computational modeling enterprise. No part of Klahr and Wallace's (1973) information processing approach to conservation was expressed as a computational model. The first production system models for different levels of conservation performance were presented in Klahr and Wallace (1976), but their account of the transition between such stages was not a computational model, nor was Klahr's (1984) elaboration of that process. At that time, it was not clear how to build a production system for number conservation that could undergo the necessary self-modification. And although Wallace, Klahr and Bluff (1987) proposed a general theory of cognitive development in information processing terms, only parts of it were implemented as computational models. Not until 1991 were the ideas about the transition between conservation performance levels completely expressed in the computational model described in this chapter (Simon, Newell & Klahr, 1991).

Another interesting aspect of the Simon and Klahr model is its very fine grained focus on a single cognitive change resulting from a single training study. Thus Simon and Klahr deal with the problem of a theory of the environment — mentioned earlier — by limiting their attention to a context in which they could be sure of children's initial performance, exposure to training, and final performance. Although only a single study is modeled, their Q-Soar model is designed to be consistent with the rest of the vast literature on conservation.

Connectionist Models

Connectionist models are less an architecture than a set of shared assumptions about the nature of neural computation, common learning rules, and a common vocabulary. In his chapter in this volume, McClelland succinctly characterizes the fundamental character of connectionist models:

> On this approach — also sometimes called the parallel-distributed processing or PDP approach — information processing takes place through the interactions of large numbers of simple, neuronlike processing units, arranged into modules. An active representation — such as the representation one may have of a current perceptual situation, for example, or of an appropriate overt response — is a distributed pattern of activation, over several modules, representing different aspects of the event or experience, perhaps at many levels of description. Processing in such systems occurs through the propagation of activation among the units, through weighted excitatory and inhibitory connections.
>
> As already suggested, the knowledge in a connectionist system is stored in the connection weights: It is they that determine what representations we form when we perceive the world and what responses these representations will lead us to execute. Such knowledge has several essential characteristics: First it is inchoate, implicit, completely opaque to verbal description. Second, even in its implicit form it is not necessarily accessible to all tasks; rather it can be used only when the units it connects are actively involved in performing the task. Third, it can approximate symbolic knowledge arbitrarily closely, but it may not; it admits of states that are cumbersome at best to describe by rules; and fourth, its acquisition can proceed gradually, through a simple, experience-driven process. (pp. 158–159)

McClelland goes on to present a connectionist model of how children learn to make correct predictions about the balance scale in a variety of weight and distance configurations. In both its general advocacy of the merits of connectionist models for cognitive development and description of his specific model, the chapter is particularly lucid. It is exemplary in presenting the fundamental connectionist argument about the importance of implicit knowledge and the "graded, embedded, nonsymbolic character" (p. 158) of children's developing knowledge.

Although an extensive empirical literature is used to justify the choice of problem, it strikes me that there is an incompatibility between the underlying theory and the form of the data. The underlying theory holds that children have graded knowledge about the balance scale, and that they have to resolve conflicting response tendencies in order to produce a response. This is consistent with an emerging view that children are more often than not faced with conflicting choices among multiple strategies (Siegler & Jenkins, 1989) or responses (Horobin & Acredolo, 1989). Indeed, it has been argued that the procedures used in almost all rule assessments distort the underlying nature of children's knowledge because they force children to choose a single response, even though they may endorse multiple responses. In such cases, children are likely to give the most probable one, but the data are interpreted as if that response was the only one entertained by the child. As Acredolo and O'Connor (1989) put it:

> From a methodological perspective, the severe limitations of the forced-choice procedure should be acknowledged. Most of the reasoning and logic tasks used in research and applied settings are presented in a forced-choice format, but this procedure allows us to see only individuals' preferences and not their certainties. The selection of a correct answer does not mean that an individual appreciates that answer as necessarily correct, and the selection of an incorrect answer does not mean that an individual has unequivocally dismissed the correct alternative. Moreover, the addition of multiple trials, requests for justifications, and the presentation of counter suggestions will not guarantee the detection of uncertainty. If the modal aspects of judgments are of any interest, and it is suggested here that they should be of much greater interest than has been the case, then alternatives to the standard force-choice procedure must be found. (p. 15)

Thus, it seems to me that connectionists, in accepting the notion of multiple competing responses, should not be matching their models to data produced by the forced-choice techniques, but should, instead, be evaluating their models against responses based on the type of assessment procedures advocated by Acredolo and O'Connor.

Finally, a word about the training regimen. Like Siegler and Shipley, McClelland proposes an explicit set of training experiences for his model. But whereas Siegler and Shipley present a plausible case for children experiencing a thousand or so exposures to single-digit addition problems, I question McClelland's assumption of children's exposure to thousands of balance-scale problems with feedback. What in the child's environment could possibly correspond to that assumption? The "see-saw" argument strikes me as implausible (especially because liability fears have caused most cities to remove see-saws from playgrounds!).

Shultz et al. provide another example of connectionist modeling of developmental processes. Their chapter is unusual in two regards. First, they describe a model that uses a learning algorithm — cascade correlation — that differs from the much more commonly used "backprop" model. They argue that cascade correlation is better able to capture the distinction between assimilation and accommodation than are other computational models. (I address this claim at some length later in the chapter.) Second, they demonstrate the generality of their approach by indicating how the same model can be used to account for developmental patterns in five quite distinct domains. Furthermore, they show how computational modeling can be used to precisely address questions about the influence of environmental biases or prestructured (nativist) biases.

This is an impressive demonstration of how computational models can facilitate focused discussion of fundamental development issues. Of course, this clarity makes it easy to find fault. My principle criticisms of the models in this chapter are with the authors' assumptions about the role of strategy and their assumptions about the nature of the child's experience in the domain.

With respect to the former, let me summarize how the seriation model works once it has learned how to seriate an array. It is given a disordered array, and it selects *which* item to move and *where* to move it. Then that action is executed (by processes not modeled here) and the resulting array is then presented to the network again, so that it can choose the next element and its desired location. During training, the decision about the correct choice of *which* and *where* is determined by the use of a single strategy, even though both Young (1976) and Baylor and Gascon (1974) demonstrated that children use many different strategies on these problems, and often mix elements of strategies midway through a seriation attempt. Thus, although the decision to separately represent *which* and *where* in isolated modules is ingenious, and obviously effective, the resulting networks fail to capture the emergence of the kind of multiple strategies that others in this volume have argued for.

With respect to training sequences, I found the Shultz et al. assumptions about exposure to balance scale patterns more plausible and subtle than those made by McClelland for the same problem. Shultz et al. have included three-element sets, as well as a bias toward sets that are only partially disordered. They make the reasonable argument that such sets are likely to induce children to create transitive orderings, and, at the same time, make it easy for them to do so.

Nevertheless, the fidelity of the assumptions implicit in such training sequences remains an open question, and one that plays a central role in the evaluation of computational models. As already noted, it is an area where we still have a lot to learn. Perhaps one reason why the most impressive connectionist models of development are in the area of language acquisition (cf. MacWhinney, 1987) is that it is a domain in which the input history has been massively documented.

FAMILY SQUABBLES: PASSIONATE, BUT FAMILY NONETHELESS

Although connectionist forays into cognitive development are often accompanied by the dismissal of symbolic approaches as unsuited to the task, I am unconvinced that the differences are as substantial as is sometimes claimed. Connectionist models are usually proposed as radically different from production system architectures, and more neurally plausible. However, one can ask where the fundamental differences lie: in the parallelism of the processing, in the distributed knowledge, or in the connectivity of that knowledge?

Parallelism can not be the source of the difference, because during the "match" or "recognize" phase of a production system's recognize-act cycle, the condition side of all productions are matched in parallel with all the elements in working memory.[2] In some systems, working memory is defined as the set of elements in a vast semantic memory that are above some threshold, so the match process is massively parallel and the connectivity between working memory elements and the productions is dynamic and potentially unbounded.

What about distributed knowledge? The extent to which knowledge is distributed or modularized in a production system depends entirely on the grain size that elements or productions are supposed to capture. Thus, a single production might represent a very explicit and verbalizable rule, or it might represent a small piece of processing for a complex, implicit piece of knowledge. Similarly, in PDP models, the individual element can represent knowledge at any grain size: from an individual neuron, to an assembly of neurons, to the word *neuron*. There is nothing inherent in either formulation that specifies what this grain should be, until additional constraints are imposed on the model, such as attempting to match model cycles to human reaction times.

Another purported difference between PDP models and production

---

[2]The actual implementation of this parallel match occurs in a serial Von Neuman machine. But so, too, do the implementations of the learning algorithms in PDP models. This microlevel of implementation is not regarded as part of either theoretical stance.

system models is the gradualism of the former and the abruptness of the latter. But as evidenced by some of the models in this book, one can create a production system architecture with continuously varying strengths of productions—hence, production systems can exhibit gradualism. Conversely, the higher order derivatives of different learning functions in connectionist systems can assume large values. Given the appropriate grain size on a performance window, such models would appear to be undergoing discontinuous changes (cf. Newell's 1972 classic analysis of process-structure distinctions in developmental psychology).

Although my attempt to minimize the differences between the two major approaches might seem to reflect the bias of one who has worked only with production-system models, the same point has also been made by connectionist advocates:

> Most of the modifications incorporated in the most recent symbolic models have narrowed the gap between symbolic and network models. . . . First, a large number of rules at a fine grain of analysis (microrules) can capture more of the subtleties of behavior than a smaller number of rules at a larger grain of analysis. Second, rule selection, and perhaps rule application as well, can be made to operate in parallel. Third, the ability to satisfy soft constraints can be gained by adding a strength parameter to each rule and incorporating procedures that use those values in selecting rules. Fourth, resilience to damage can be gained by building redundancy into the rule system (e.g., making multiple copies of each rule). Fifth, increased attention can be given to learning algorithms (such as the genetic algorithm [Holland, 1975; Koza, 1992]), knowledge compilation and "chunking" of rules into larger units [Anderson, 1983; Newell, 1990], and ways of applying old knowledge to new problems (such as analogy [Falkenheiner, Forbus, & Gentner, 1989]).
>
> There presently is no adequate research base for determining what differences in empirical adequacy might result from these differences, but the differences are likely to be small enough that empirical adequacy will not be the primary determinant of the fate of symbolic versus connectionist models. Within either tradition, if a particular inadequacy is found, design innovations that find some way around the failure are likely to be forthcoming. Personal taste, general assumptions about cognition, the sociology of science, and a variety of other factors can be expected to govern the individual choices that together will determine what approaches to cognitive modeling will gain dominance. (Bechtel & Abrahamsen, 1991, pp. 18–19)

Perhaps the difference in these approaches is in the rhetoric. Whereas production system descriptions are burdened with a pedestrian terminology of *matching, recognizing, acting, cycles* and *chunking,* connectionist models enjoy the lyrical characterizations of such things as *cascade correlation, graceful degradation, optimal harmony, victory, temperature,* and *epochs*. In their full ecstasy, their advocates even invoke Biblical expressiveness: "it comes to pass . . ." says McClelland of how his balance scale model learns to encode weight.

As you can see, I am unable to resist teasing my connectionist friends. However, I would like to end this section on a more serious — and constructive — note. The literature is filled with extensive — at times acrimonious — debates about what each type of computational model can or can not do. To some extent, these debates have been healthy. Clearly, there are important pragmatic and theoretical differences in attempts to create computational models of developmental phenomena. But I believe that the internecine battle between the symbolic and subsymbolic camps has overstated the differences and ignored the fact that the two approaches share some important properties. Perhaps the most important of these is the commitment to stating all assumptions about processes and mechanisms with an exactness unattainable in other forms of theorizing. We need to disavow strong prior commitments to one form or another, and instead, exploit whatever tools are available and develop new tools as necessary, in order to achieve our goal of understanding the process of cognitive development.

THIS STUFF IS HARD. BUT WHAT IS THE ALTERNATIVE?

The chapters in this book are not always easy reading. Compared to the standard fare of developmental theory, these chapters introduce a bewildering variety of technical terms, concepts, notation, and representations. Understanding them requires a familiarity with a technical language that is unlikely to have been a major part of the graduate training of most developmentalists. Both production systems and connectionist models involve new concepts, new terminology, even new reading styles (when following an account of how a model is organized, how it runs, and how it is matched to the data).

I think this communication problem is a temporary stage in the development of the field. It derives from two aspects of this still-emerging field. The first is that there is not yet a common language or even a set of fully shared assumptions among computational modelers. The second is that, because of the unusually high variance in the technical backgrounds of their potential readers, authors of chapters describing the models must make arbitrary assumptions about the amount of background and level of detail to include. It is as if we were in the early days of multidimensional scaling, or analysis of variance, and each author had to describe the idiosyncratic approach he or she had taken to do the statistical analysis. Unlike today's writers, the author of such early papers could not assume that the reader had taken several courses on the technical aspects of the analysis before seeing the application to the context under discussion.

Nevertheless, these chapters are worth the struggle. Each one of them describes — in various degrees of detail and completeness — a computational model of some important aspect of cognitive development. My enthusiasm for this kind of work derives from the conviction that, for all of their complexity, computational models like these represent the most promising direction for increasing our understanding of cognitive development.

If you find this claim too brash, then consider the alternative: the theory-as-words. In cognitive development, this form of theory is exemplified by the following quotation from the master (Piaget, 1937/1954):

> The superficial accommodation of the beginnings of thought and the distorting assimilation of reality to the self are therefore at first undifferentiated and they operate in opposite directions. They are undifferentiated because the immediate experience which characterizes the former always, in the last analysis, consists in considering the personal point of view as the expression of the absolute and thus in subjecting the appearance of things to an egocentric assimilation, just as this assimilation is necessarily on a par with a direct perception that excludes the construction of a rational system of relations. But at the beginning, however undifferentiated may be these accommodative operations and those in which assimilation may be discerned, they work in opposite directions. Precisely because immediate experience is accompanied by an assimilation of perceptions to the schemata of personal activity or modeled after it, accommodation to the inner workings of things is constantly impeded by it. Inversely, assimilation of things to the self is constantly held in check by the resistance necessitating this accommodation, since there is involved at least the appearance of reality, which is not unlimitedly pliant to the subject's will. So also, on the social plane, the constraint imposed by the opinion of others thwarts egocentrism and vice versa, although the two attitudes of imitation of others and assimilation to the self are constantly coexistent and reveal the same difficulties of adaptation to reciprocity and true cooperation.
>
> Gradually, as the child's thought evolves, assimilation and accommodation are differentiated and become increasingly complementary. In the realm of representation of the world this means, on the one hand, that accommodation, instead of remaining on the surface of experience, penetrates it more and more deeply, that is, under the chaos of appearances it seeks regularities and becomes capable of real experimentations to establish them. On the other hand assimilation, instead of reducing phenomena to the concepts inspired by personal activity, incorporates them in the system of relationships rising from the more profound activity on intelligence itself. True experience and deductive construction thus become simultaneously separate and correlative[.]
> (pp. 43–44)

The passage is from one of Piaget's first explications of assimilation and accommodation. Although it has a certain poetic beauty, as a scientist, I do not understand it, I do not know how to test it, and I doubt that any two readers will interpret it in the same way.

Now consider the chapters in this book. Perhaps you found some ambiguities in these expositions that left you as puzzled as did the Piagetian excerpt. But note a crucial difference: In each case there is an explicit computational model. The chapter is only an explication of that model: *it is not the model itself*. You can, if you so desire, obtain a copy of the code, and run the model on your own. With a bit of effort, you can know precisely how Siegler and Shipley's ASCM chooses among addition strategies, or how Halford et al.'s TRIMM learns to make transitive inferences, or what McClelland's model starts with, how it learns, and what it "knows" at the end of the learning process. You can examine a computational model, adjust its parameters, alter its environmental input, and so on. You might even write your own account of what the model does, and how it works. Not so with the Piagetian account, or with any verbal model. *The only instantiation of the theory is the text account,* and the ambiguity of textual theories engenders a subdiscipline of interpretation — particularly in Piaget's case (e.g., Beilin, 1989; Chapman, 1988; Flavell, 1963; Furth, 1969; Ginsberg & Opper, 1969; Gruber & Vonèche, 1977).

The sharp contrast between these two modes of theorizing produces what some regard as a weakness of computational models, but what is in fact their very strength: the relative ease with which one can make pointed criticisms of the plausibility of their assumptions, mechanisms, or mappings to human behavior. The inherent ambiguity of verbal theories makes them invulnerable to such criticism because there are no explicit assumptions to evaluate. The precise assumptions are left as (implicit) exercises for the reader. In contrast, you may question the plausibility of the strategy choice algorithm in Siegler's ASCM model, or the training set in McClelland's balance scale model, or the assumption about prior knowledge in Halford's model. But for each question, there is a specific operation that you (or the theorist) could try out on the model, and observe its effect. The discussion by Shultz et al. about the differences between their cascade correlation model and McClelland's back propagation model of the same phenomenon exemplifies the new forum of such sharply focused dialogues.

WHY THESE TASKS? RETHINKING
OUR DEVELOPMENTAL DROSOPHILIA

As genetics needs its model organisms, its *Drosophilia* and *Neurospora*, so psychology needs standard task environments around which knowledge and understanding can cumulate.

                                                                                    –Simon and Chase (1973)

Simon and Chase go on to contend that the use of such "standard task environments" enables research to cumulate by addressing different aspects of human thinking in a small number of rich, but well-understood and easily replicable, contexts. In the early days of computer simulation, this role was well-served by games such as chess, and puzzles such as the Tower of Hanoi (Anzai & Simon, 1979; Klahr & Robinson, 1981; Simon, 1975).

Developmental psychology has its own set of standard tasks, due largely to Piaget. The vast array of tasks he introduced has had a pervasive influence on the field. Many thousands of studies using his basic tasks have been run in the past 60 years or so, and variants continue to be invented. So it is not surprising that four of the six computational models in this volume deal with problems that were first used by Piaget to index the stages of children's cognitive development (transitive inference, balance scale prediction, conservation of number, time–speed–distance problems).[3]

However, as new computational models begin to raise new questions, it may be prudent to question our inclination to use Piagetian tasks simply because they already have an extensive empirical base. This is not to suggest throwing out the baby and so forth, for it is still possible to utilize the existing tasks effectively. Nevertheless, as these new models enable us to ask new questions about old tasks as well as to suggest entirely novel tasks, the issue of task choice may warrant more attention than it has received.

THOUGHT AS FOOD? ESCHEWING ASSIMILATION AND ACCOMMODATION

Developmentalists of all stripes — including computational modelers — seem to feel obliged to comment on the extent to which their theories can be placed in correspondence with the Piagetian notions of assimilation and accommodation. For example, consider the mapping by Shultz et al.:

> Using Piaget's terms, one can conceptualize three general types of cognitive encounters in cascade-correlation nets: assimilation, assimilative learning, and accommodation. Pure assimilation occurs without learning. It is represented in cascade correlation by correct generalization to novel problems without either weight changes or hidden unit recruitment. Assimilative learning occurs by weight adjustment, but without hidden unit recruitment. Here the network learns new patterns that do not require nonlinear changes in representational power. Accommodation occurs via hidden unit recruitment when new patterns cannot be learned without nonlinear increases in computational power. (p. 255)

---

[3]Indeed, in our monograph on information processing models of cognitive development (Klahr & Wallace, 1976), we dutifully worked our way through a series of production system models for the basic Piagetian tasks: class inclusion, transitivity, and conservation.

In a sportsmanlike effort, Shultz et al. concede (a bit) to other models' abilities to characterize assimilation and accommodation:

> Adaptation through assimilation and accommodation can also be reinterpreted through rule-based and back-propagation perspectives, but with less satisfactory results. In a rule-based learning system like Soar, assimilation could be construed as rule-firing and accommodation as chunking new rules through impasse-driven search. In back-propagation learning, accommodation could be viewed in terms of weight adjustment and assimilation as the absence of such adjustment. (p. 256)

These attempts to map the new computational constructs to precomputational theoretical constructs are not limited to the present volume. Consider the following from Bechtel and Abrahamsen's (1991) introductory text on connectionism:

> Connectionism could be viewed as a modern mechanism for achieving stage-like states by means of the heretofore somewhat mysterious processes of accommodation and assimilation. Specifically, assimilation can be interpreted in terms of the tendency of an interactive network to settle into the most appropriate of its stable (attractor) states (see Hinton & Shallice, 1989) when input is presented to it; in Piaget's language, this is the schema to which the experience has been assimilated. Accommodation can be interpreted as the changes in activations as well as weights that occur in order to assimilate the experience. (That is, transient state changes and learning are highly interrelated both in connectionist networks and in Piaget's notion of accommodation. The assimilation of any experience involves both of these aspects of accommodation.) (p. 271)

But why bother with such an exercise? Assimilation and accommodation have been with us so long that it is easy to forget that they are not empirical regularities demanding a theoretical account. Instead, they are obscure theoretical constructs, imported by Piaget as analogies from the biology of the digestive process. Attempts to map these constructs to computational models are as unconstrained as are the initial constructs. Indeed, the quotations cited reveal a distressing amount of variability in such mapping efforts. Similar comments apply to attempted mappings between modern computational models and other aspects of Piaget's theoretical language such as the INRC group. In summary, I believe we should abandon the criterion of how well computational models can account for assimilation and accommodation — or any other precomputational metaphors — because the criterion is uninformative and unnecessary.

CONCLUSION

I opened this chapter with a quotation from John Flavell that succinctly characterizes the challenge that the contributors to this volume implicitly accepted. I close it with another Flavell insight that characterizes and justifies their response to that challenge:

> "Simple models will just not do for human cognition." (Flavell & Wohlwill, 1969, p. 74)

ACKNOWLEDGMENTS

I thank Brian MacWhinney, Robert Siegler, and the editors of this volume for suggestions on how to improve earlier drafts of this chapter.

REFERENCES

Acredelo, C., & O'Connor, J. (1989). *A reconsideration of children's certainty of conservation: New procedures for assessing children's sense of certainty, necessity, and possibility.* Unpublished manuscript. University of California, Davis, Department of Applied Behavioral Sciences.

Anderson, J. R. (1983). *The architecture of cognition.* Cambridge, MA: Harvard University Press.

Anderson, J. R. (1993). *Rules of the mind.* Hillsdale, NJ: Lawrence Erlbaum Associates.

Anderson, J. R., Kline, P. J., & Beasley, C. M., Jr. (1978). *A general learning theory and its application to schema abstraction* (Tech. Rep. No. 78-2). Pittsburgh, PA: Carnegie Mellon University, Department of Psychology.

Anzai, Y., & Simon, H. A. (1979). The theory of learning by doing. *Psychological Review, 86,* 124–140.

Baylor, G. W., & Gascon, J. (1974). An information processing theory of aspects of the development of weight seriation in children. *Cognitive Psychology, 6,* 1–40.

Bechtel, W., & Abrahamsen, A. (1991). *Connectionism and the mind: An introduction to parallel processing in networks.* Cambridge, MA: Basil Blackwell.

Beilin, H. (1989). Piagetian theory. In R. Vasta (Ed.), Six theories of child development: Revised formulations and current issues. *Annals of Child Development, 6,* 85–132.

Chapman, M. (1988). *Constructive evolution: Origin and development of Piaget's thought.* New York: Cambridge University Press.

Falkenhainer, B., Forbus, K. D., & Gentner, D. (1989). The structure-mapping engine: Algorithm and examples. *Artificial Intelligence, 41,* 1–63.

Flavell, J. H. (1963). *The developmental psychology of Jean Piaget.* Princeton, NJ: Van Nostrand.

Flavell, J. H. (1984). Discussion. In R. J. Sternberg (Ed.). *Mechanisms of cognitive development* (pp. 187–210). New York: Freeman.

Flavell, J. H., & Wohlwill, J. F. (1969). Formal and functional aspects of cognitive development. In D. Elkind & J. H. Flavell (Eds.), *Studies in cognitive development* (pp. 67–120). New York: Oxford University Press.

Furth, H. G. (1969). *Piaget and knowledge: Theoretical foundations.* Englewood Cliffs, NJ: Prentice-Hall.

Ginsburg, H., & Opper, S. (1969). *Piaget's theory of intellectual development: An introduction.* Englewood Cliffs, NJ: Prentice-Hall.

Gruber, H. E., & Vonèche, J. J. (Eds.). (1977). *The essential Piaget: An interpretive reference guide.* New York: Basic Books.

Hinton, G. E., & Shallice, T. (1989). *Lesioning a connectionist network: Investigations of acquired dyslexia* (Tech. Rep. No. CRG–TR–89–3). Toronto, Canada: University of Toronto.

Holland, J. H. (1975). *Adaptation in natural and artificial systems*. Ann Arbor, MI: University of Michigan Press.

Horobin, K., & Acredolo, C. (1989). The impact of probability judgments on reasoning about multiple possibilities. *Child Development, 60,* 183–200.

Klahr, D. (1980). Information processing models of cognitive development. In R. Klewe & H. Spada (Eds.), *Developmental models of thinking* (pp. 127–162). New York: Academic Press.

Klahr, D. (1984). Transition processes in quantitative development. In R. Sternberg (Ed.), *Mechanisms of cognitive development* (pp. 101–139). San Francisco: Freeman.

Klahr, D. (1992). Information processing approaches to cognitive development. In M. H. Bornstein & M. E. Lamb (Eds.), *Developmental psychology: An advanced textbook* (3rd ed., pp. 273–336). Hillsdale, NJ: Lawrence Erlbaum Associates.

Klahr, D., & Robertson, M. (1981). Formal assessment of problen solving and planning processes in preschool children. *Cognitive Psychology,13,* 113–148.

Klahr, D., & Wallace, J. G. (1970a). The development of serial completion strategies: An information processing analysis. *British Journal of Psychology, 61,* 243–257.

Klahr, D., & Wallace, J. G. (1970b). An information processing analysis of some Piagetian experimental tasks. *Cognitive Psychology, 1,* 358–387.

Klahr, D., & Wallace, J. G. (1973). The role of quantification operators in the development of conservation of quantity. *Cognitive Psychology, 4,* 301–327.

Klahr, D., & Wallace, J. G. (1976). *Cognitive development: An information-processing view.* Hillsdale, NJ: Lawrence Erlbaum Associates.

Koza, J. R. (1992). *Genetic programming: On the programming of computers by means of natural selection and genetics.* Cambridge, MA: Bradford.

MacWhinney, B. (1978). The acquisition of morphophonology. *Monographs of the Society for Research in Child Development, 43* (Whole No. 1).

MacWhinney, B. J. (Ed.). (1987). *Mechanisms of language acquisition.* Hillsdale, NJ: Lawrence Erlbaum Associates.

MacWhinney, B., Leinbach, J., Taraban, R., & McDonald, J. (1989). Language learning: Cues or rules? *Journal of Memory and Language, 28,* 255–277.

McClelland, J. L. & Rumelhart, D. E. (1988). *Explorations in parallel distributed processing: A handbook of models, programs, and exercises* [IBM PC edition]. Boston: MA: MIT Press.

McCloskey, M. (1991). Networks and theories: The place of connectionism in cognitive science. *Psychological Science, 2*(6), 387–395

Neches, R., Langley, P., & Klahr, D. (1987). Learning, development and productions systems. In D. Klahr, P. Langley, & R. Neches (Eds.), *Production system models of learning and development* (pp. 1–54). Cambridge, MA: MIT Press.

Newell, A. (1972). A note on process-structure distinctions in developmental psychology. In S. Farnham-Diggory (Ed.), *Information processing in children* (pp. 126–143). New York: Academic Press.

Newell, A. (1973). Production systems: Models of control structures. In W. G. Chase (Ed.), *Visual information processing* (pp. 463–526). New York: Academic Press.

Newell, A. (1990). *Unified theories of cognition.* Cambridge, MA: Harvard University Press.

Piaget, J. (1954). *The construction of reality in the child* (M. Cook, Trans.). New York: Basic Books. (Original work published 1937)

Rumelhart, D. E., & McClelland, J. L. (1986). *Parallel distributed processing: Explorations in the microstructure of cognition.* Cambridge, MA: MIT Press.

Siegler, R. S., & Jenkins, E. (1989). *How children discover new strategies*. Hillsdale, NJ: Lawrence Erlbaum Associates.

Siegler, R. S., & Shrager, J. (1984). Strategy choices in addition and subtraction: How do children know what to do? In C. Sophian (Ed.), *Origins of cognitive skills* (pp. 229–293). Hillsdale, NJ: Lawrence Erlbaum Associates.

Simon, H. A. (1962). An information processing theory of intellectual development. *Monographs of the Society for Research in Child Development, 27* (2, Serial No. 82).

Simon, H. A. (1975). The functional equivalence of problem-solving skills. *Cognitive Psychology, 7*, 268–288.

Simon, H. A., & Chase, W. G. (1973). Skill in chess. *American Scientist, 61*(4), 394–403.

Simon, H. A. & Kotovsky, K. (1963). Human acquisition of concepts for sequential patterns. *Psychological Review, 70*, 534–546.

Simon, T., Newell, A., & Klahr, D. (1991). A computational account of children's learning about number conservation. In D. Fisher & M. Pazzani (Eds.), *Concept formation: knowledge and experience in unsupervised learning* (pp. 423–462). San Mateo, CA: Morgan Kauffman.

Van Lehn, K. (Ed.). (1991). *Architectures for intelligence: The 22nd Carnegie Mellon Symposium on Cognition*. Hillsdale, NJ: Lawrence Erlbaum Associates.

Wallace, J. G., Klahr, D., & Bluff, K. (1987). A self-modifying production system for conservation acquisition. In D. Klahr, P. Langley, & R. Neches (Eds.), *Production system models of learning and development* (pp. 359–435). Cambridge, MA: MIT Press.

Waterman, D. (1975). Adaptive production systems. In *Proceedings of the Fourth International Joint Conference on Artificial Intelligence*. Cambridge, MA: MIT, Artificial Intelligence Laboratory.

Young, R. M. (1976). *Seriation by children: An artificial intelligence analysis of a Piagetian task*. Basel, Switzerland: Birkhauser.

Author Index

["

Subject Index